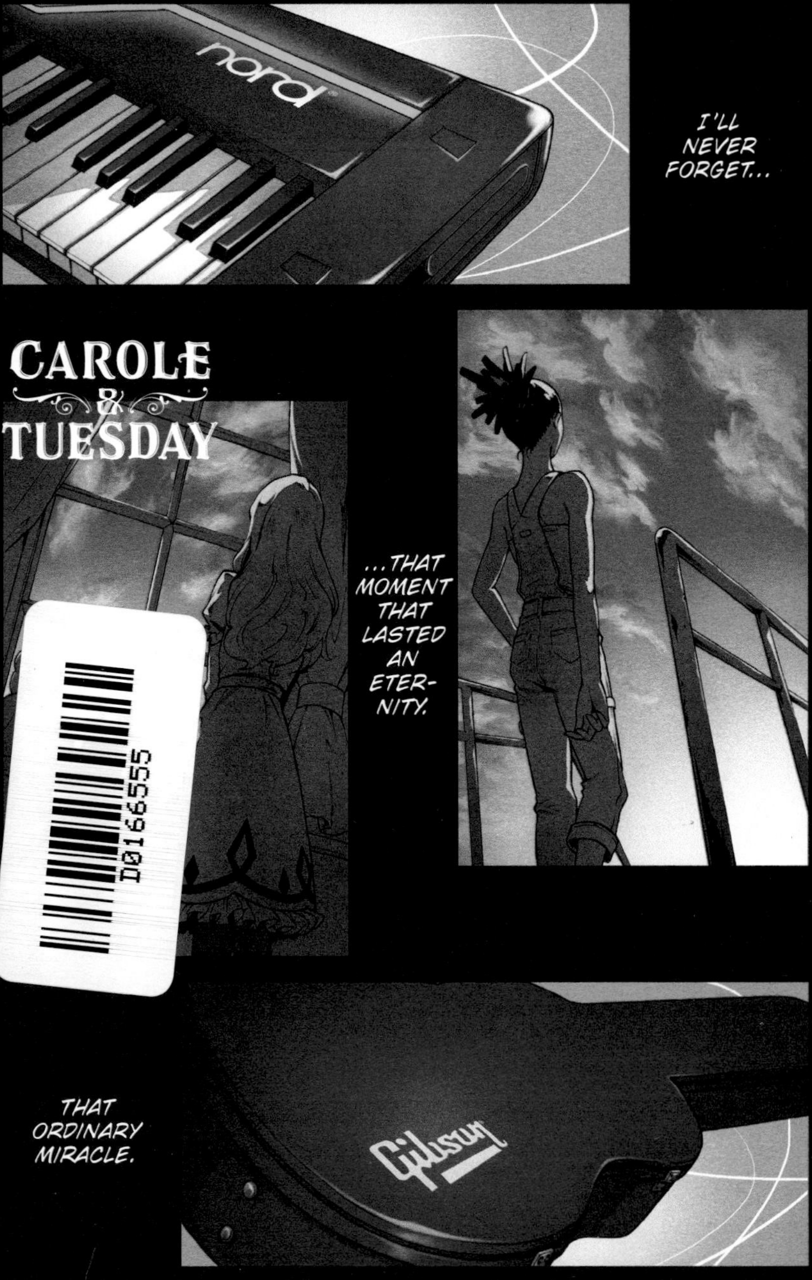
I'LL NEVER FORGET...
...THAT MOMENT THAT LASTED AN ETER-NITY.
CAROLE & TUESDAY
THAT ORDINARY MIRACLE.

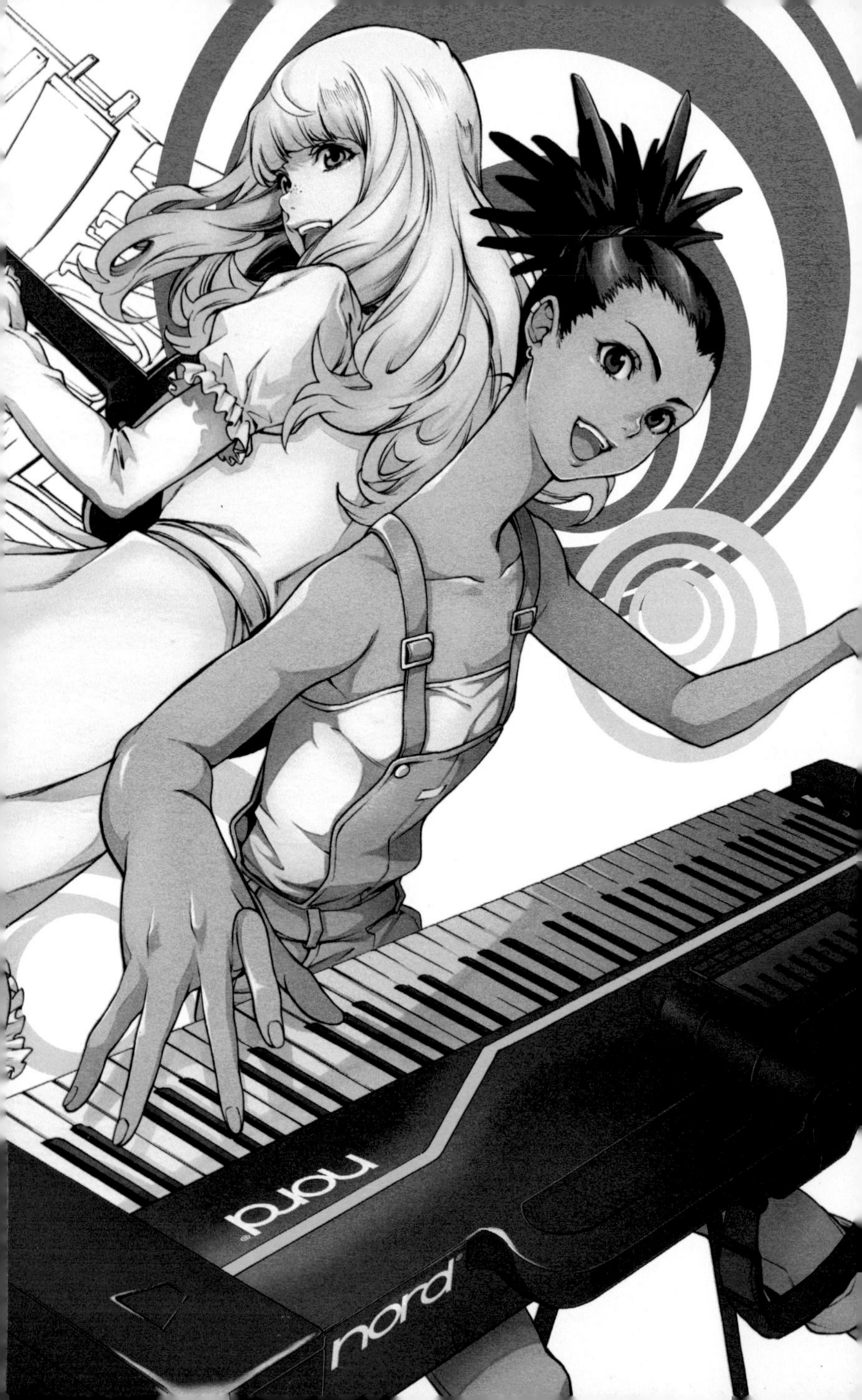
nord
nord
nord

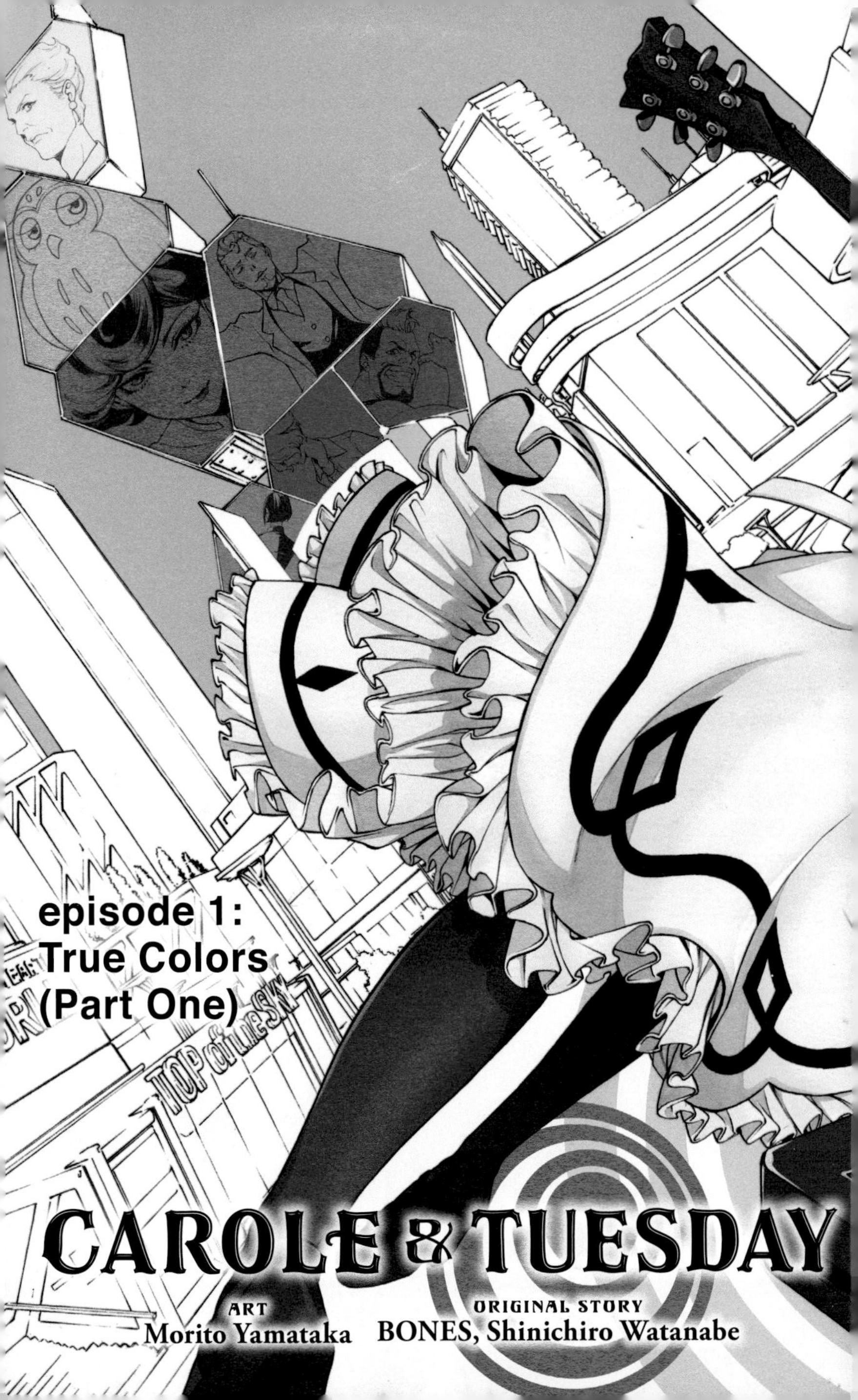
episode 1:
True Colors
(Part One)
CAROLE & TUESDAY
ART
Morito Yamataka
ORIGINAL STORY
BONES, Shinichiro Watanabe

CONTENTS

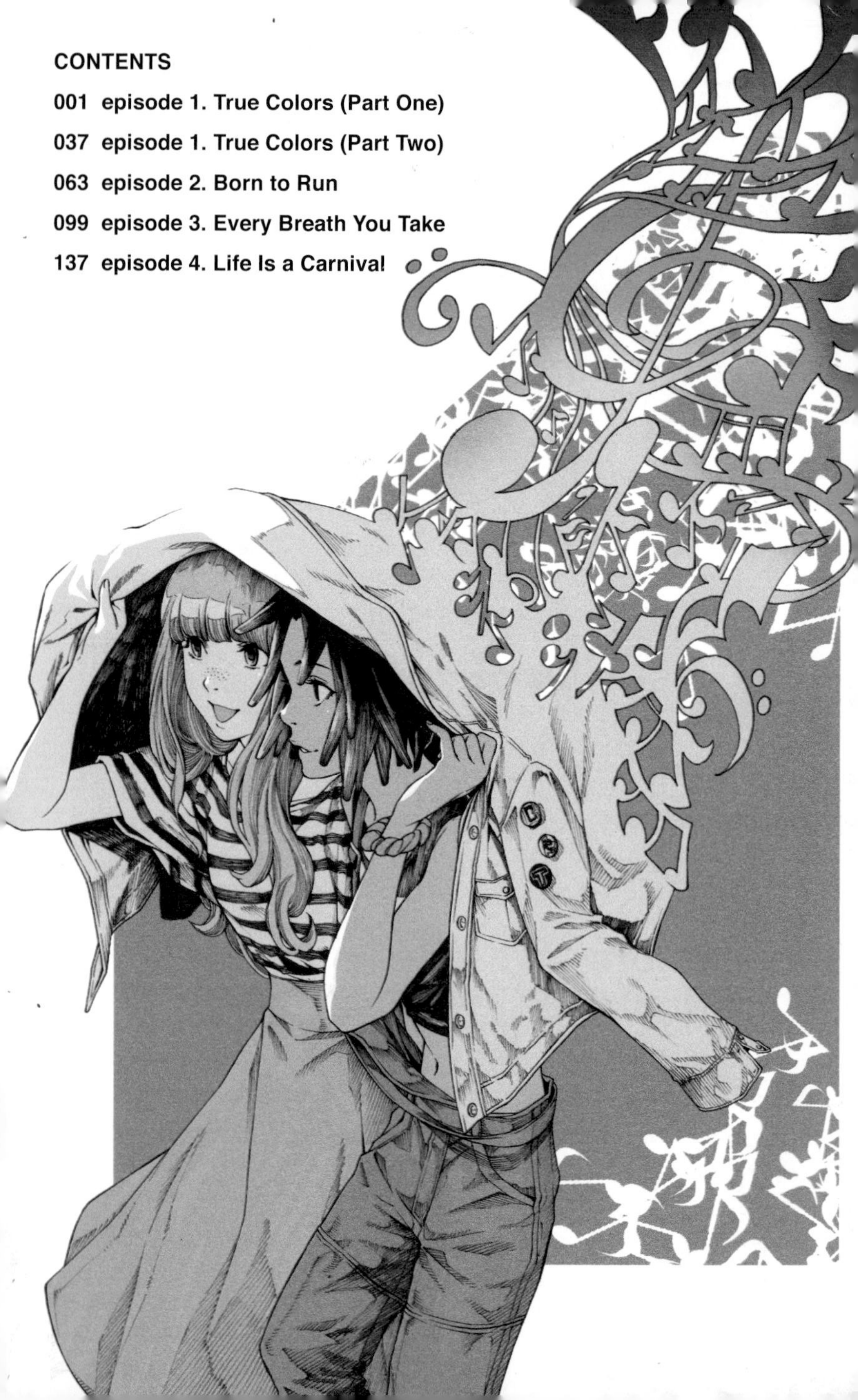

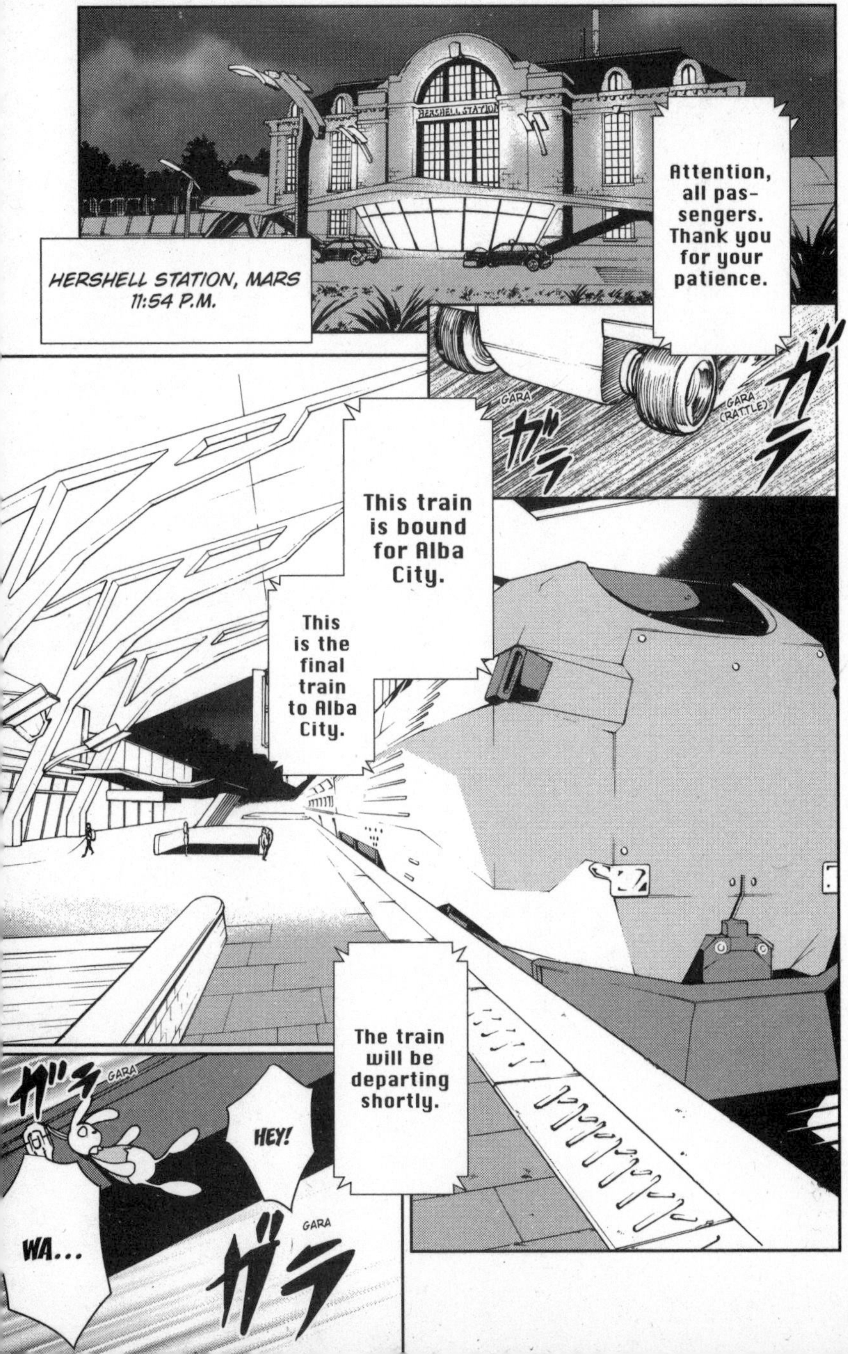
HERSHELL STATION
Attention, all pas-sengers. Thank you for your patience.
HERSHELL STATION, MARS
11:54 P.M.
GARA (RATTLE)
GARA
This train is bound for Alba City.
This is the final train to Alba City.
The train will be departing shortly.
GARA
HEY!
GARA
WA...

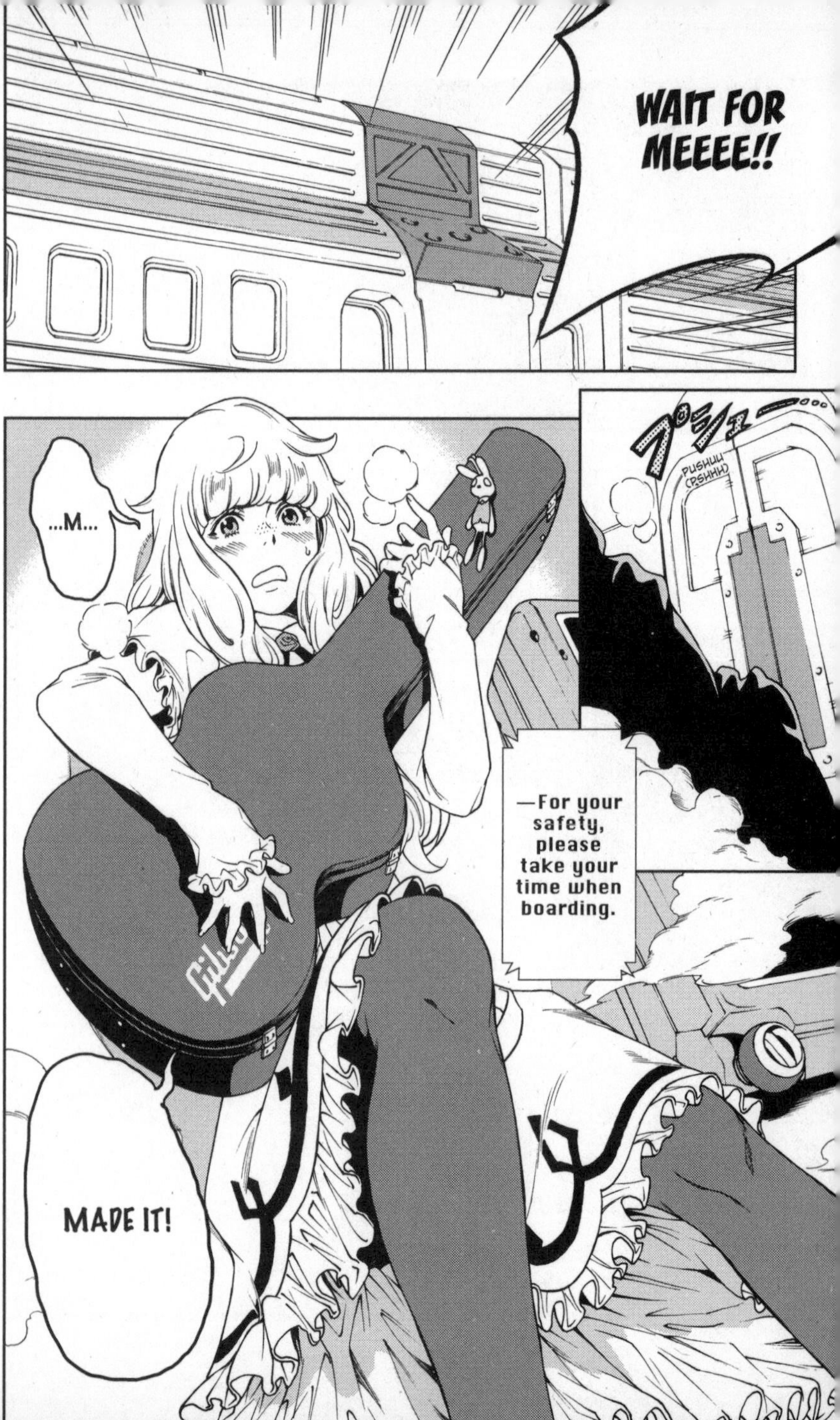

WAIT FOR MEEEE!!
PUSHUU (PSHHH)
...M...
—For your safety, please take your time when boarding.
MADE IT!

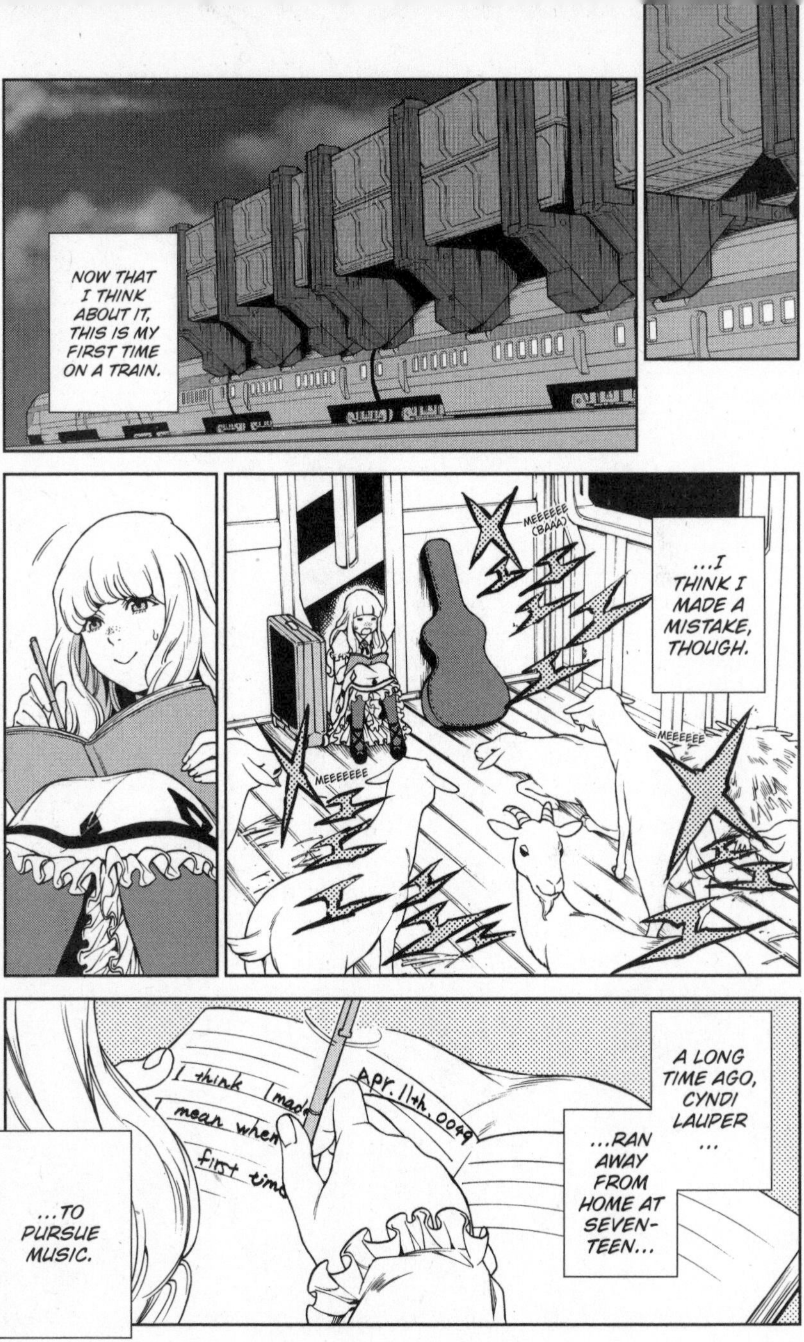
NOW THAT I THINK ABOUT IT, THIS IS MY FIRST TIME ON A TRAIN.
...I THINK I MADE A MISTAKE, THOUGH.
MEEEEEE (BAAA)
MEEEEEE
MEEEEEEE
A LONG TIME AGO, CYNDI LAUPER...
...RAN AWAY FROM HOME AT SEVEN-TEEN...
...TO PURSUE MUSIC.

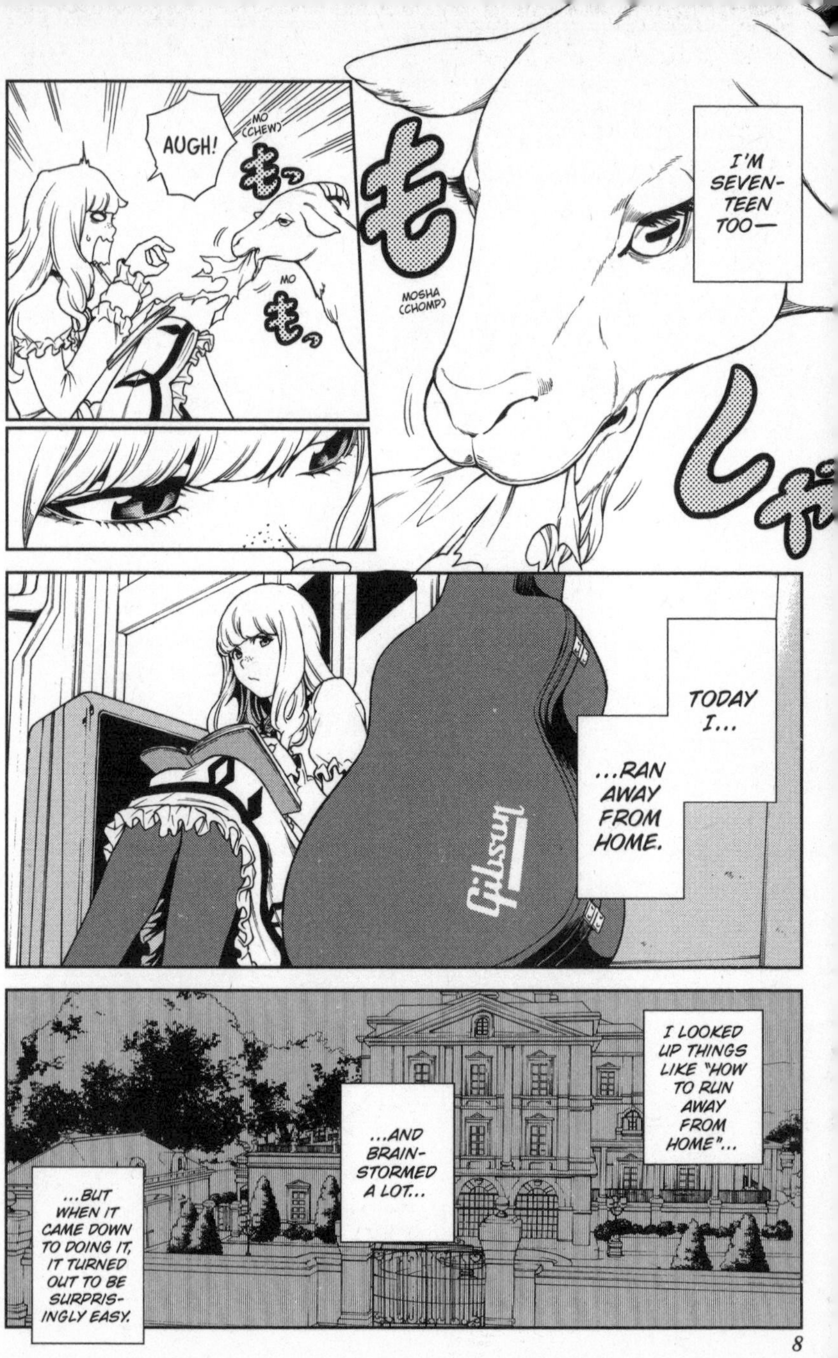
I'M SEVEN-TEEN TOO—
も
MOSHA (CHOMP)
しゃ
AUGH!
MO (CHEW)
もっ
MO
もっ
TODAY I...
...RAN AWAY FROM HOME.
Gibson
I LOOKED UP THINGS LIKE "HOW TO RUN AWAY FROM HOME"...
...AND BRAIN-STORMED A LOT...
...BUT WHEN IT CAME DOWN TO DOING IT, IT TURNED OUT TO BE SURPRIS-INGLY EASY.

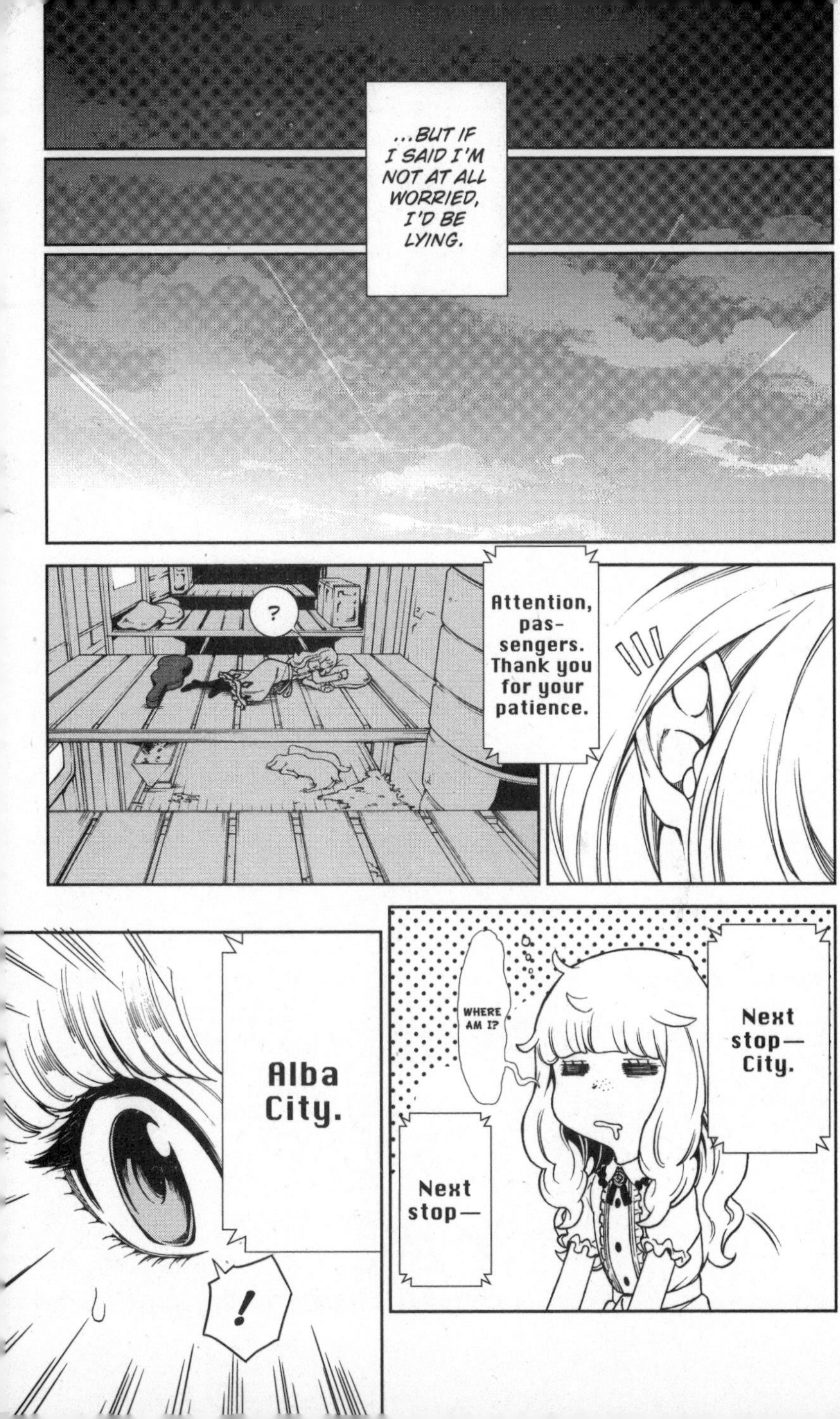
...BUT IF I SAID I'M NOT AT ALL WORRIED, I'D BE LYING.
Attention, pas-sengers. Thank you for your patience.
?
Next stop— City.
WHERE AM I?
Next stop—
Alba City.
!

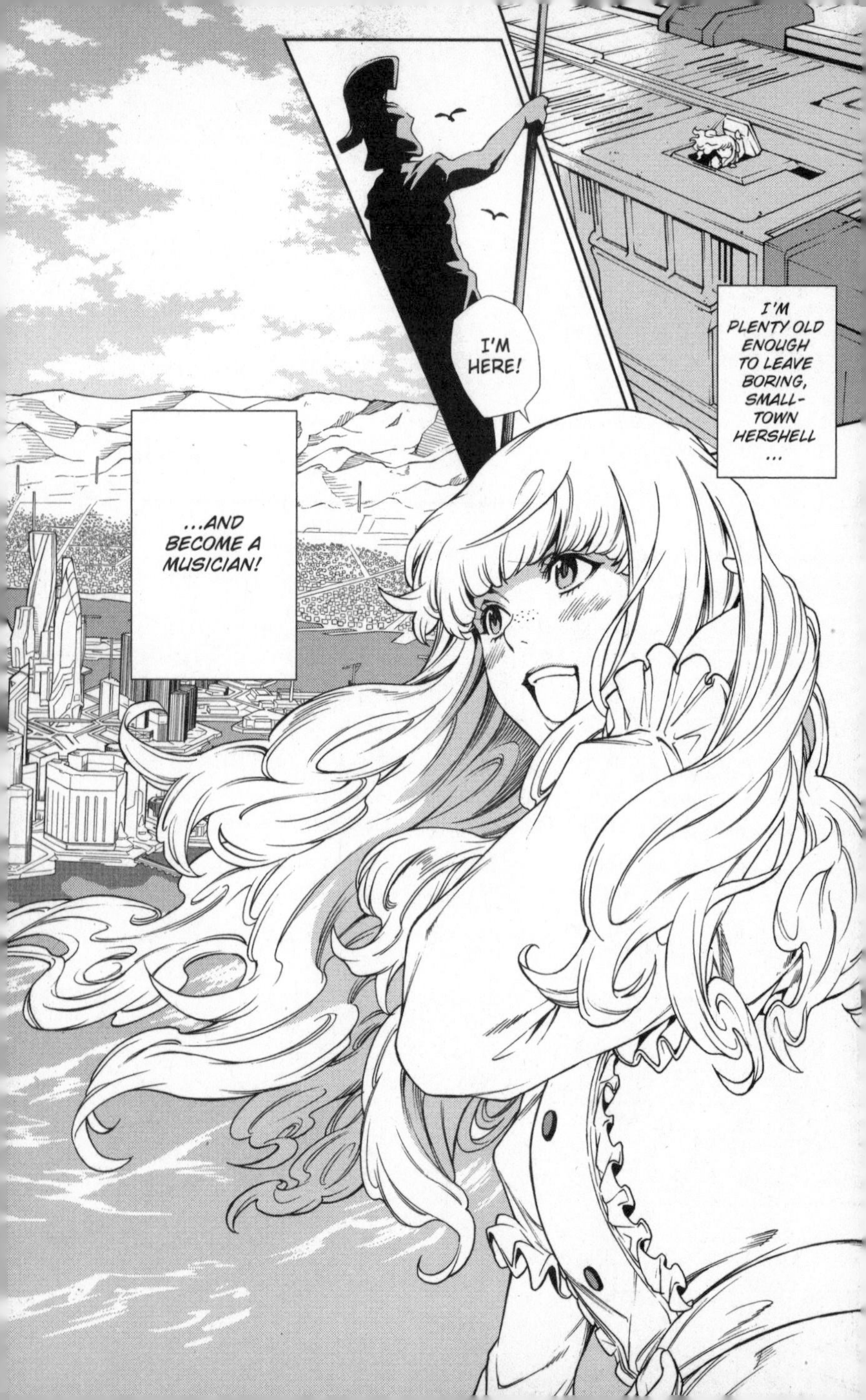
I'M PLENTY OLD ENOUGH TO LEAVE BORING, SMALL-TOWN HERSHELL ...
I'M HERE!
...AND BECOME A MUSICIAN!

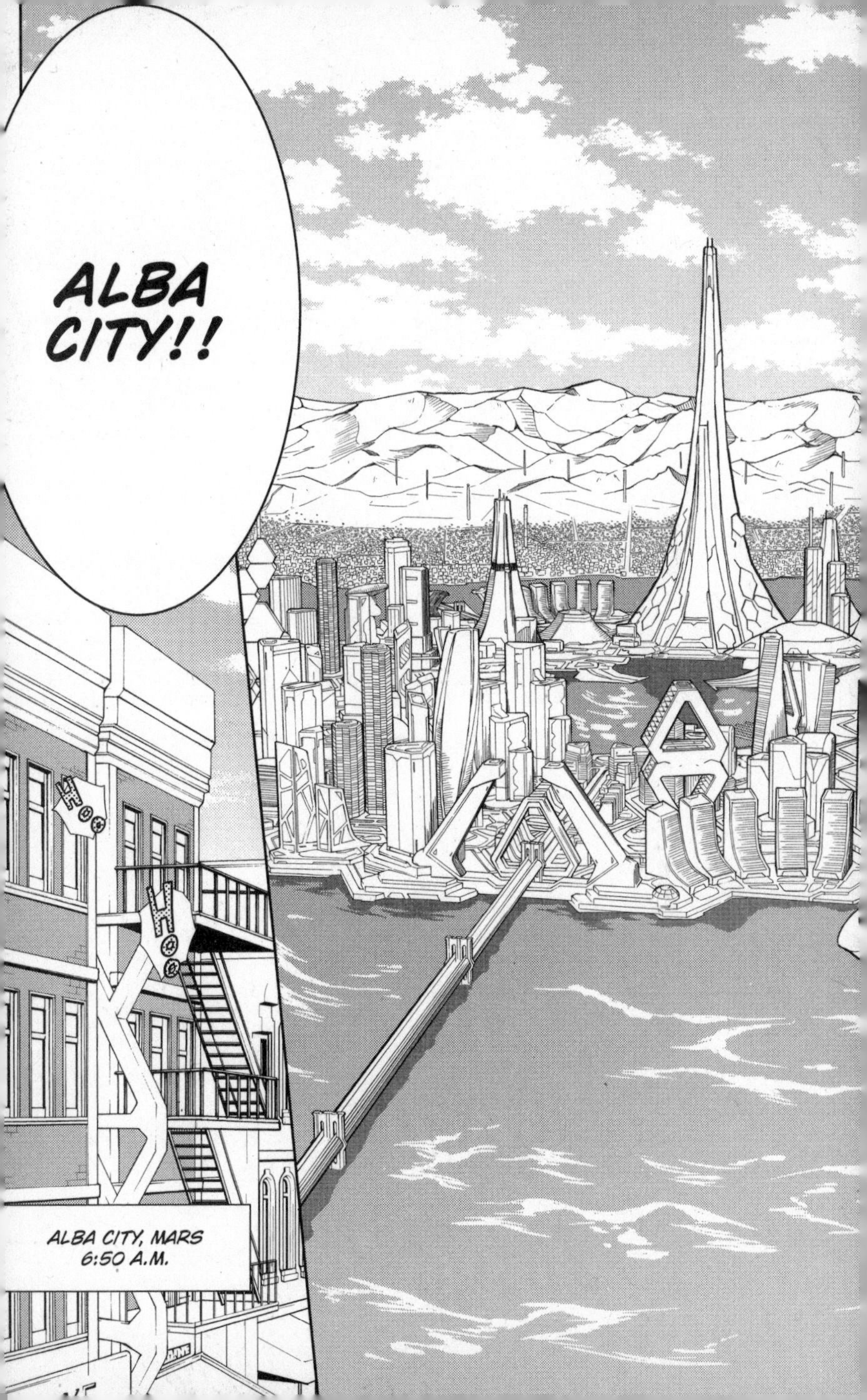
ALBA CITY!!
ALBA CITY, MARS
6:50 A.M.

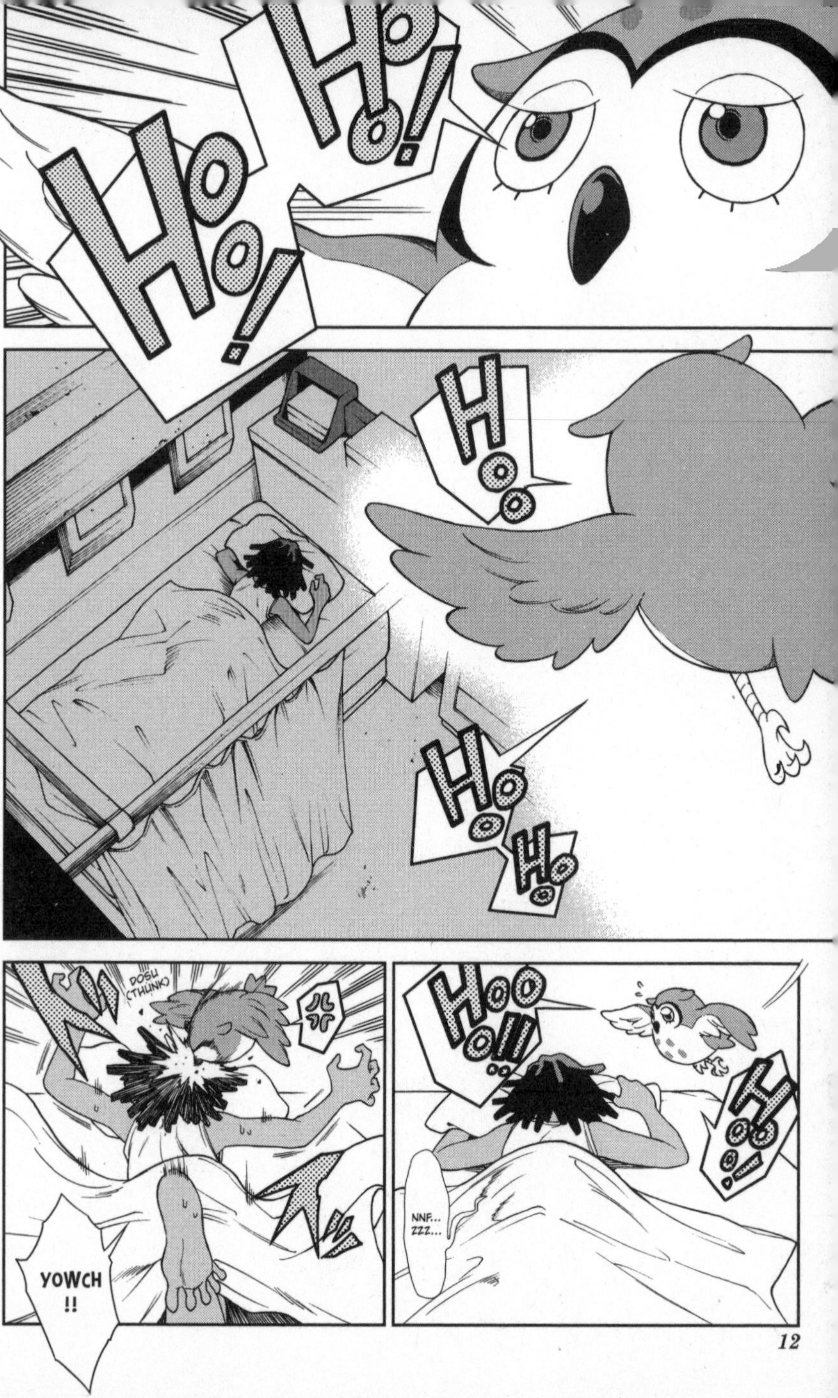
HOO!
HOO!!
HOO
HOO
HOO
HOOO!!
HOO!
NNF...
ZZZ...
DOSU (THUNK)
YOWCH !!

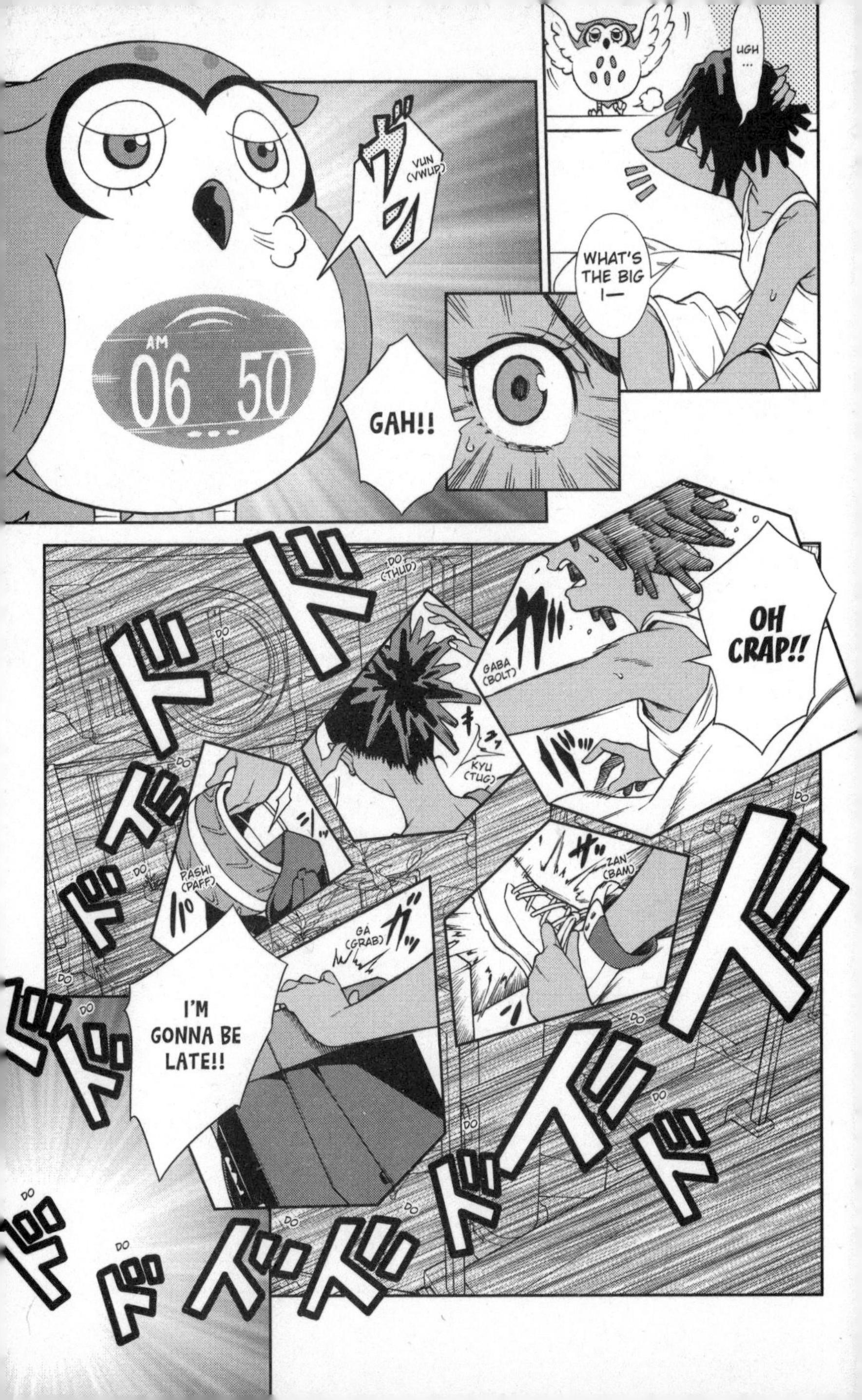
UGH ...
WHAT'S THE BIG I—
GAH!!
VUN (VWUP)
AM 06 50
OH CRAP!!
GABA (BOLT)
KYU (TUG)
ZAN (BAM)
DO (THUD)
PASHI (PAFF)
GA (GRAB)
I'M GONNA BE LATE!!
DO
DO
DO
DO
DO
DO
DO
DO
DO
DO

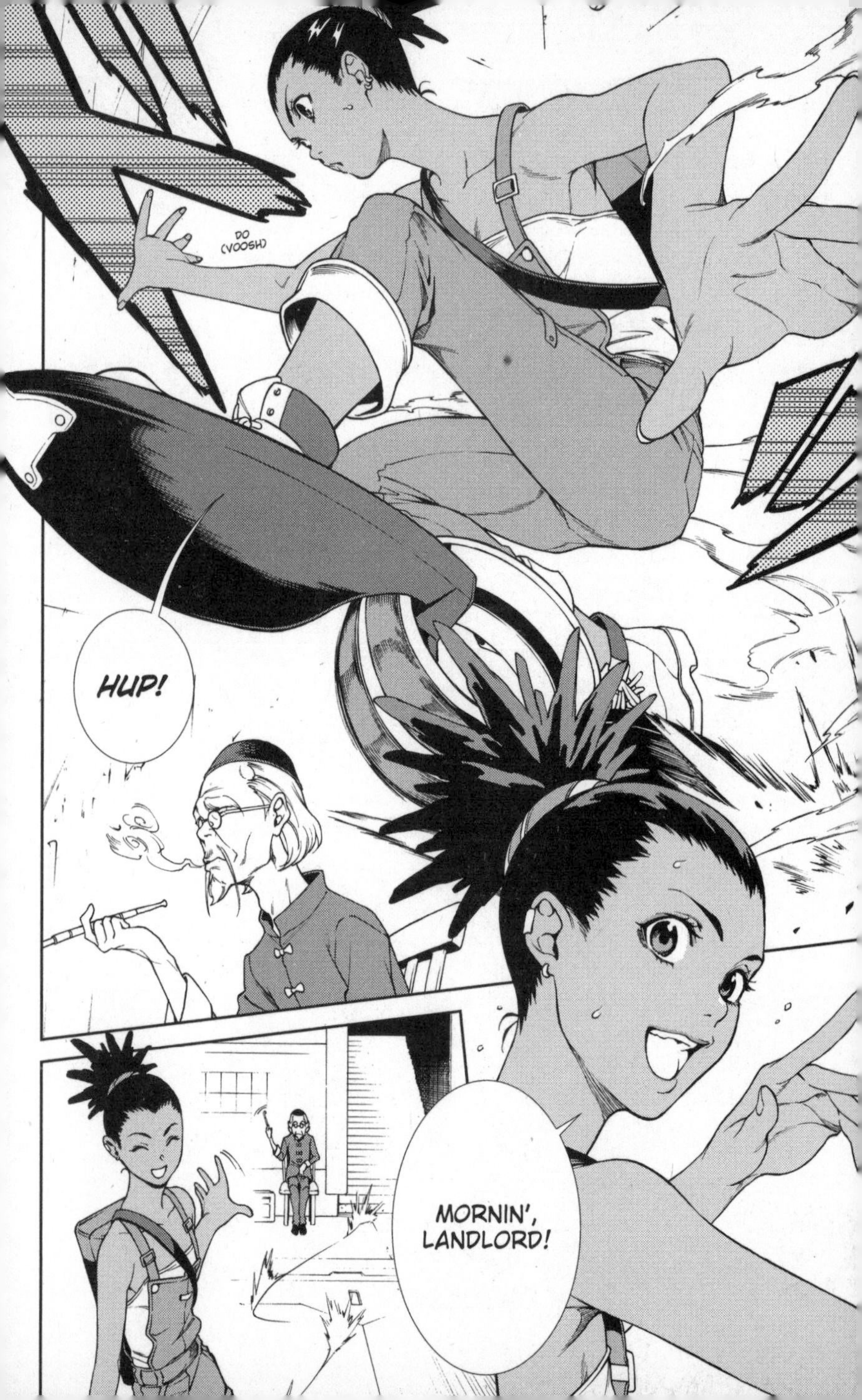
DO (VOOSH)
HUP!
MORNIN', LANDLORD!

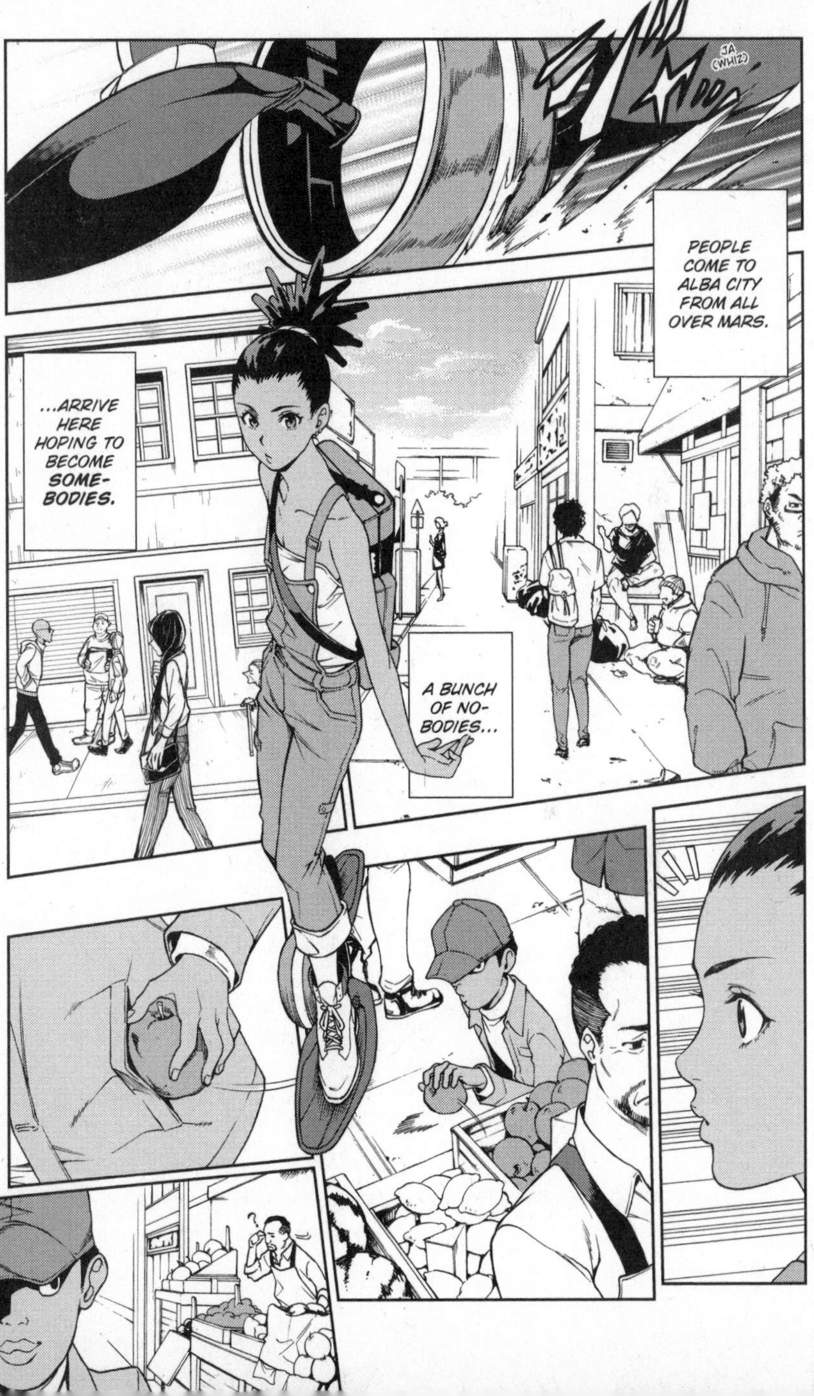
JA (WHIZ)
PEOPLE COME TO ALBA CITY FROM ALL OVER MARS.
A BUNCH OF NO-BODIES...
...ARRIVE HERE HOPING TO BECOME SOME-BODIES.

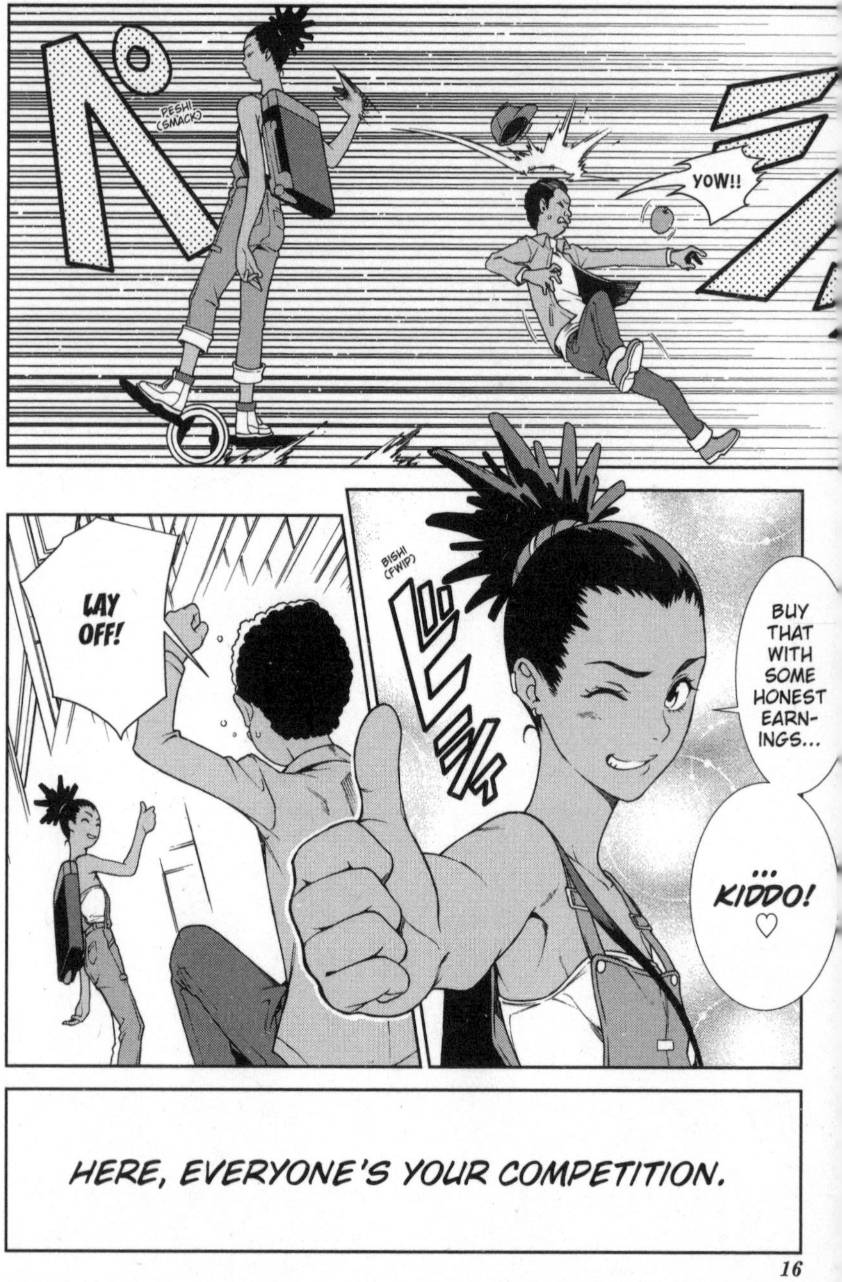
YOW!!
PESHI (SMACK)
BUY THAT WITH SOME HONEST EARN-INGS...
BISHI (FWIP)
...KIDDO! ♡
LAY OFF!
HERE, EVERYONE'S YOUR COMPETITION.

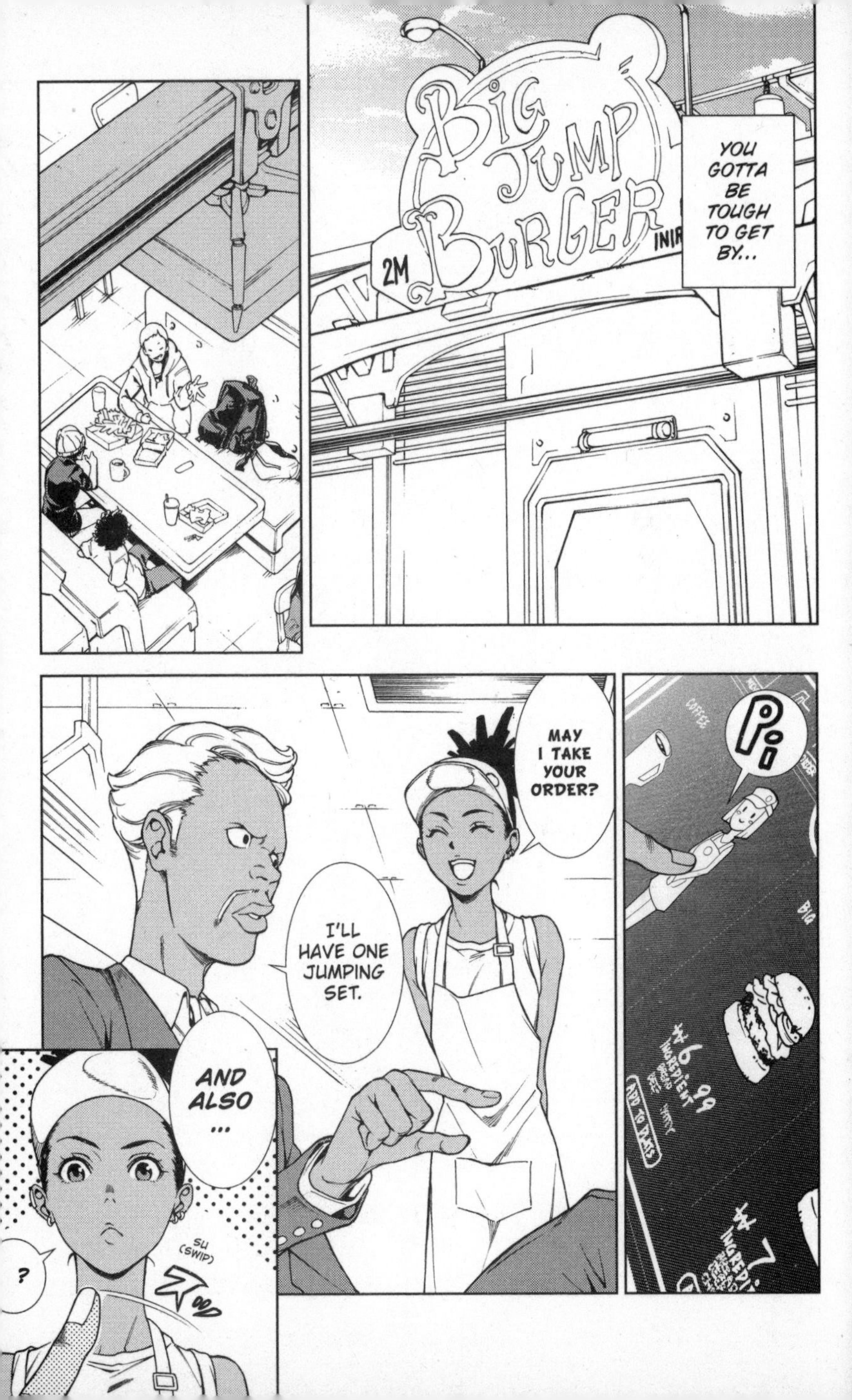
BIG JUMP BURGER
2M
YOU GOTTA BE TOUGH TO GET BY...
COFFEE
Pi
MAY I TAKE YOUR ORDER?
I'LL HAVE ONE JUMPING SET.
AND ALSO ...
?
SU (SWIP)

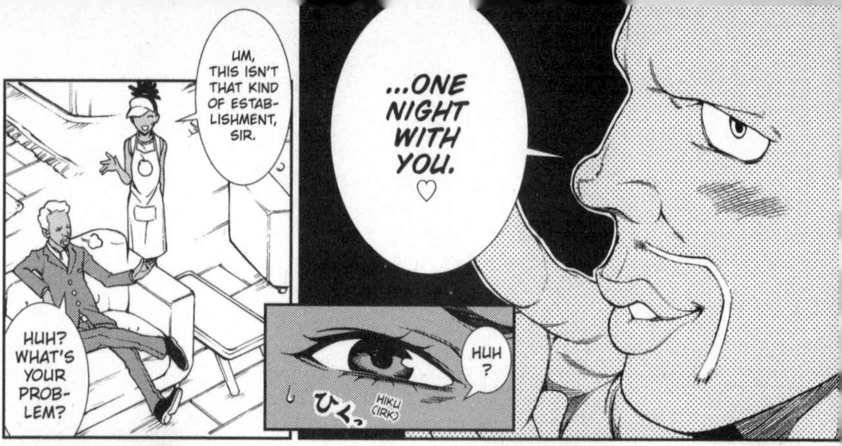
...ONE NIGHT WITH YOU. ♡
UM, THIS ISN'T THAT KIND OF ESTAB-LISHMENT, SIR.
HUH? WHAT'S YOUR PROB-LEM?
HUH?
HIKU (IRK)

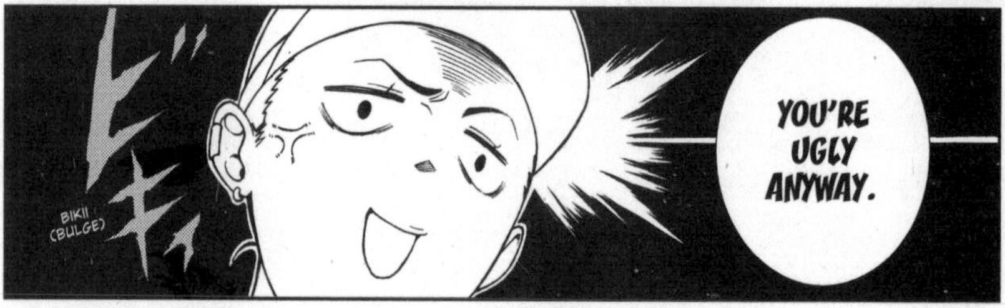
YOU'RE UGLY ANYWAY.
BIKII (BULGE)

...AND YOU WON'T MAKE IT IF YOU STOP MOVING.

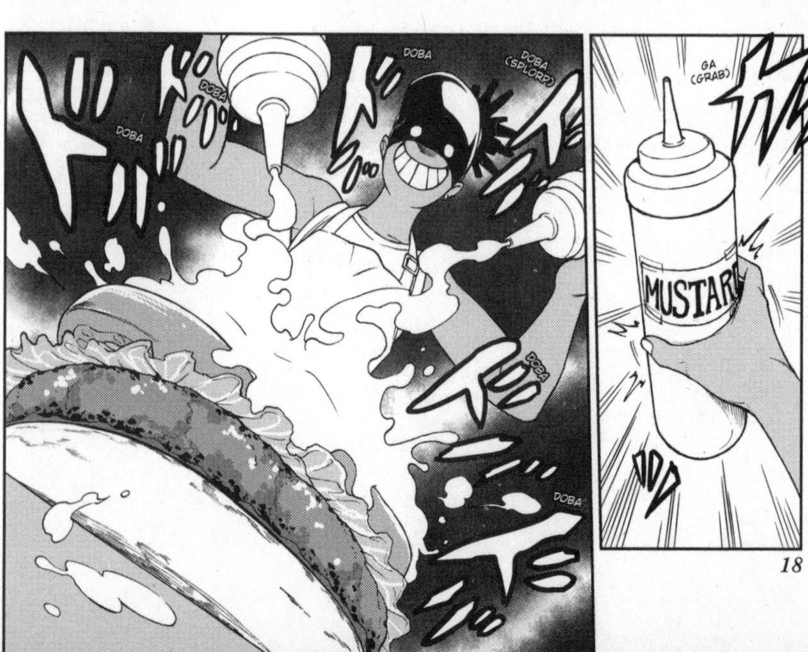
GA (GRAB)
MUSTAR
DOBA (SPLORP)
DOBA
DOBA
DOBA
DOBA
DOBA

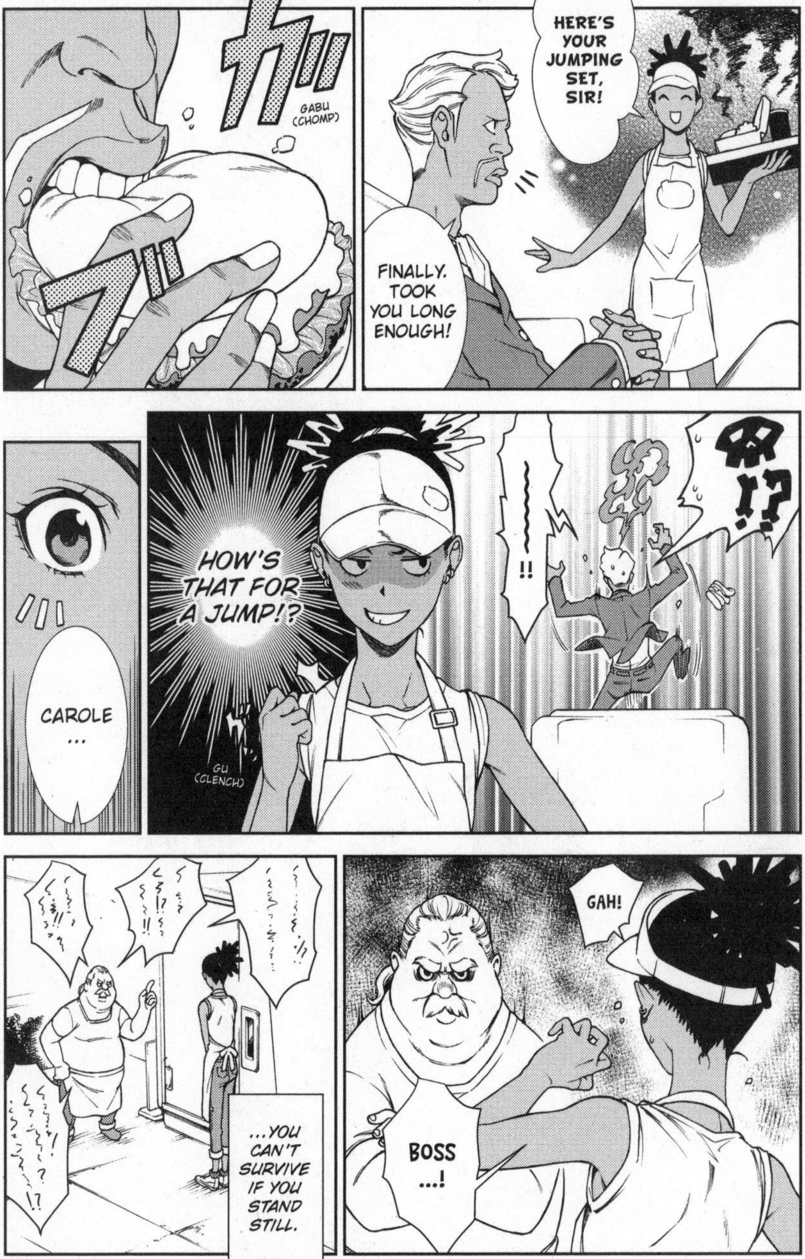
HERE'S YOUR JUMPING SET, SIR!
FINALLY. TOOK YOU LONG ENOUGH!
GABU (CHOMP)
!!
HOW'S THAT FOR A JUMP!?
GU (CLENCH)
CAROLE ...
GAH!
BOSS ...!
...YOU CAN'T SURVIVE IF YOU STAND STILL.

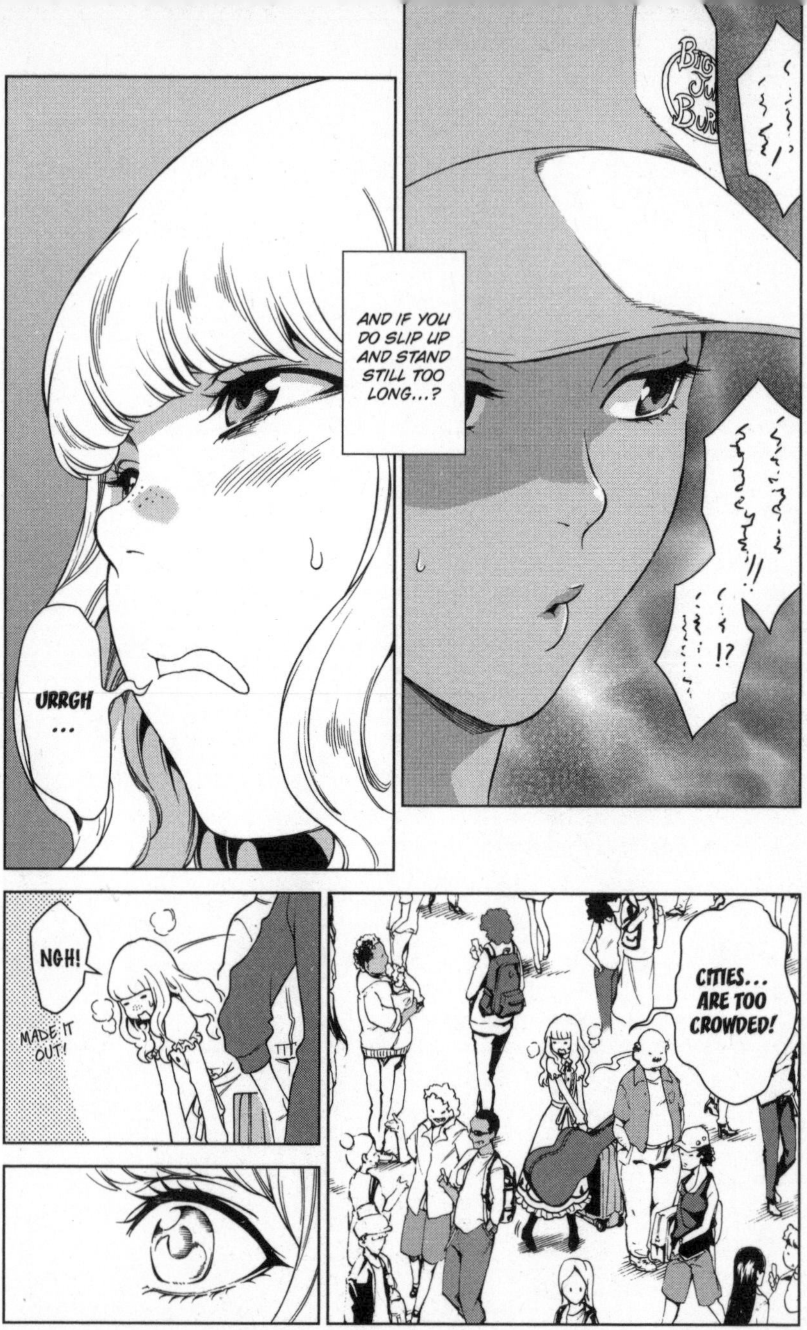
AND IF YOU DO SLIP UP AND STAND STILL TOO LONG...?
URRGH ...
CITIES... ARE TOO CROWDED!
NGH!
MADE IT OUT!

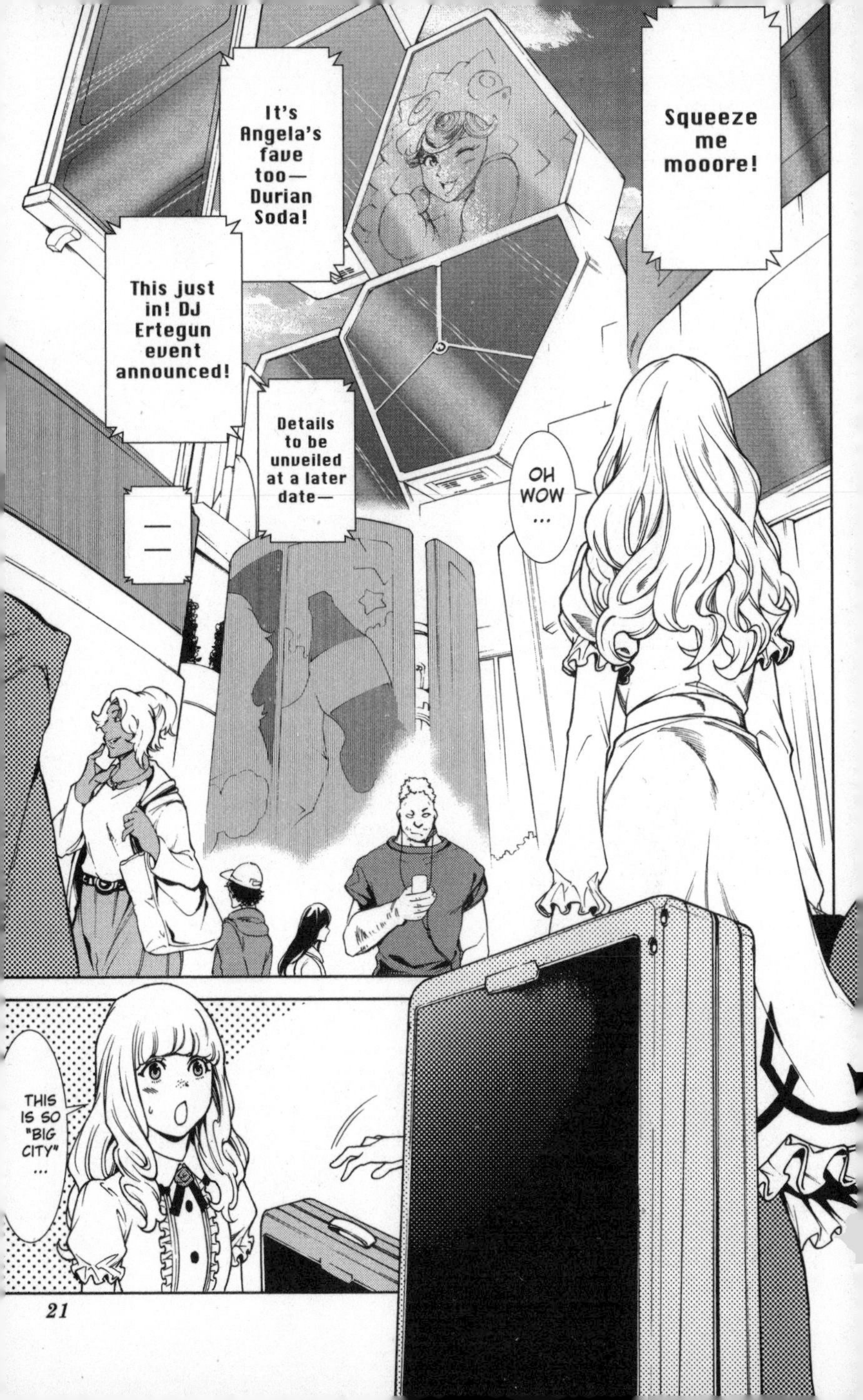

Squeeze me mooore!
It's Angela's fave too— Durian Soda!
This just in! DJ Ertegun event announced!
Details to be unveiled at a later date—
— —
OH WOW ...
THIS IS SO "BIG CITY" ...

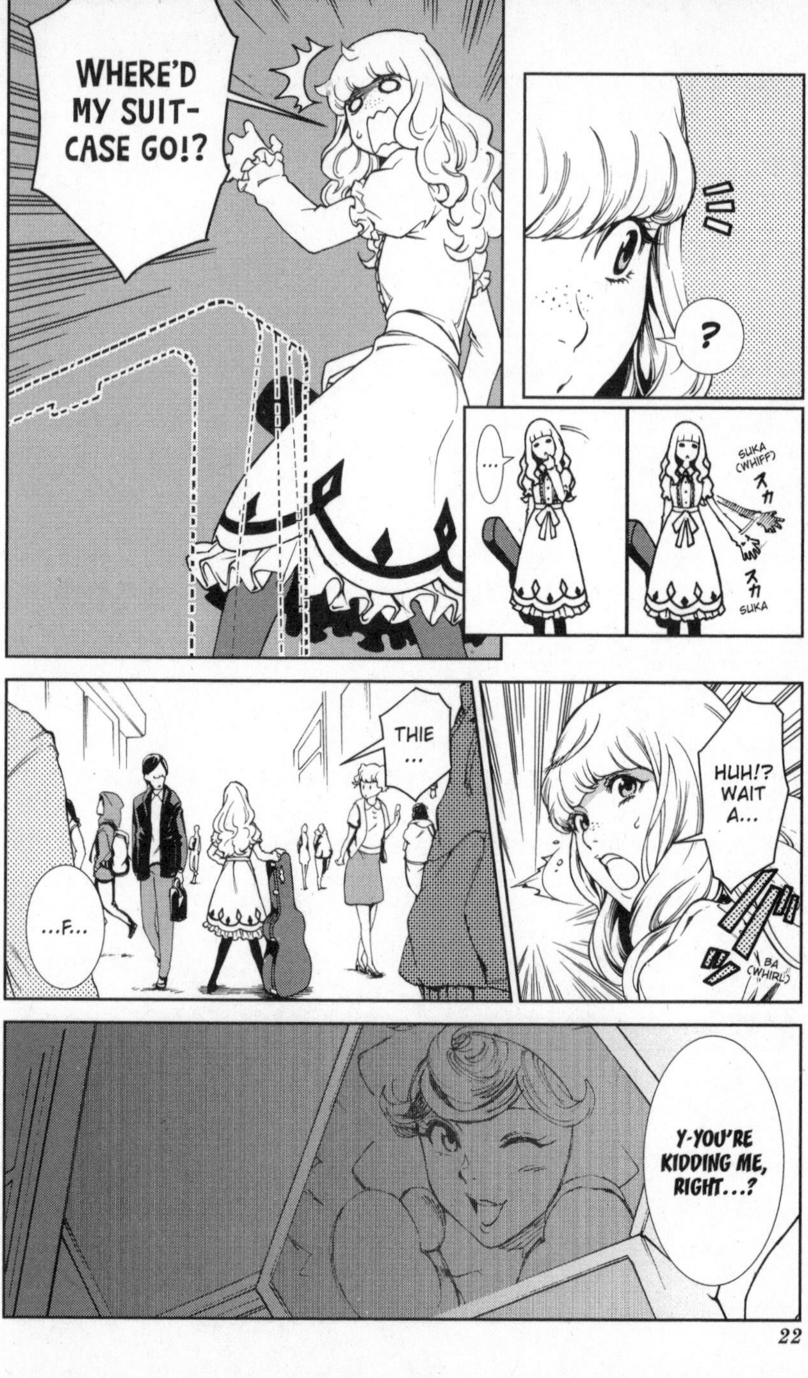
?
SUKA (WHIFF)
スカ
スカ
SUKA
...
WHERE'D MY SUIT-CASE GO!?
HUH!? WAIT A...
BA (WHIRL)
THIE ...
...F...
Y-YOU'RE KIDDING ME, RIGHT...?

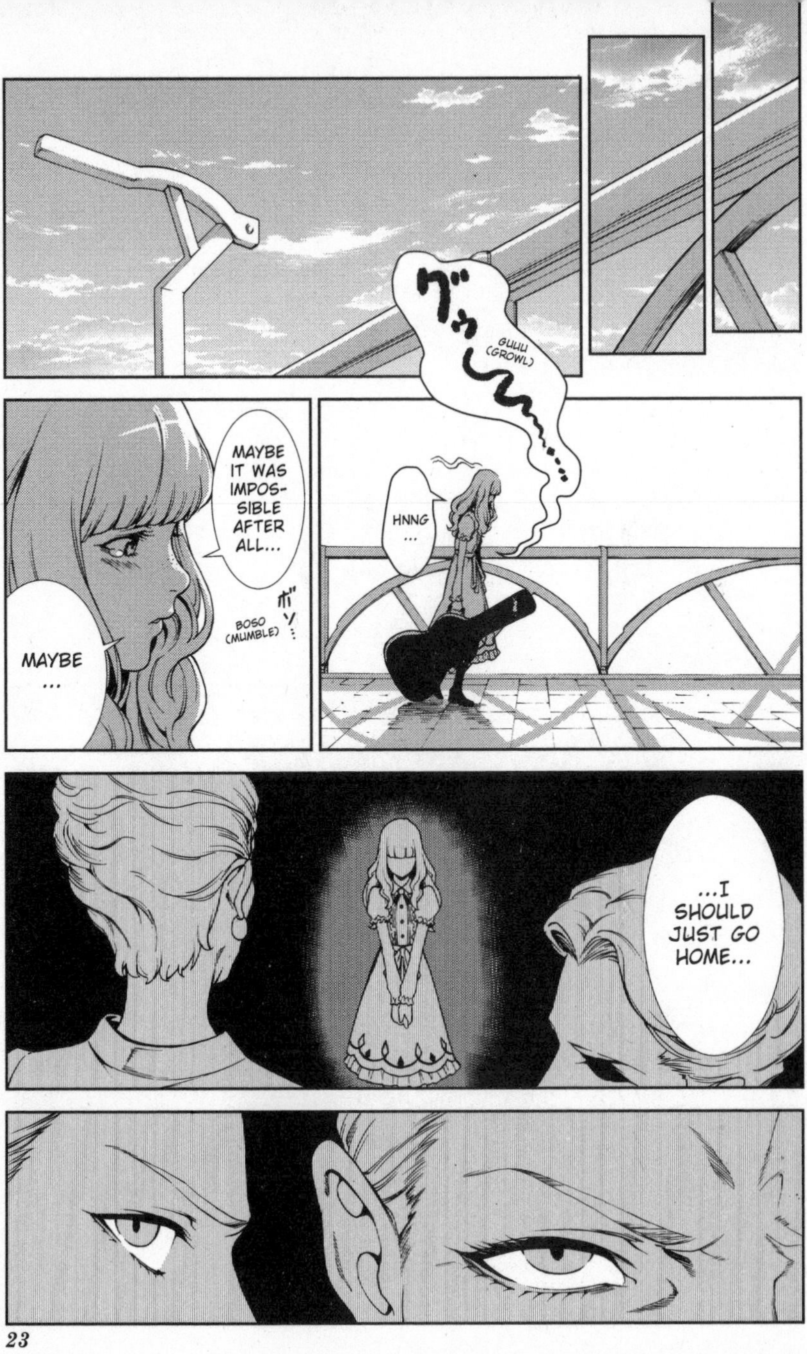

グゥ
GUUU (GROWL)
HNNG ...
MAYBE IT WAS IMPOSSIBLE AFTER ALL...
ボソ
BOSO (MUMBLE)
MAYBE ...
...I SHOULD JUST GO HOME...

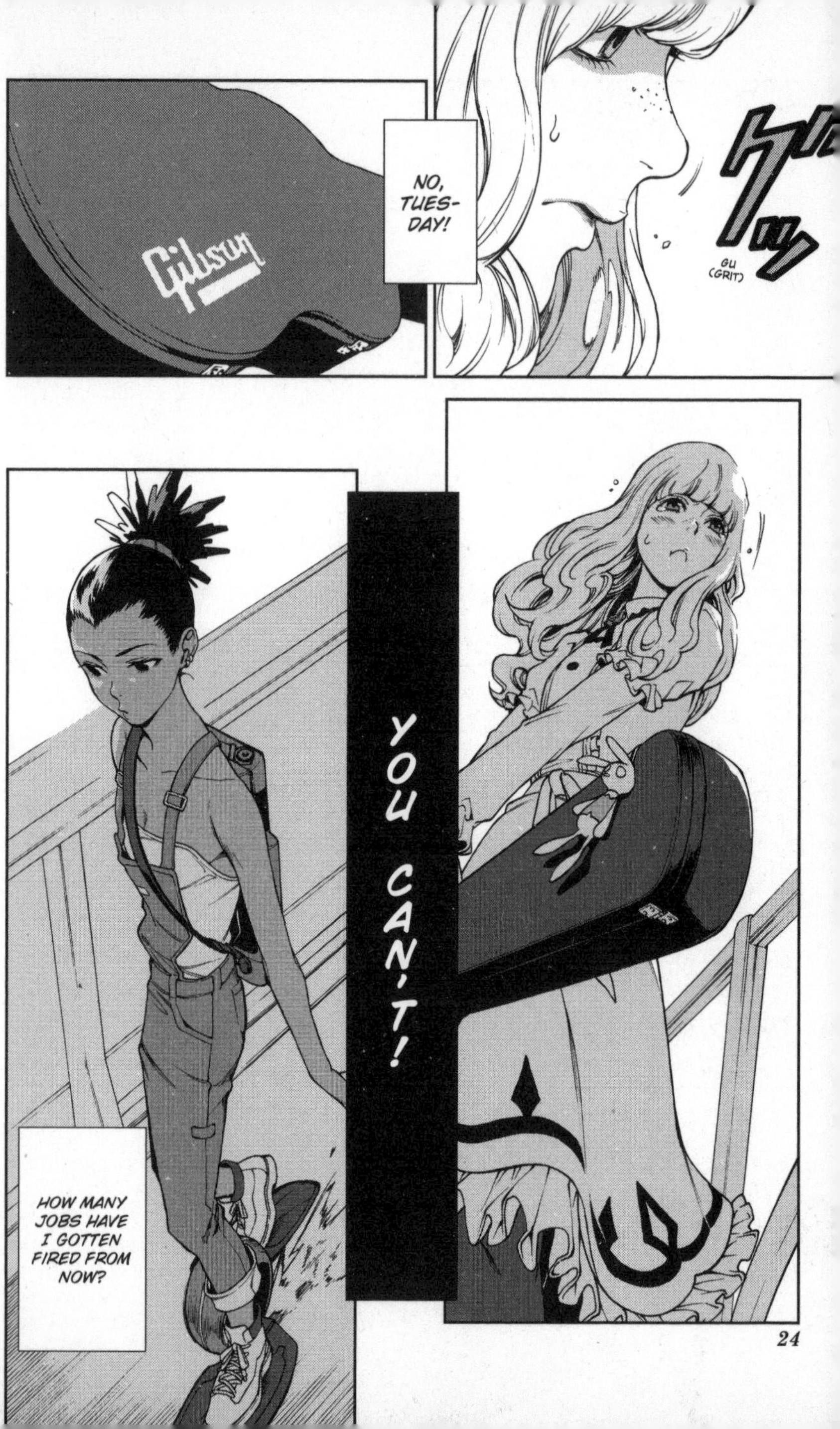
GU
(GRIT)
NO, TUES-DAY!
YOU CAN'T!
HOW MANY JOBS HAVE I GOTTEN FIRED FROM NOW?

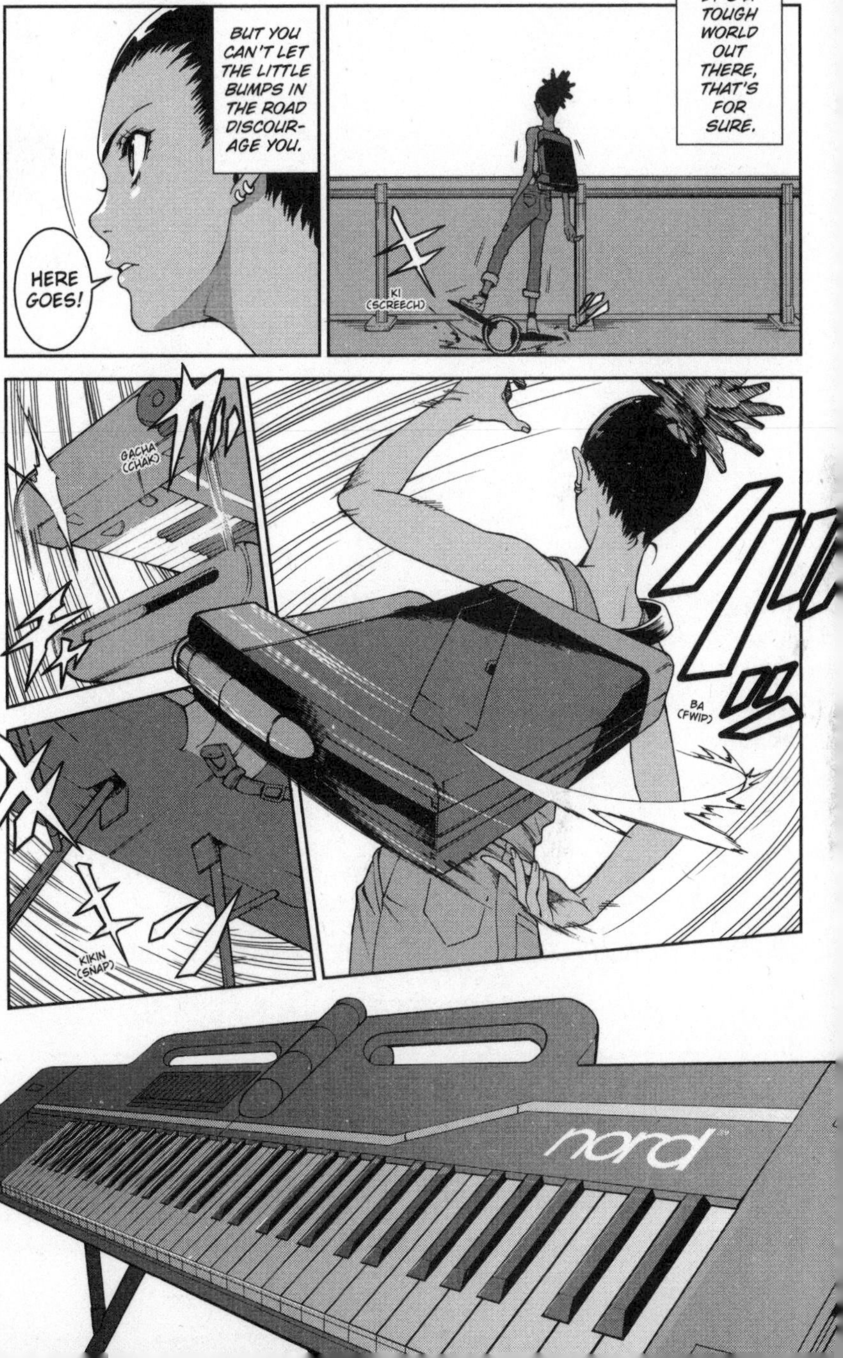
IT'S A TOUGH WORLD OUT THERE, THAT'S FOR SURE.
KI (SCREECH)
BUT YOU CAN'T LET THE LITTLE BUMPS IN THE ROAD DISCOURAGE YOU.
HERE GOES!
BA (FWIP)
GACHA (CHAK)
KIKIN (SNAP)
nord

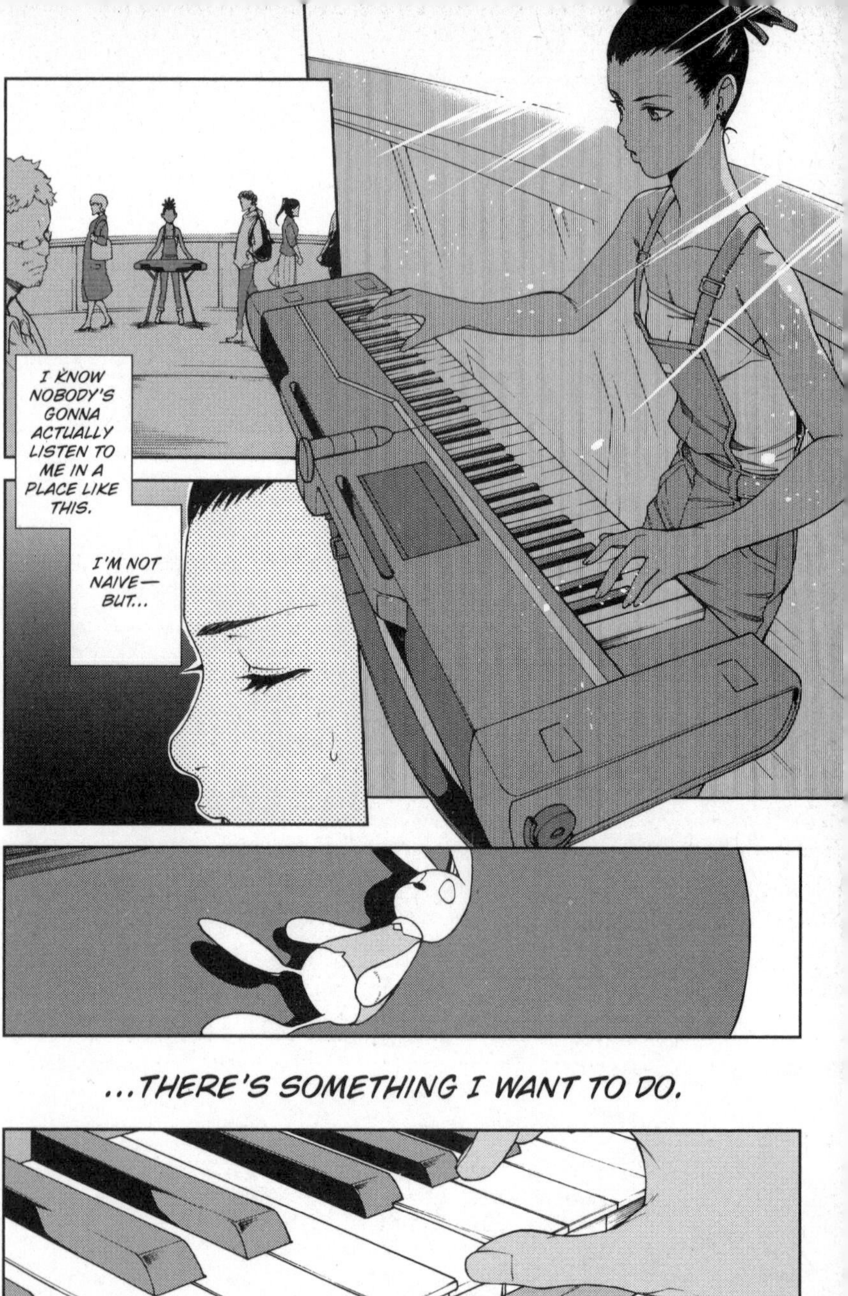
I KNOW NOBODY'S GONNA ACTUALLY LISTEN TO ME IN A PLACE LIKE THIS.
I'M NOT NAIVE— BUT...
...THERE'S SOMETHING I WANT TO DO.

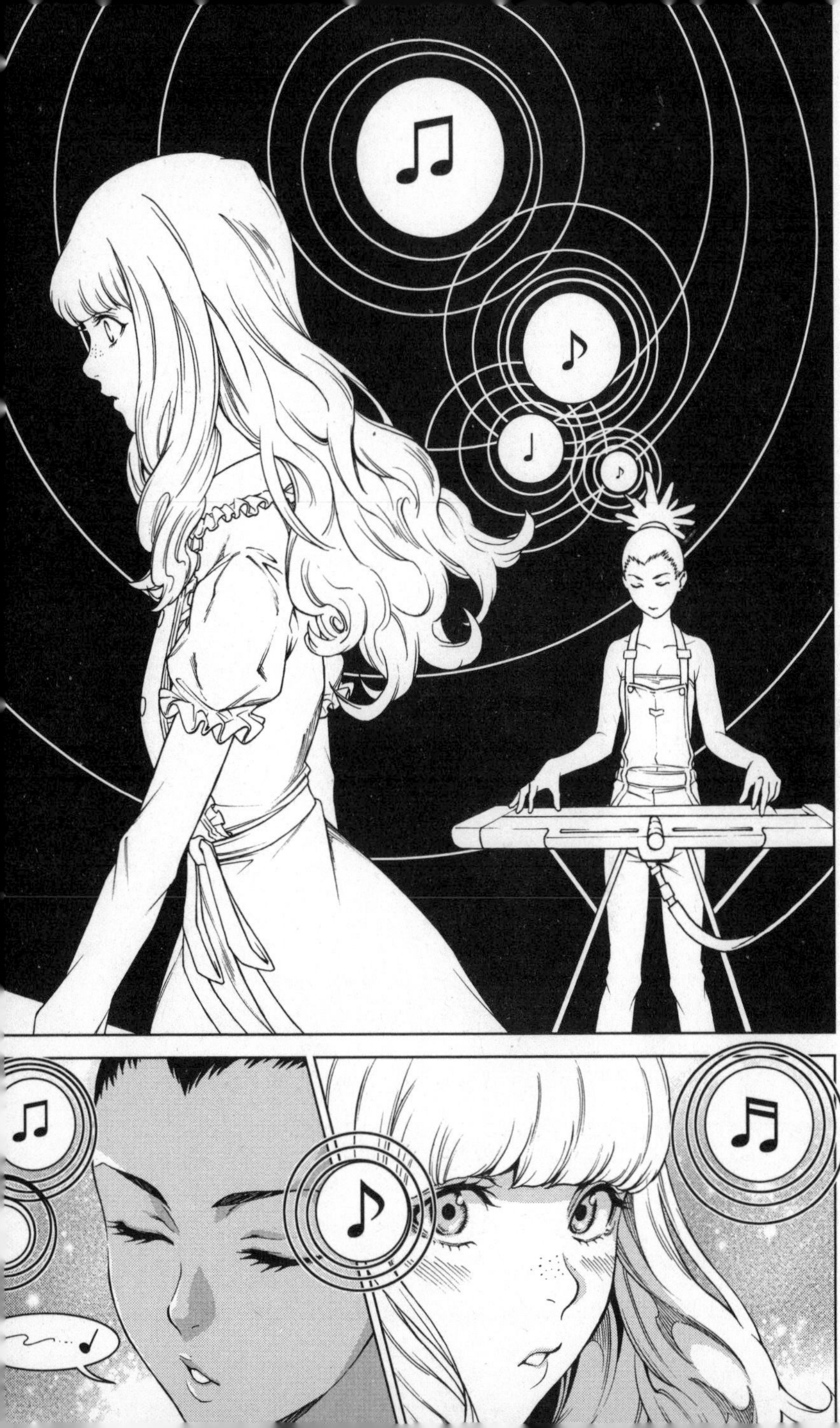

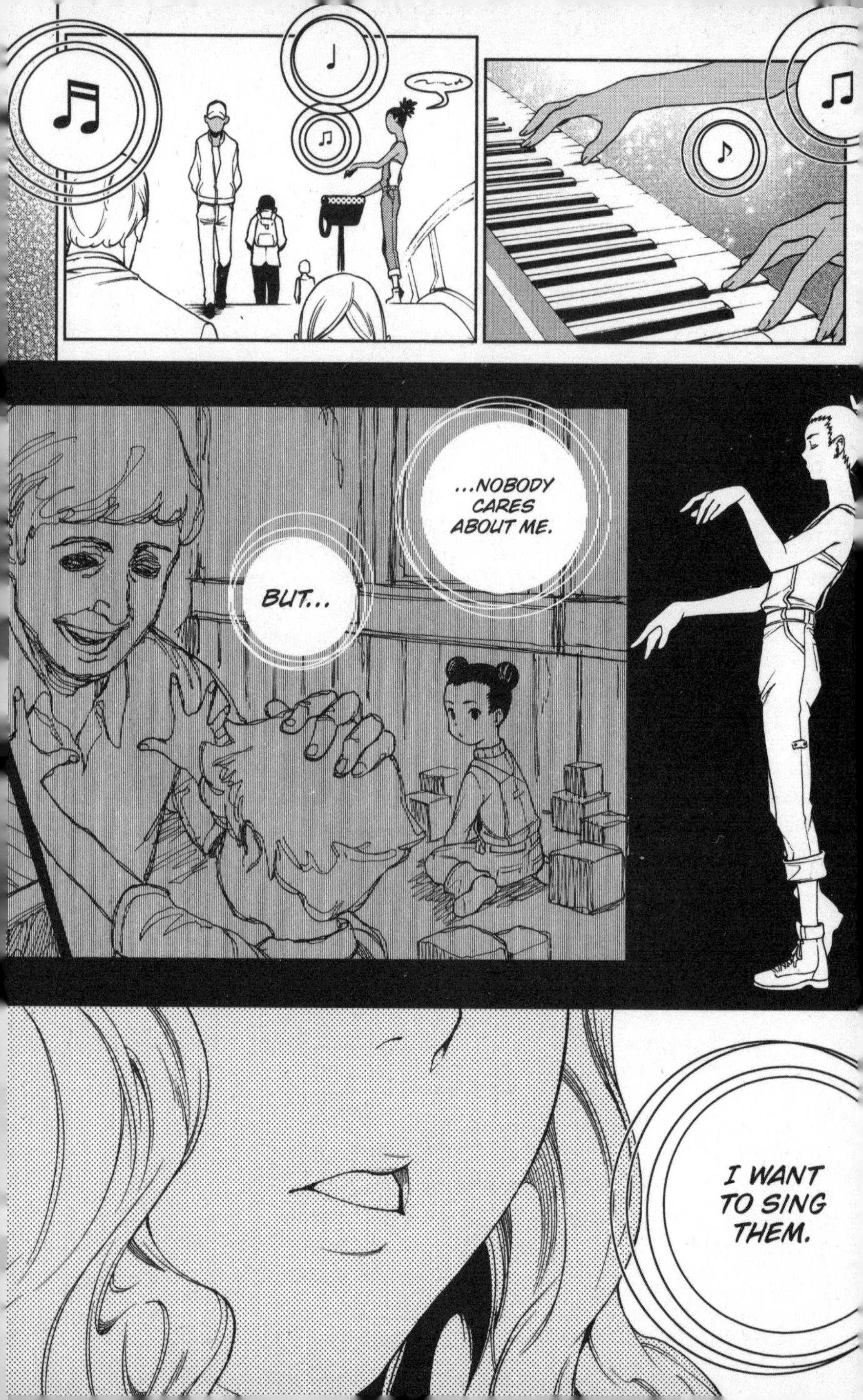
...NOBODY CARES ABOUT ME.
BUT...
I WANT TO SING THEM.

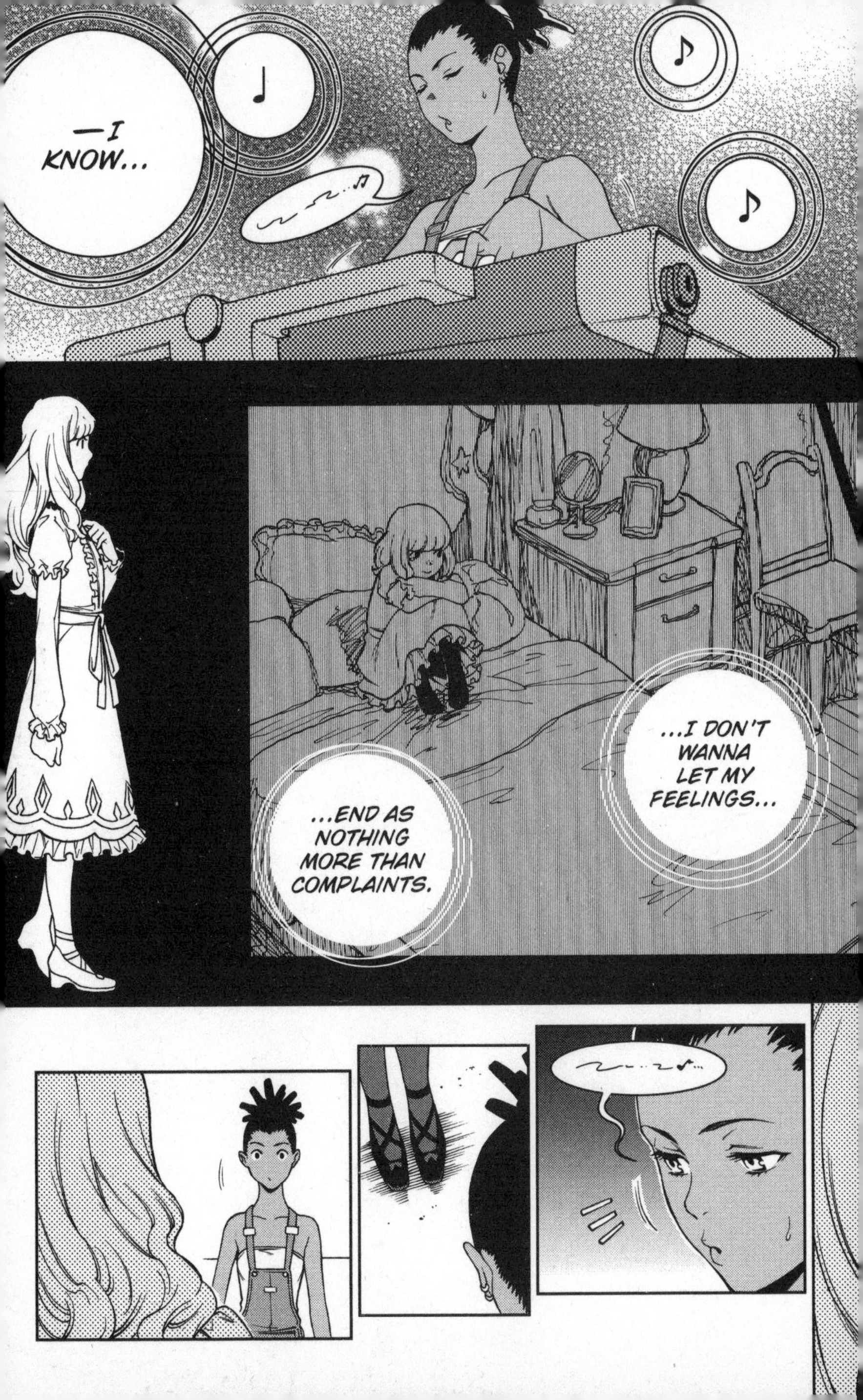
—I KNOW...
...I DON'T WANNA LET MY FEELINGS...
...END AS NOTHING MORE THAN COMPLAINTS.

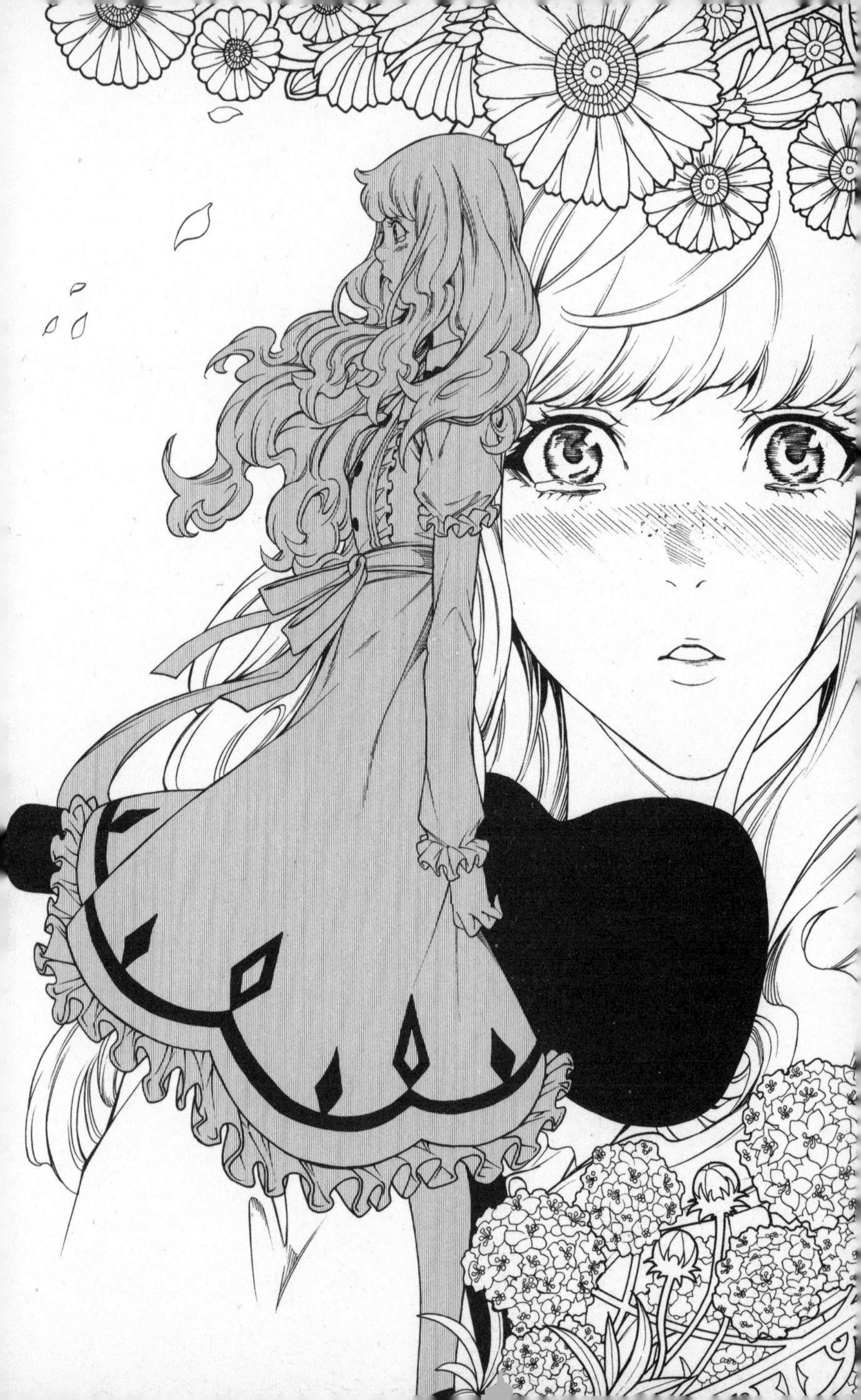

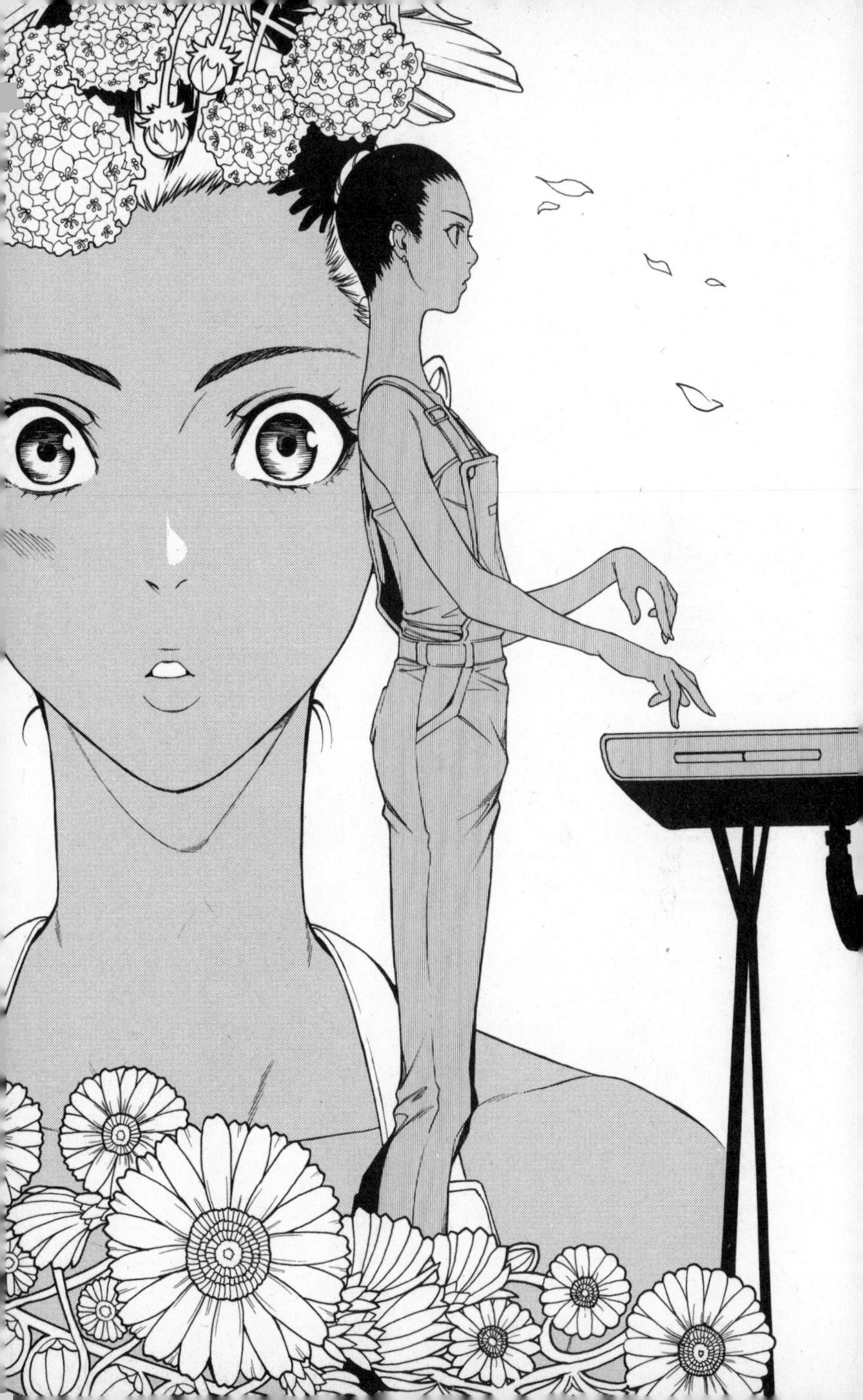

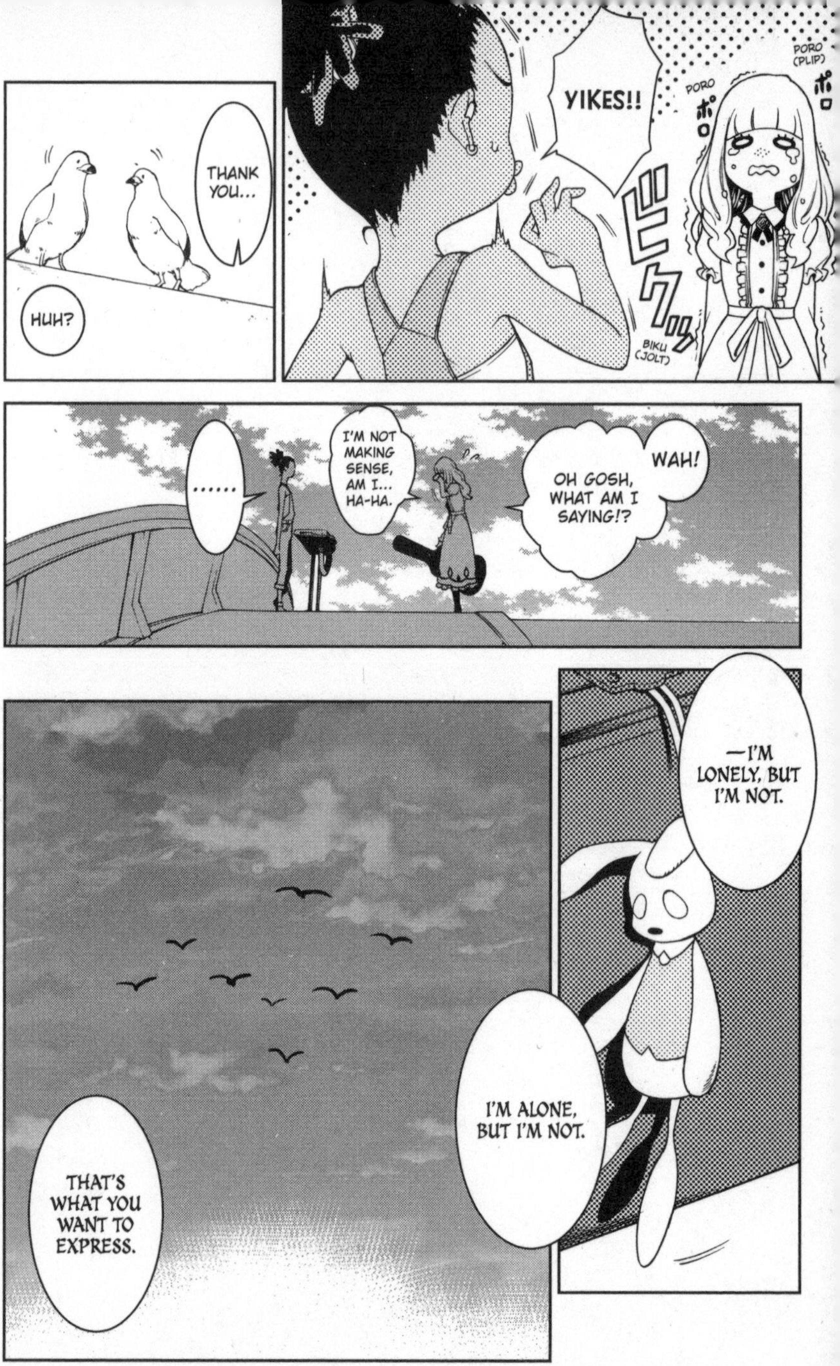
PORO (PLIP)
ポロ
PORO
ポロ
YIKES!!
ビクッ
BIKU (JOLT)
THANK YOU...
HUH?
WAH!
OH GOSH, WHAT AM I SAYING!?
I'M NOT MAKING SENSE, AM I... HA-HA.
......
—I'M LONELY, BUT I'M NOT.
I'M ALONE, BUT I'M NOT.
THAT'S WHAT YOU WANT TO EXPRESS.

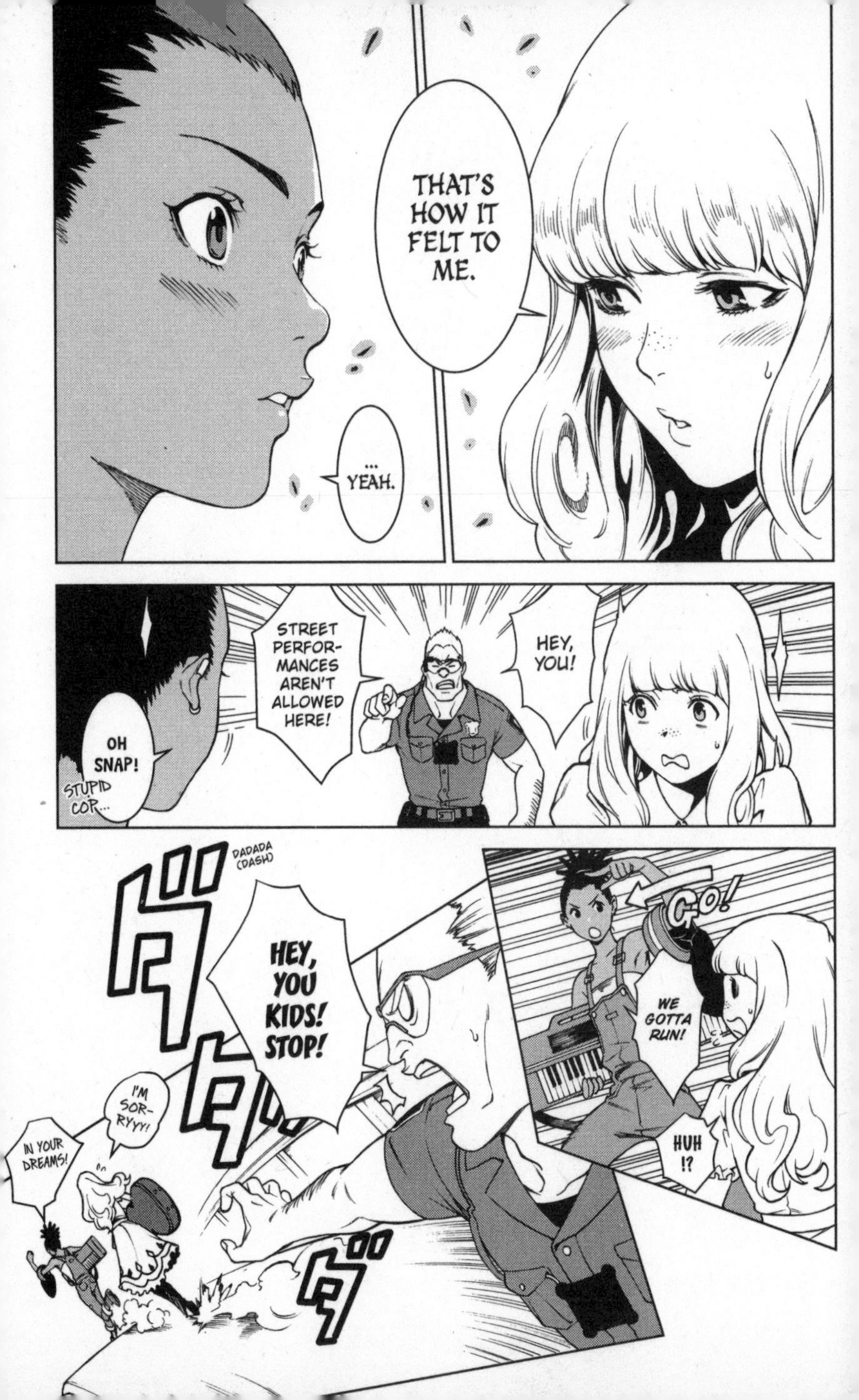
THAT'S HOW IT FELT TO ME.
... YEAH.
HEY, YOU!
STREET PERFORMANCES AREN'T ALLOWED HERE!
OH SNAP!
STUPID COP...
GO!
WE GOTTA RUN!
HUH !?
DADADA (DASH)
HEY, YOU KIDS! STOP!
I'M SORRYYY!
IN YOUR DREAMS!

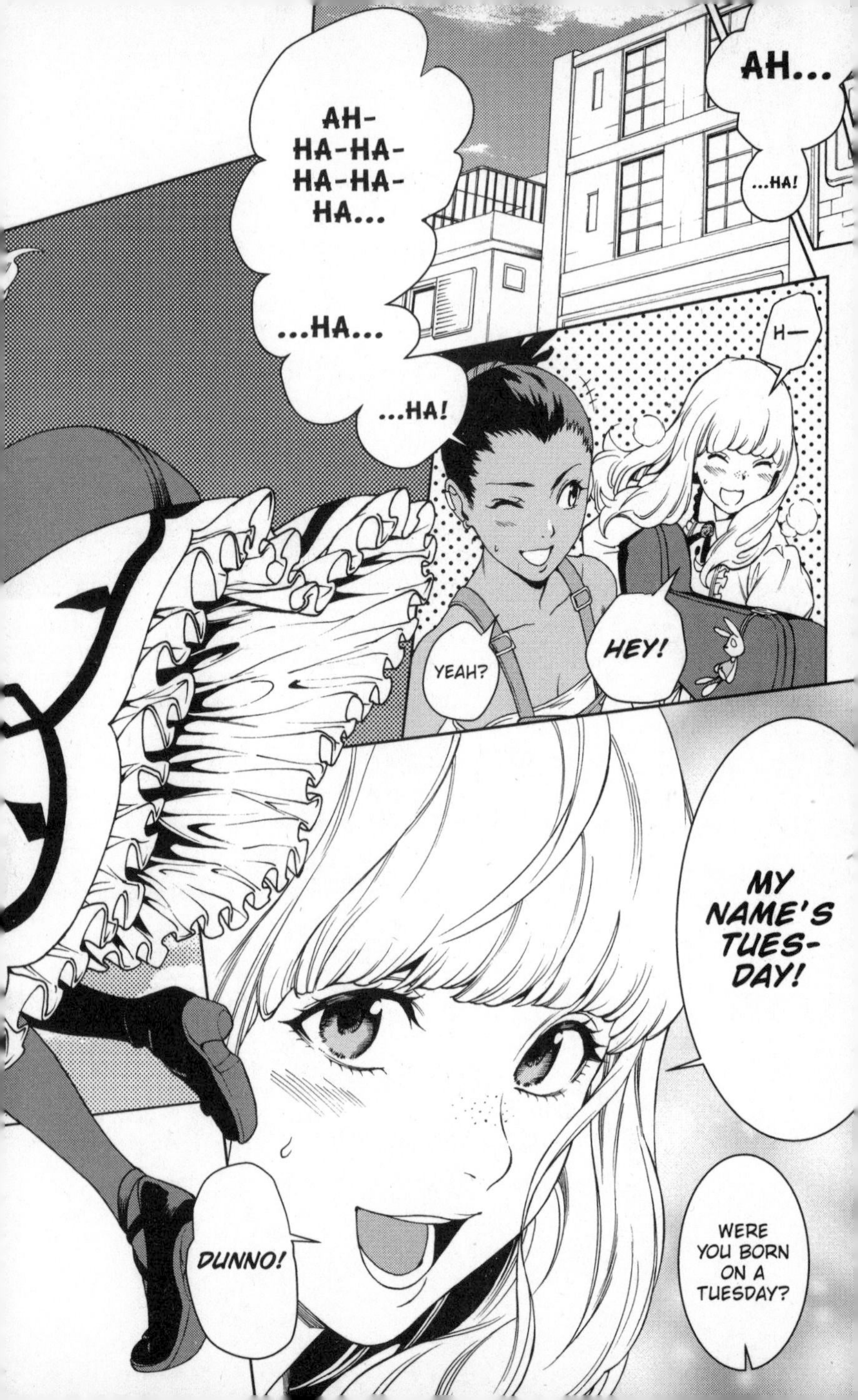
AH...
...HA!
AH-HA-HA-HA-HA-HA...
...HA...
...HA!
H—
HEY!
YEAH?
MY NAME'S TUES-DAY!
WERE YOU BORN ON A TUESDAY?
DUNNO!

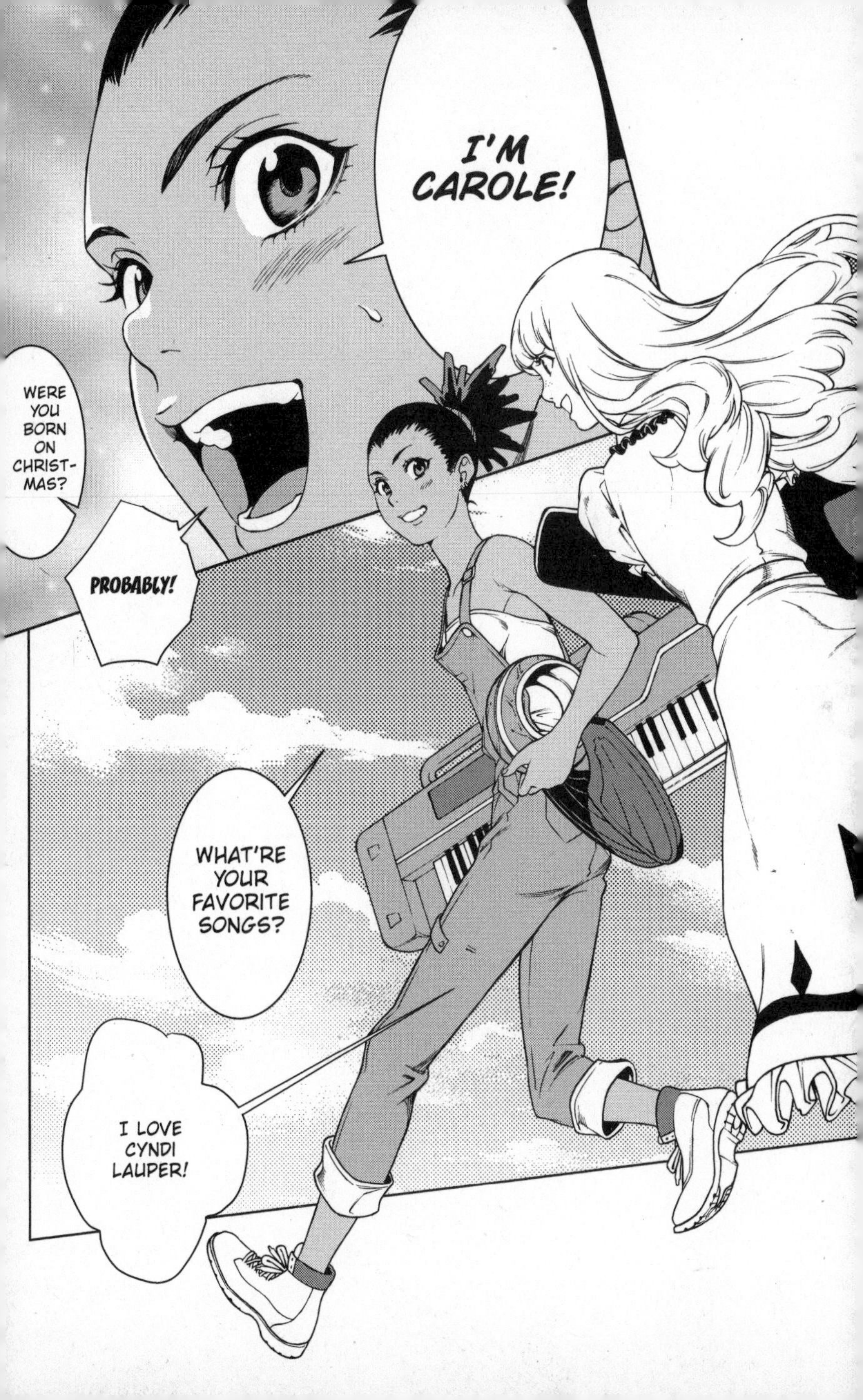
I'M CAROLE!
WERE YOU BORN ON CHRISTMAS?
PROBABLY!
WHAT'RE YOUR FAVORITE SONGS?
I LOVE CYNDI LAUPER!

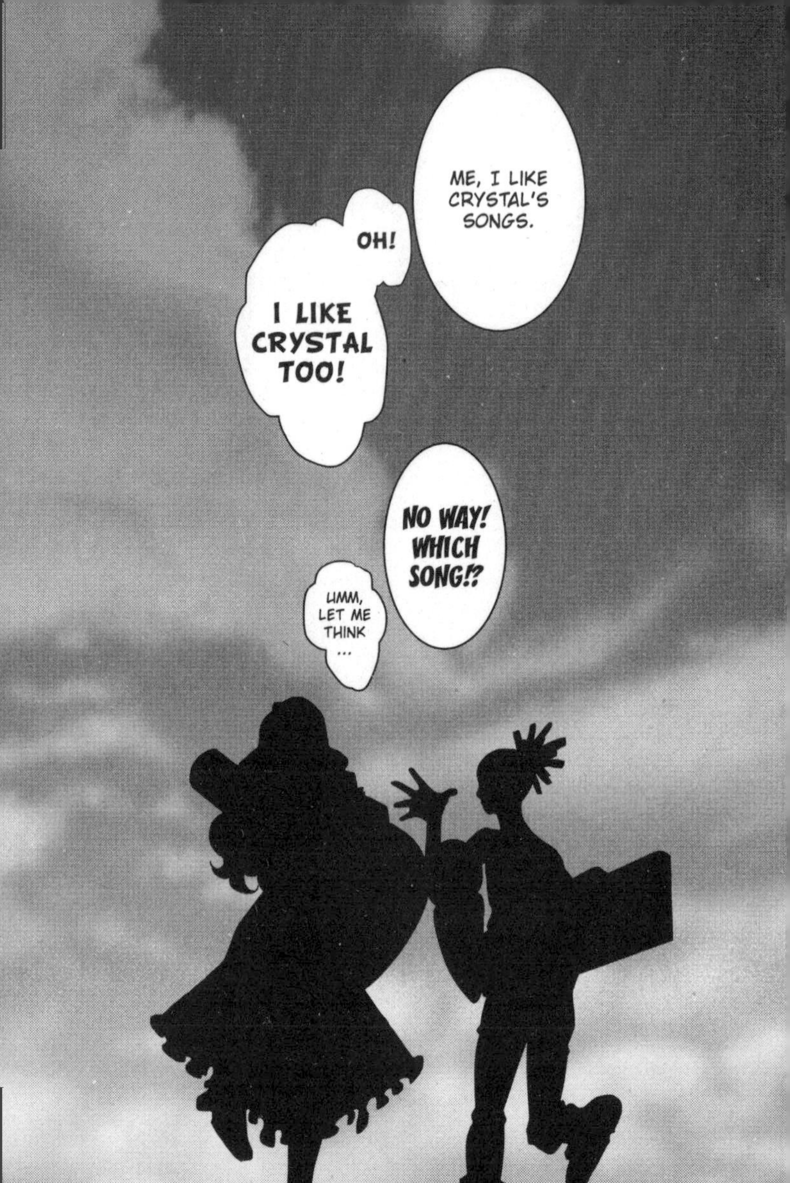
ME, I LIKE CRYSTAL'S SONGS.
OH!
I LIKE CRYSTAL TOO!
NO WAY! WHICH SONG!?
UMM, LET ME THINK ...

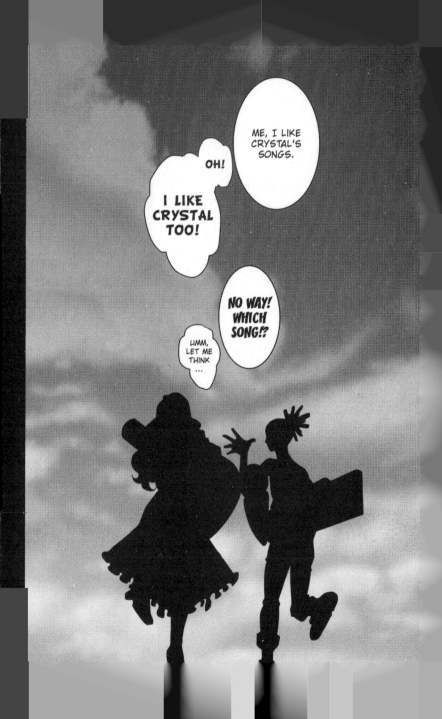

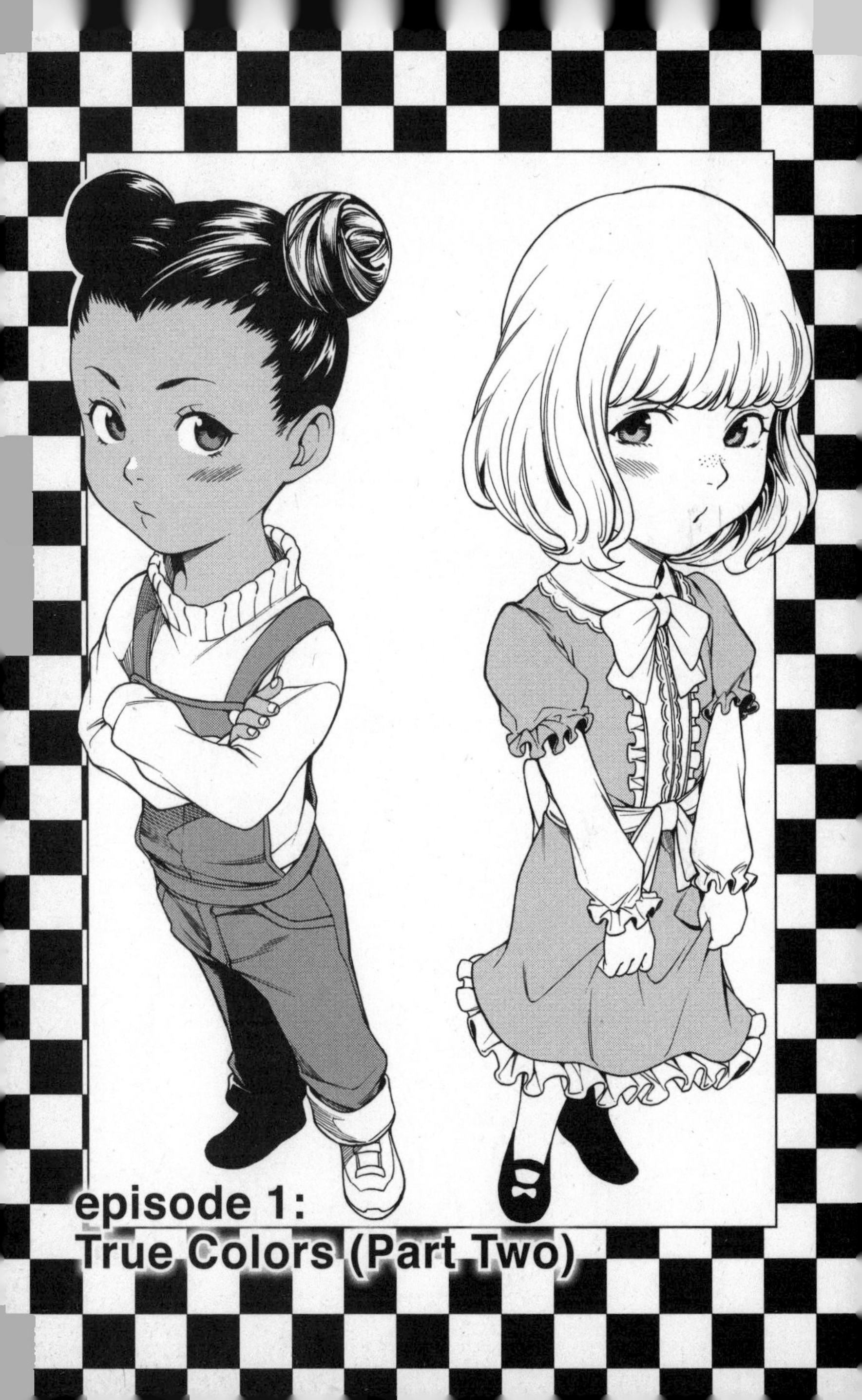

episode 1:
True Colors (Part Two)

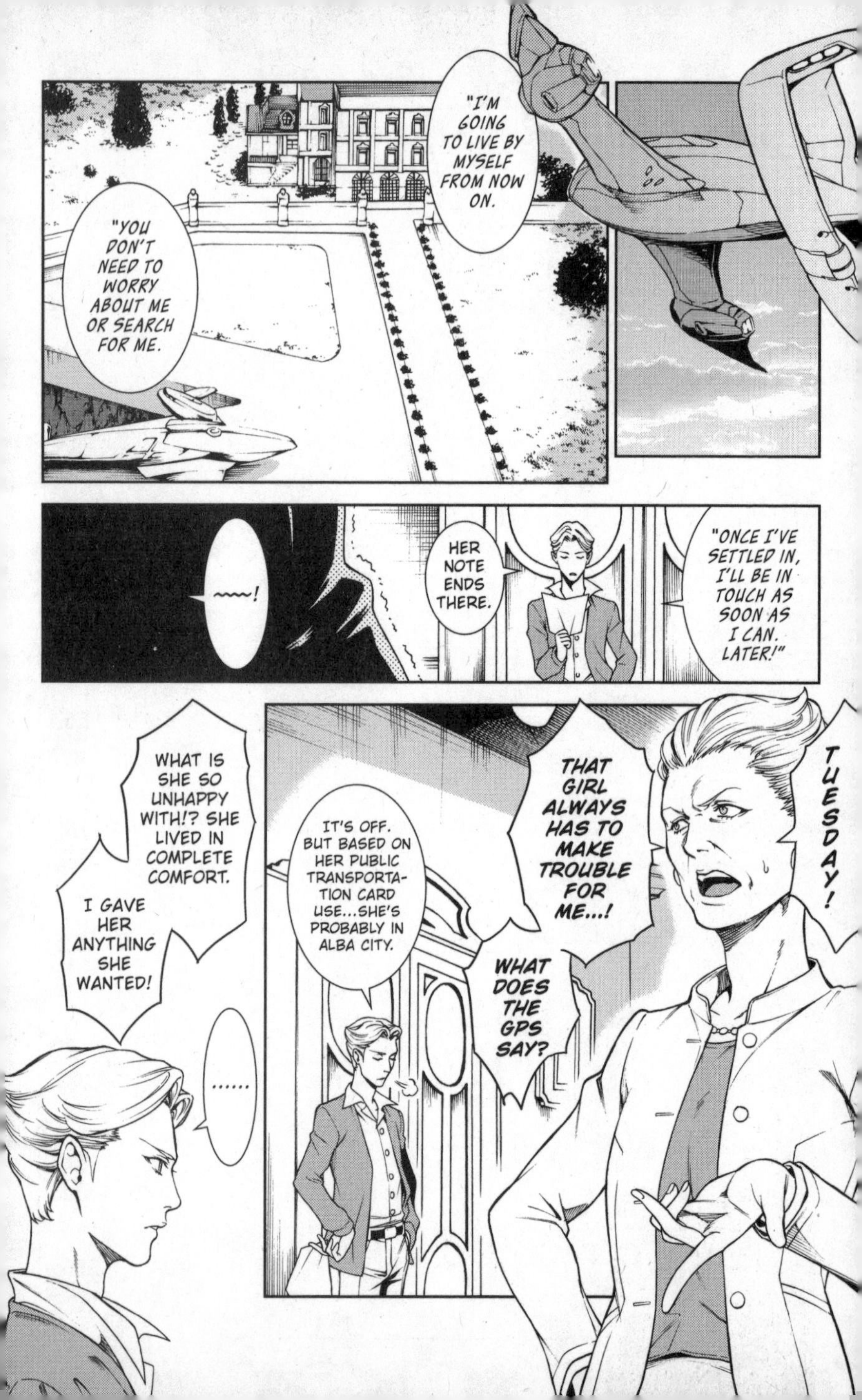
"I'M GOING TO LIVE BY MYSELF FROM NOW ON.
"YOU DON'T NEED TO WORRY ABOUT ME OR SEARCH FOR ME.
"ONCE I'VE SETTLED IN, I'LL BE IN TOUCH AS SOON AS I CAN. LATER!"
HER NOTE ENDS THERE.
~~~!
TUESDAY!
THAT GIRL ALWAYS HAS TO MAKE TROUBLE FOR ME...!
WHAT DOES THE GPS SAY?
IT'S OFF. BUT BASED ON HER PUBLIC TRANSPORTATION CARD USE...SHE'S PROBABLY IN ALBA CITY.
WHAT IS SHE SO UNHAPPY WITH!? SHE LIVED IN COMPLETE COMFORT.
I GAVE HER ANYTHING SHE WANTED!
......
~~~

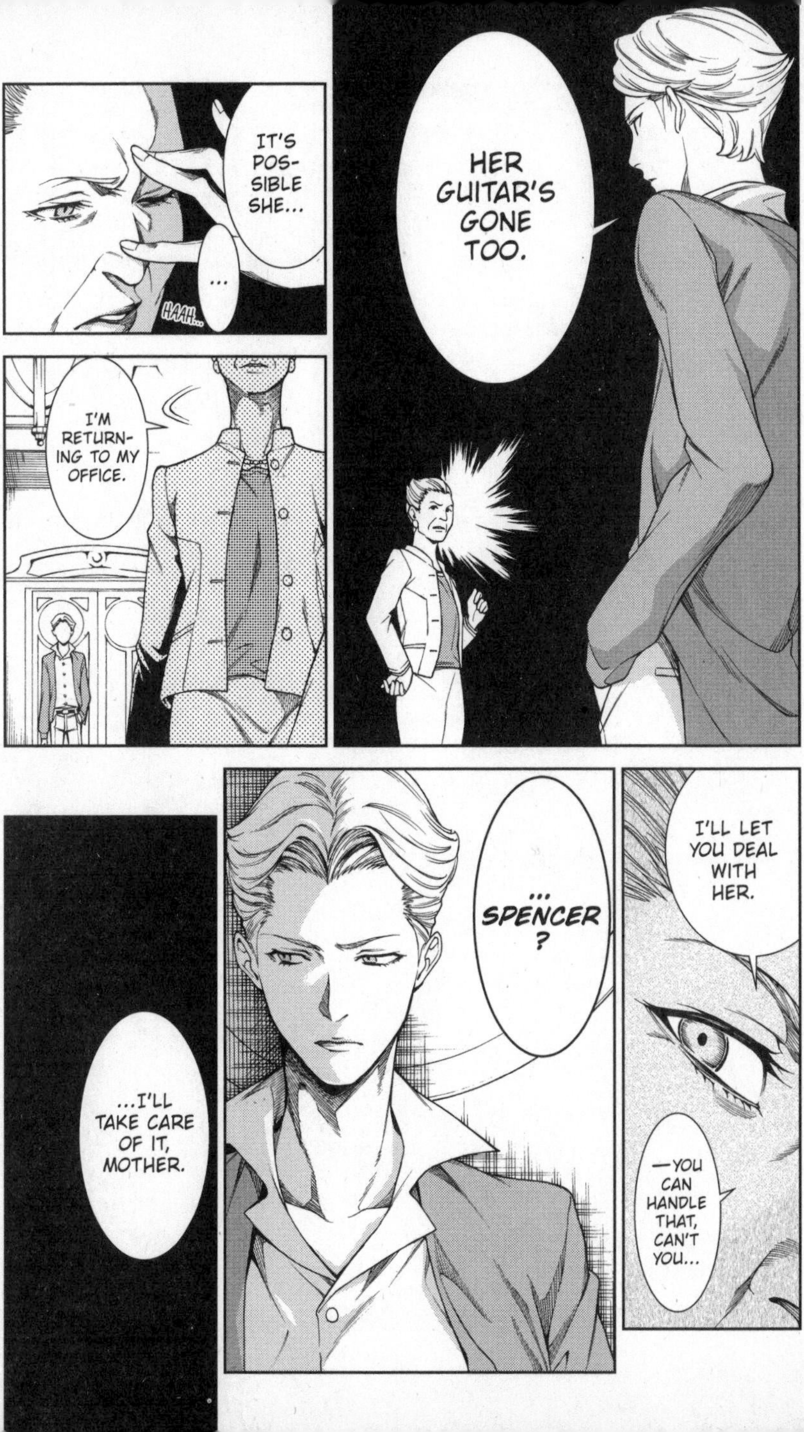
HER GUITAR'S GONE TOO.
IT'S POS-SIBLE SHE...
...
HAAH...
I'M RETURN-ING TO MY OFFICE.
I'LL LET YOU DEAL WITH HER.
—YOU CAN HANDLE THAT, CAN'T YOU...
...SPENCER?
...I'LL TAKE CARE OF IT, MOTHER.

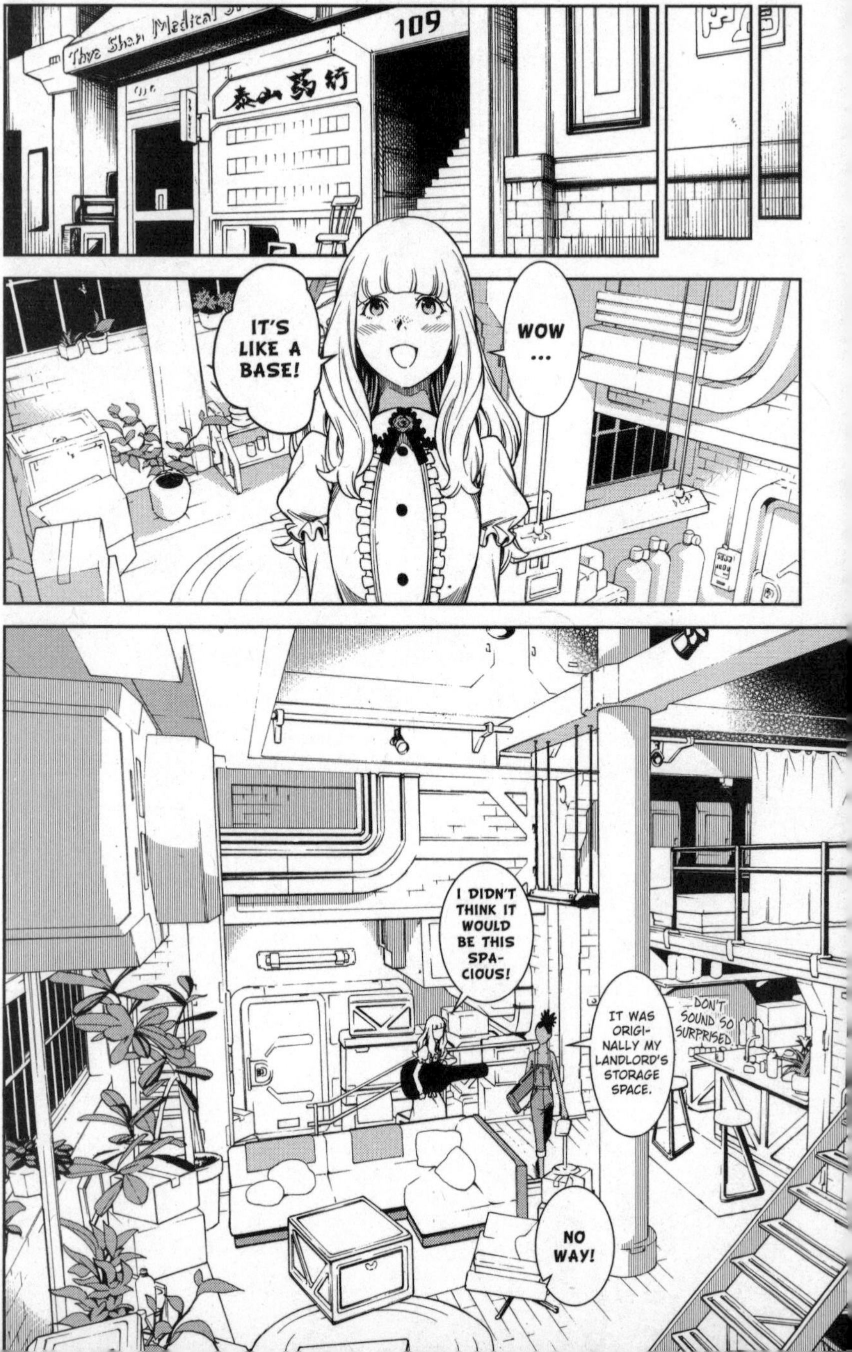
Thye Shan Medical
109
WOW ...
IT'S LIKE A BASE!
I DIDN'T THINK IT WOULD BE THIS SPACIOUS!
IT WAS ORIGINALLY MY LANDLORD'S STORAGE SPACE.
DON'T SOUND SO SURPRISED.
NO WAY!

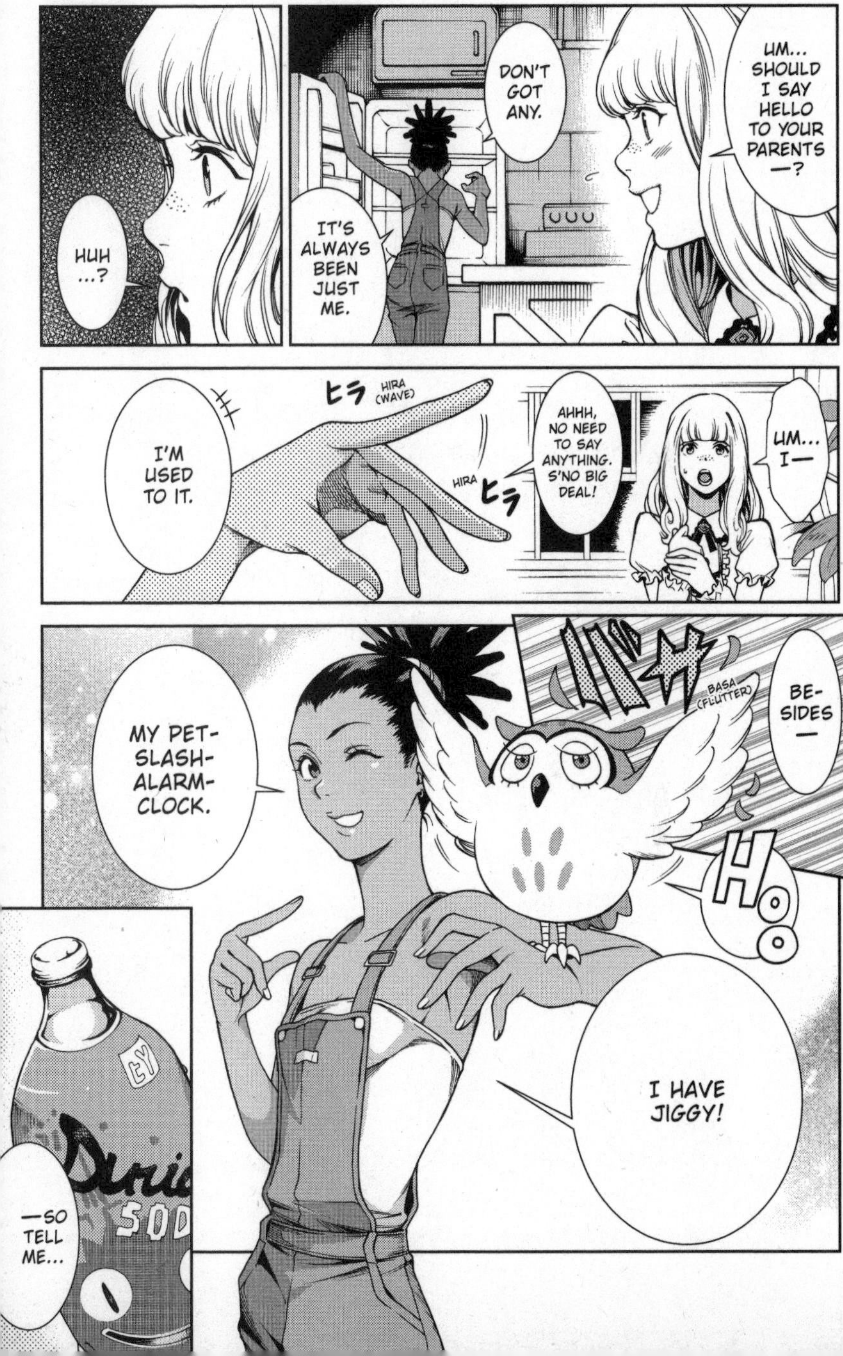
UM... SHOULD I SAY HELLO TO YOUR PARENTS—?
DON'T GOT ANY.
IT'S ALWAYS BEEN JUST ME.
HUH ...?
UM... I—
AHHH, NO NEED TO SAY ANYTHING. S'NO BIG DEAL!
HIRA (WAVE)
HIRA
I'M USED TO IT.
BE-SIDES—
BASA (FLUTTER)
HOO
I HAVE JIGGY!
MY PET-SLASH-ALARM-CLOCK.
—SO TELL ME...

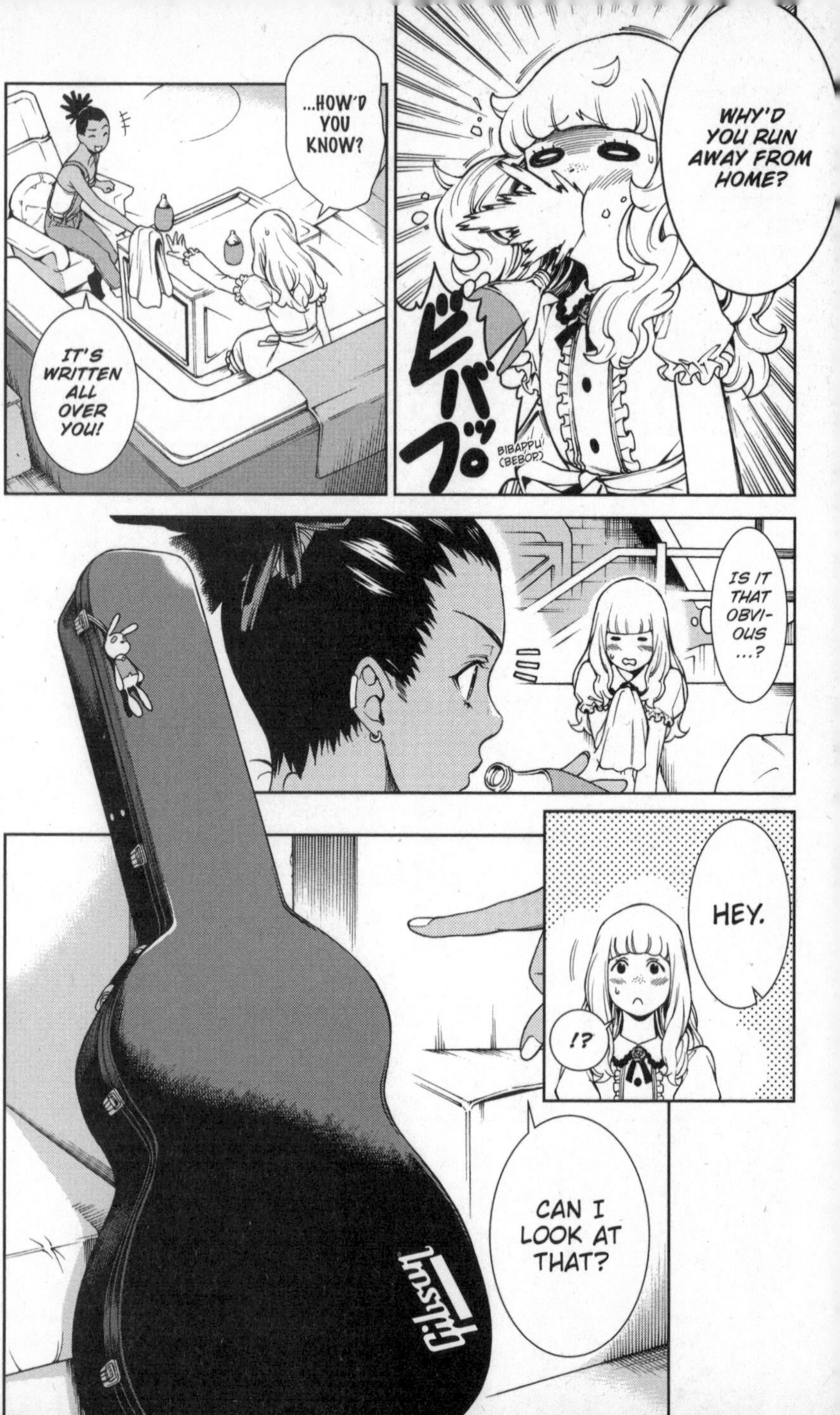
WHY'D YOU RUN AWAY FROM HOME?
BIBAPPU (BEBOP)
...HOW'D YOU KNOW?
IT'S WRITTEN ALL OVER YOU!
IS IT THAT OBVIOUS...?
HEY.
!?
CAN I LOOK AT THAT?

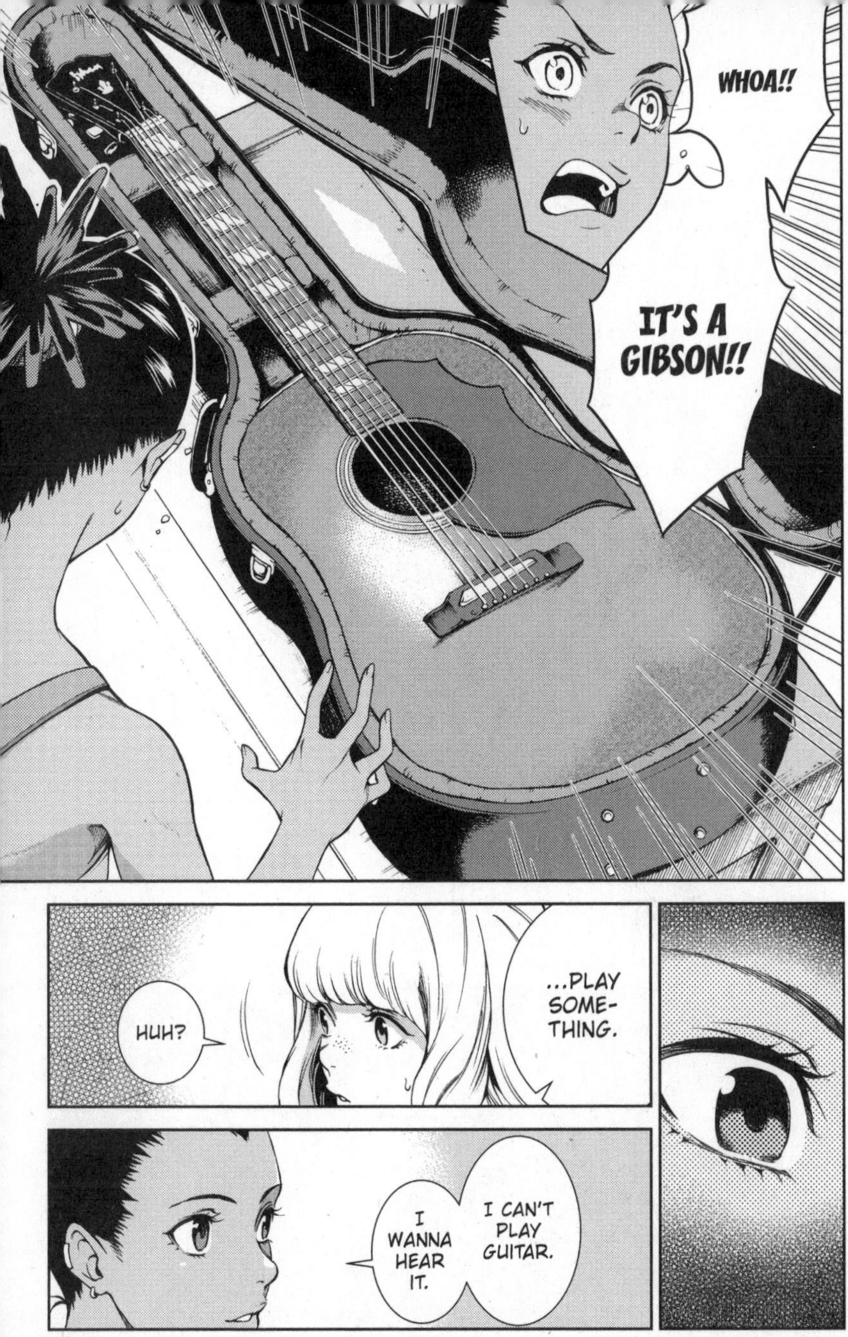
WHOA!!
IT'S A GIBSON!!
...PLAY SOME-THING.
HUH?
I CAN'T PLAY GUITAR.
I WANNA HEAR IT.

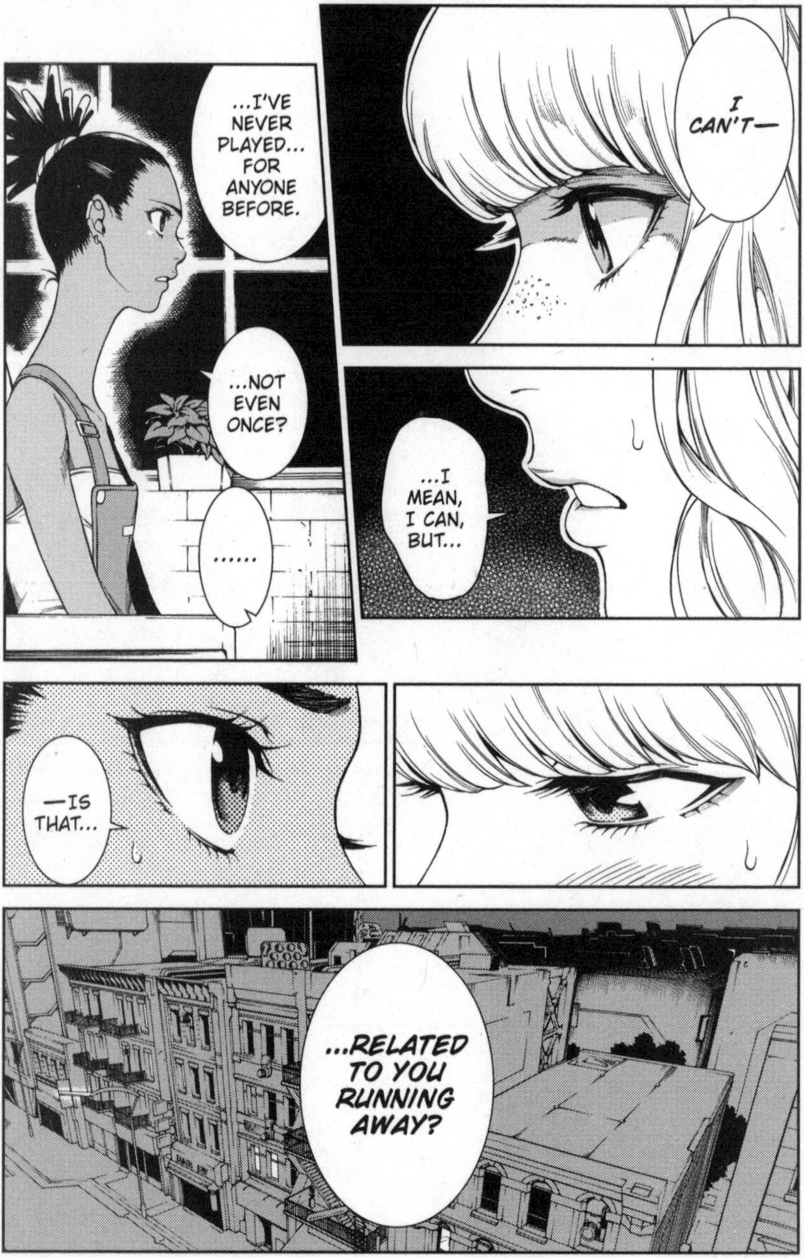
I CAN'T—
...I MEAN, I CAN, BUT...
...I'VE NEVER PLAYED... FOR ANYONE BEFORE.
...NOT EVEN ONCE?
......
—IS THAT...
...RELATED TO YOU RUNNING AWAY?

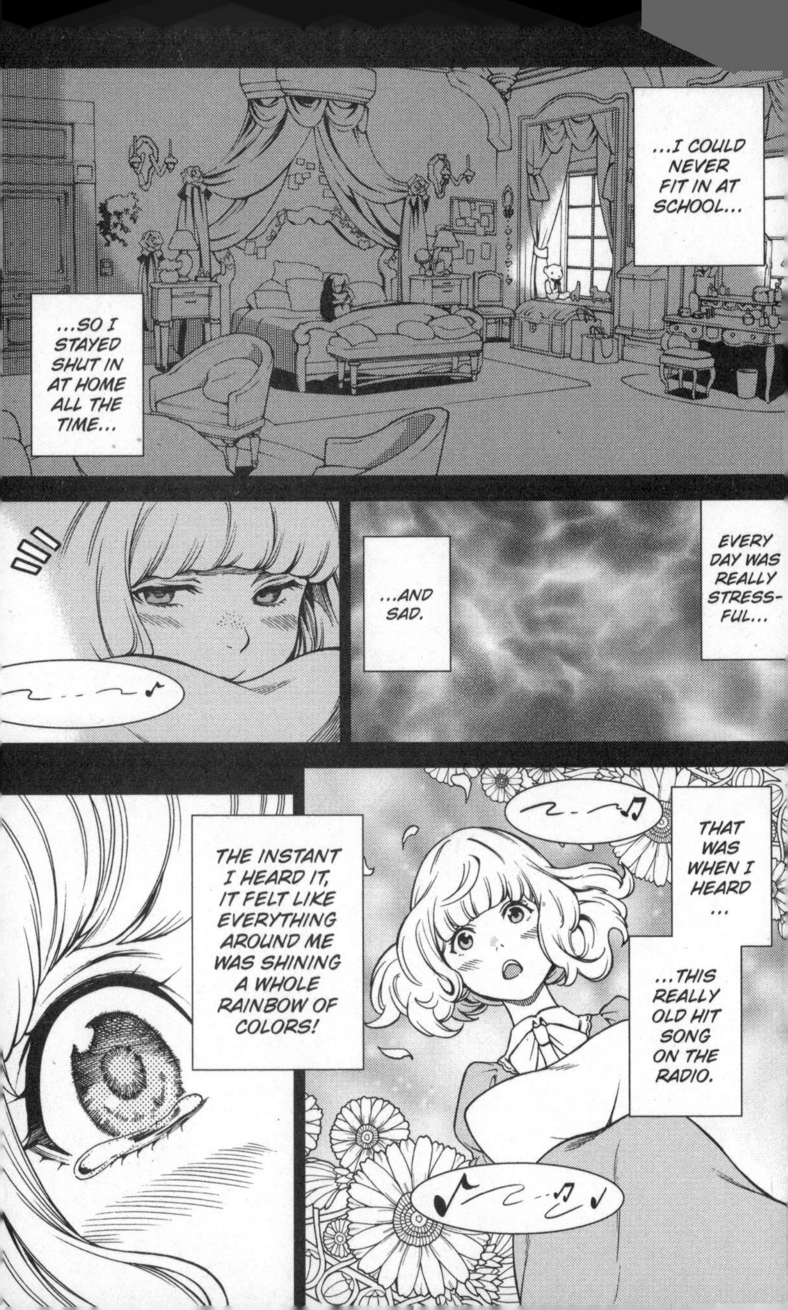
...I COULD NEVER FIT IN AT SCHOOL...
...SO I STAYED SHUT IN AT HOME ALL THE TIME...
EVERY DAY WAS REALLY STRESS-FUL...
...AND SAD.
THAT WAS WHEN I HEARD...
...THIS REALLY OLD HIT SONG ON THE RADIO.
THE INSTANT I HEARD IT, IT FELT LIKE EVERYTHING AROUND ME WAS SHINING A WHOLE RAINBOW OF COLORS!

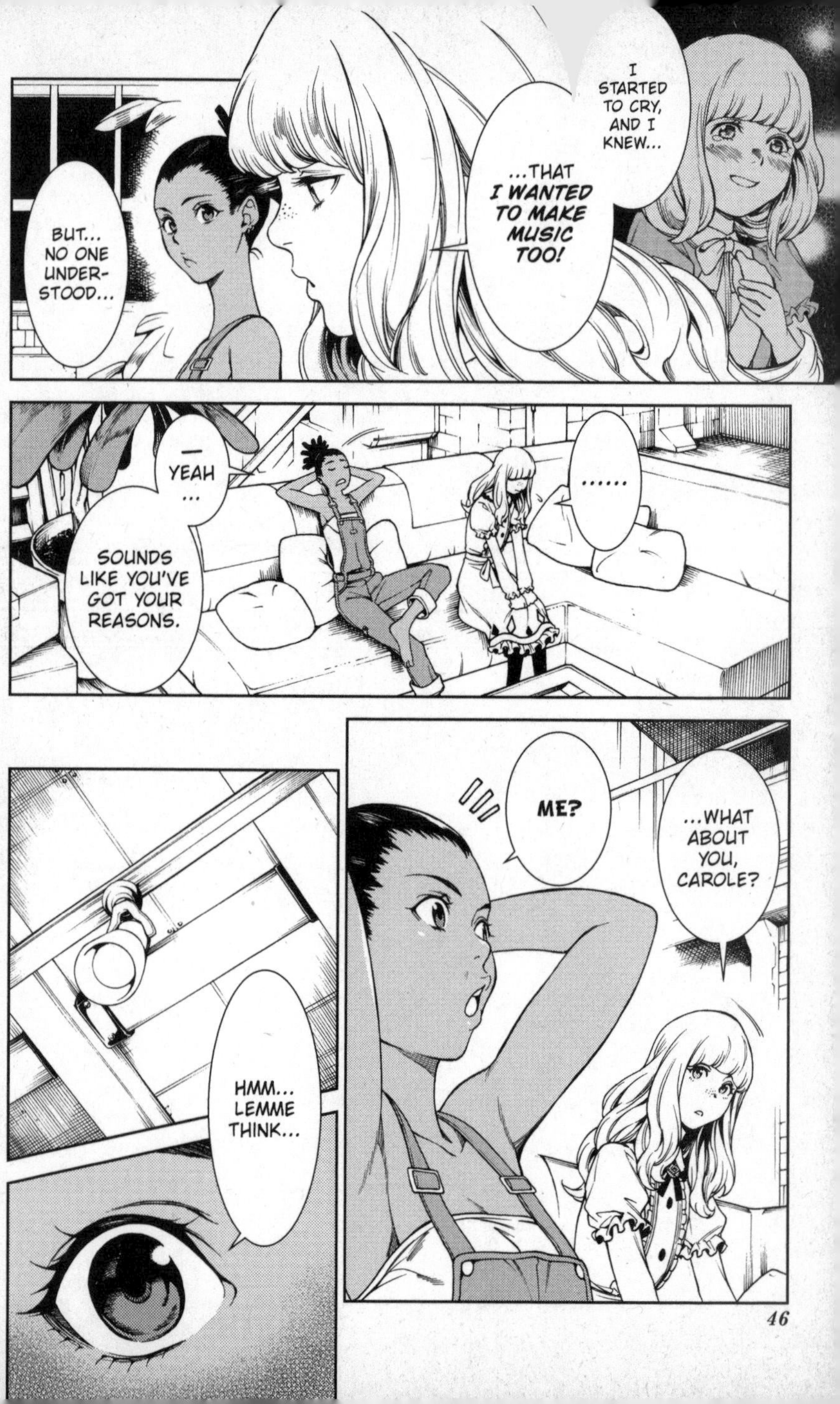
I STARTED TO CRY, AND I KNEW...
...THAT *I WANTED TO MAKE MUSIC TOO!*
BUT... NO ONE UNDER-STOOD...
......
—YEAH...
SOUNDS LIKE YOU'VE GOT YOUR REASONS.
...WHAT ABOUT YOU, CAROLE?
ME?
HMM... LEMME THINK...

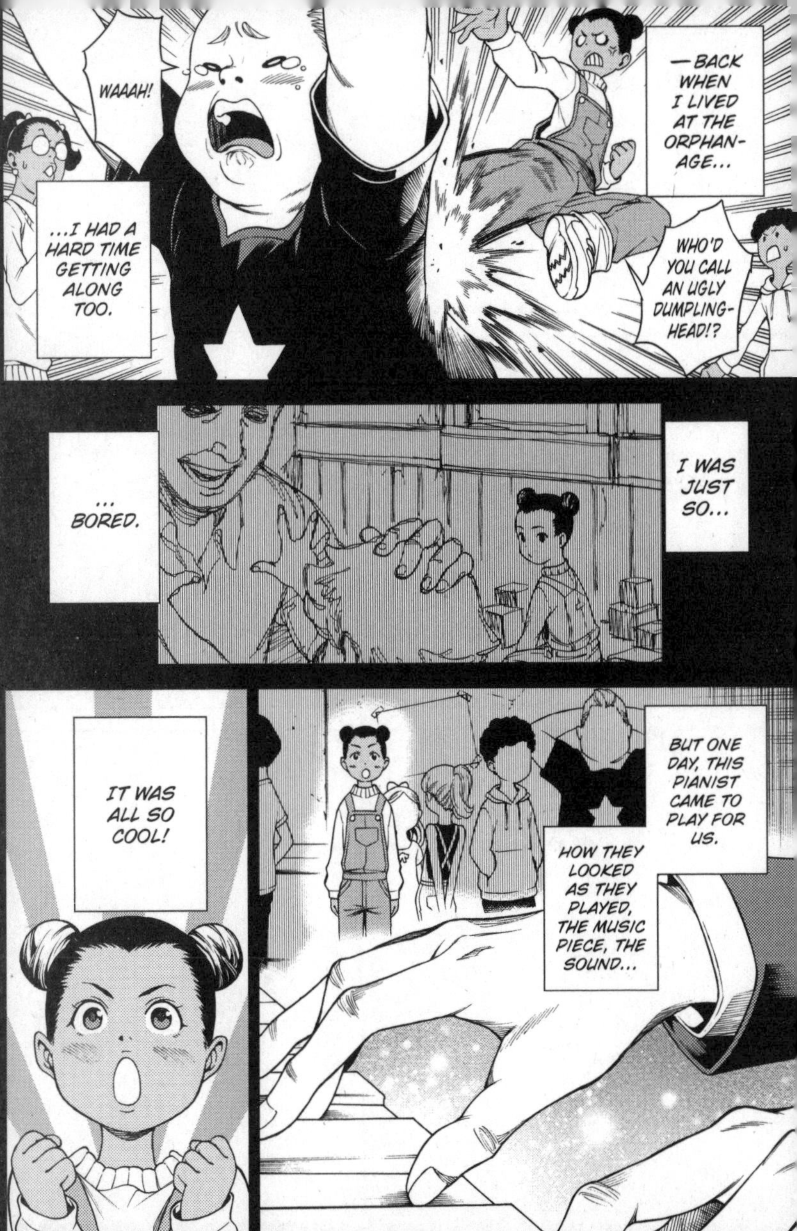
—BACK WHEN I LIVED AT THE ORPHANAGE...
WHO'D YOU CALL AN UGLY DUMPLING-HEAD!?
WAAAH!
...I HAD A HARD TIME GETTING ALONG TOO.
I WAS JUST SO...
... BORED.
BUT ONE DAY, THIS PIANIST CAME TO PLAY FOR US.
HOW THEY LOOKED AS THEY PLAYED, THE MUSIC PIECE, THE SOUND...
IT WAS ALL SO COOL!

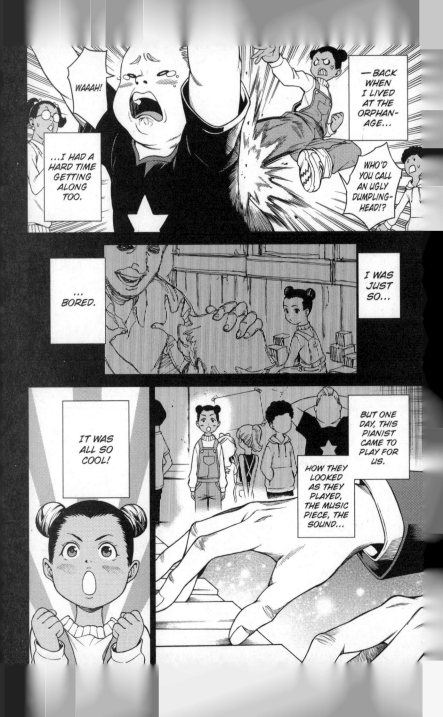

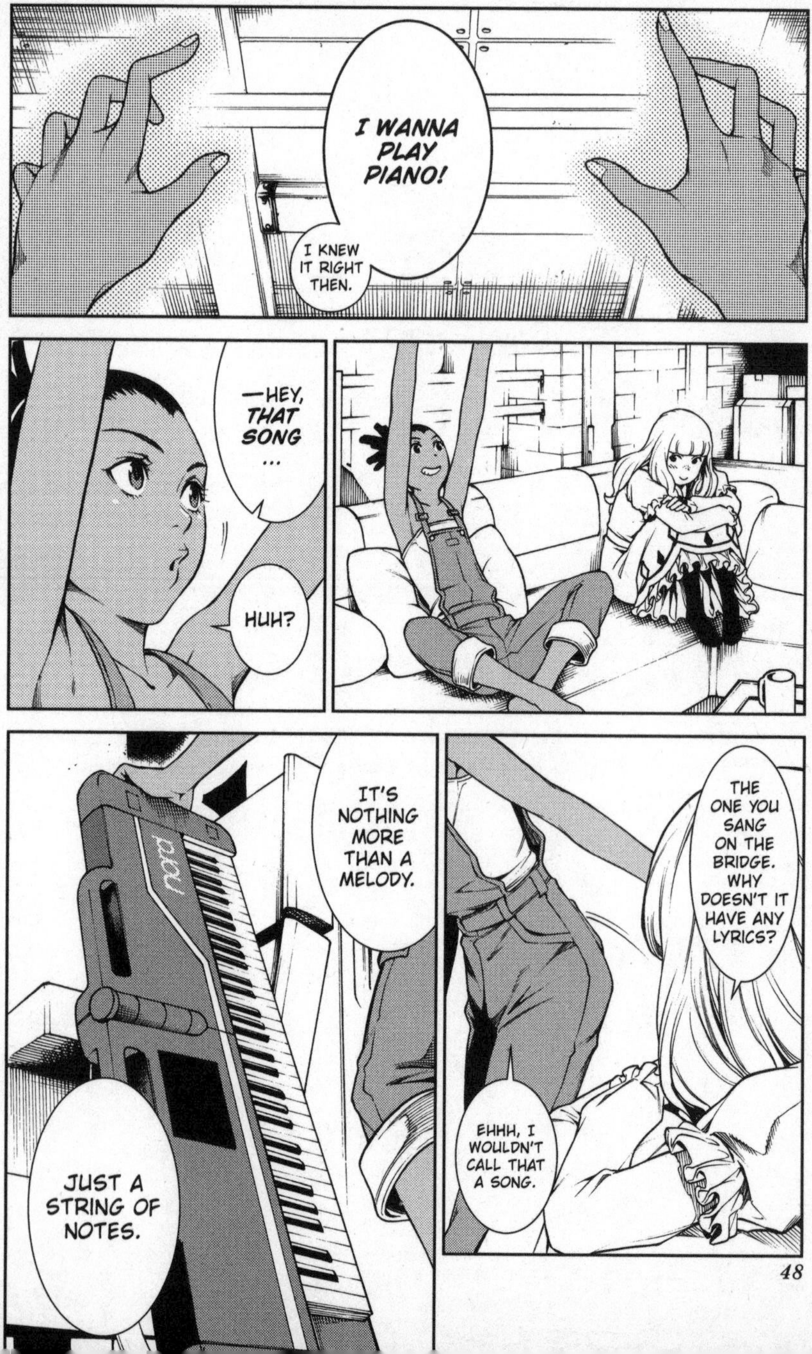
I WANNA PLAY PIANO!
I KNEW IT RIGHT THEN.
—HEY, THAT SONG ...
HUH?
THE ONE YOU SANG ON THE BRIDGE. WHY DOESN'T IT HAVE ANY LYRICS?
EHHH, I WOULDN'T CALL THAT A SONG.
IT'S NOTHING MORE THAN A MELODY.
JUST A STRING OF NOTES.

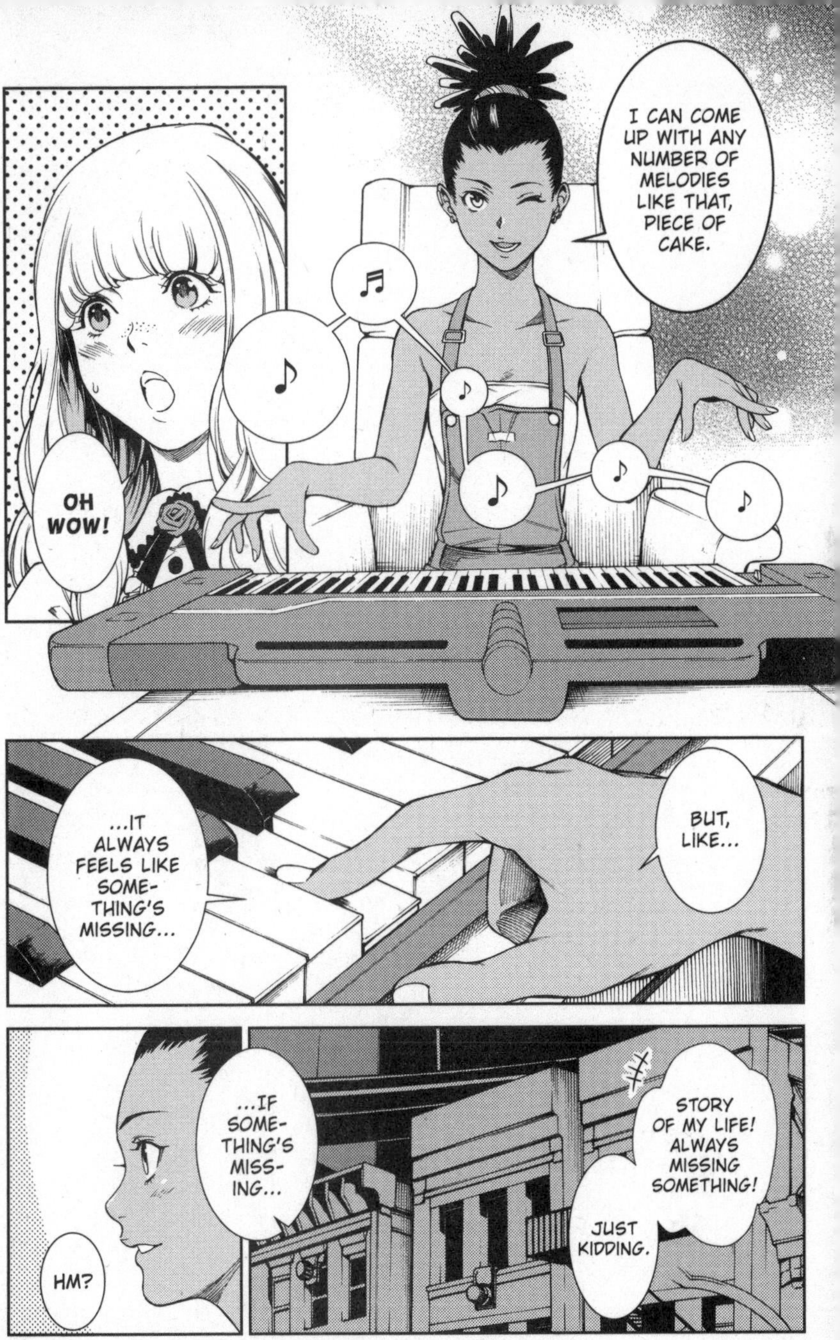

I CAN COME UP WITH ANY NUMBER OF MELODIES LIKE THAT, PIECE OF CAKE.
OH WOW!
BUT, LIKE...
...IT ALWAYS FEELS LIKE SOME-THING'S MISSING...
STORY OF MY LIFE! ALWAYS MISSING SOMETHING!
JUST KIDDING.
...IF SOME-THING'S MISS-ING...
HM?

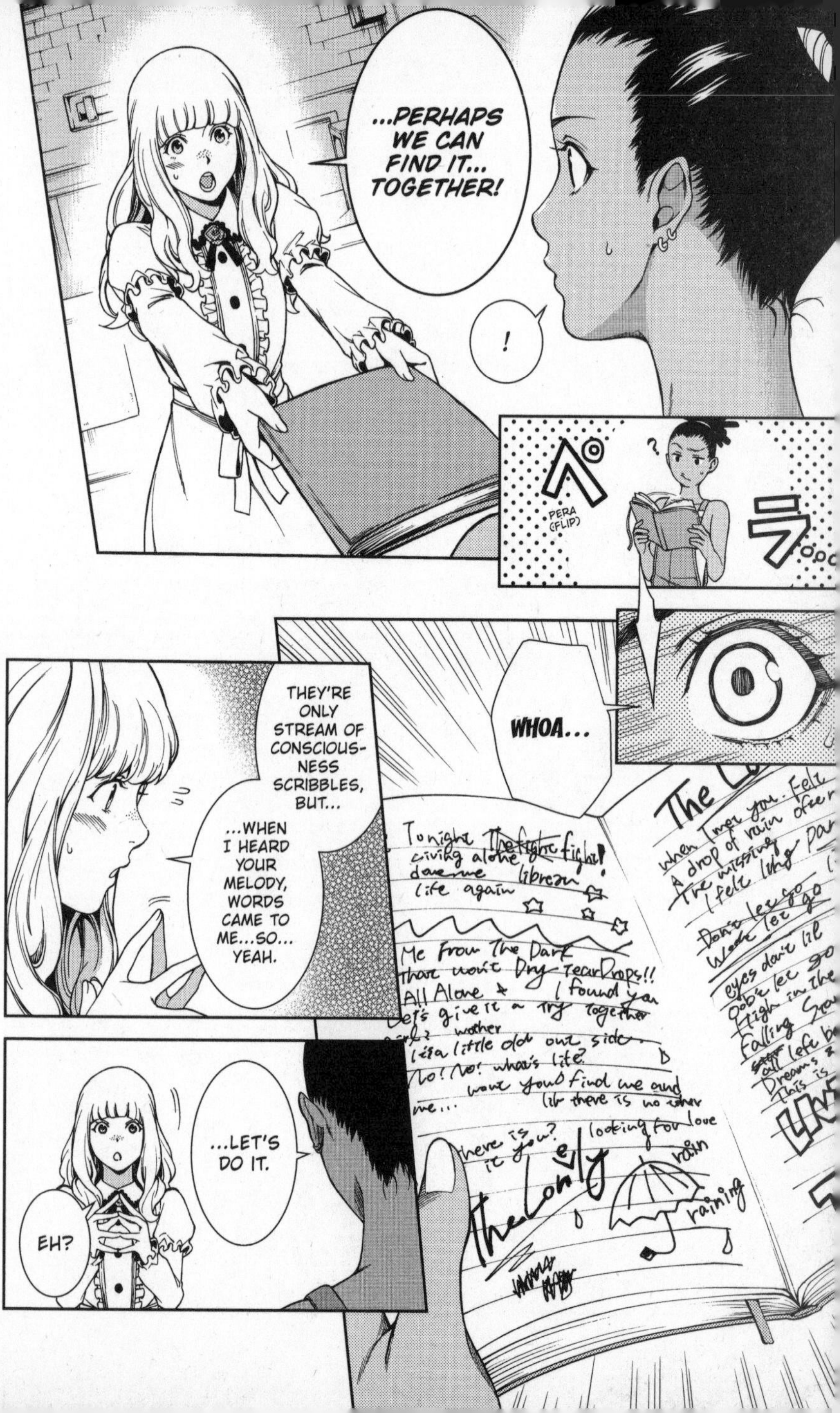
...PERHAPS WE CAN FIND IT... TOGETHER!
!
PERA (FLIP)
WHOA...
Tonight
life again
Me From The Dark
All Alone
I found you
looking for love
rain
raining
The Lonly
THEY'RE ONLY STREAM OF CONSCIOUS-NESS SCRIBBLES, BUT...
...WHEN I HEARD YOUR MELODY, WORDS CAME TO ME...SO... YEAH.
...LET'S DO IT.
EH?

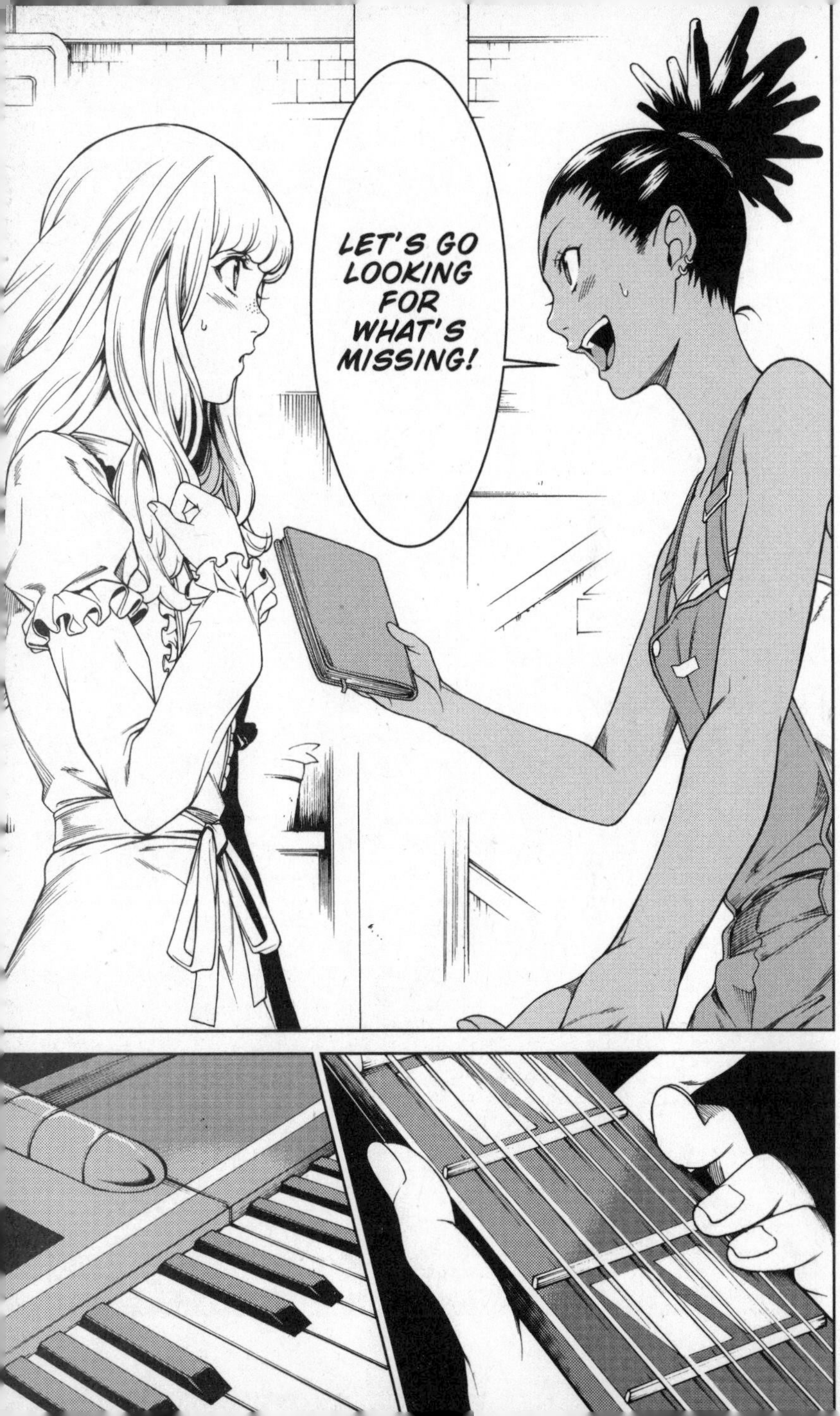
LET'S GO LOOKING FOR WHAT'S MISSING!

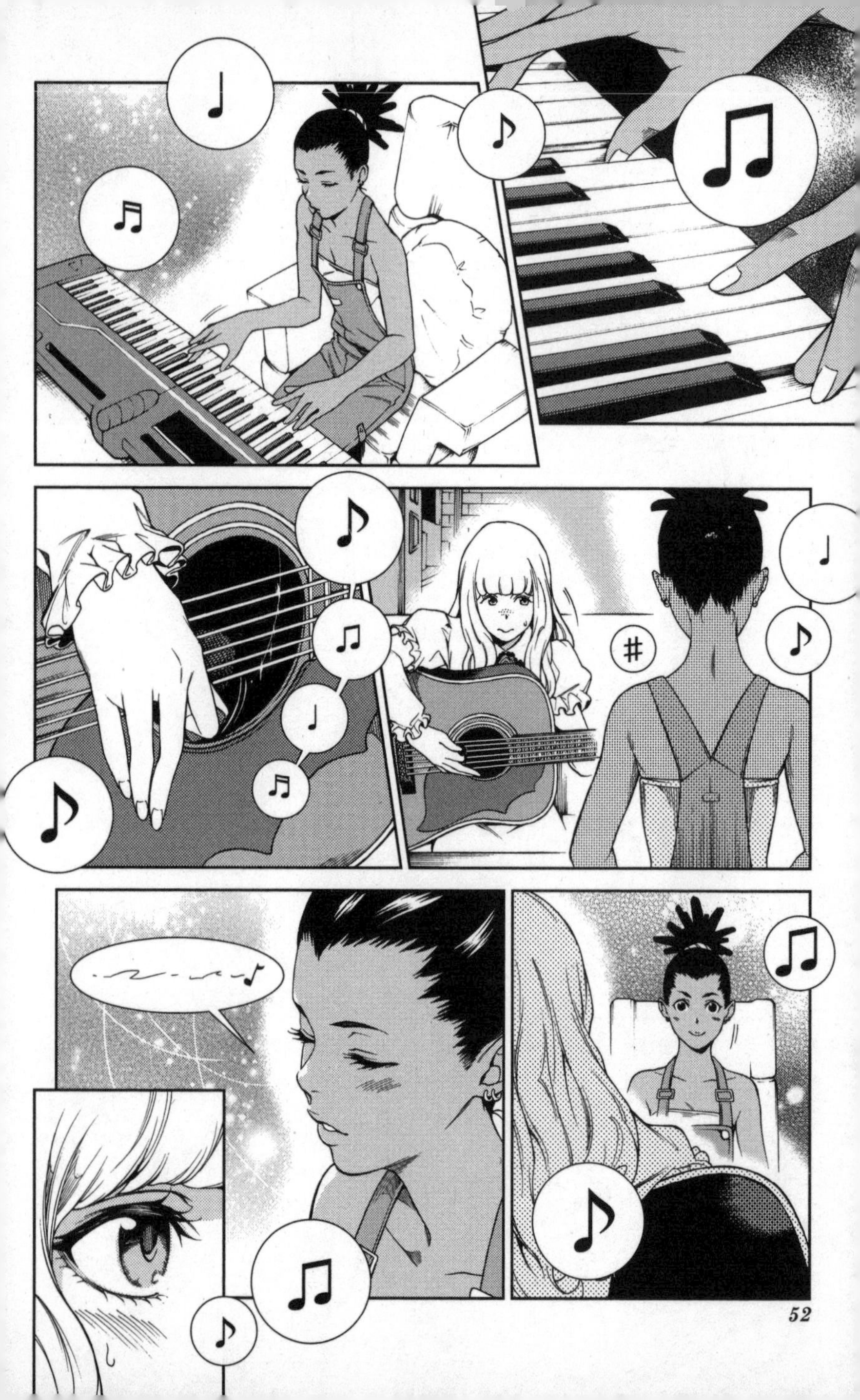

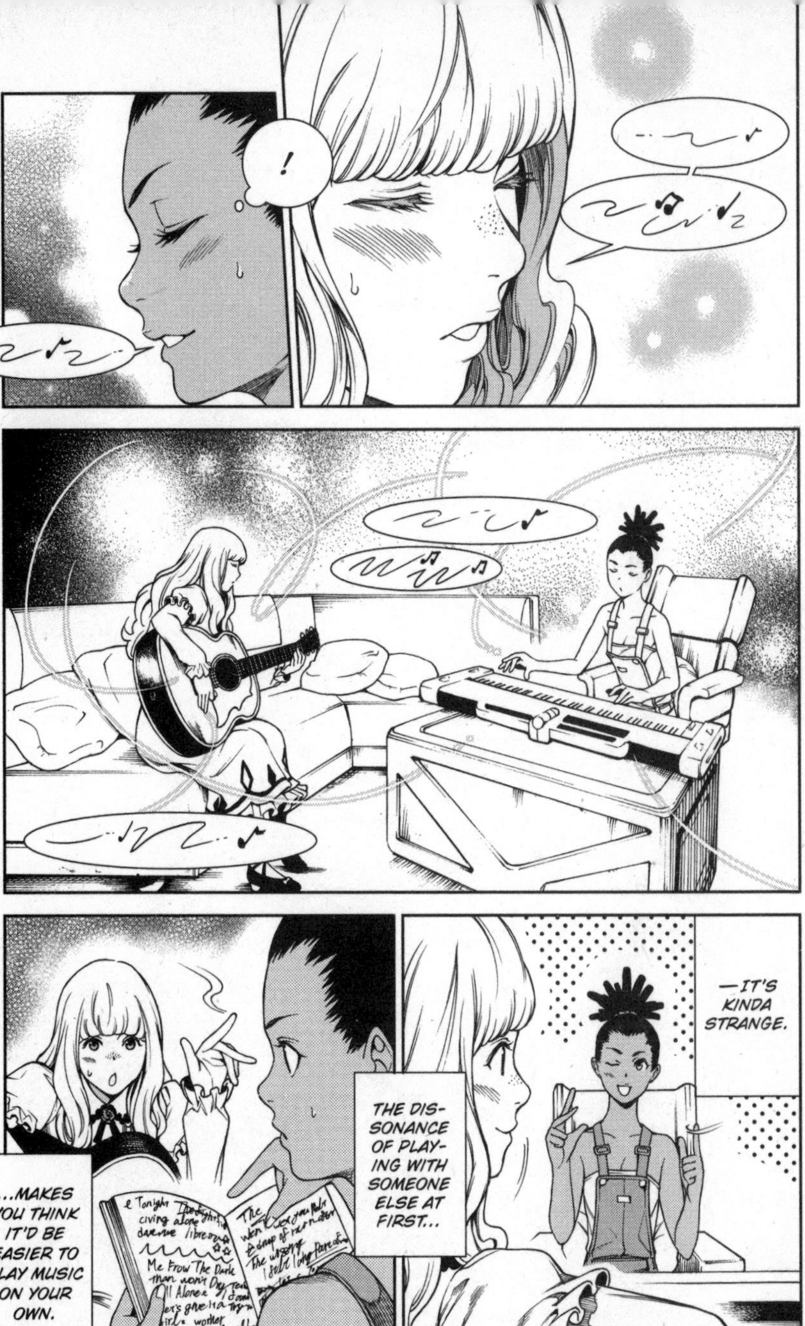
!
—IT'S KINDA STRANGE.
THE DIS-SONANCE OF PLAY-ING WITH SOMEONE ELSE AT FIRST...
...MAKES YOU THINK IT'D BE EASIER TO PLAY MUSIC ON YOUR OWN.

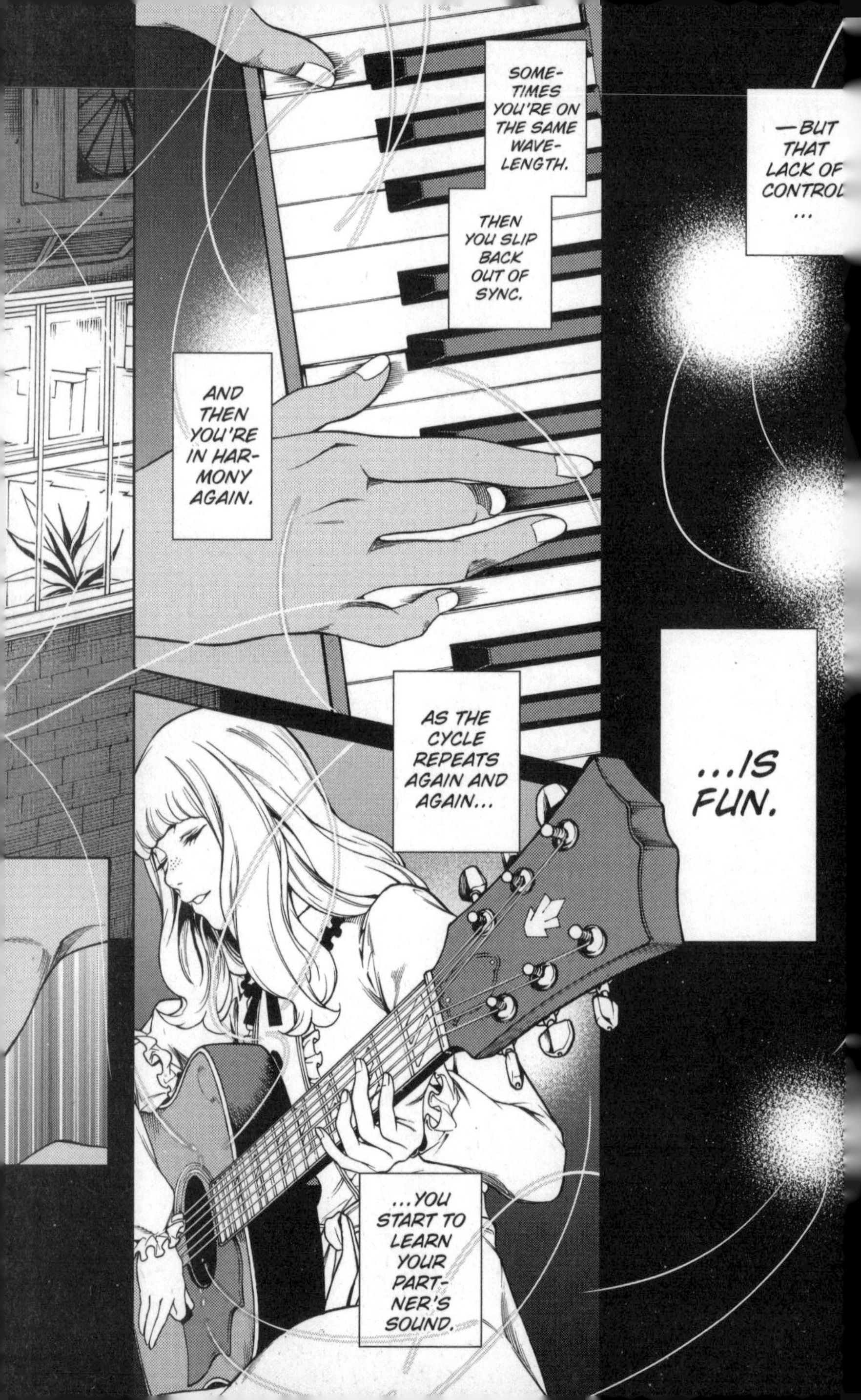
SOME-TIMES YOU'RE ON THE SAME WAVE-LENGTH.
THEN YOU SLIP BACK OUT OF SYNC.
AND THEN YOU'RE IN HAR-MONY AGAIN.
AS THE CYCLE REPEATS AGAIN AND AGAIN...
...YOU START TO LEARN YOUR PART-NER'S SOUND.
—BUT THAT LACK OF CONTROL ...
...IS FUN.

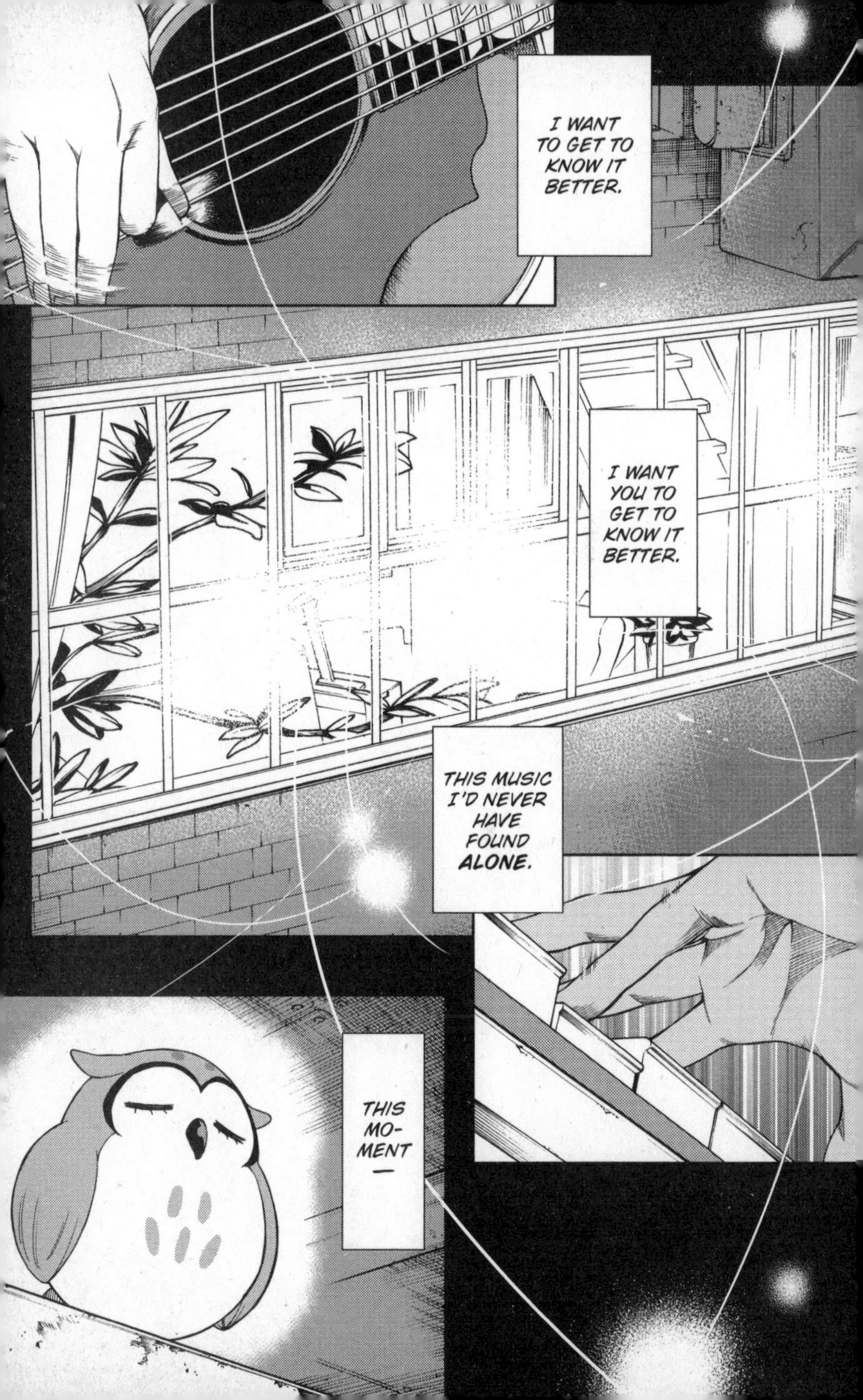
I WANT TO GET TO KNOW IT BETTER.
I WANT YOU TO GET TO KNOW IT BETTER.
THIS MUSIC I'D NEVER HAVE FOUND **ALONE.**
THIS MO-MENT —

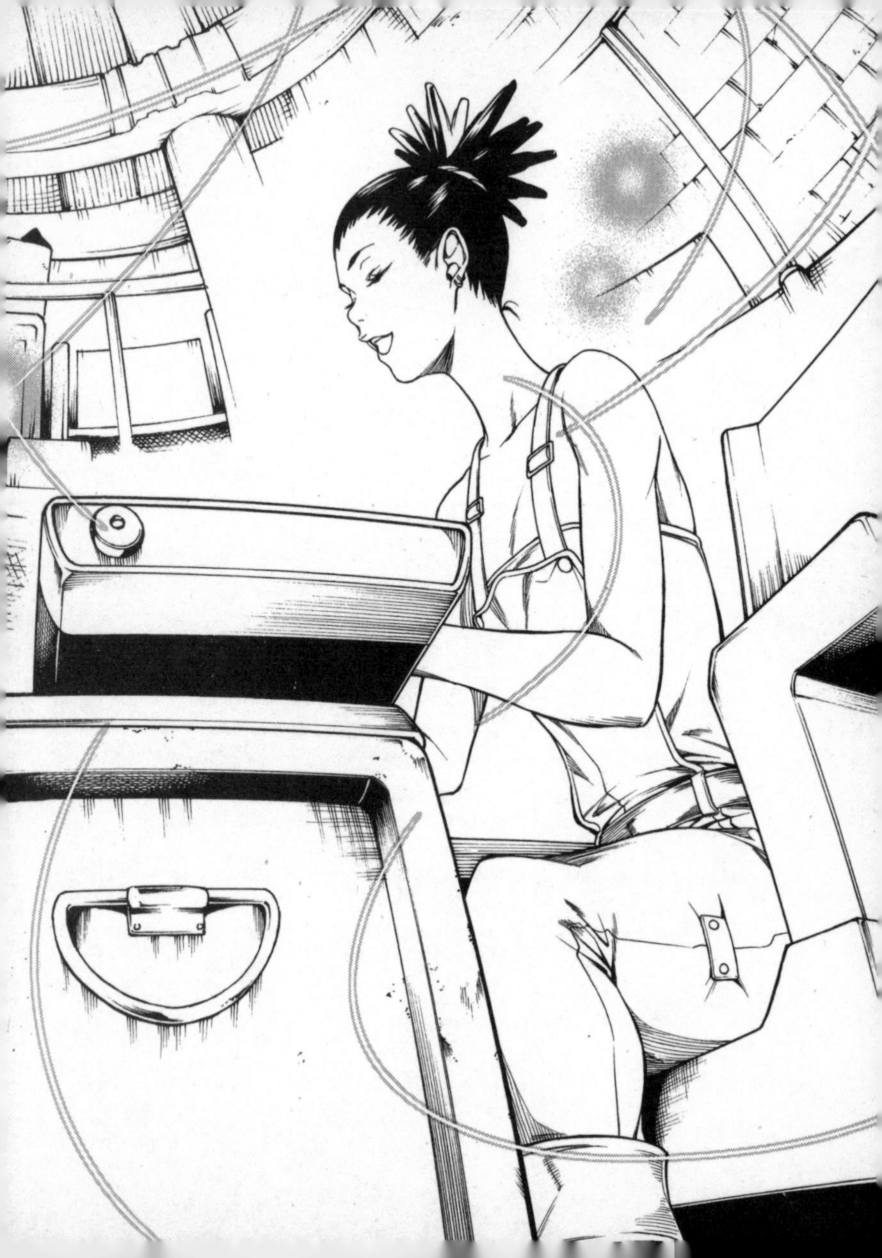

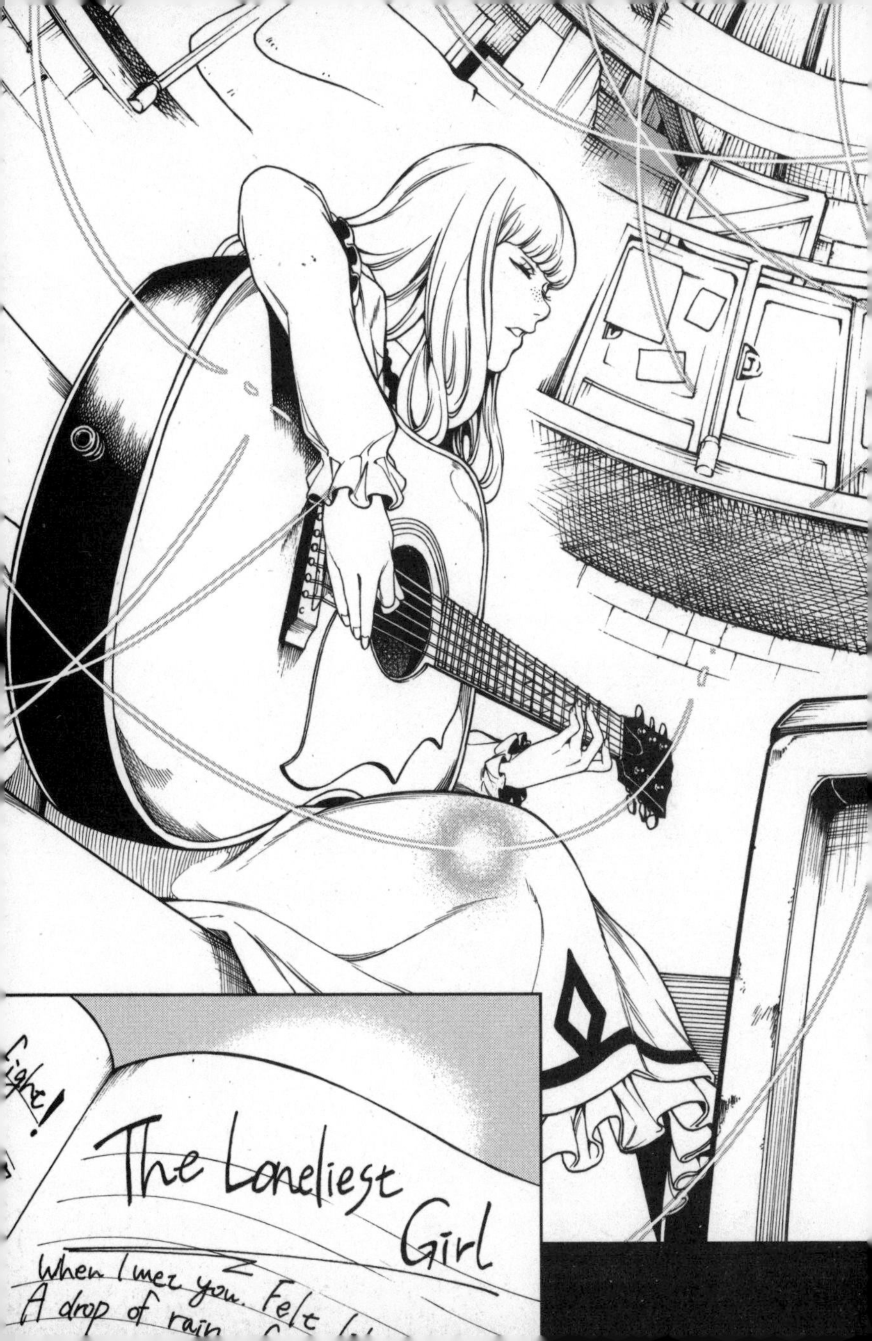

The Loneliest Girl
When I met you. Felt
A drop of rain

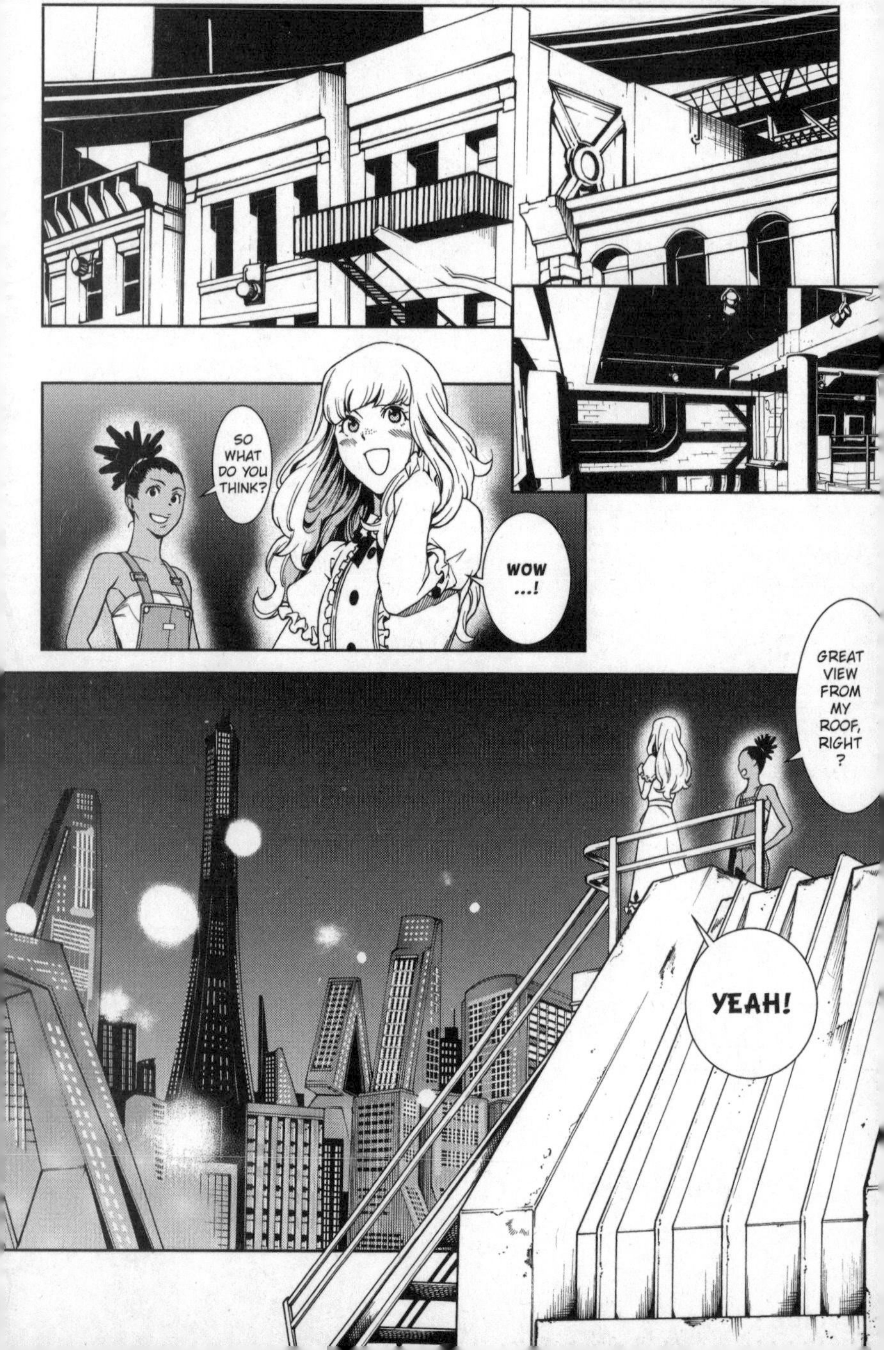
SO WHAT DO YOU THINK?
WOW ...!
GREAT VIEW FROM MY ROOF, RIGHT?
YEAH!

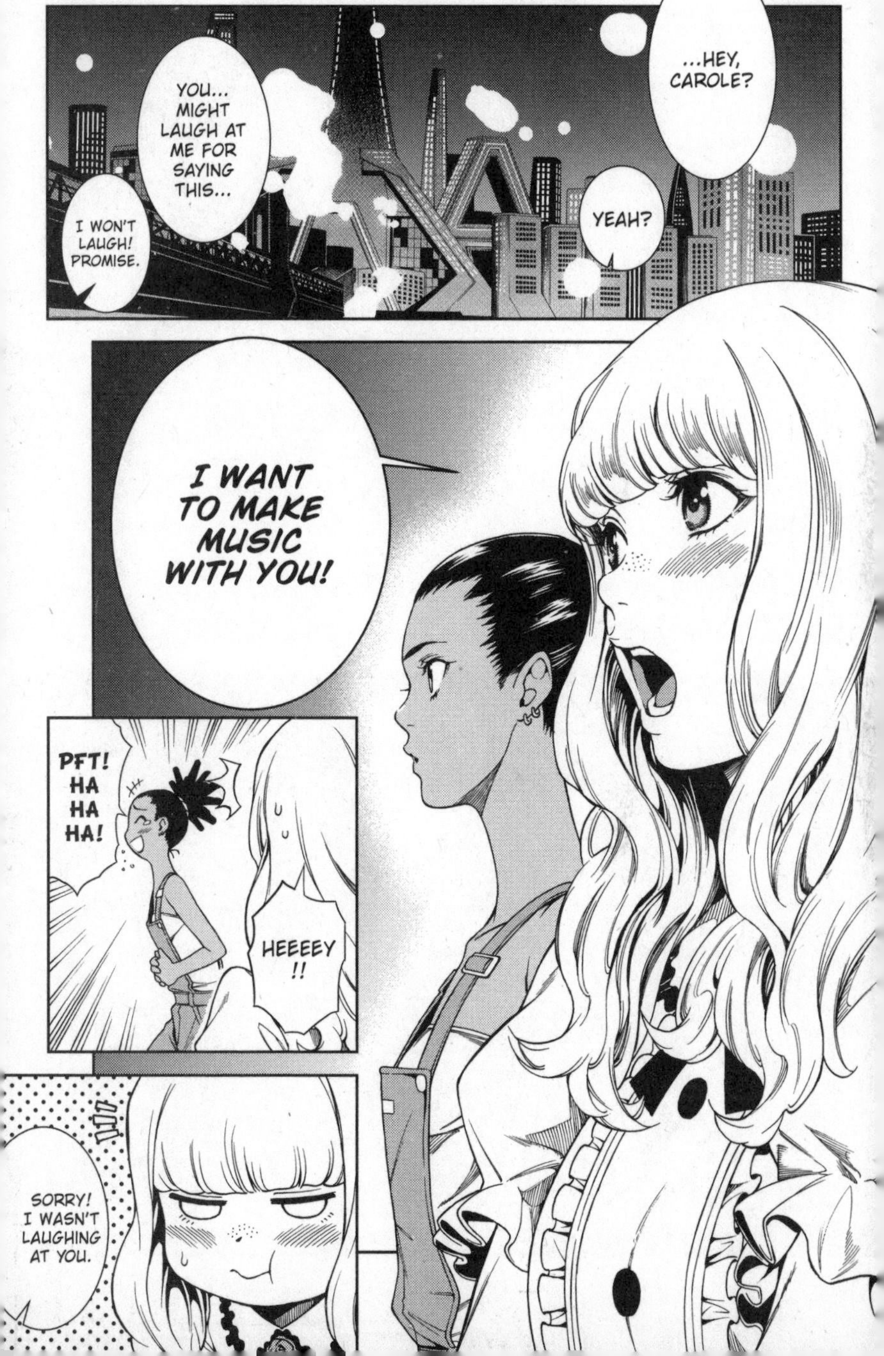
...HEY, CAROLE?
YEAH?
YOU... MIGHT LAUGH AT ME FOR SAYING THIS...
I WON'T LAUGH! PROMISE.
I WANT TO MAKE MUSIC WITH YOU!
PFT! HA HA HA!
HEEEEY !!
SORRY! I WASN'T LAUGHING AT YOU.

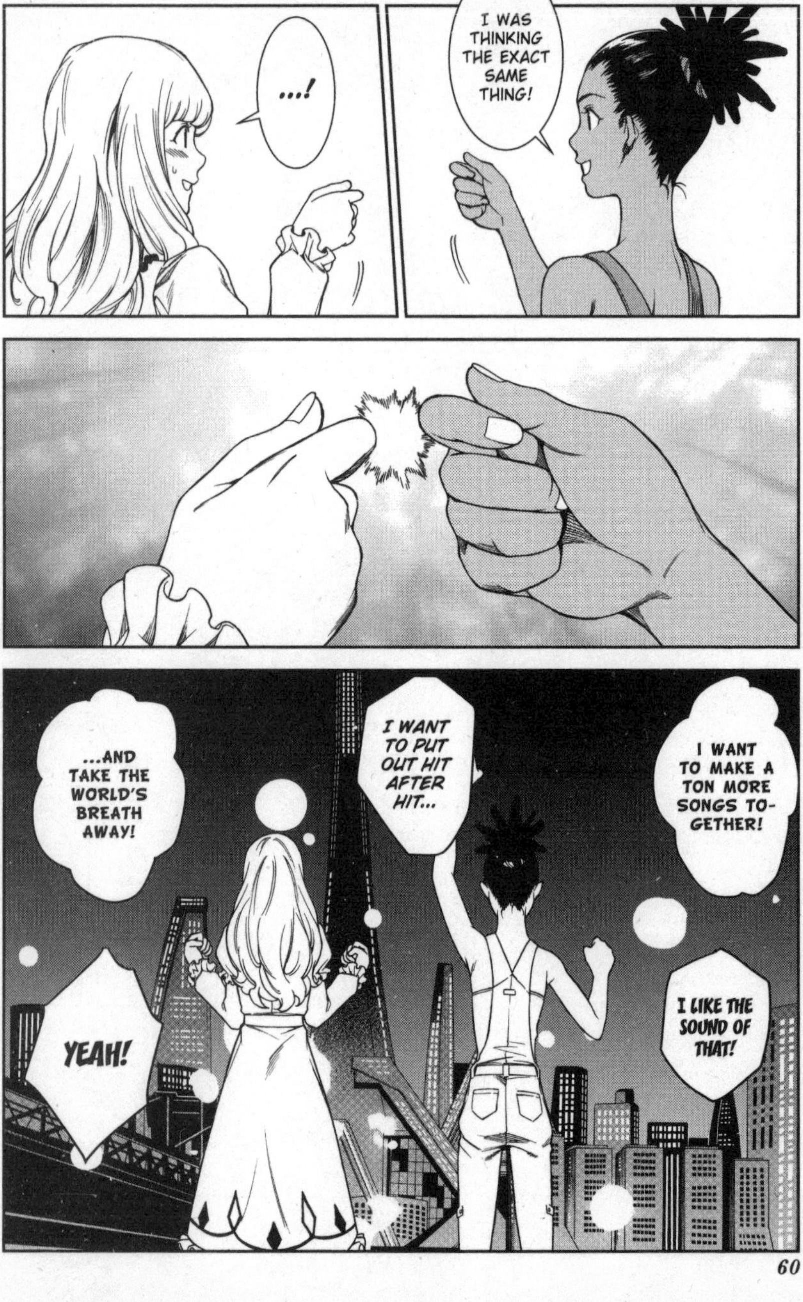
I WAS THINKING THE EXACT SAME THING!
...!
I WANT TO MAKE A TON MORE SONGS TOGETHER!
I WANT TO PUT OUT HIT AFTER HIT...
...AND TAKE THE WORLD'S BREATH AWAY!
I LIKE THE SOUND OF THAT!
YEAH!

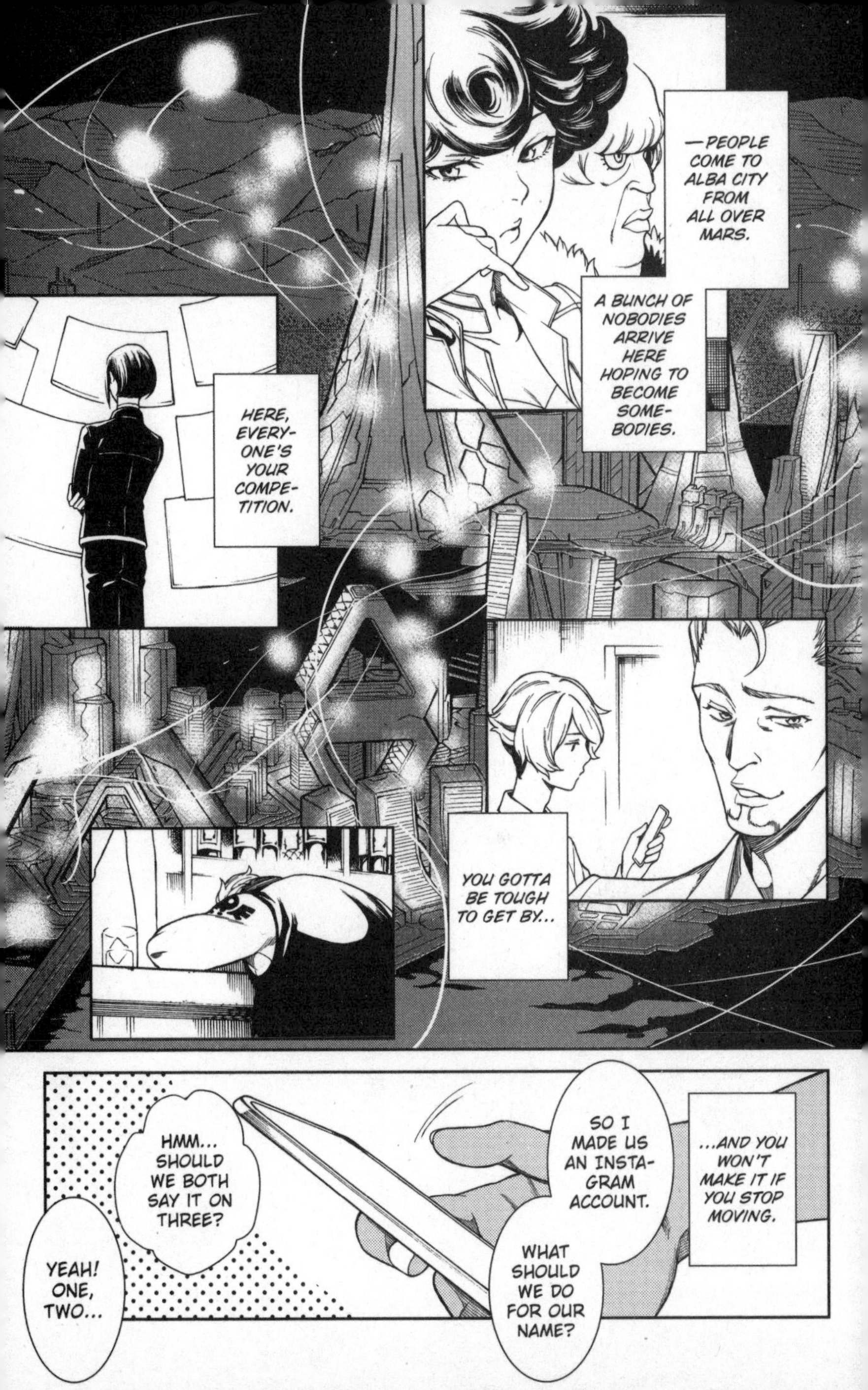
—PEOPLE COME TO ALBA CITY FROM ALL OVER MARS.
A BUNCH OF NOBODIES ARRIVE HERE HOPING TO BECOME SOME-BODIES.
HERE, EVERY-ONE'S YOUR COMPE-TITION.
YOU GOTTA BE TOUGH TO GET BY...
...AND YOU WON'T MAKE IT IF YOU STOP MOVING.
SO I MADE US AN INSTA-GRAM ACCOUNT.
WHAT SHOULD WE DO FOR OUR NAME?
HMM... SHOULD WE BOTH SAY IT ON THREE?
YEAH! ONE, TWO...

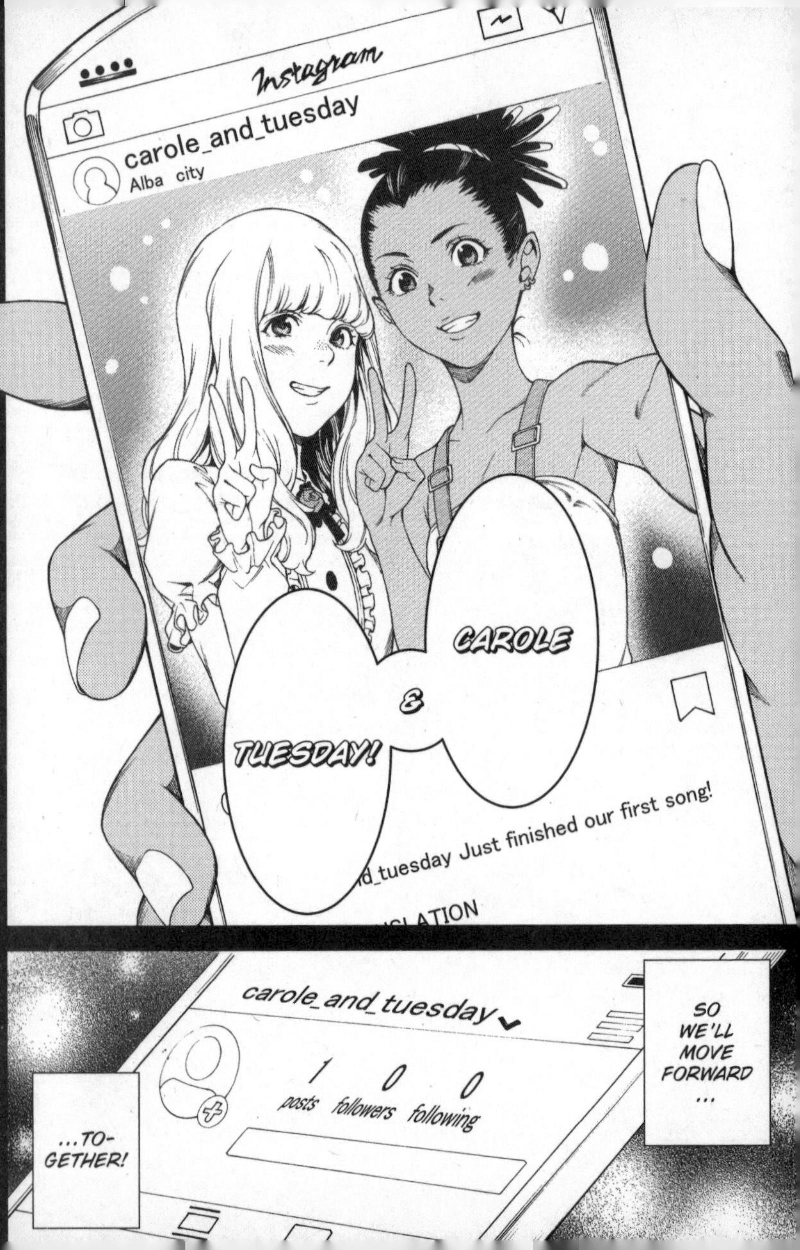
Instagram
carole_and_tuesday
Alba city
CAROLE & TUESDAY!
d_tuesday Just finished our first song!
SO WE'LL MOVE FORWARD...
...TO-GETHER!
carole_and_tuesday
1 posts 0 followers 0 following

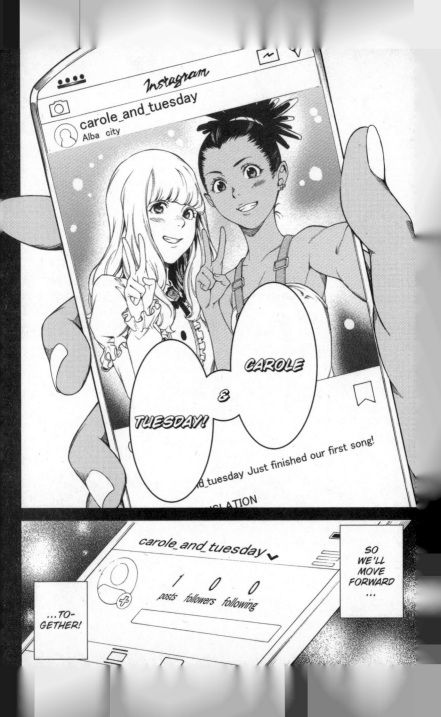

episode 2: Born to Run

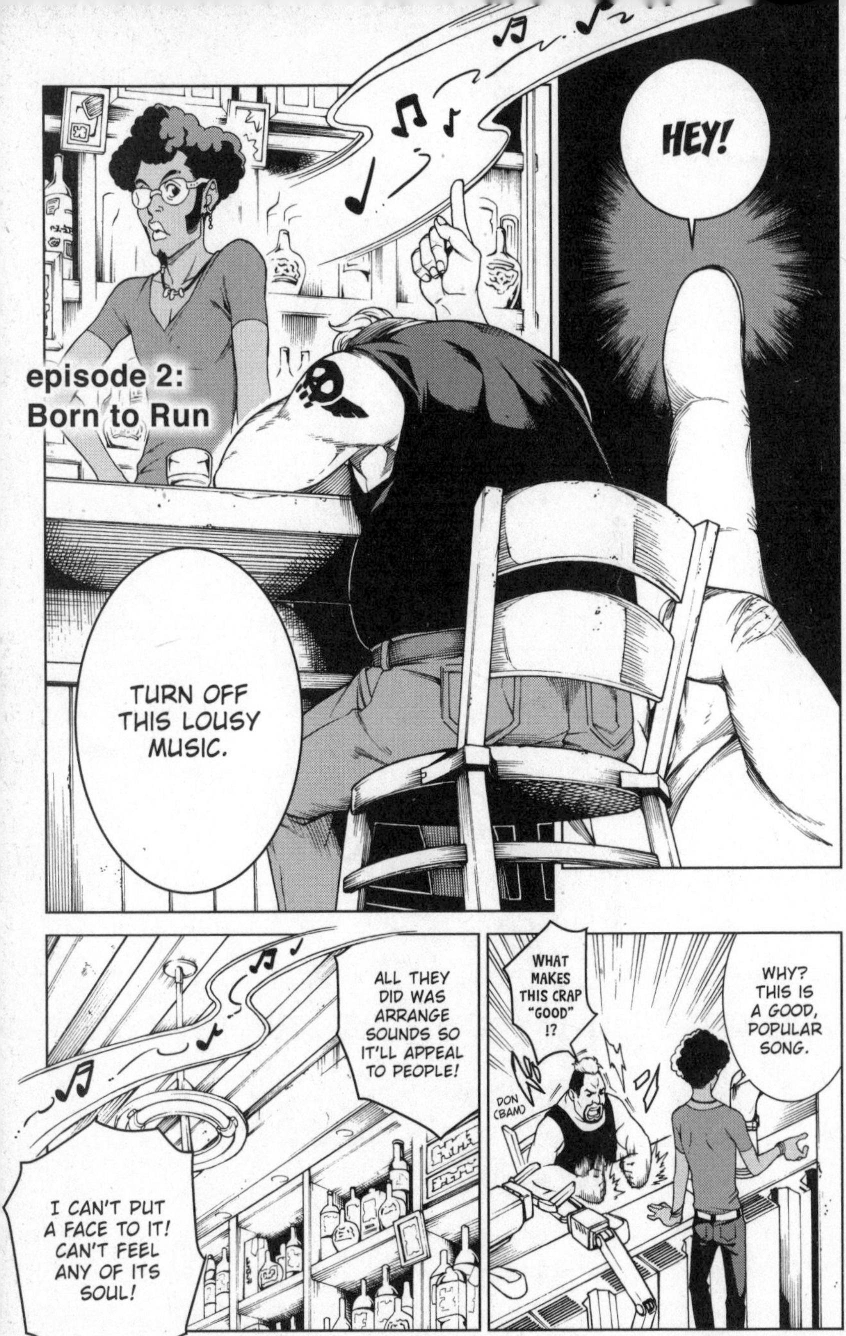
HEY!
TURN OFF THIS LOUSY MUSIC.
WHY? THIS IS A GOOD, POPULAR SONG.
WHAT MAKES THIS CRAP "GOOD" !?
DON (BAM)
ALL THEY DID WAS ARRANGE SOUNDS SO IT'LL APPEAL TO PEOPLE!
I CAN'T PUT A FACE TO IT! CAN'T FEEL ANY OF ITS SOUL!

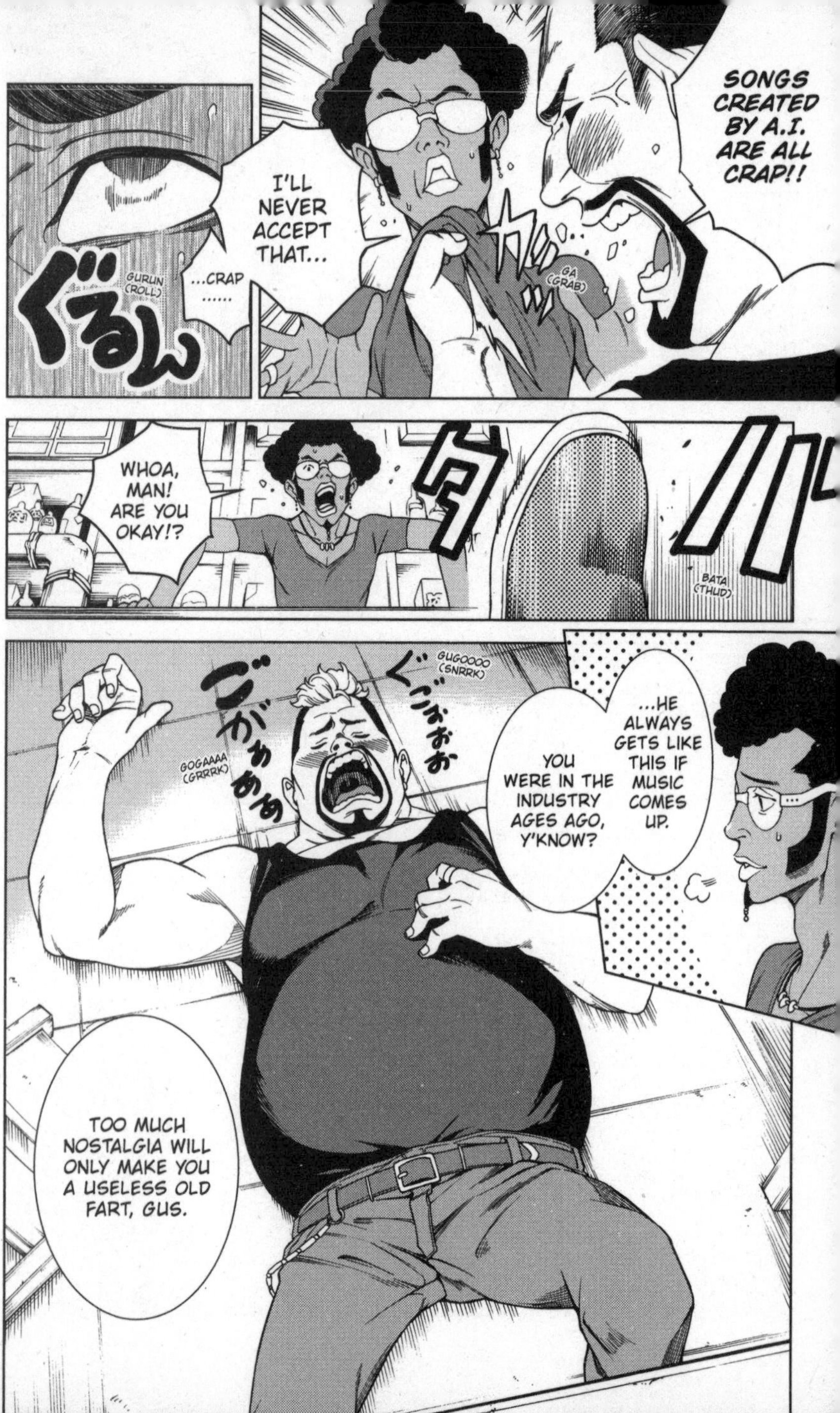
SONGS CREATED BY A.I. ARE ALL CRAP!!
I'LL NEVER ACCEPT THAT...
GA (GRAB)
...CRAP ......
GURUN (ROLL)
ぐるん
BATA (THUD)
WHOA, MAN! ARE YOU OKAY!?
...HE ALWAYS GETS LIKE THIS IF MUSIC COMES UP.
YOU WERE IN THE INDUSTRY AGES AGO, Y'KNOW?
GUGOOOO (SNRRK)
GOGAAAA (GRRRK)
TOO MUCH NOSTALGIA WILL ONLY MAKE YOU A USELESS OLD FART, GUS.

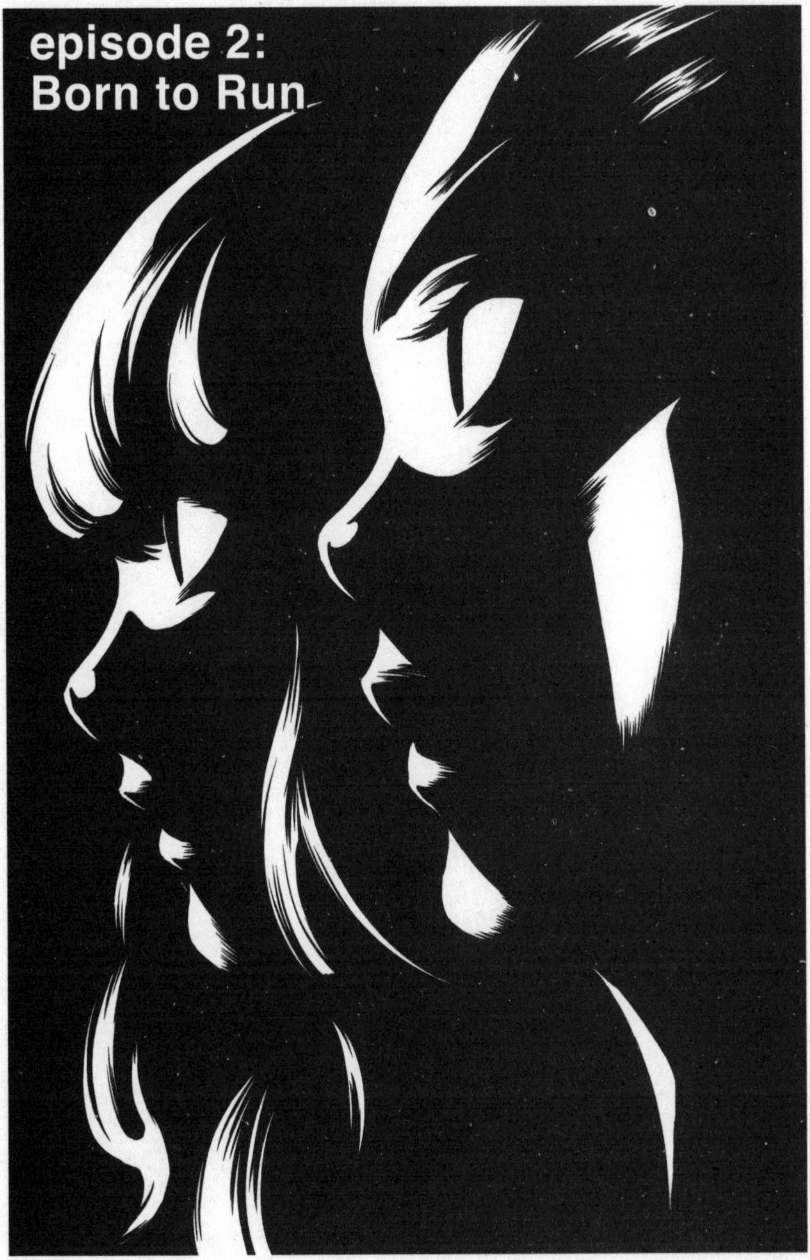
episode 2:
Born to Run

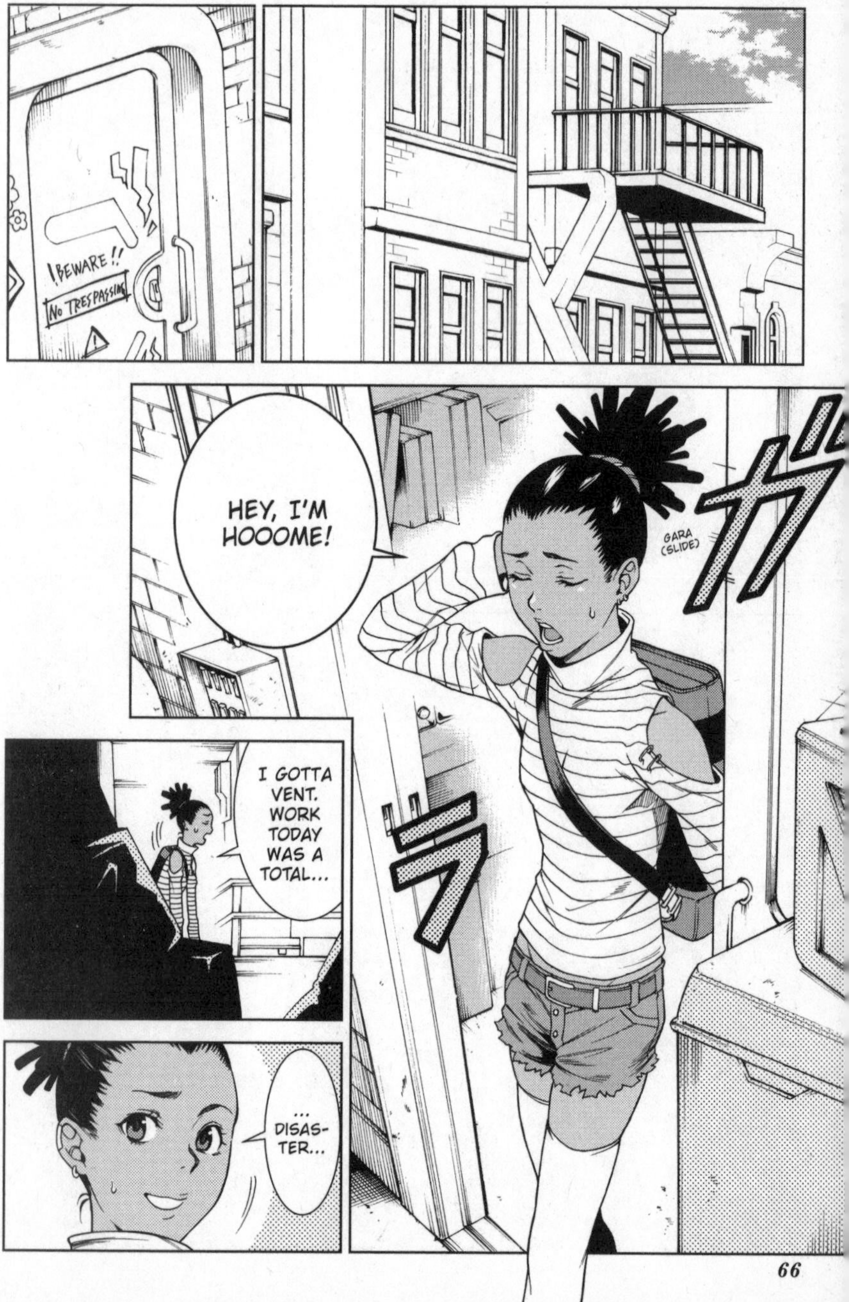
¡BEWARE!!
NO TRESPASSING
ガ
GARA (SLIDE)
HEY, I'M HOOOME!
ラ
I GOTTA VENT. WORK TODAY WAS A TOTAL...
...DISAS-TER...

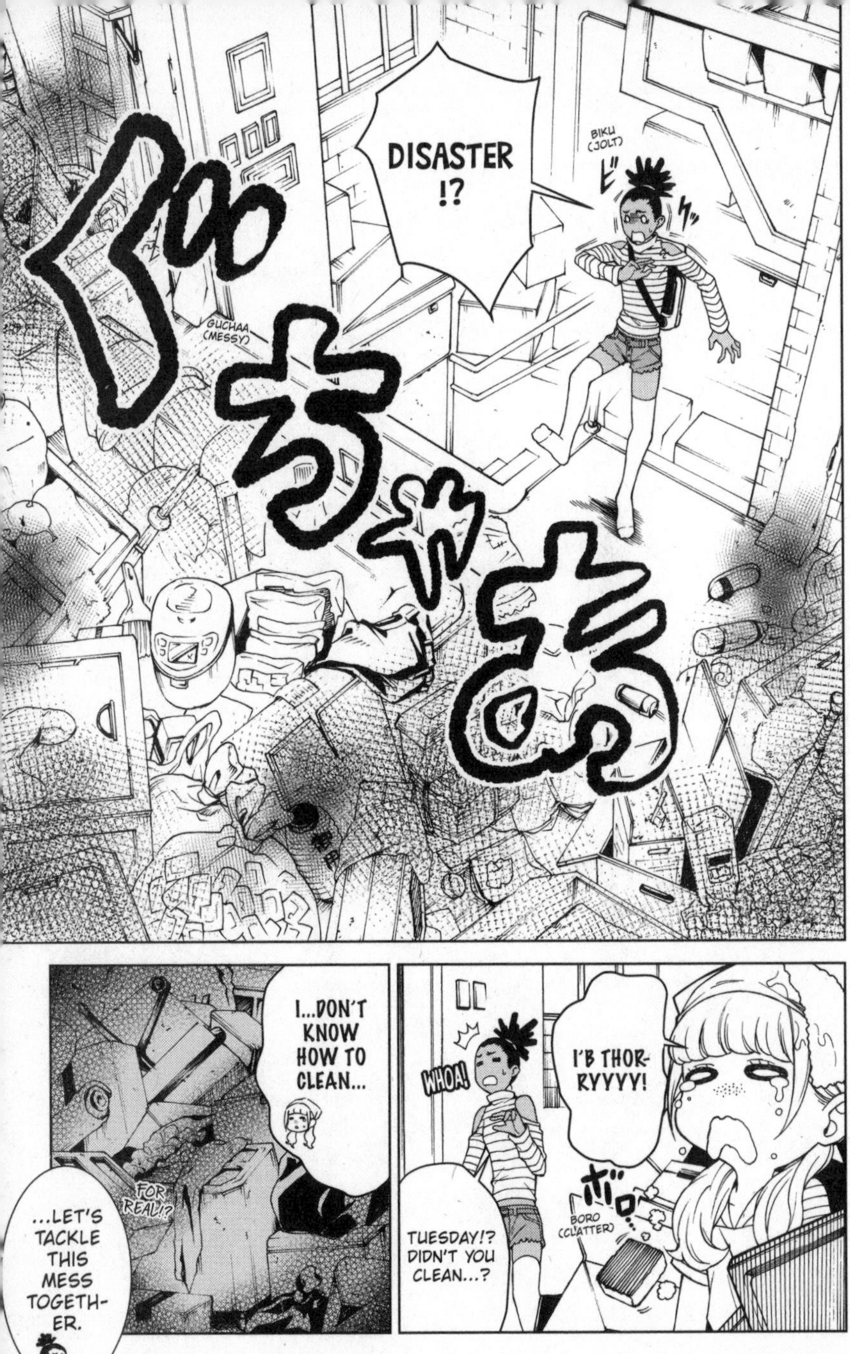
BIKU (JOLT)
DISASTER !?
GUCHAA (MESSY)
I'B THOR-RYYYY!
WHOA!
BORO (CLATTER)
TUESDAY!? DIDN'T YOU CLEAN...?
I...DON'T KNOW HOW TO CLEAN...
FOR REAL!?
...LET'S TACKLE THIS MESS TOGETH-ER.

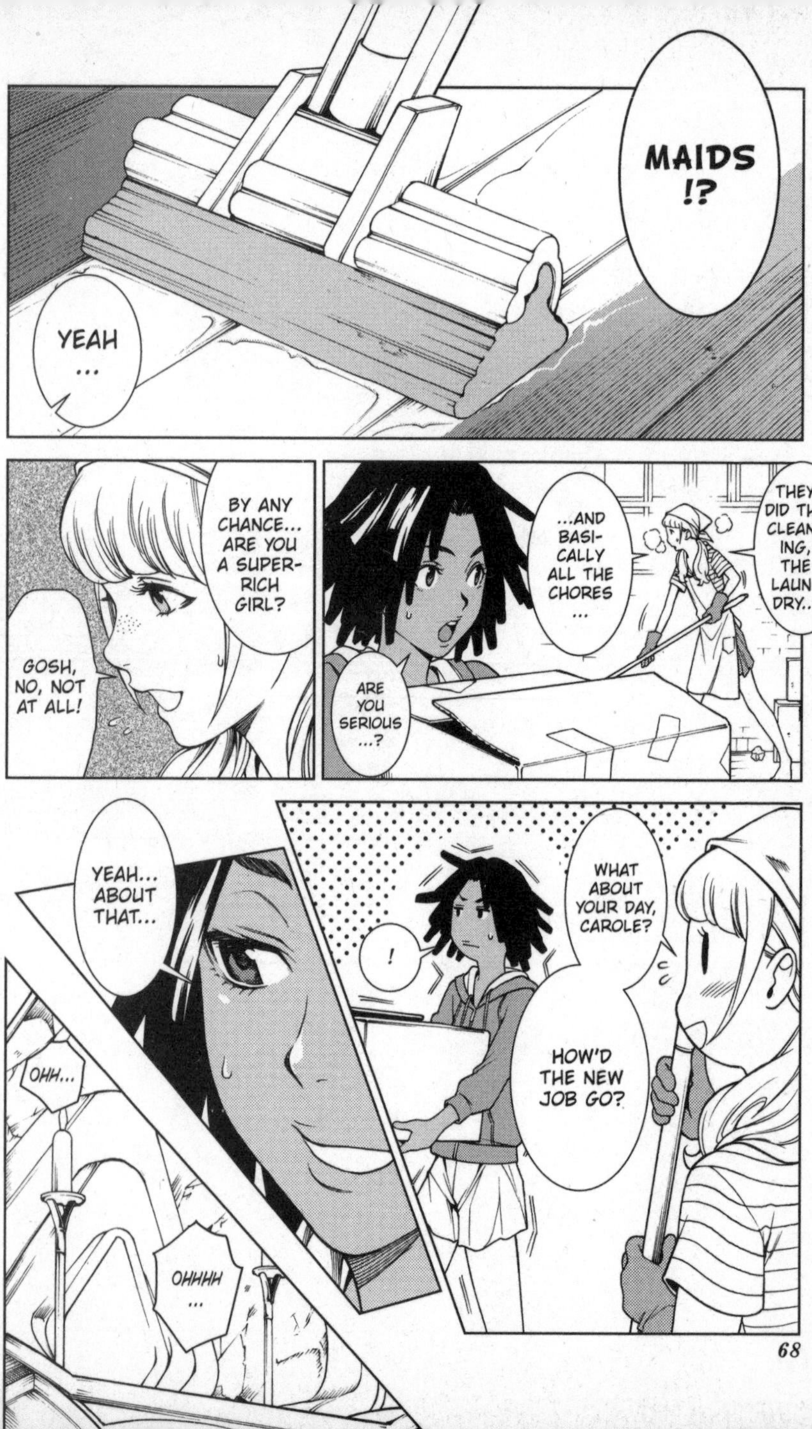
MAIDS !?
YEAH ...
THEY DID THE CLEANING, THE LAUNDRY...
...AND BASICALLY ALL THE CHORES ...
ARE YOU SERIOUS ...?
BY ANY CHANCE... ARE YOU A SUPER-RICH GIRL?
GOSH, NO, NOT AT ALL!
WHAT ABOUT YOUR DAY, CAROLE?
!
HOW'D THE NEW JOB GO?
YEAH... ABOUT THAT...
OHH...
OHHHH ...

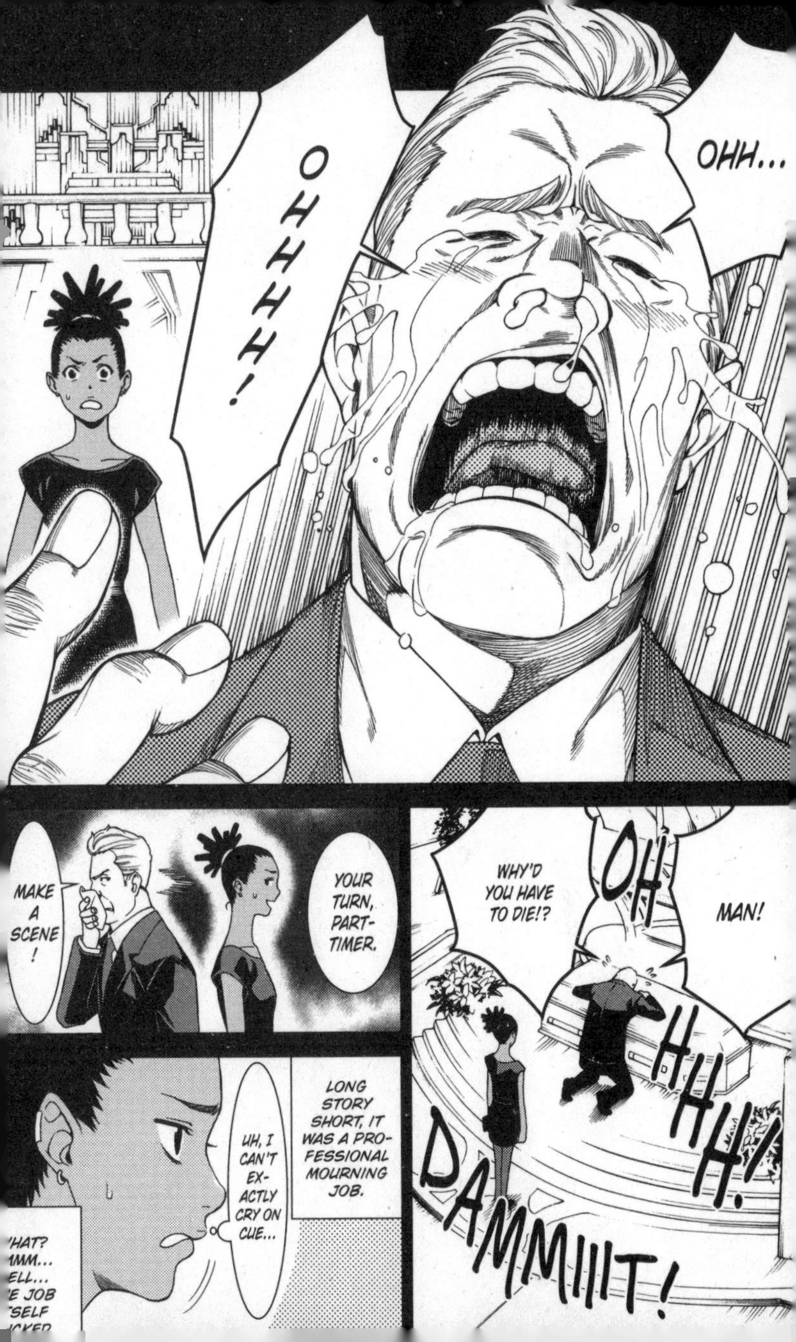
OHH...
OHHHHH!
WHY'D YOU HAVE TO DIE!?
OHHHHH!
MAN!
DAMMIIIT!
YOUR TURN, PART-TIMER.
MAKE A SCENE!
LONG STORY SHORT, IT WAS A PROFESSIONAL MOURNING JOB.
UH, I CAN'T EXACTLY CRY ON CUE...
HAT? MMM... ELL... E JOB TSELF

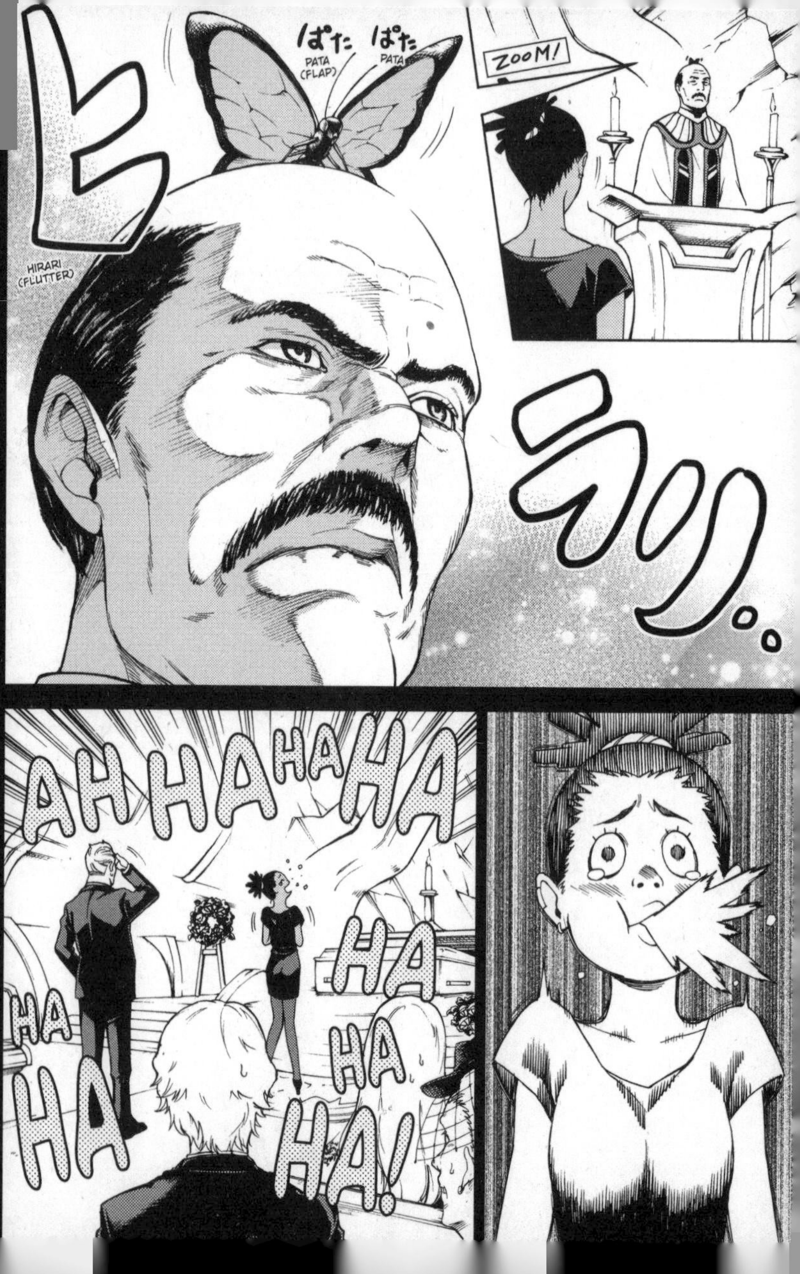
ZOOM!
ぱた ぱた
PATA (FLAP) PATA
ヒ
HIRARI (FLUTTER)
ラリ。。
AHHAHAHAHA
HA
HA
HA!
HA
HA

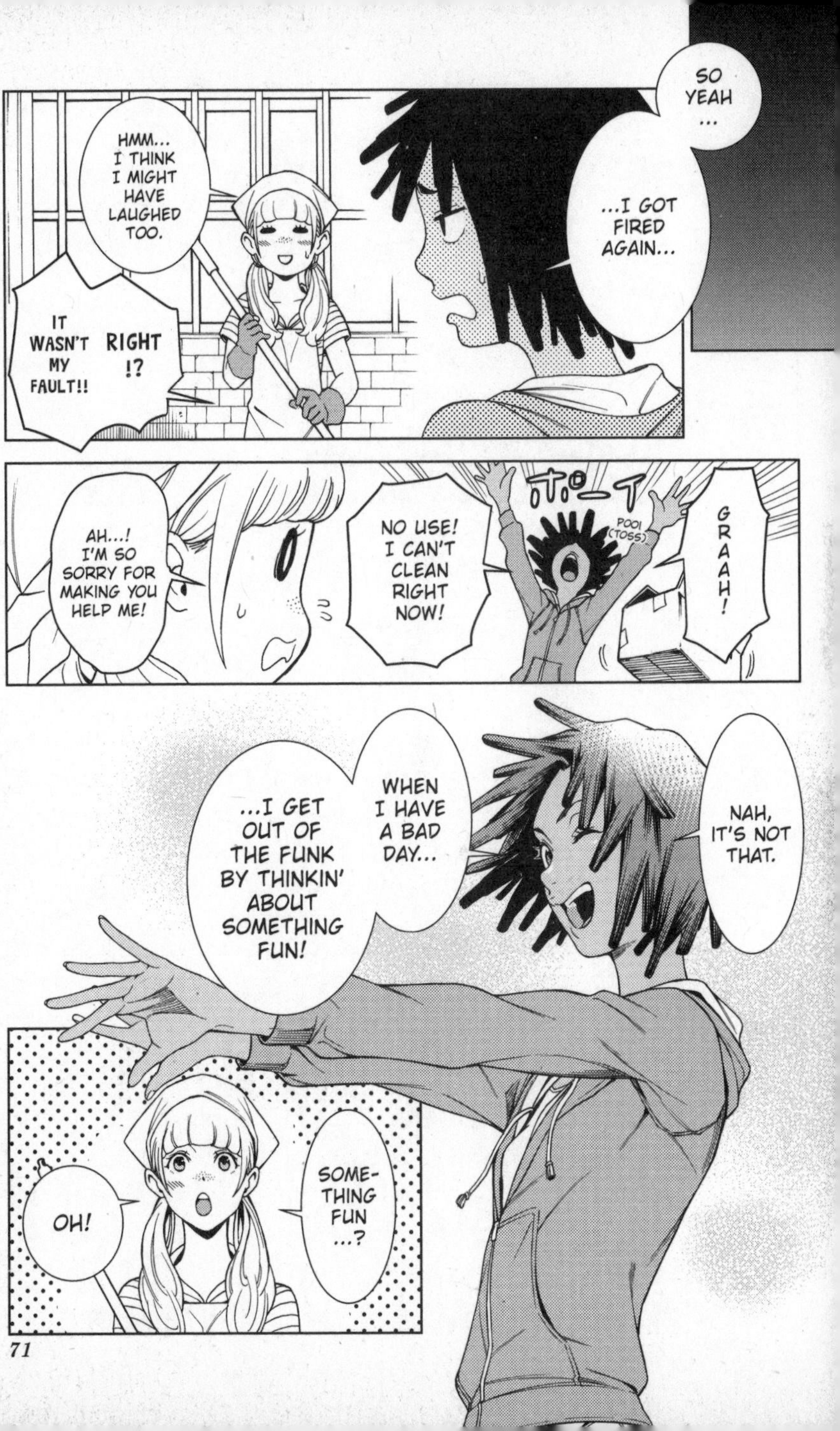
SO YEAH ...
...I GOT FIRED AGAIN...
HMM... I THINK I MIGHT HAVE LAUGHED TOO.
IT WASN'T MY FAULT!! RIGHT !?
GRAAH!
POOI (TOSS)
NO USE! I CAN'T CLEAN RIGHT NOW!
AH...! I'M SO SORRY FOR MAKING YOU HELP ME!
NAH, IT'S NOT THAT.
WHEN I HAVE A BAD DAY...
...I GET OUT OF THE FUNK BY THINKIN' ABOUT SOMETHING FUN!
SOME-THING FUN ...?
OH!

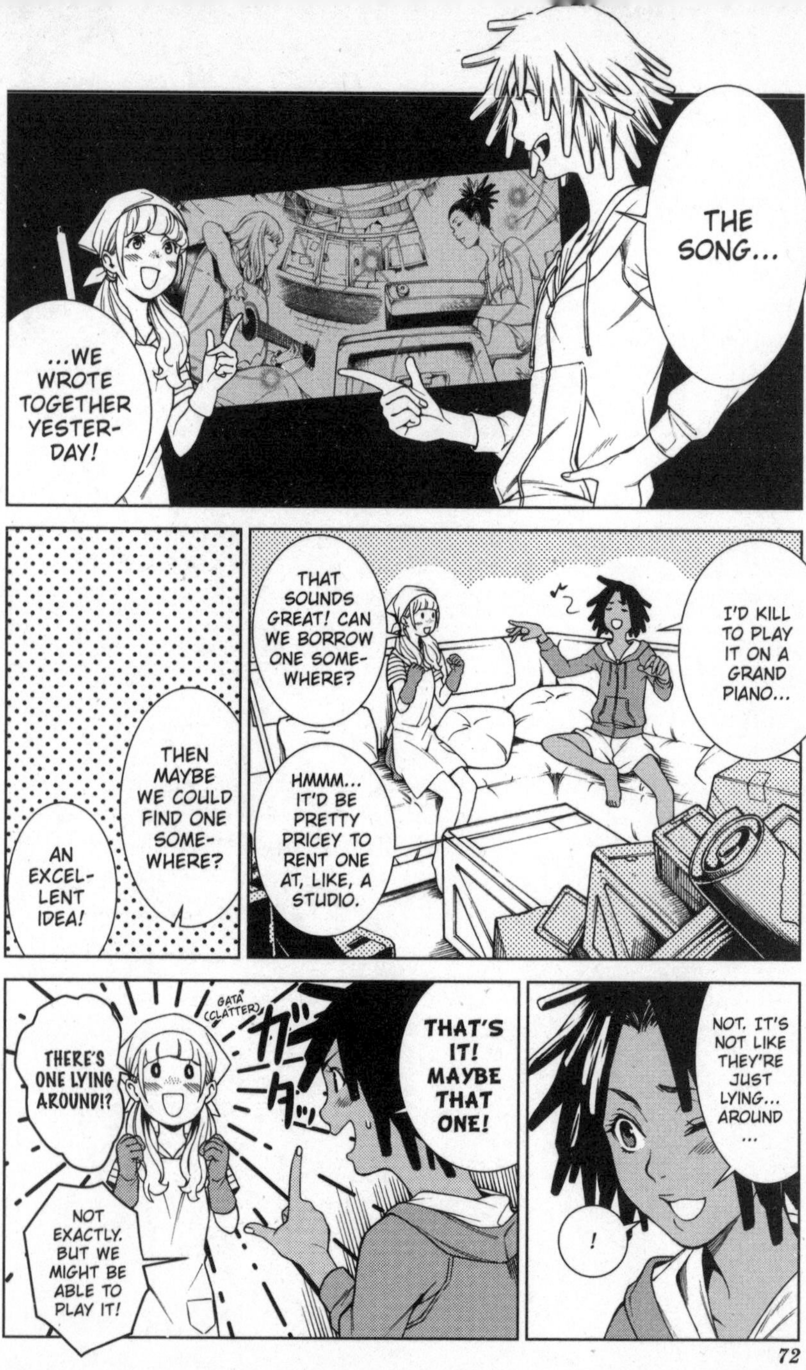
THE SONG...
...WE WROTE TOGETHER YESTER-DAY!
I'D KILL TO PLAY IT ON A GRAND PIANO...
THAT SOUNDS GREAT! CAN WE BORROW ONE SOME-WHERE?
HMMM... IT'D BE PRETTY PRICEY TO RENT ONE AT, LIKE, A STUDIO.
THEN MAYBE WE COULD FIND ONE SOME-WHERE?
AN EXCEL-LENT IDEA!
NOT. IT'S NOT LIKE THEY'RE JUST LYING... AROUND ...
!
THAT'S IT! MAYBE THAT ONE!
GATA (CLATTER)
THERE'S ONE LYING AROUND!?
NOT EXACTLY. BUT WE MIGHT BE ABLE TO PLAY IT!

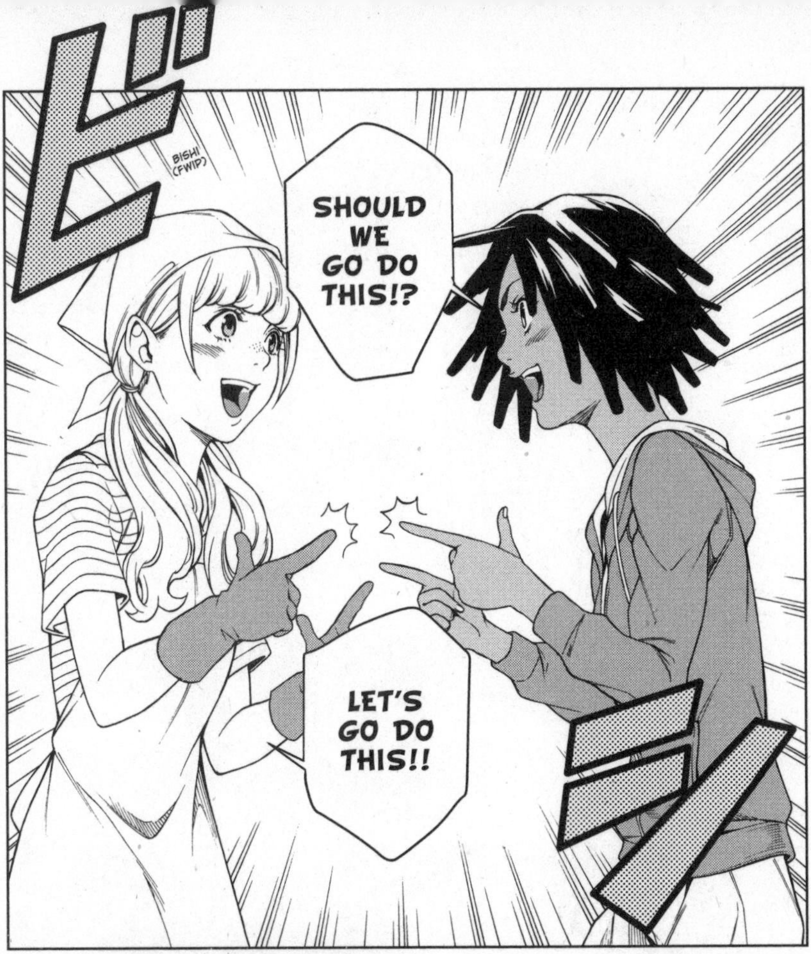
SHOULD WE GO DO THIS!?
BISHI (FWIP)
LET'S GO DO THIS!!

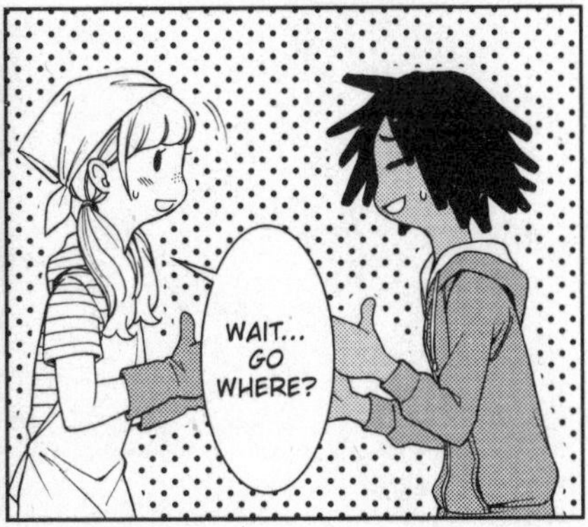
WAIT... GO WHERE?

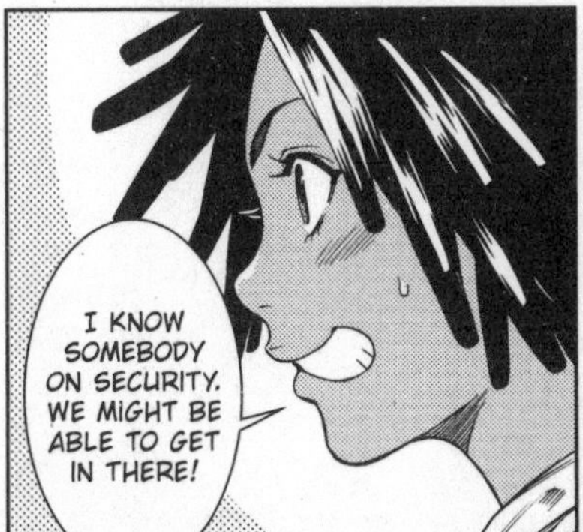
I KNOW SOMEBODY ON SECURITY. WE MIGHT BE ABLE TO GET IN THERE!

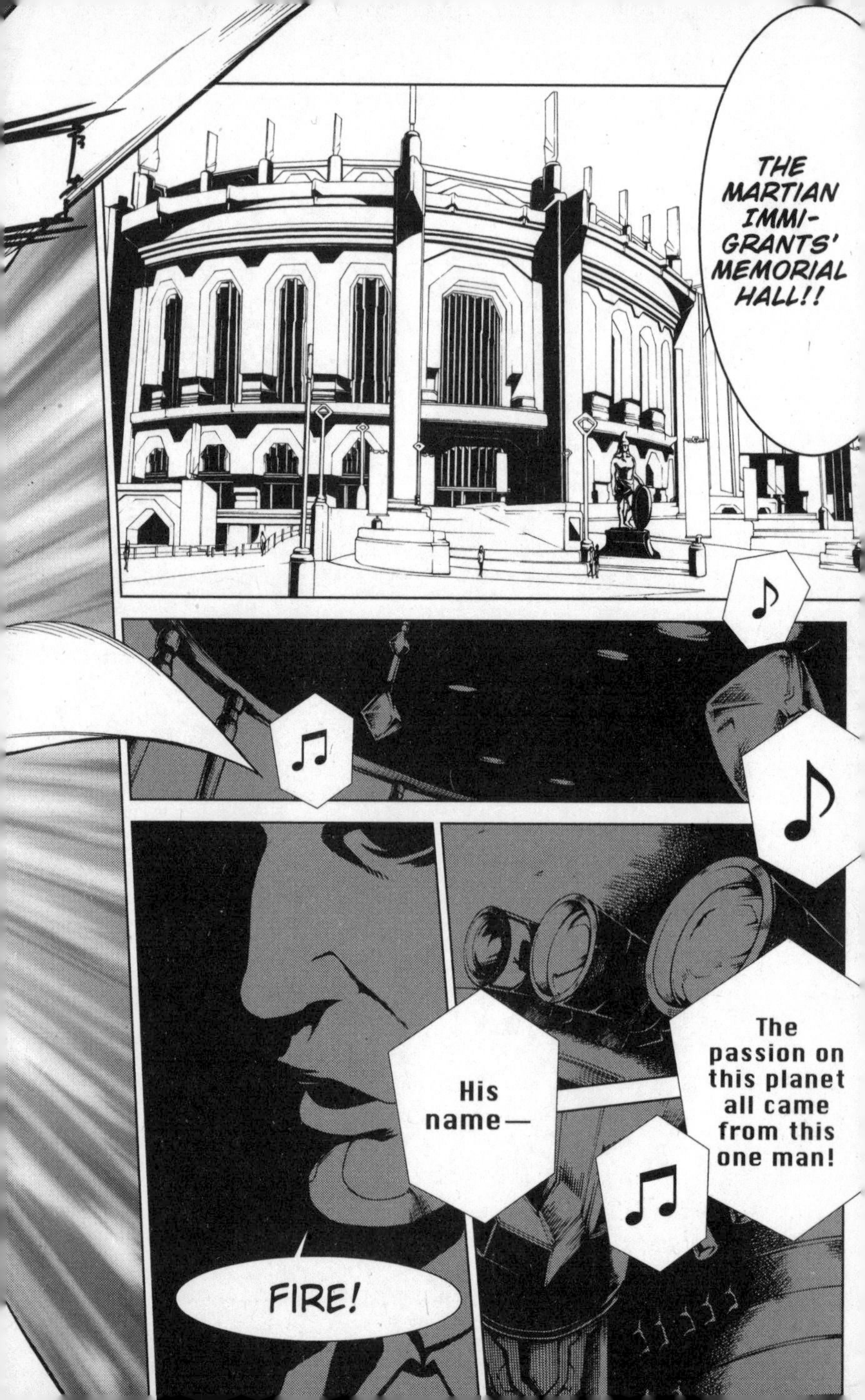
THE MARTIAN IMMI-GRANTS' MEMORIAL HALL!!
The passion on this planet all came from this one man!
His name—
FIRE!

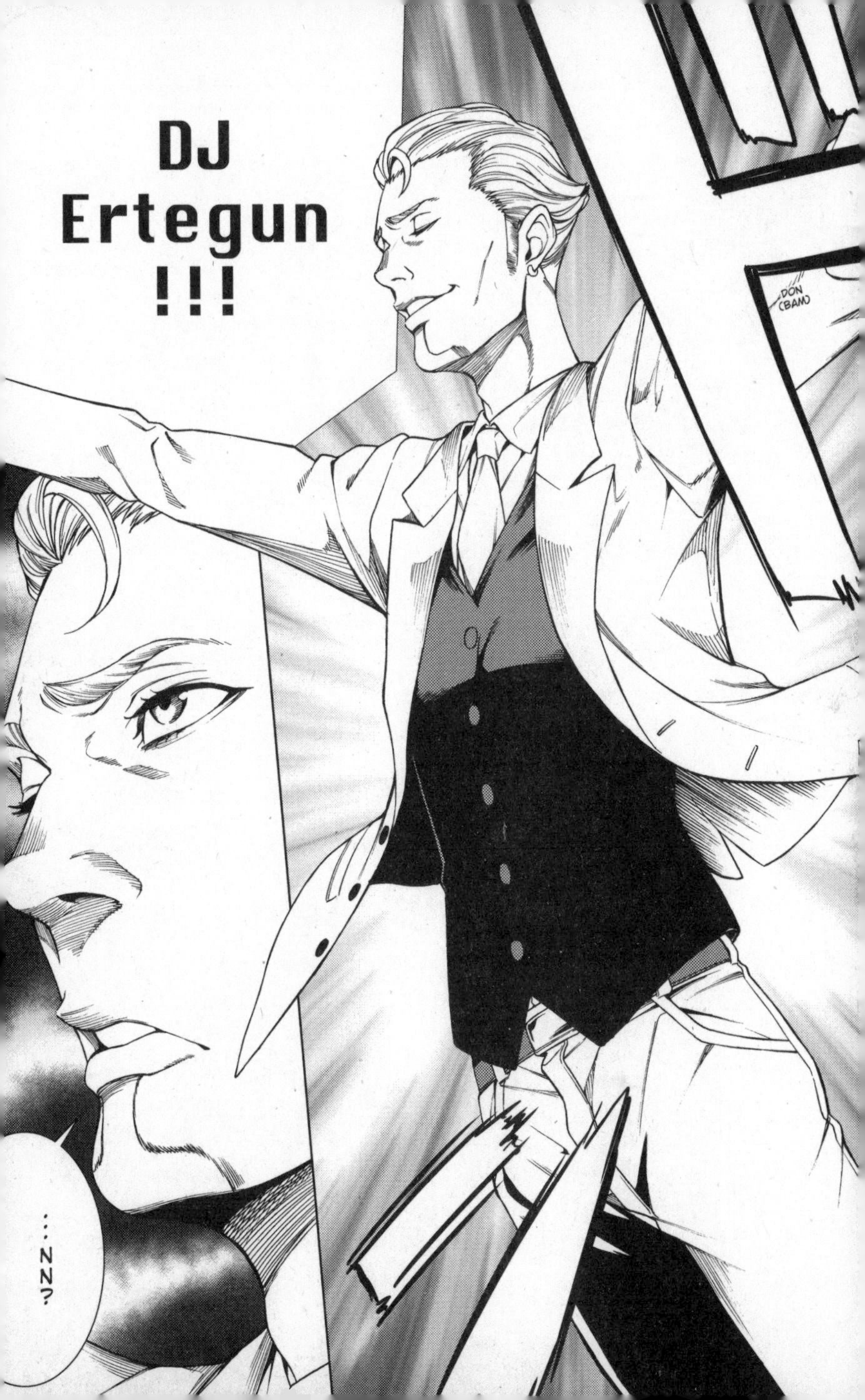
DON
(BAM)
DJ Ertegun !!!
...NN?

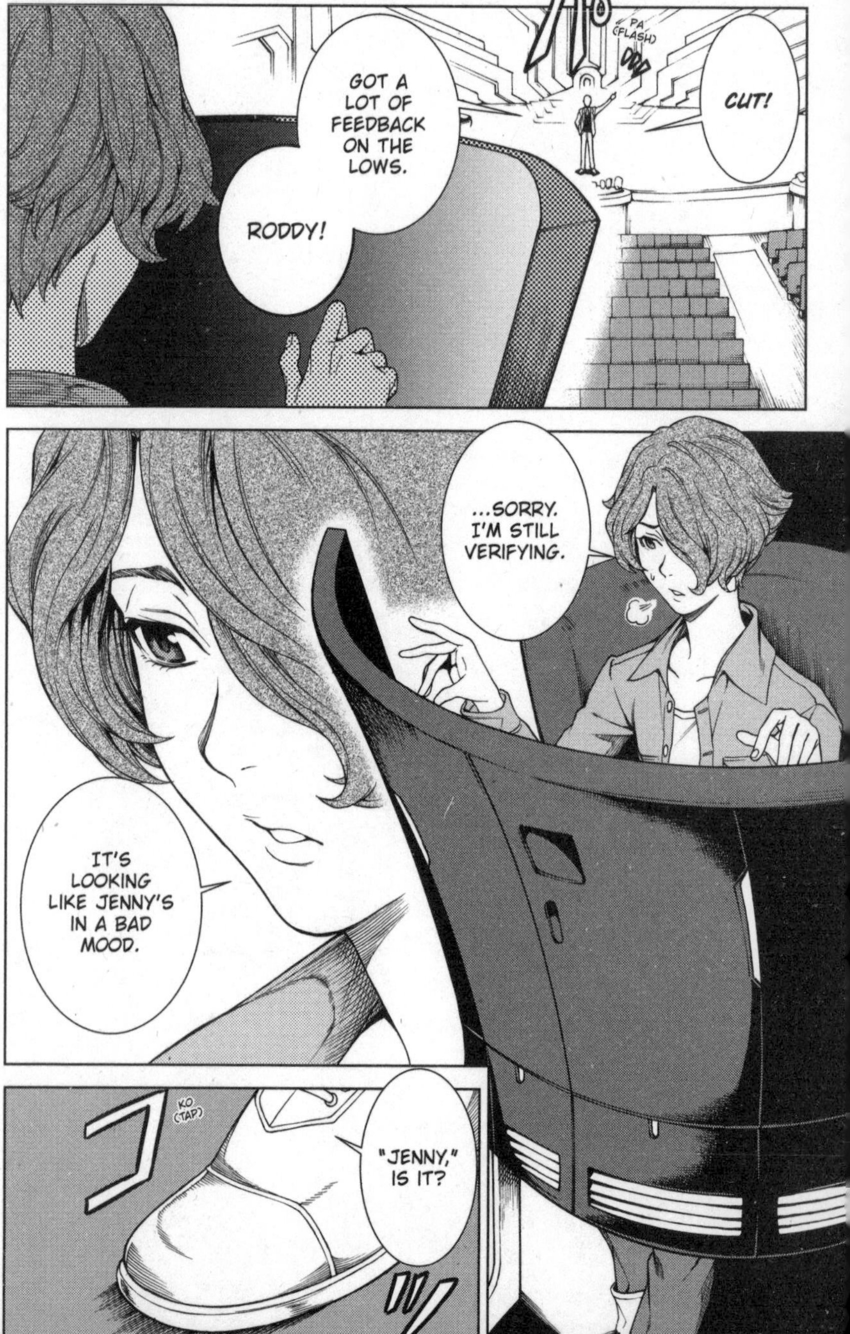
CUT!
PA (FLASH)
GOT A LOT OF FEEDBACK ON THE LOWS.
RODDY!
...SORRY. I'M STILL VERIFYING.
IT'S LOOKING LIKE JENNY'S IN A BAD MOOD.
"JENNY," IS IT?
KO (TAP)

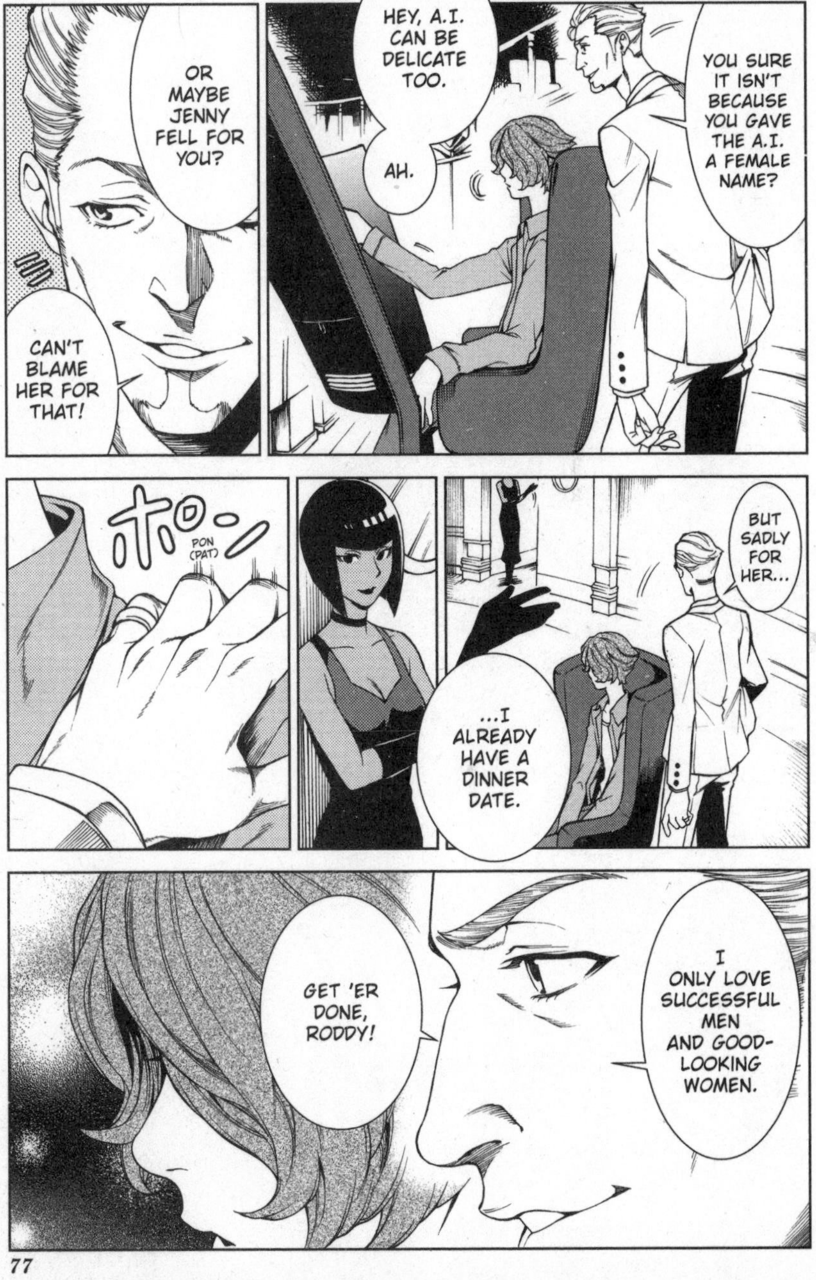
YOU SURE IT ISN'T BECAUSE YOU GAVE THE A.I. A FEMALE NAME?
HEY, A.I. CAN BE DELICATE TOO.
AH.
OR MAYBE JENNY FELL FOR YOU?
CAN'T BLAME HER FOR THAT!
BUT SADLY FOR HER...
...I ALREADY HAVE A DINNER DATE.
PON (PAT)
I ONLY LOVE SUCCESSFUL MEN AND GOOD-LOOKING WOMEN.
GET 'ER DONE, RODDY!

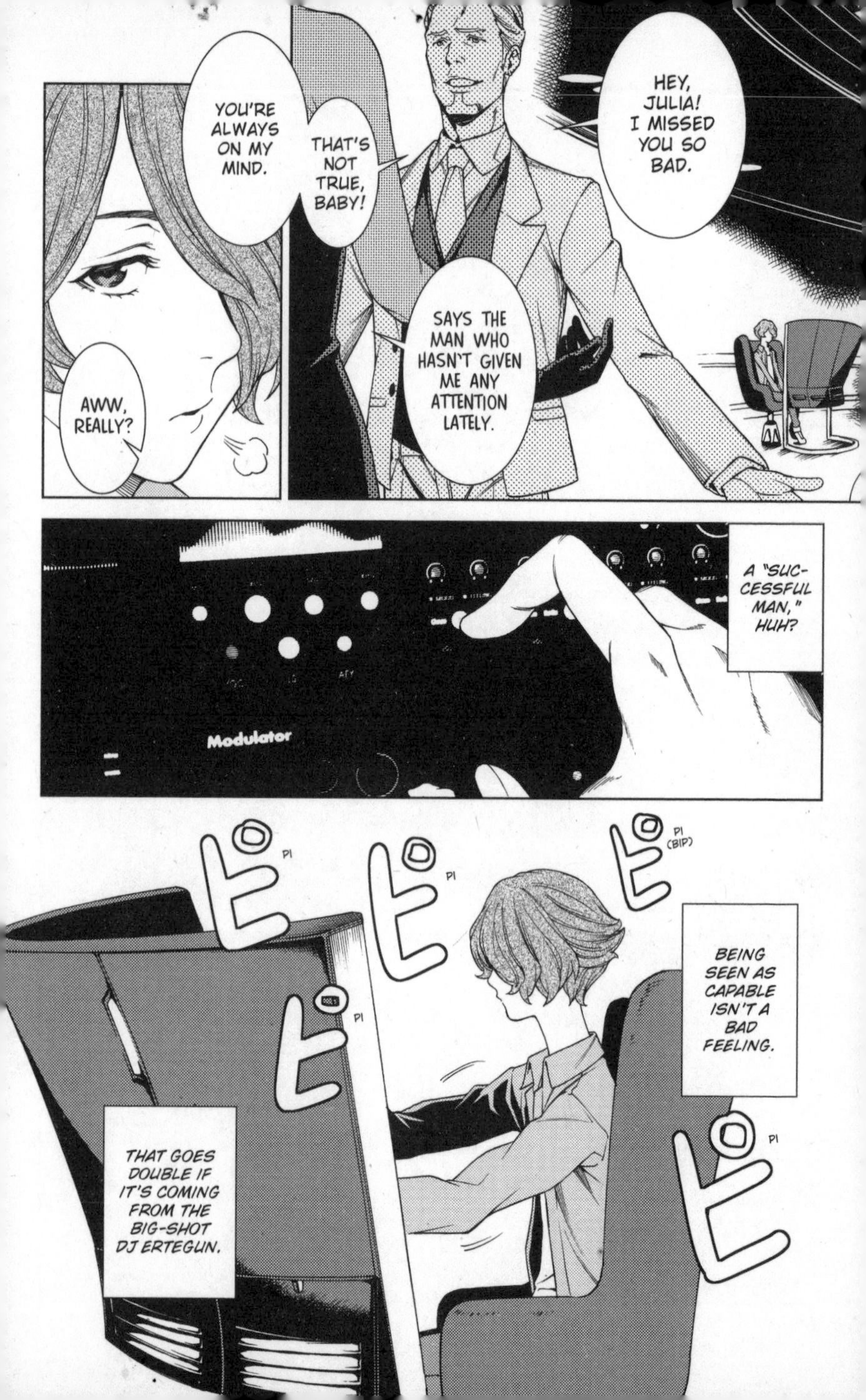
HEY, JULIA! I MISSED YOU SO BAD.
SAYS THE MAN WHO HASN'T GIVEN ME ANY ATTENTION LATELY.
THAT'S NOT TRUE, BABY!
YOU'RE ALWAYS ON MY MIND.
AWW, REALLY?
A "SUC-CESSFUL MAN," HUH?
Modulator
ピ PI (BIP)
ピ PI
ピ PI
BEING SEEN AS CAPABLE ISN'T A BAD FEELING.
ピ PI
ピ PI
THAT GOES DOUBLE IF IT'S COMING FROM THE BIG-SHOT DJ ERTEGUN.

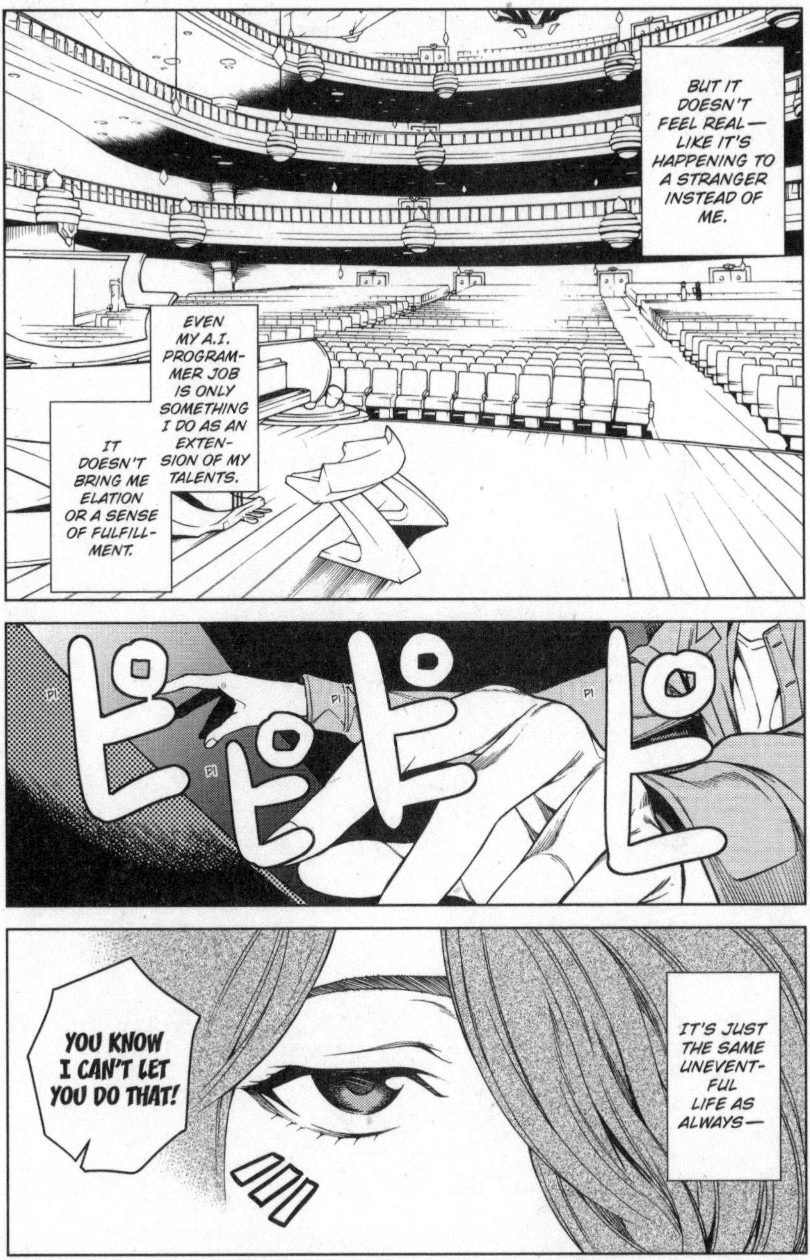
BUT IT DOESN'T FEEL REAL—LIKE IT'S HAPPENING TO A STRANGER INSTEAD OF ME.
EVEN MY A.I. PROGRAMMER JOB IS ONLY SOMETHING I DO AS AN EXTENSION OF MY TALENTS.
IT DOESN'T BRING ME ELATION OR A SENSE OF FULFILLMENT.
PI
PI
PI
PI
IT'S JUST THE SAME UNEVENTFUL LIFE AS ALWAYS—
YOU KNOW I CAN'T LET YOU DO THAT!

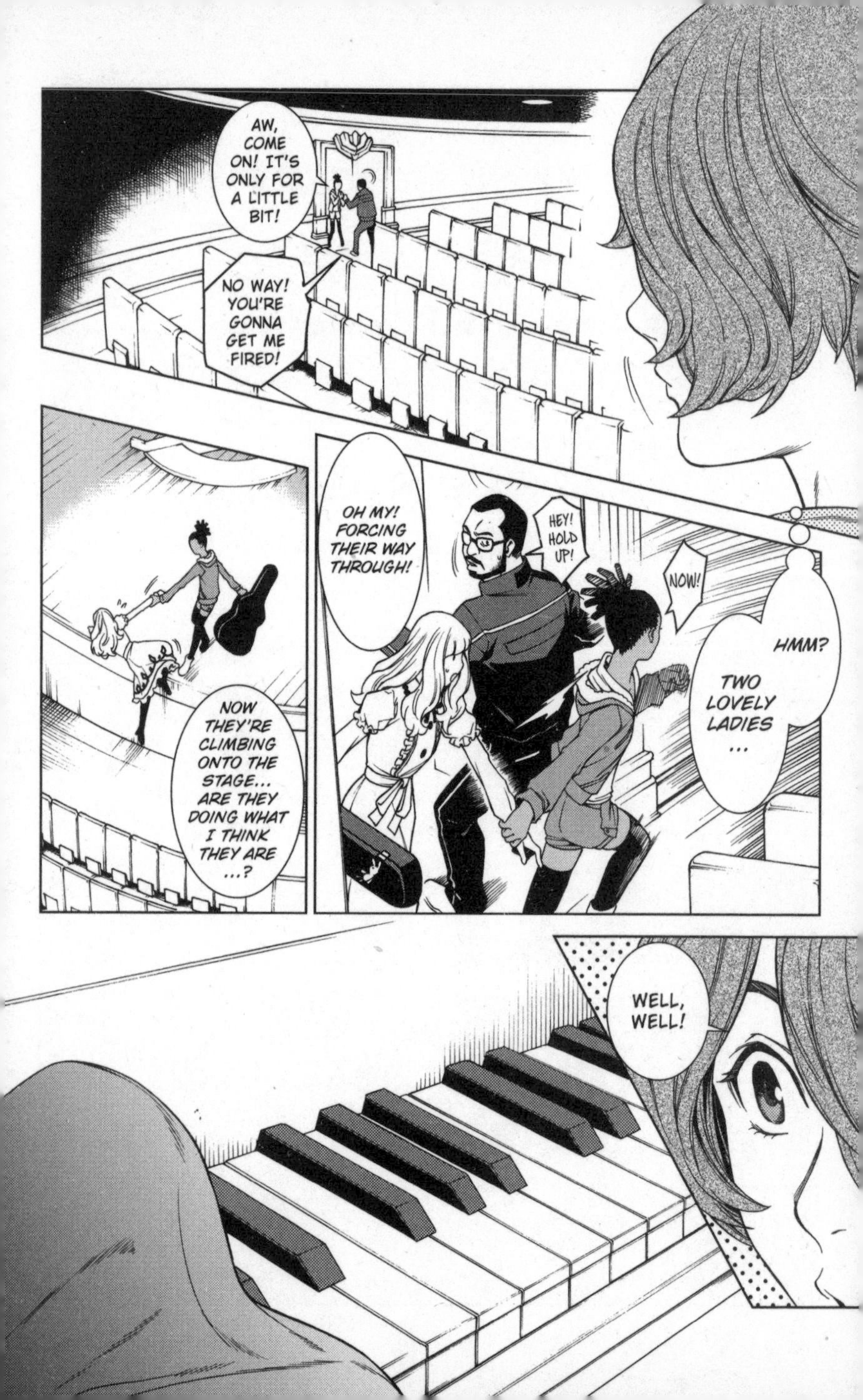
AW, COME ON! IT'S ONLY FOR A LITTLE BIT!
NO WAY! YOU'RE GONNA GET ME FIRED!
HMM?
TWO LOVELY LADIES ...
NOW!
HEY! HOLD UP!
OH MY! FORCING THEIR WAY THROUGH!
NOW THEY'RE CLIMBING ONTO THE STAGE... ARE THEY DOING WHAT I THINK THEY ARE ...?
WELL, WELL!

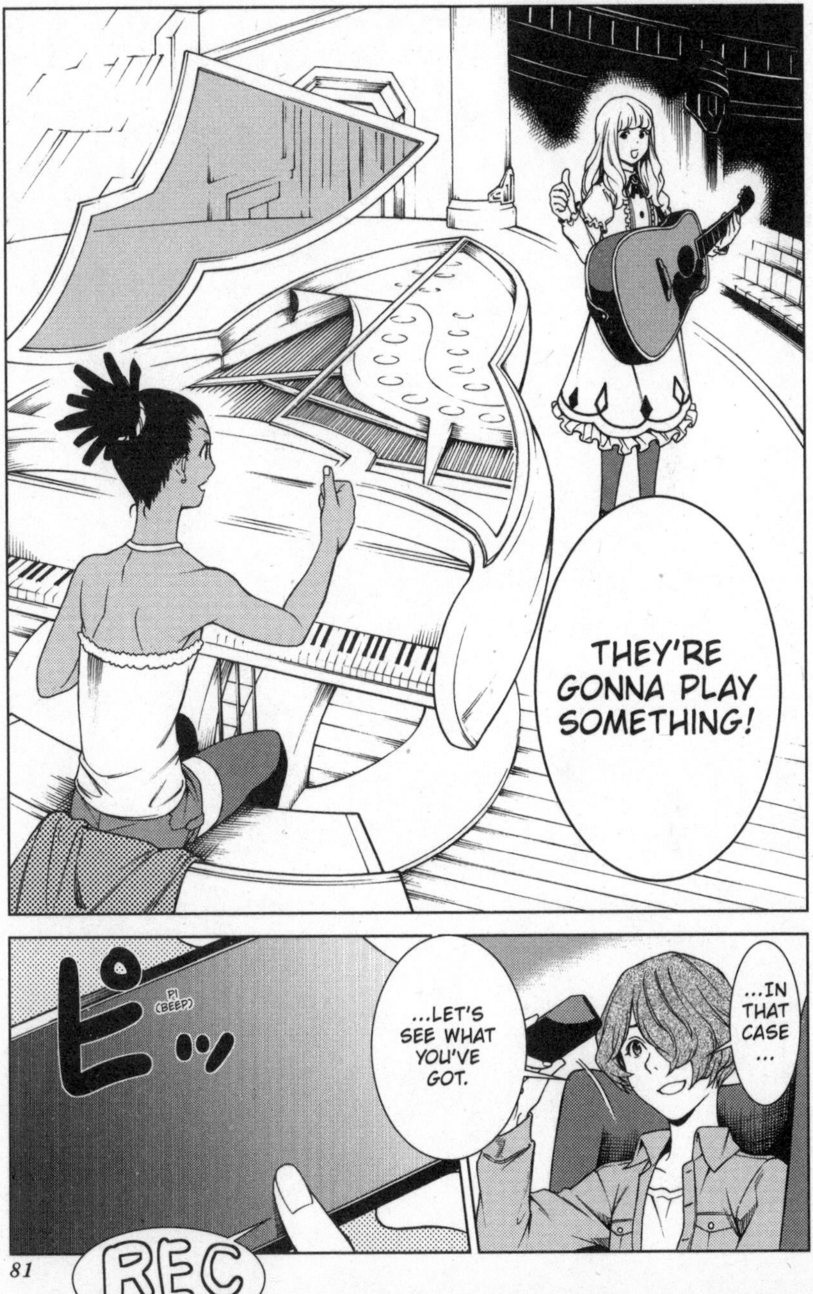
THEY'RE GONNA PLAY SOMETHING!
...IN THAT CASE...
...LET'S SEE WHAT YOU'VE GOT.
PI (BEEP)
REC

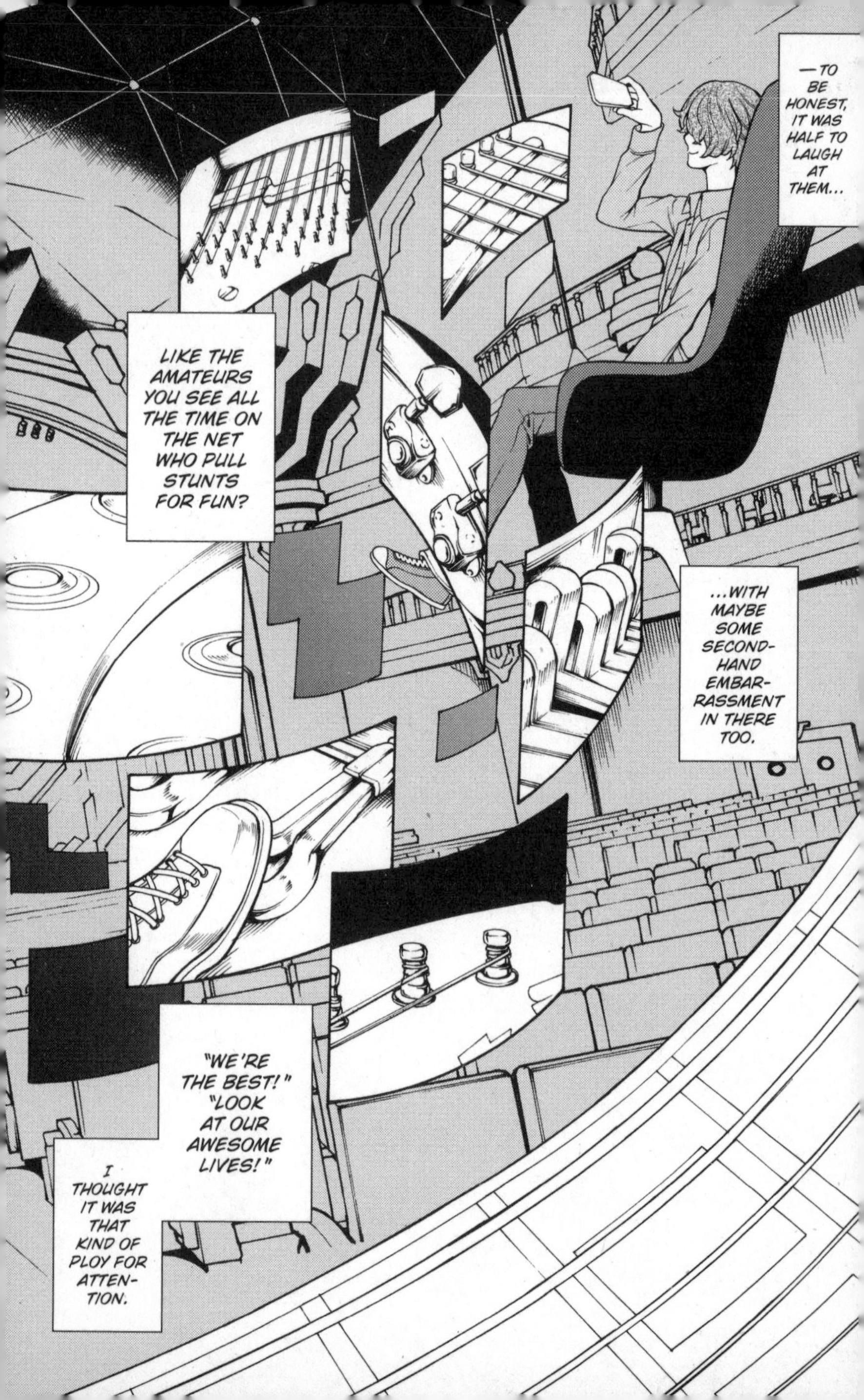
—TO BE HONEST, IT WAS HALF TO LAUGH AT THEM...
...WITH MAYBE SOME SECOND-HAND EMBARRASSMENT IN THERE TOO.
LIKE THE AMATEURS YOU SEE ALL THE TIME ON THE NET WHO PULL STUNTS FOR FUN?
"WE'RE THE BEST!" "LOOK AT OUR AWESOME LIVES!"
I THOUGHT IT WAS THAT KIND OF PLOY FOR ATTENTION.

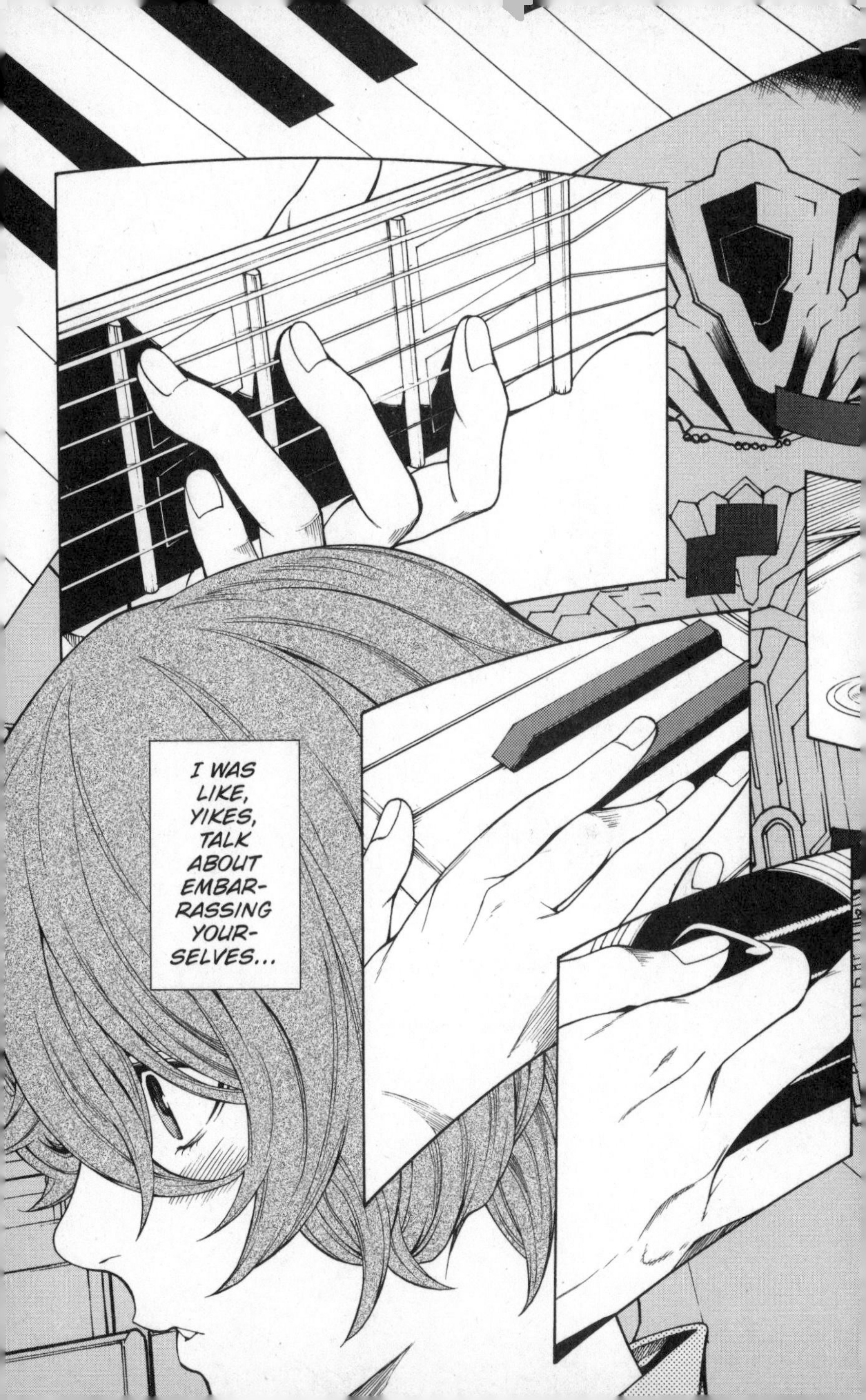
I WAS LIKE, YIKES, TALK ABOUT EMBARRASSING YOURSELVES...

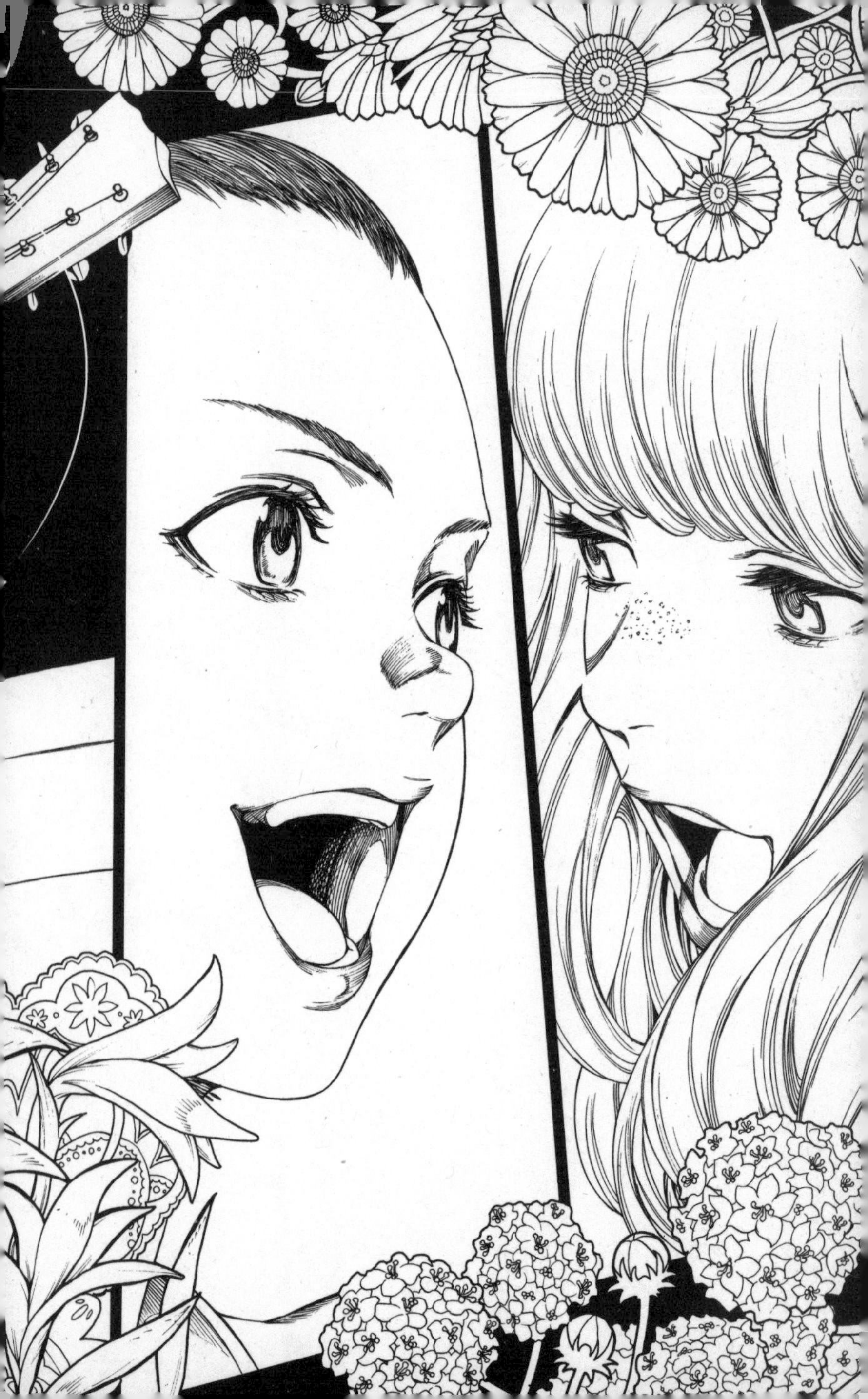

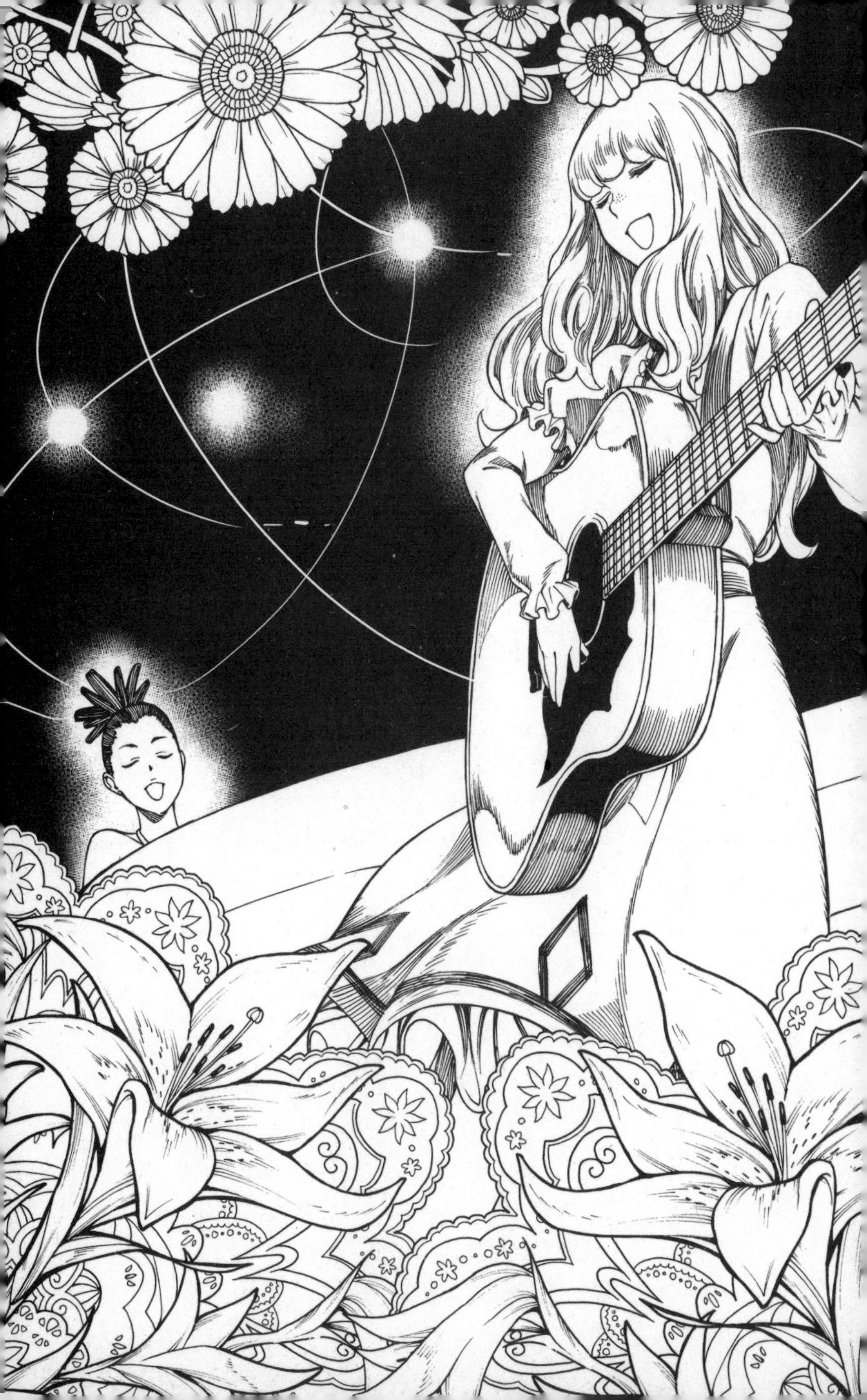

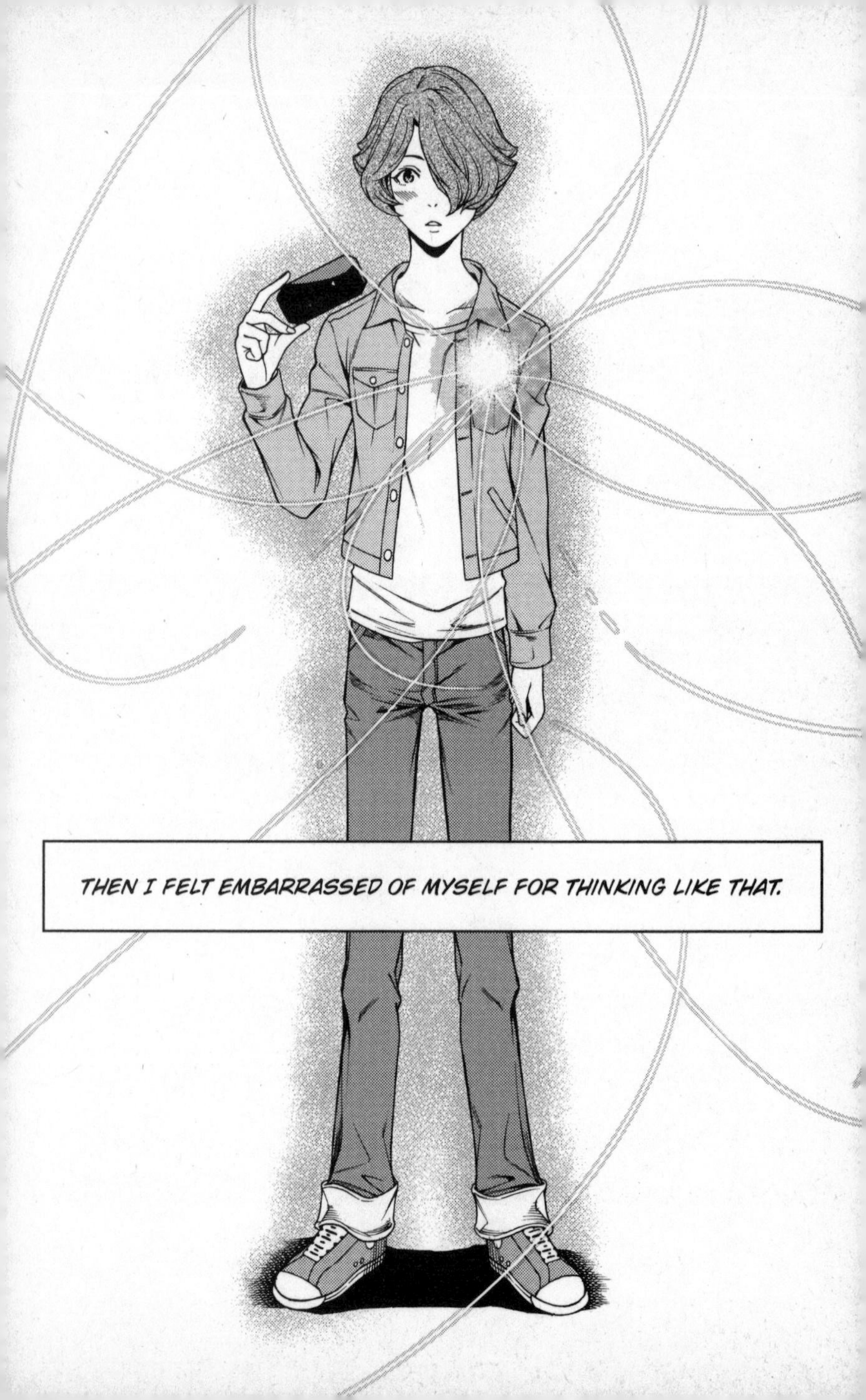
THEN I FELT EMBARRASSED OF MYSELF FOR THINKING LIKE THAT.

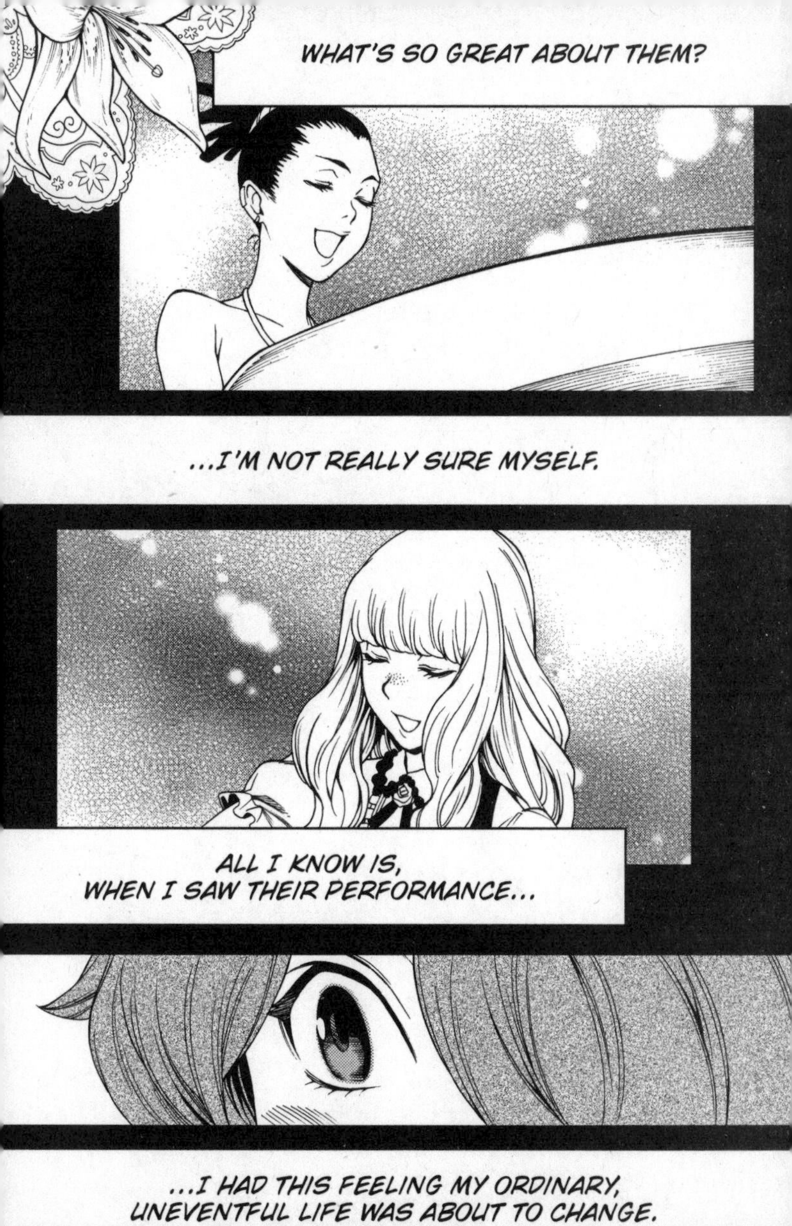
WHAT'S SO GREAT ABOUT THEM?
...I'M NOT REALLY SURE MYSELF.
ALL I KNOW IS, WHEN I SAW THEIR PERFORMANCE...
...I HAD THIS FEELING MY ORDINARY, UNEVENTFUL LIFE WAS ABOUT TO CHANGE.

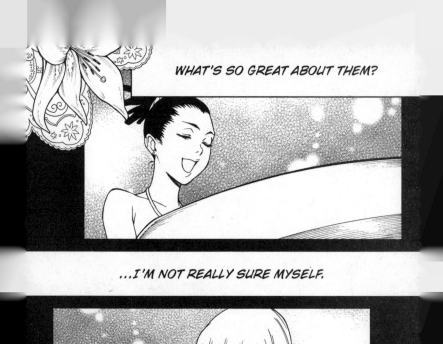

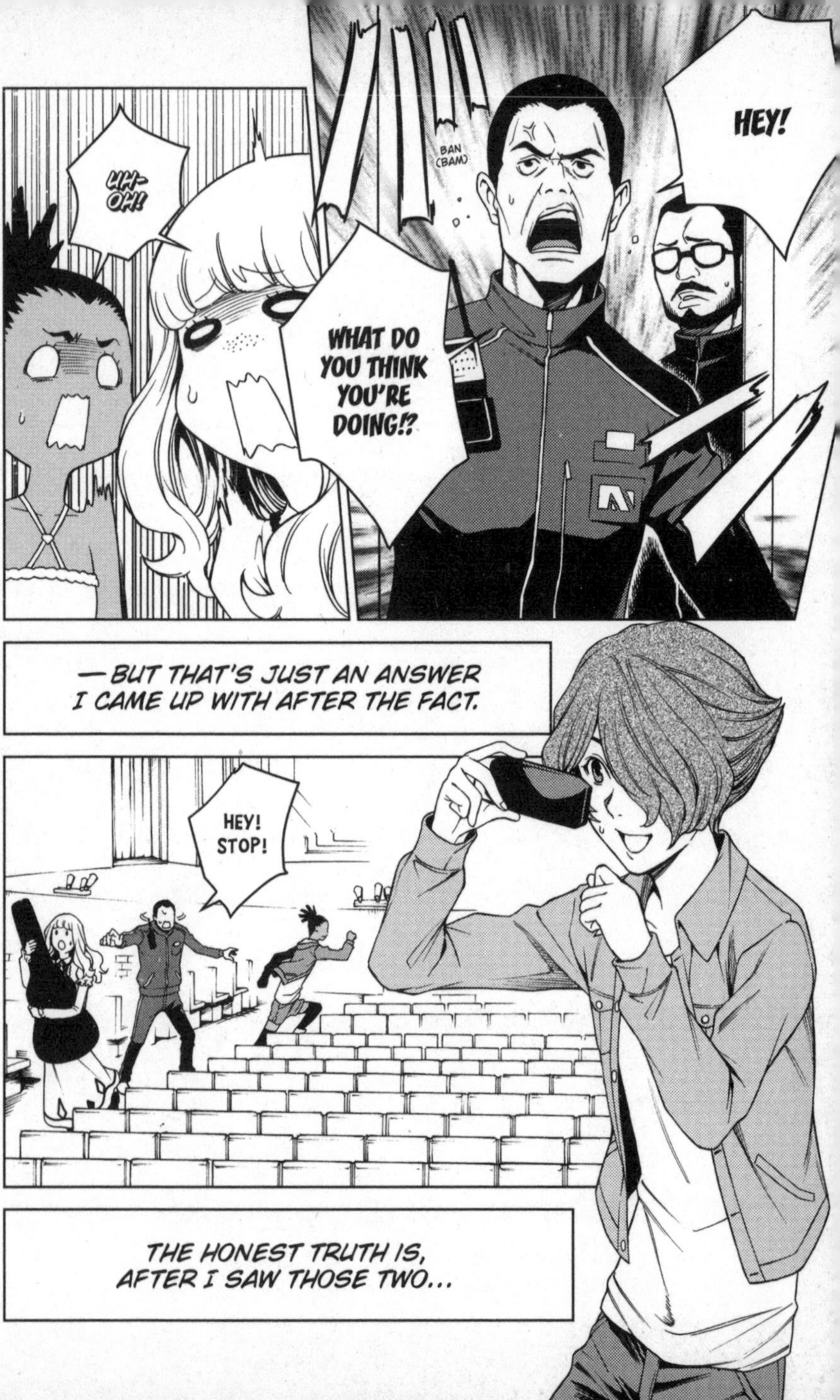
HEY!
BAN (BAM)
WHAT DO YOU THINK YOU'RE DOING!?
UH-OH!
—BUT THAT'S JUST AN ANSWER I CAME UP WITH AFTER THE FACT.
HEY! STOP!
THE HONEST TRUTH IS, AFTER I SAW THOSE TWO...

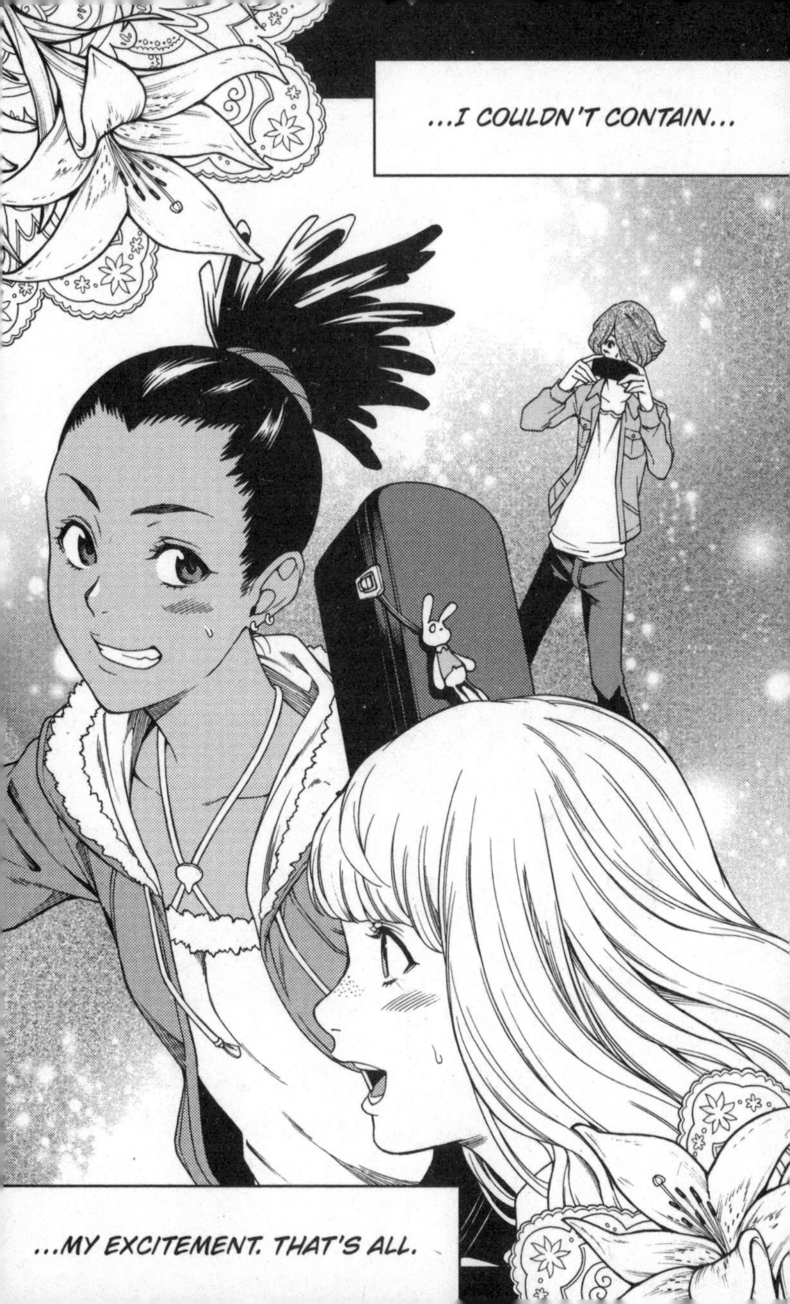
...I COULDN'T CONTAIN...
...MY EXCITEMENT. THAT'S ALL.

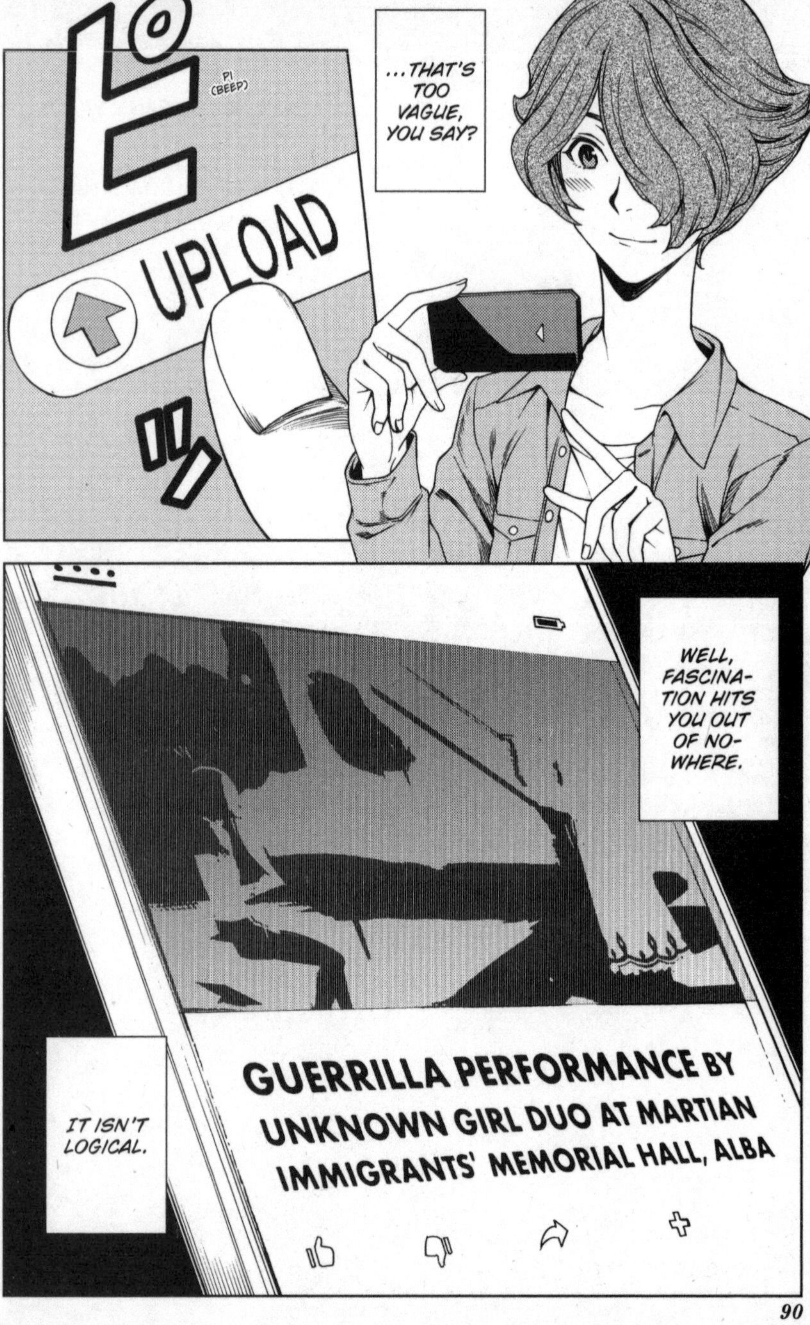
...THAT'S TOO VAGUE, YOU SAY?
PI (BEEP)
UPLOAD
WELL, FASCINATION HITS YOU OUT OF NOWHERE.
GUERRILLA PERFORMANCE BY UNKNOWN GIRL DUO AT MARTIAN IMMIGRANTS' MEMORIAL HALL, ALBA
IT ISN'T LOGICAL.

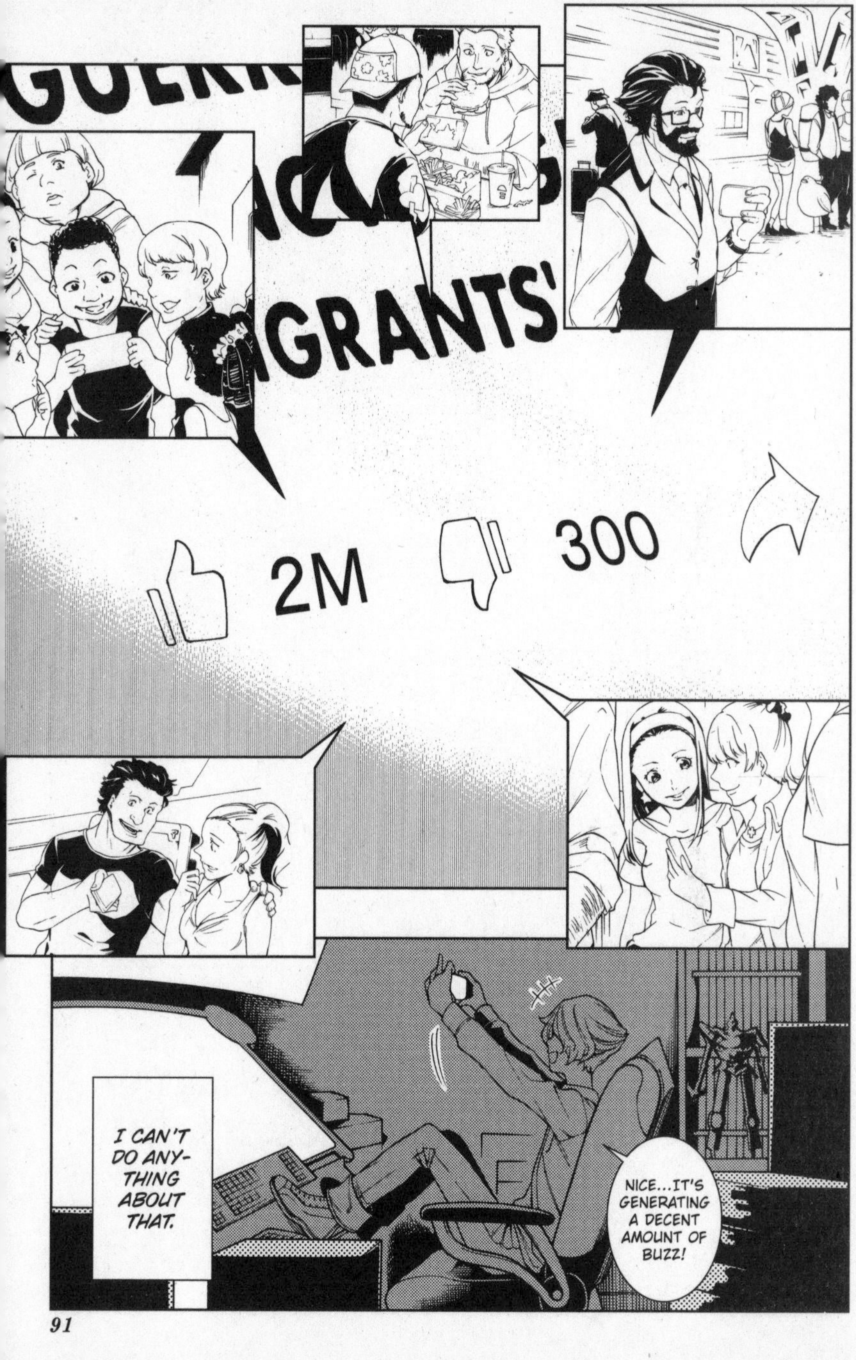
GUERR
IGRANTS'
2M
300
NICE...IT'S GENERATING A DECENT AMOUNT OF BUZZ!
I CAN'T DO ANYTHING ABOUT THAT.

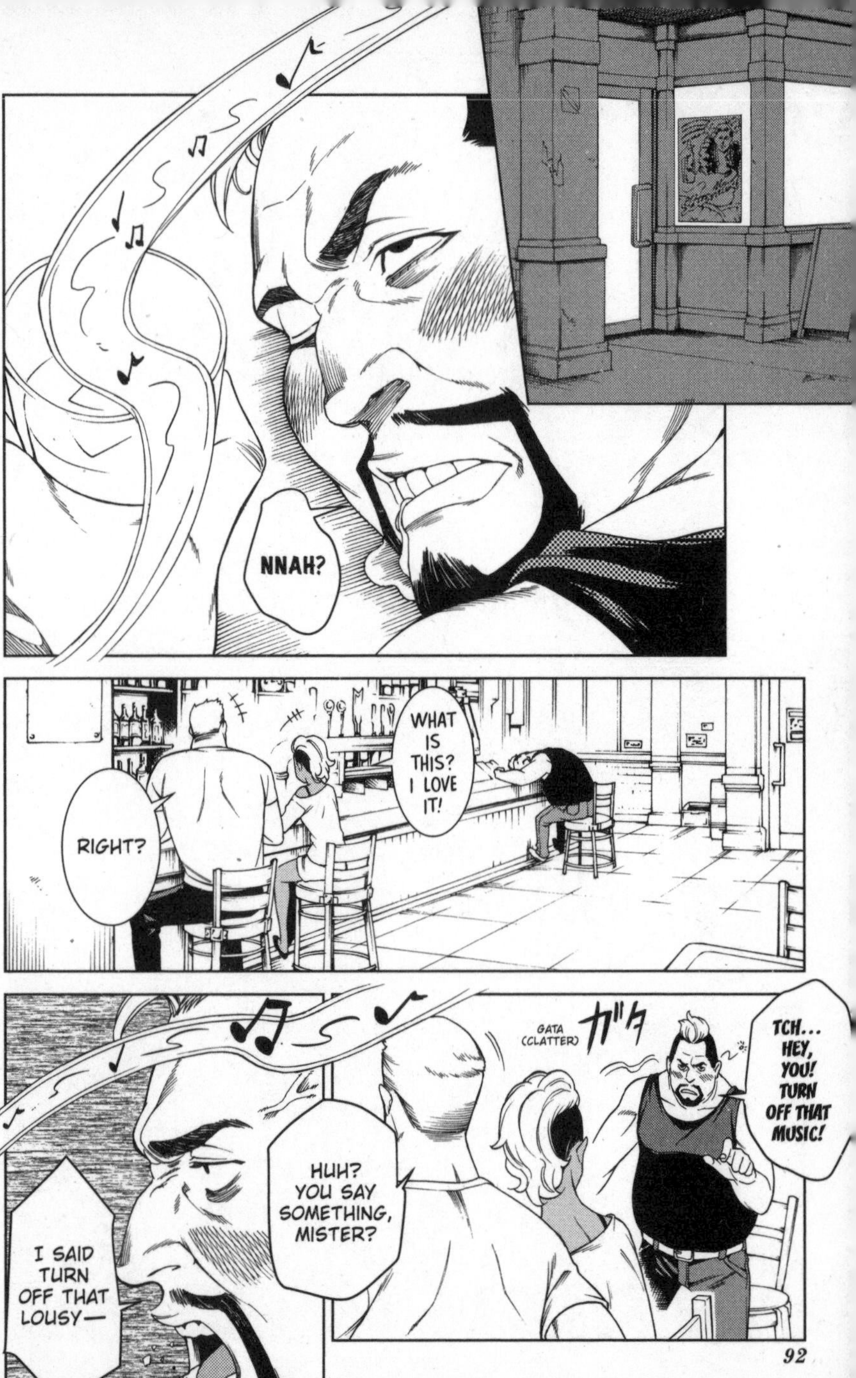
NNAH?
WHAT IS THIS? I LOVE IT!
RIGHT?
GATA (CLATTER) ガタ
TCH... HEY, YOU! TURN OFF THAT MUSIC!
HUH? YOU SAY SOMETHING, MISTER?
I SAID TURN OFF THAT LOUSY—

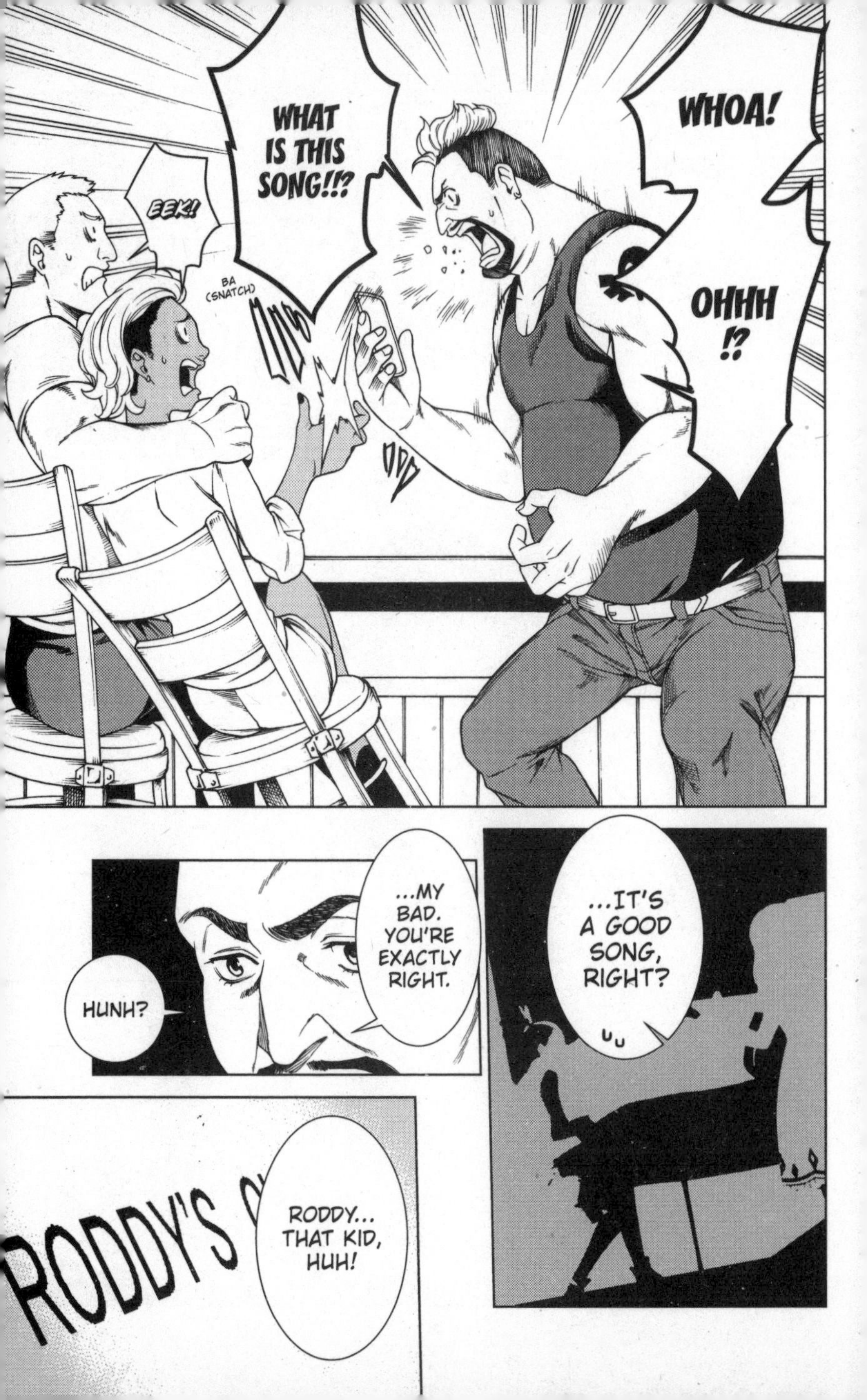
WHOA!
OHHH !?
WHAT IS THIS SONG!!?
BA (SNATCH)
EEK!!
...IT'S A GOOD SONG, RIGHT?
...MY BAD. YOU'RE EXACTLY RIGHT.
HUNH?
RODDY... THAT KID, HUH!
RODDY'S

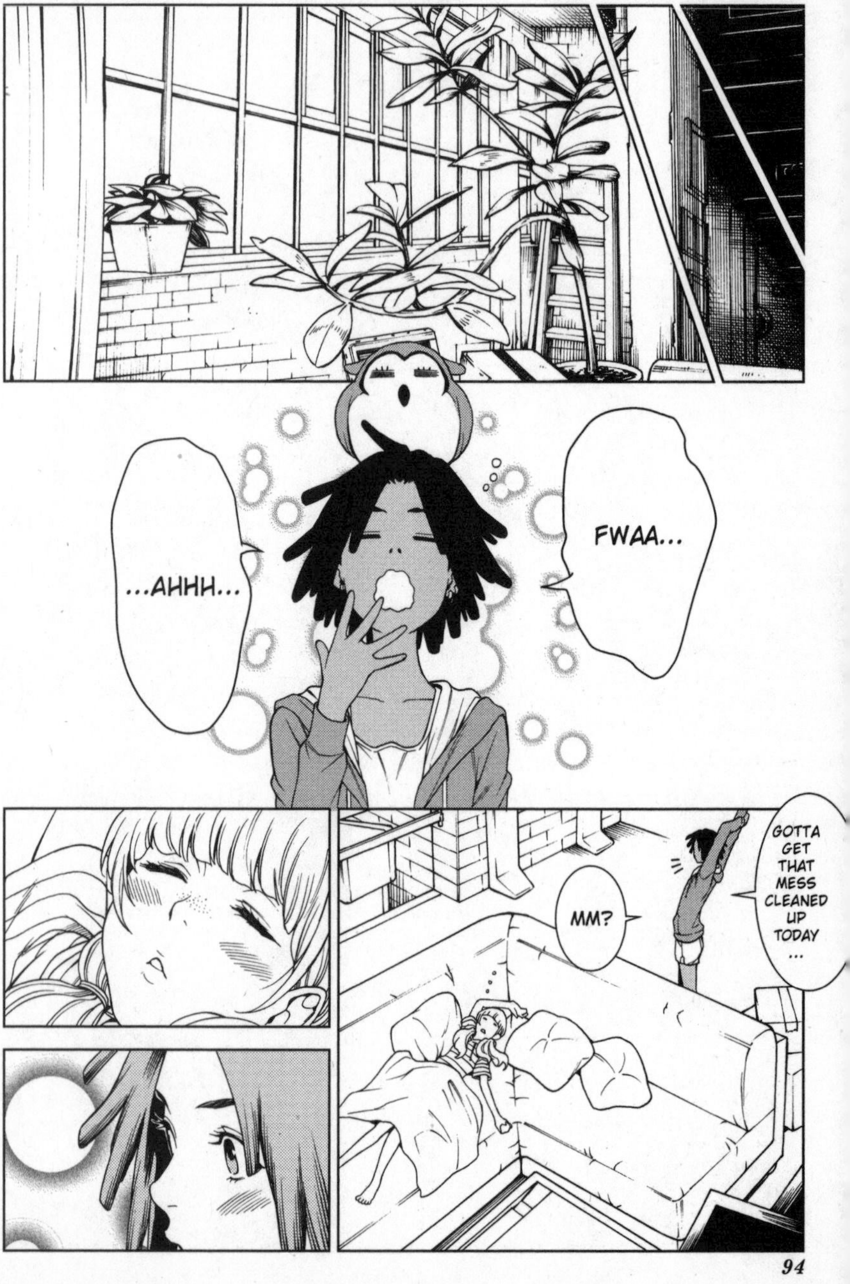
FWAA...
...AHHH...
GOTTA GET THAT MESS CLEANED UP TODAY ...
MM?

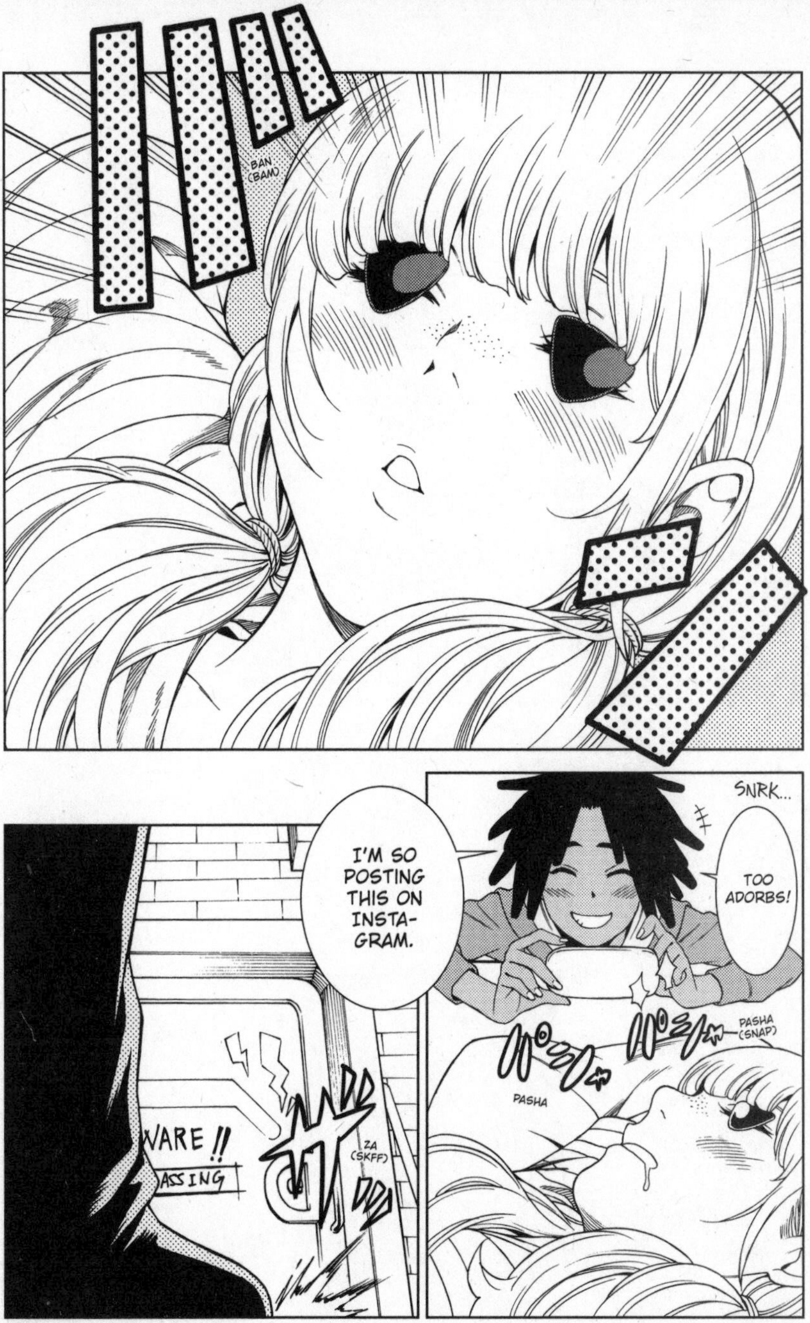
BAN (BAM)
SNRK...
TOO ADORBS!
I'M SO POSTING THIS ON INSTA-GRAM.
PASHA (SNAP)
PASHA
ZA (SKFF)
WARE !!
ASSING

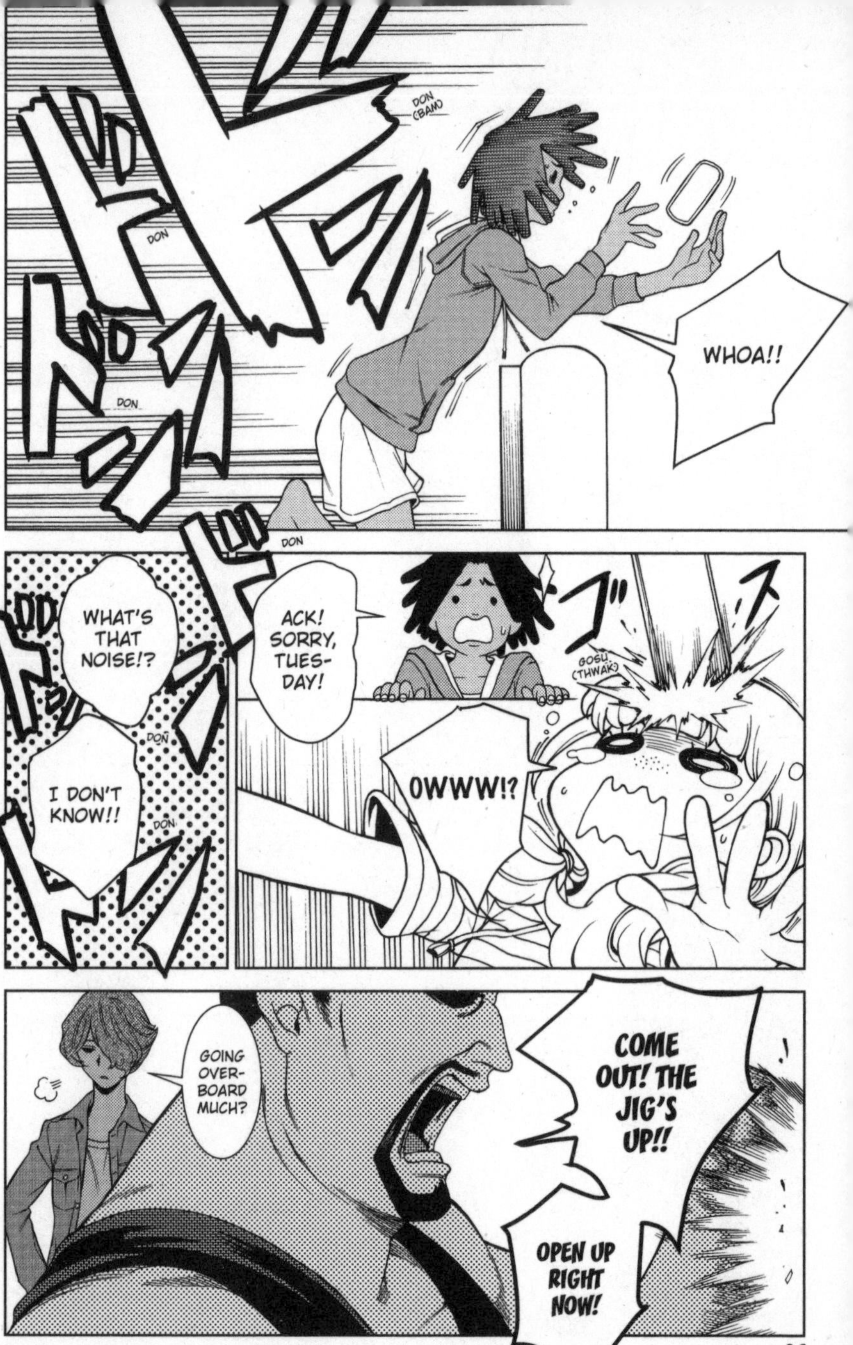
DON (BAM)
WHOA!!
DON
DON
DON
ACK! SORRY, TUES-DAY!
GOSU (THWAK)
OWWW!?
WHAT'S THAT NOISE!?
DON
I DON'T KNOW!!
DON
COME OUT! THE JIG'S UP!!
OPEN UP RIGHT NOW!
GOING OVER-BOARD MUCH?

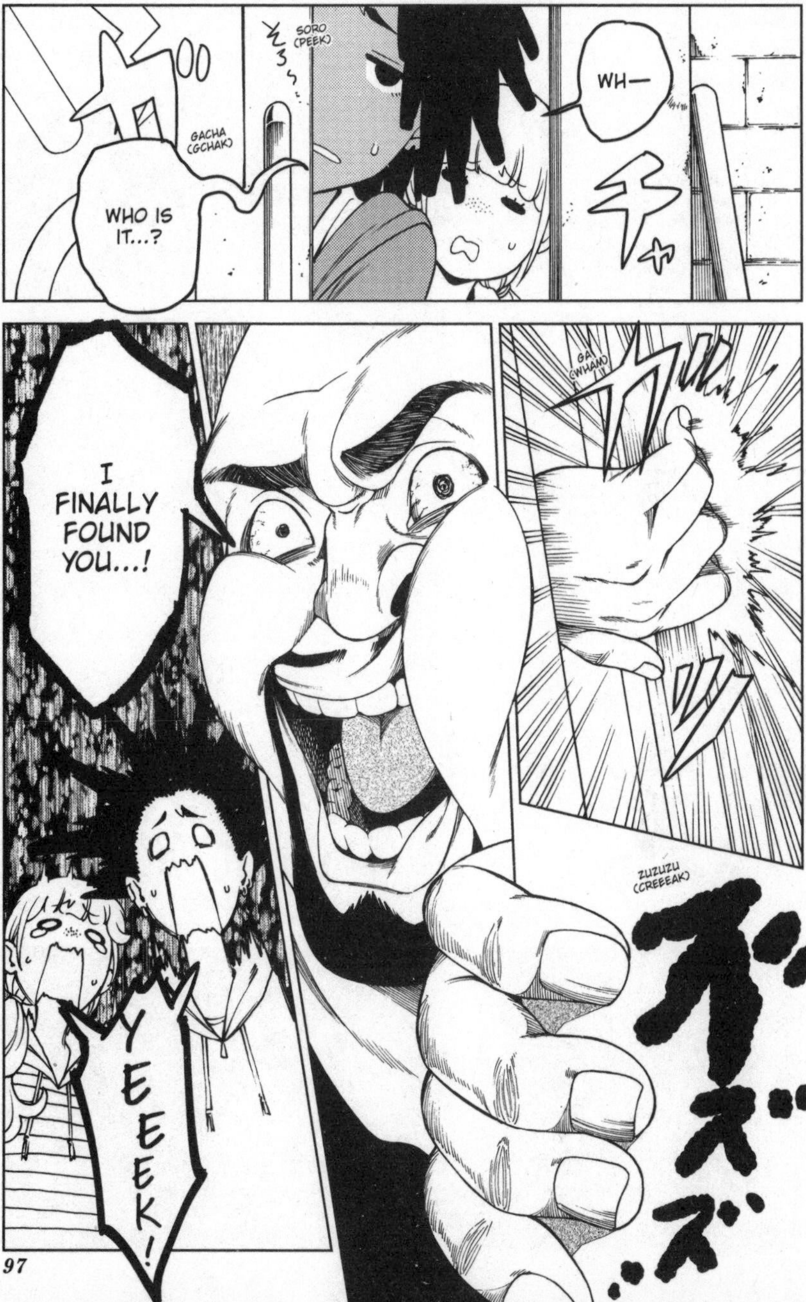
WH—
SORO (PEEK)
GACHA (GCHAK)
WHO IS IT...?
GA (WHAM)
I FINALLY FOUND YOU...!
ZUZUZU (CREEEAK)
YEEEK!

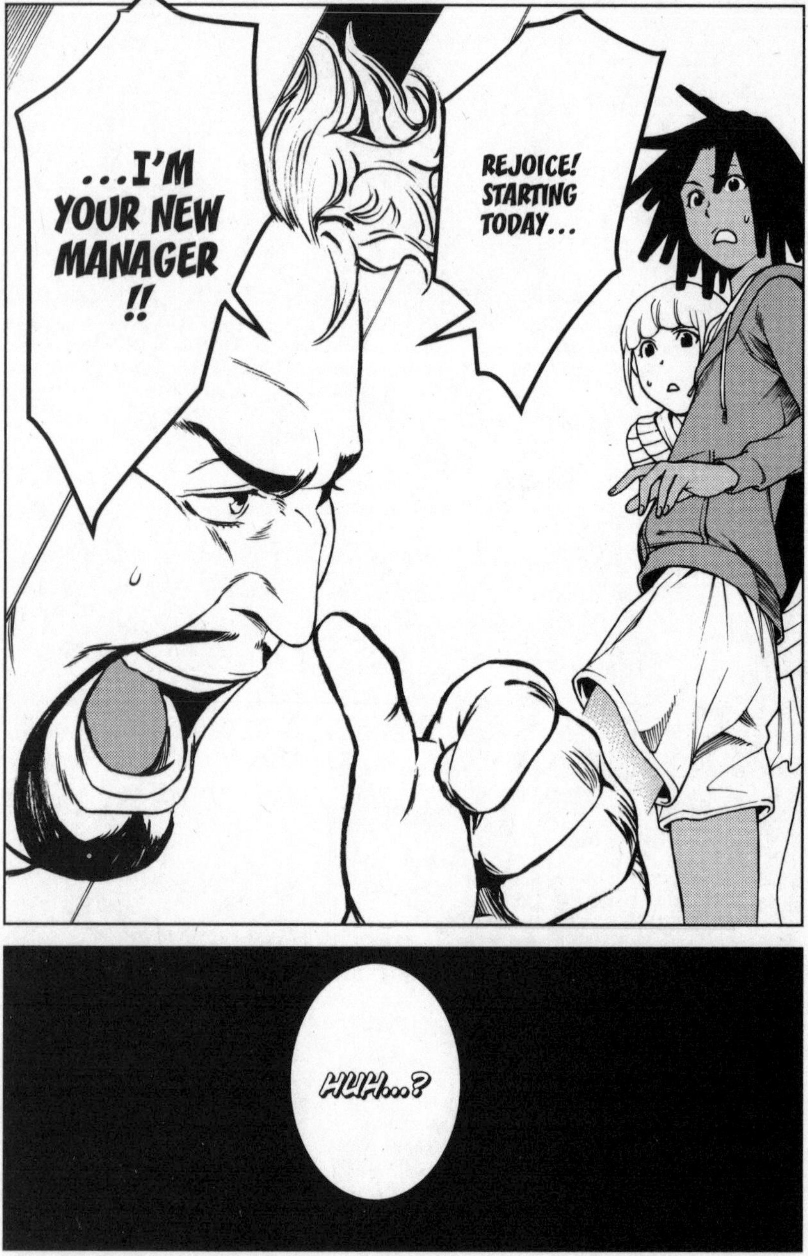
REJOICE! STARTING TODAY...
...I'M YOUR NEW MANAGER!!
HUH...?

END

episode 3: Every Breath You Take

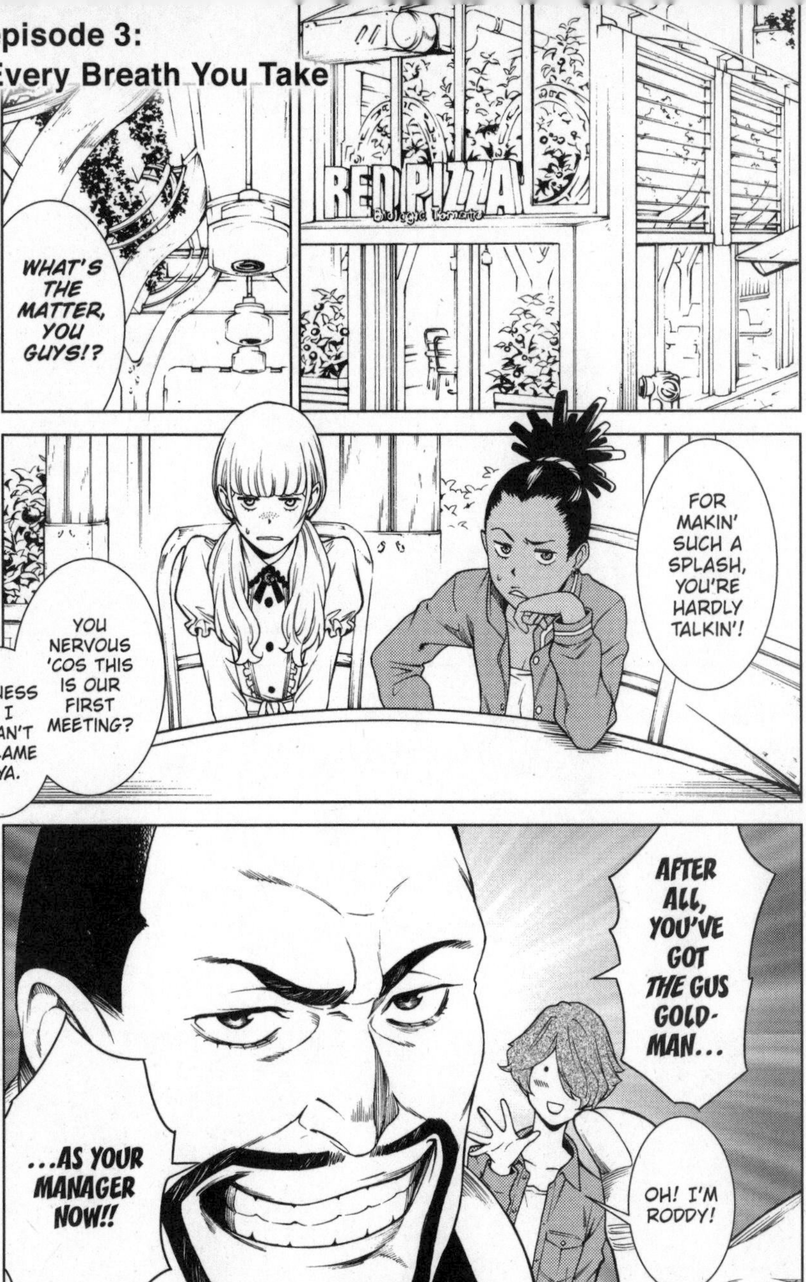

RED PIZZA
WHAT'S THE MATTER, YOU GUYS!?
FOR MAKIN' SUCH A SPLASH, YOU'RE HARDLY TALKIN'!
YOU NERVOUS 'COS THIS IS OUR FIRST MEETING?
GUESS I CAN'T BLAME YA.
AFTER ALL, YOU'VE GOT THE GUS GOLDMAN...
...AS YOUR MANAGER NOW!!
OH! I'M RODDY!

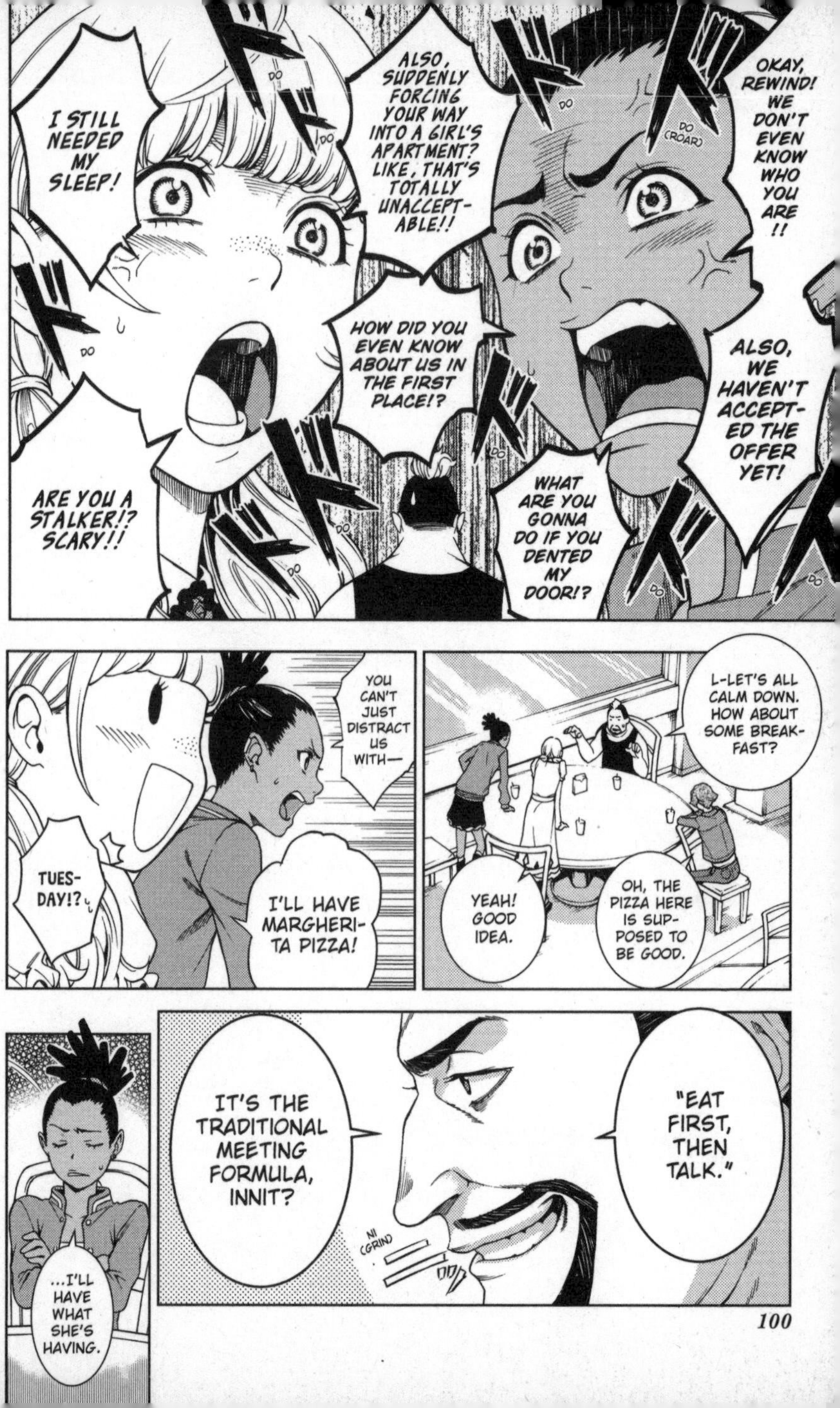
DO
DO (ROAR)
OKAY, REWIND! WE DON'T EVEN KNOW WHO YOU ARE!!
ALSO, WE HAVEN'T ACCEPTED THE OFFER YET!
DO
DO
ALSO, SUDDENLY FORCING YOUR WAY INTO A GIRL'S APARTMENT? LIKE, THAT'S TOTALLY UNACCEPTABLE!!
DO
DO
WHAT ARE YOU GONNA DO IF YOU DENTED MY DOOR!?
HOW DID YOU EVEN KNOW ABOUT US IN THE FIRST PLACE!?
DO
DO
I STILL NEEDED MY SLEEP!
DO
ARE YOU A STALKER!? SCARY!!
L-LET'S ALL CALM DOWN. HOW ABOUT SOME BREAKFAST?
OH, THE PIZZA HERE IS SUPPOSED TO BE GOOD.
YEAH! GOOD IDEA.
YOU CAN'T JUST DISTRACT US WITH—
I'LL HAVE MARGHERITA PIZZA!
TUES-DAY!?
"EAT FIRST, THEN TALK."
IT'S THE TRADITIONAL MEETING FORMULA, INNIT?
NI (GRIN)
...I'LL HAVE WHAT SHE'S HAVING.

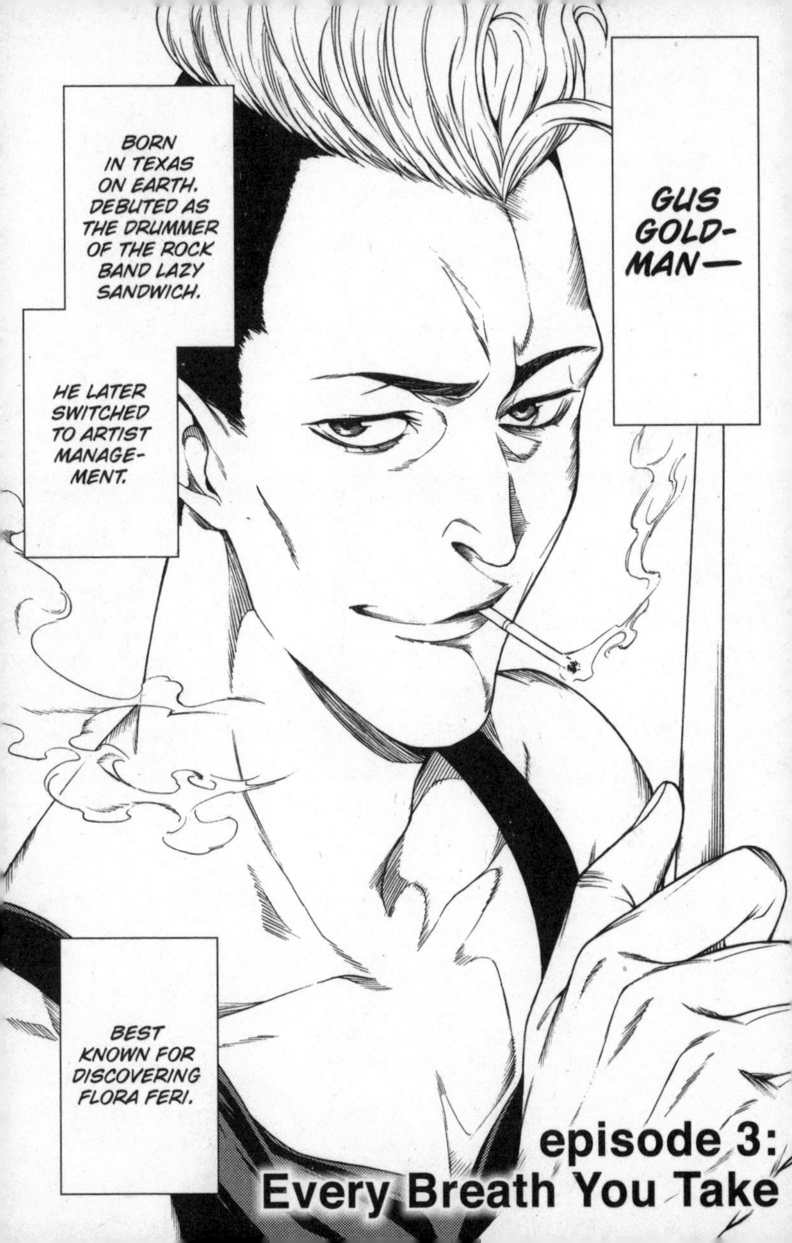
GUS GOLD-MAN—
BORN IN TEXAS ON EARTH. DEBUTED AS THE DRUMMER OF THE ROCK BAND LAZY SANDWICH.
HE LATER SWITCHED TO ARTIST MANAGE-MENT.
BEST KNOWN FOR DISCOVERING FLORA FERI.

episode 3: Every Breath You Take

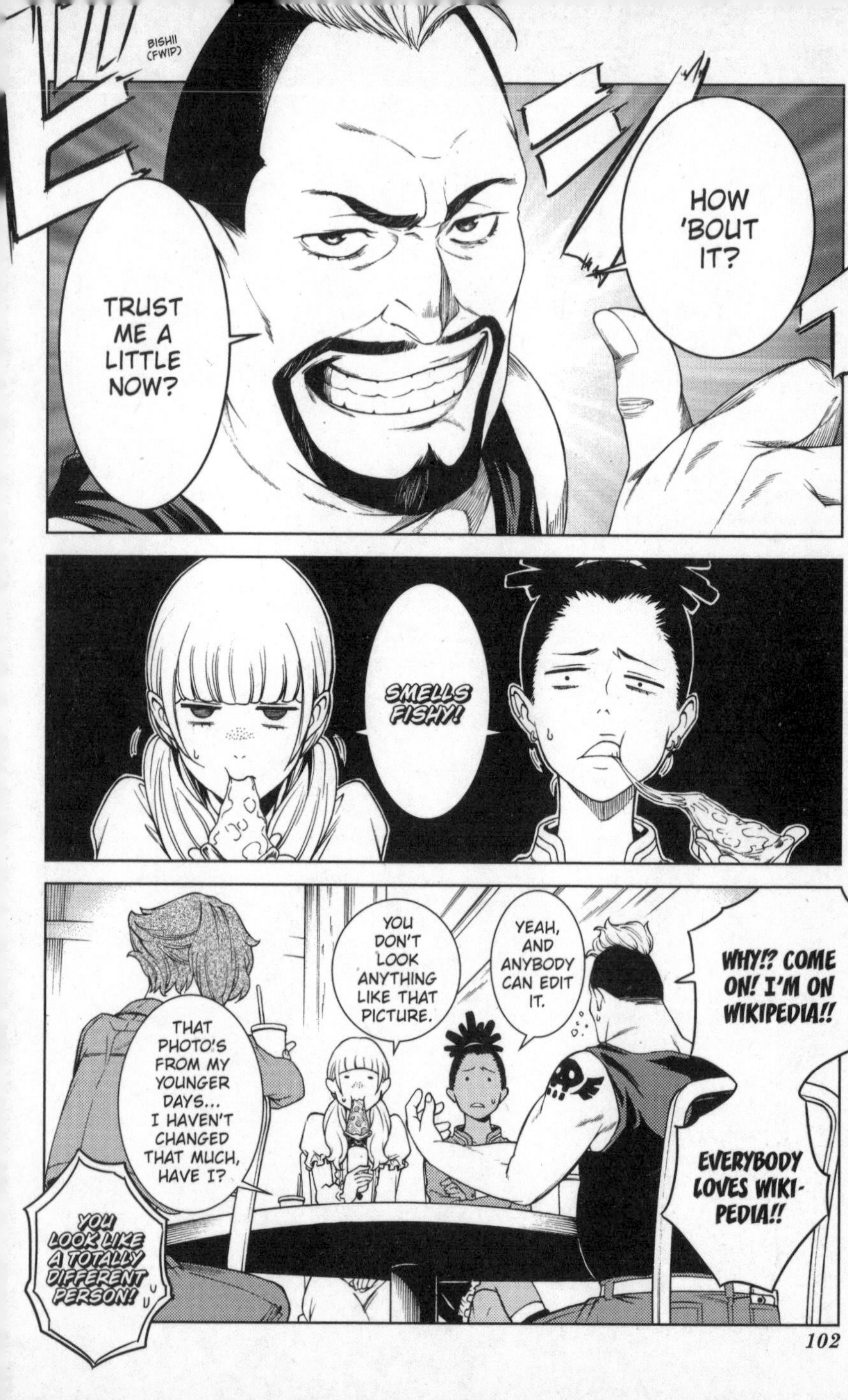
BISHII (FWIP)
HOW 'BOUT IT?
TRUST ME A LITTLE NOW?
SMELLS FISHY!
WHY!? COME ON! I'M ON WIKIPEDIA!!
YEAH, AND ANYBODY CAN EDIT IT.
YOU DON'T LOOK ANYTHING LIKE THAT PICTURE.
EVERYBODY LOVES WIKI-PEDIA!!
THAT PHOTO'S FROM MY YOUNGER DAYS... I HAVEN'T CHANGED THAT MUCH, HAVE I?
YOU LOOK LIKE A TOTALLY DIFFERENT PERSON!

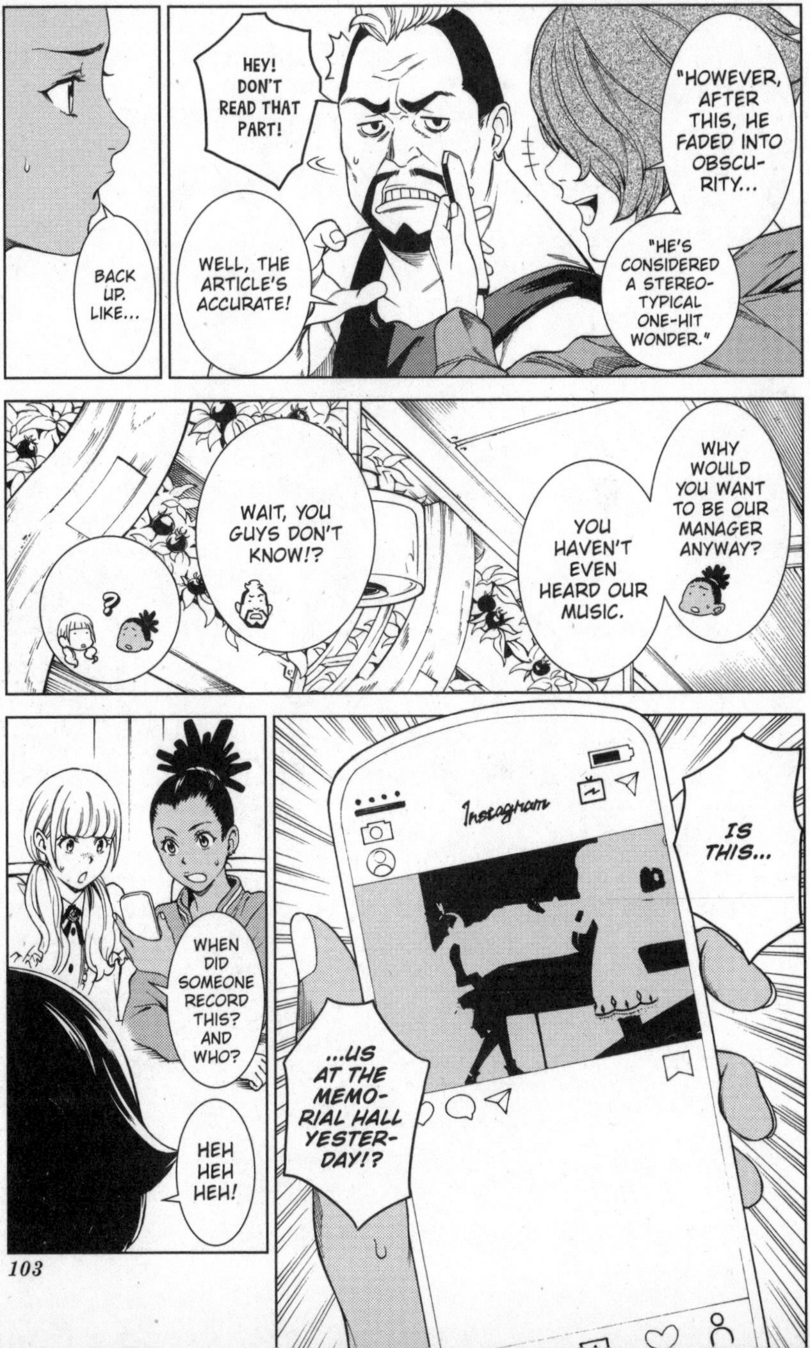
"HOWEVER, AFTER THIS, HE FADED INTO OBSCURITY...
"HE'S CONSIDERED A STEREOTYPICAL ONE-HIT WONDER."
HEY! DON'T READ THAT PART!
WELL, THE ARTICLE'S ACCURATE!
BACK UP. LIKE...
WHY WOULD YOU WANT TO BE OUR MANAGER ANYWAY?
YOU HAVEN'T EVEN HEARD OUR MUSIC.
WAIT, YOU GUYS DON'T KNOW!?
?
IS THIS...
Instagram
...US AT THE MEMORIAL HALL YESTERDAY!?
WHEN DID SOMEONE RECORD THIS? AND WHO?
HEH HEH HEH!

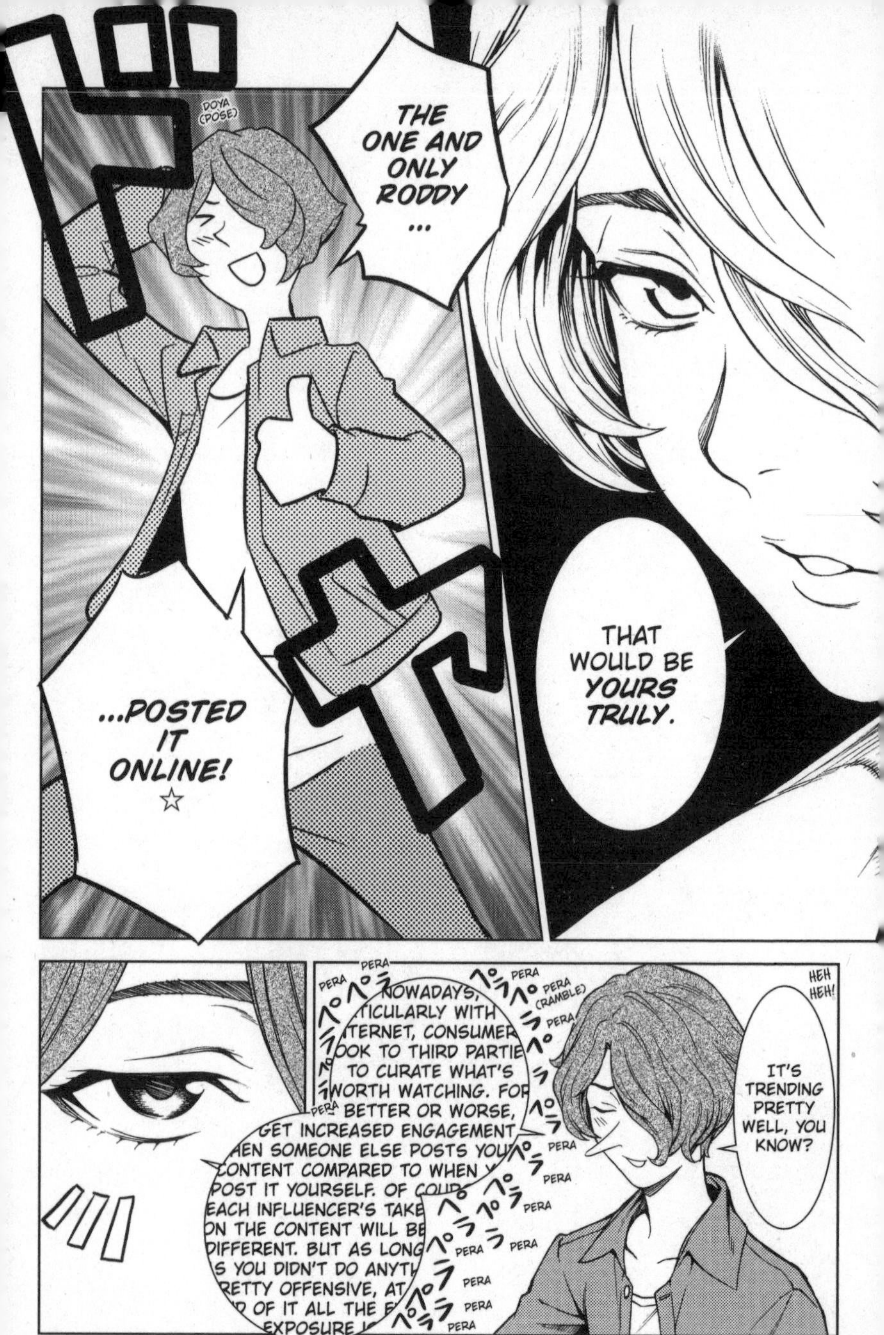
THE ONE AND ONLY RODDY ...
THAT WOULD BE YOURS TRULY.
DOYA (POSE)
...POSTED IT ONLINE! ☆
HEH HEH!
IT'S TRENDING PRETTY WELL, YOU KNOW?
PERA PERA (RAMBLE)
NOWADAYS, TICULARLY WITH TERNET, CONSUMER OOK TO THIRD PARTIE TO CURATE WHAT'S WORTH WATCHING. FOR BETTER OR WORSE,
GET INCREASED ENGAGEMENT HEN SOMEONE ELSE POSTS YOU CONTENT COMPARED TO WHEN POST IT YOURSELF. OF COU EACH INFLUENCER'S TAKE ON THE CONTENT WILL BE DIFFERENT. BUT AS LONG S YOU DIDN'T DO ANYTH RETTY OFFENSIVE, AT OF IT ALL THE EXPOSURE
PERA PERA PERA PERA PERA PERA PERA

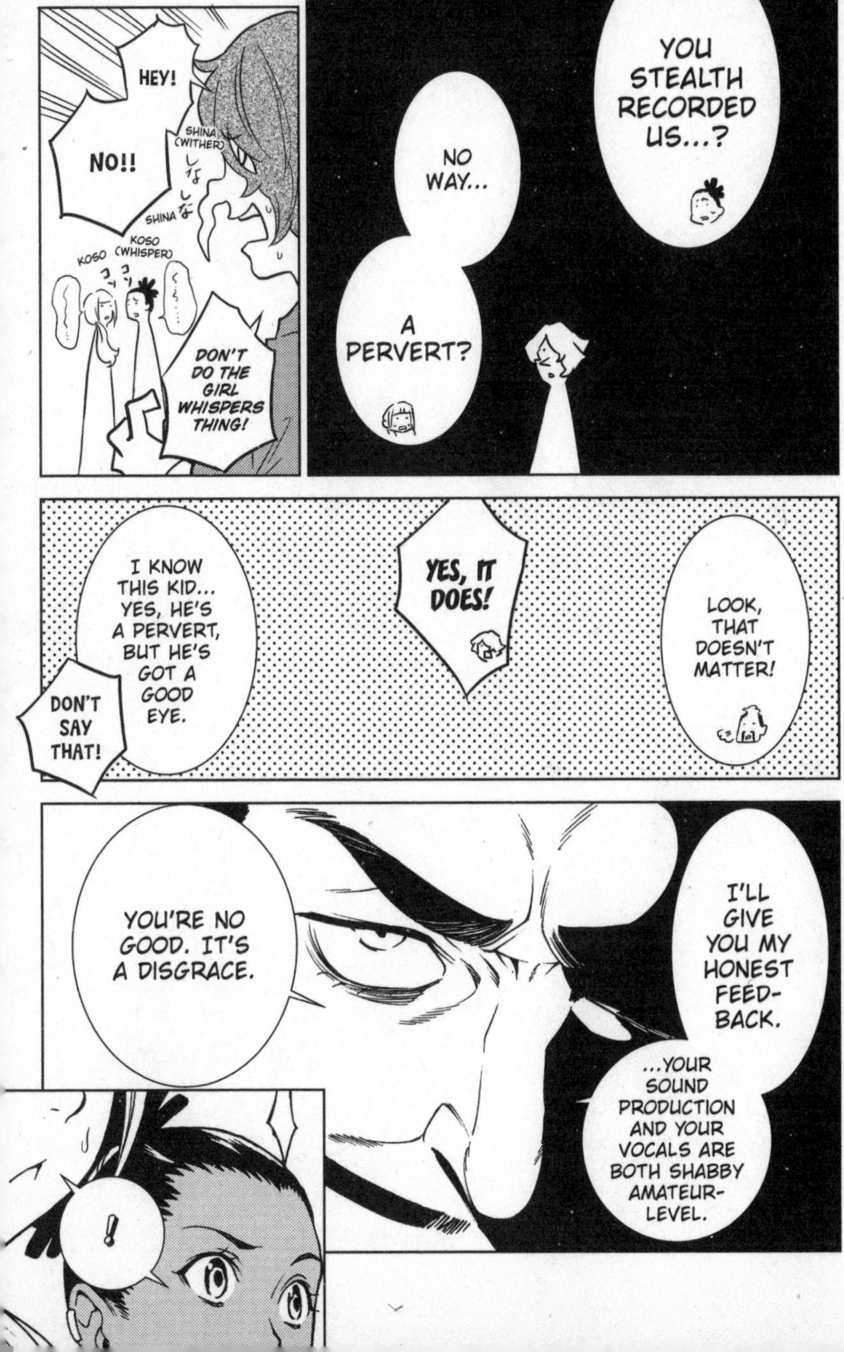
YOU STEALTH RECORDED US...?
NO WAY...
A PERVERT?
HEY!
NO!!
SHINA (WITHER)
SHINA
KOSO (WHISPER)
KOSO
DON'T DO THE GIRL WHISPERS THING!
LOOK, THAT DOESN'T MATTER!
YES, IT DOES!
I KNOW THIS KID... YES, HE'S A PERVERT, BUT HE'S GOT A GOOD EYE.
DON'T SAY THAT!
I'LL GIVE YOU MY HONEST FEED-BACK.
...YOUR SOUND PRODUCTION AND YOUR VOCALS ARE BOTH SHABBY AMATEUR-LEVEL.
YOU'RE NO GOOD. IT'S A DISGRACE.
!

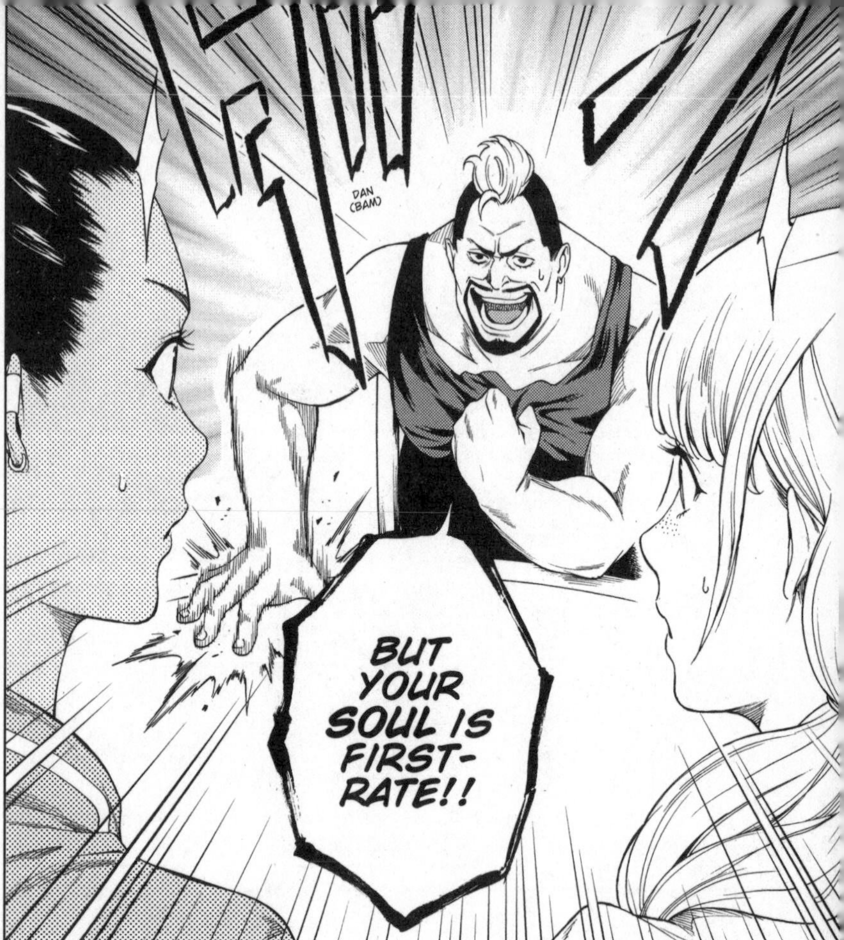
DAN (BAM)
BUT YOUR SOUL IS FIRST-RATE!!

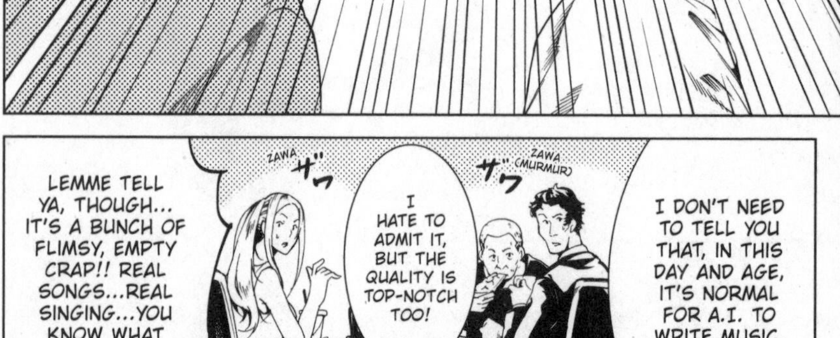
I DON'T NEED TO TELL YOU THAT, IN THIS DAY AND AGE, IT'S NORMAL FOR A.I. TO WRITE MUSIC.
ZAWA (MURMUR)
I HATE TO ADMIT IT, BUT THE QUALITY IS TOP-NOTCH TOO!
ZAWA
LEMME TELL YA, THOUGH... IT'S A BUNCH OF FLIMSY, EMPTY CRAP!! REAL SONGS...REAL SINGING...YOU KNOW WHAT IT IS?

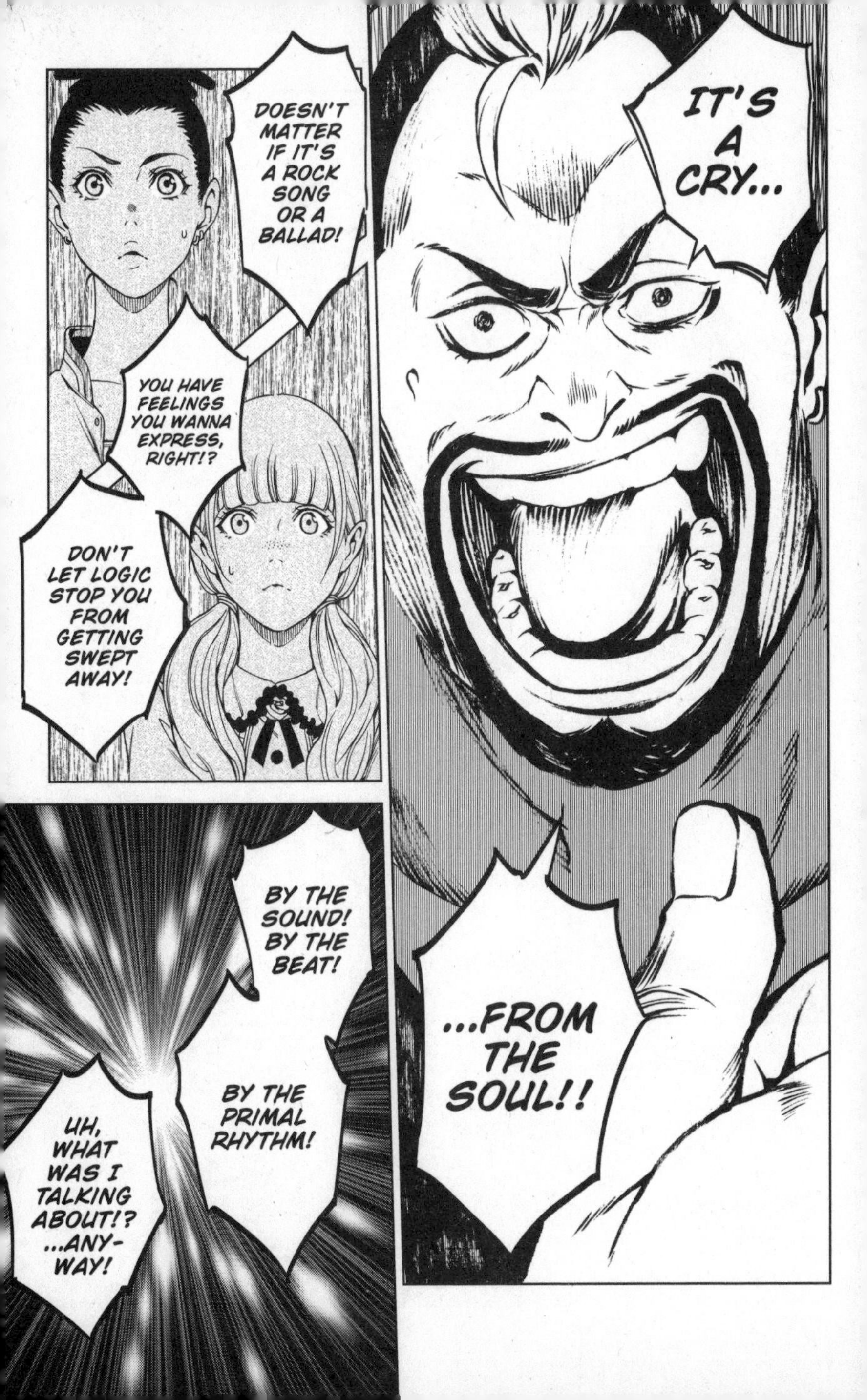
IT'S A CRY...
...FROM THE SOUL!!
DOESN'T MATTER IF IT'S A ROCK SONG OR A BALLAD!
YOU HAVE FEELINGS YOU WANNA EXPRESS, RIGHT!?
DON'T LET LOGIC STOP YOU FROM GETTING SWEPT AWAY!
BY THE SOUND! BY THE BEAT!
BY THE PRIMAL RHYTHM!
UH, WHAT WAS I TALKING ABOUT!? ...ANY-WAY!

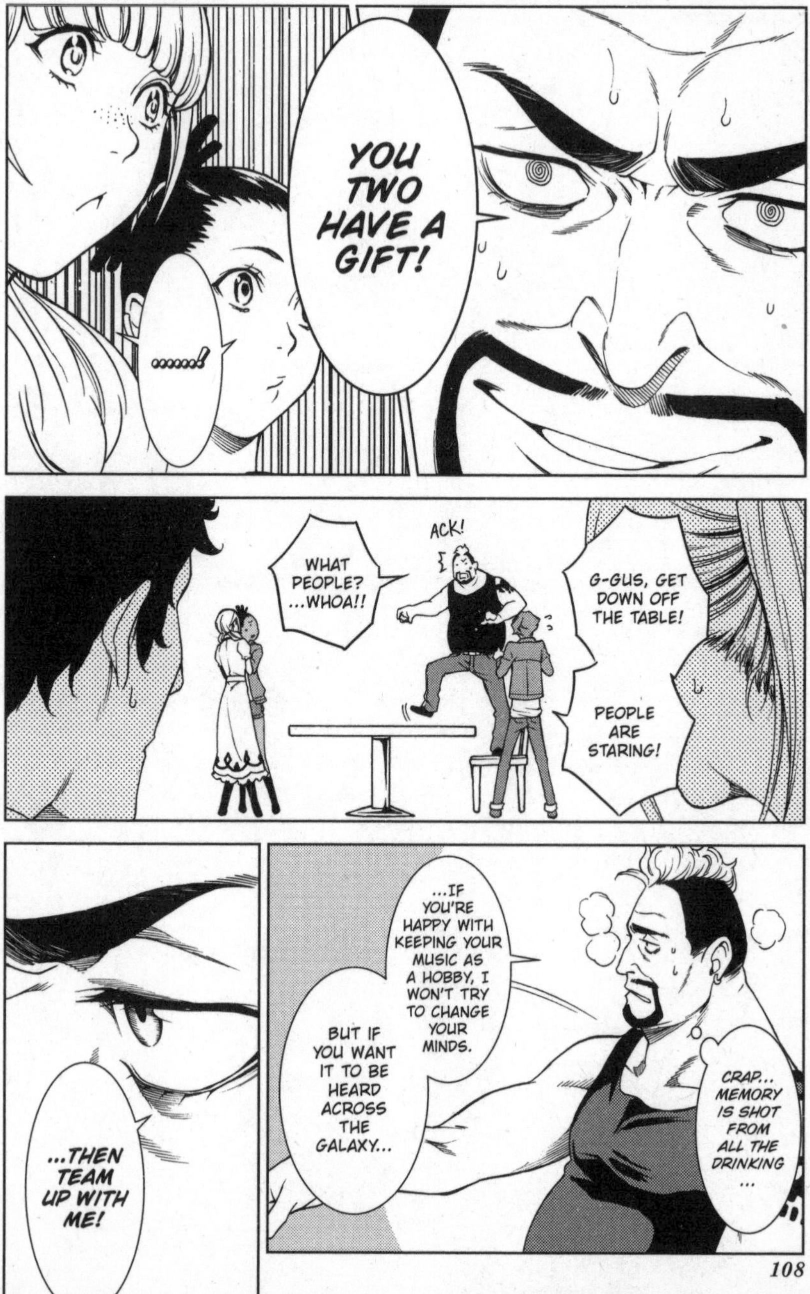
YOU TWO HAVE A GIFT!
.......!
G-GUS, GET DOWN OFF THE TABLE!
PEOPLE ARE STARING!
ACK!
WHAT PEOPLE? ...WHOA!!
CRAP... MEMORY IS SHOT FROM ALL THE DRINKING...
...IF YOU'RE HAPPY WITH KEEPING YOUR MUSIC AS A HOBBY, I WON'T TRY TO CHANGE YOUR MINDS.
BUT IF YOU WANT IT TO BE HEARD ACROSS THE GALAXY...
...THEN TEAM UP WITH ME!

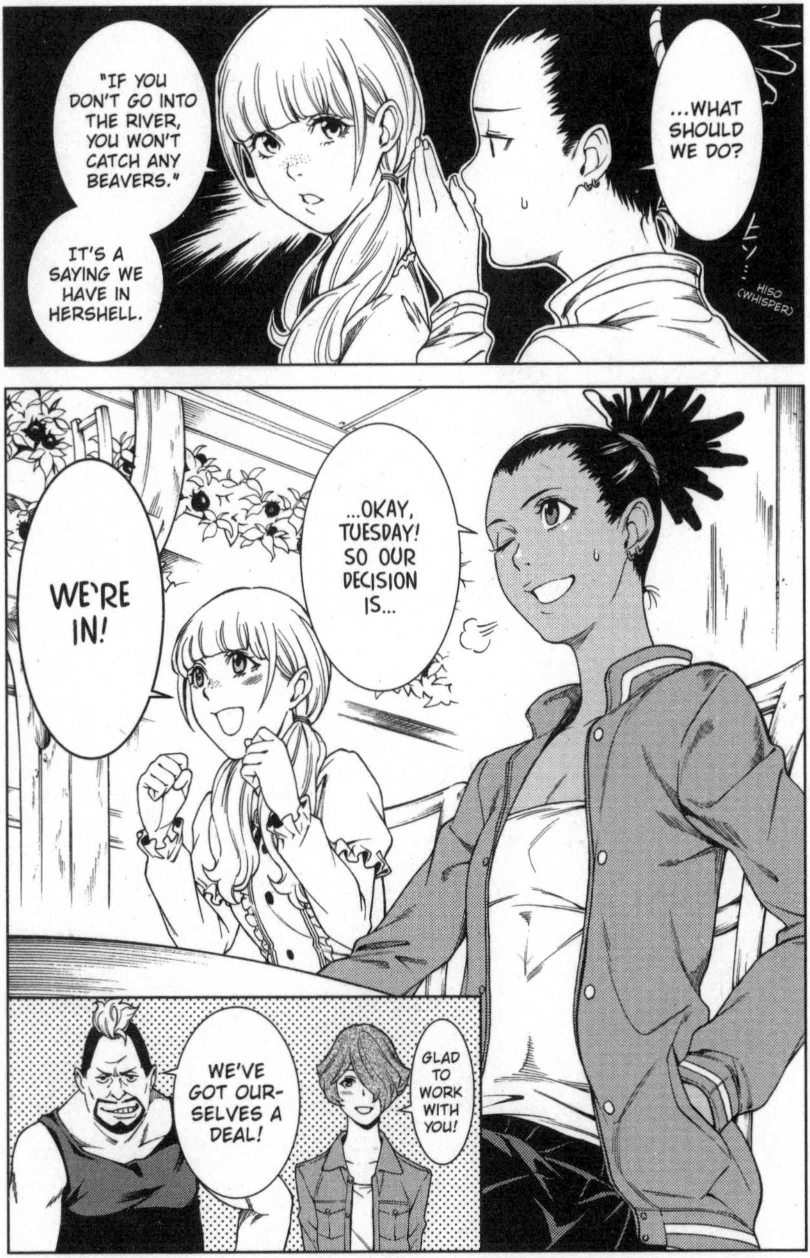
HISO (WHISPER)
...WHAT SHOULD WE DO?
"IF YOU DON'T GO INTO THE RIVER, YOU WON'T CATCH ANY BEAVERS."
IT'S A SAYING WE HAVE IN HERSHELL.
...OKAY, TUESDAY! SO OUR DECISION IS...
WE'RE IN!
GLAD TO WORK WITH YOU!
WE'VE GOT OUR-SELVES A DEAL!

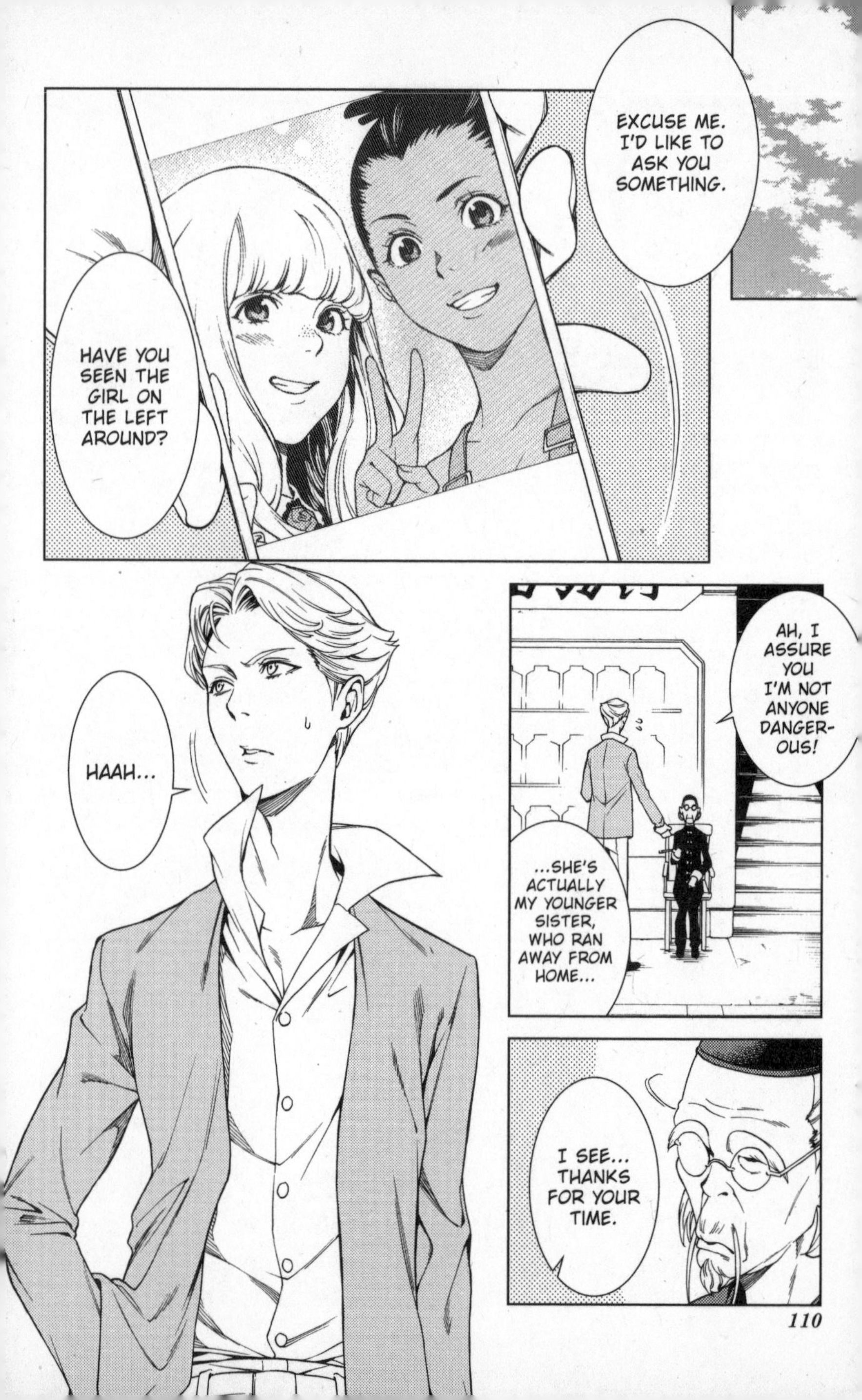
EXCUSE ME. I'D LIKE TO ASK YOU SOMETHING.
HAVE YOU SEEN THE GIRL ON THE LEFT AROUND?
AH, I ASSURE YOU I'M NOT ANYONE DANGER-OUS!
...SHE'S ACTUALLY MY YOUNGER SISTER, WHO RAN AWAY FROM HOME...
I SEE... THANKS FOR YOUR TIME.
HAAH...

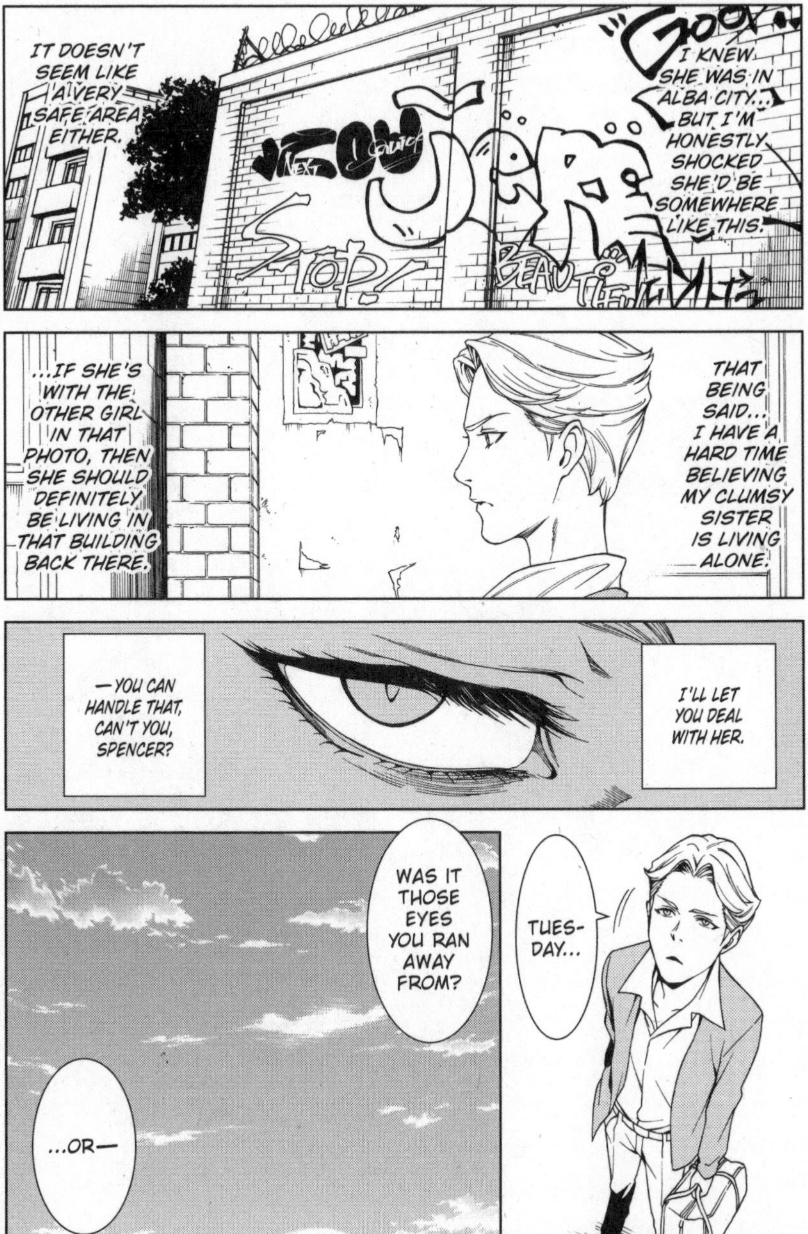
I KNEW SHE WAS IN ALBA CITY... BUT I'M HONESTLY SHOCKED SHE'D BE SOMEWHERE LIKE THIS.
IT DOESN'T SEEM LIKE A VERY SAFE AREA EITHER.
THAT BEING SAID... I HAVE A HARD TIME BELIEVING MY CLUMSY SISTER IS LIVING ALONE.
...IF SHE'S WITH THE OTHER GIRL IN THAT PHOTO, THEN SHE SHOULD DEFINITELY BE LIVING IN THAT BUILDING BACK THERE.
I'LL LET YOU DEAL WITH HER.
—YOU CAN HANDLE THAT, CAN'T YOU, SPENCER?
TUES-DAY...
WAS IT THOSE EYES YOU RAN AWAY FROM?
...OR—

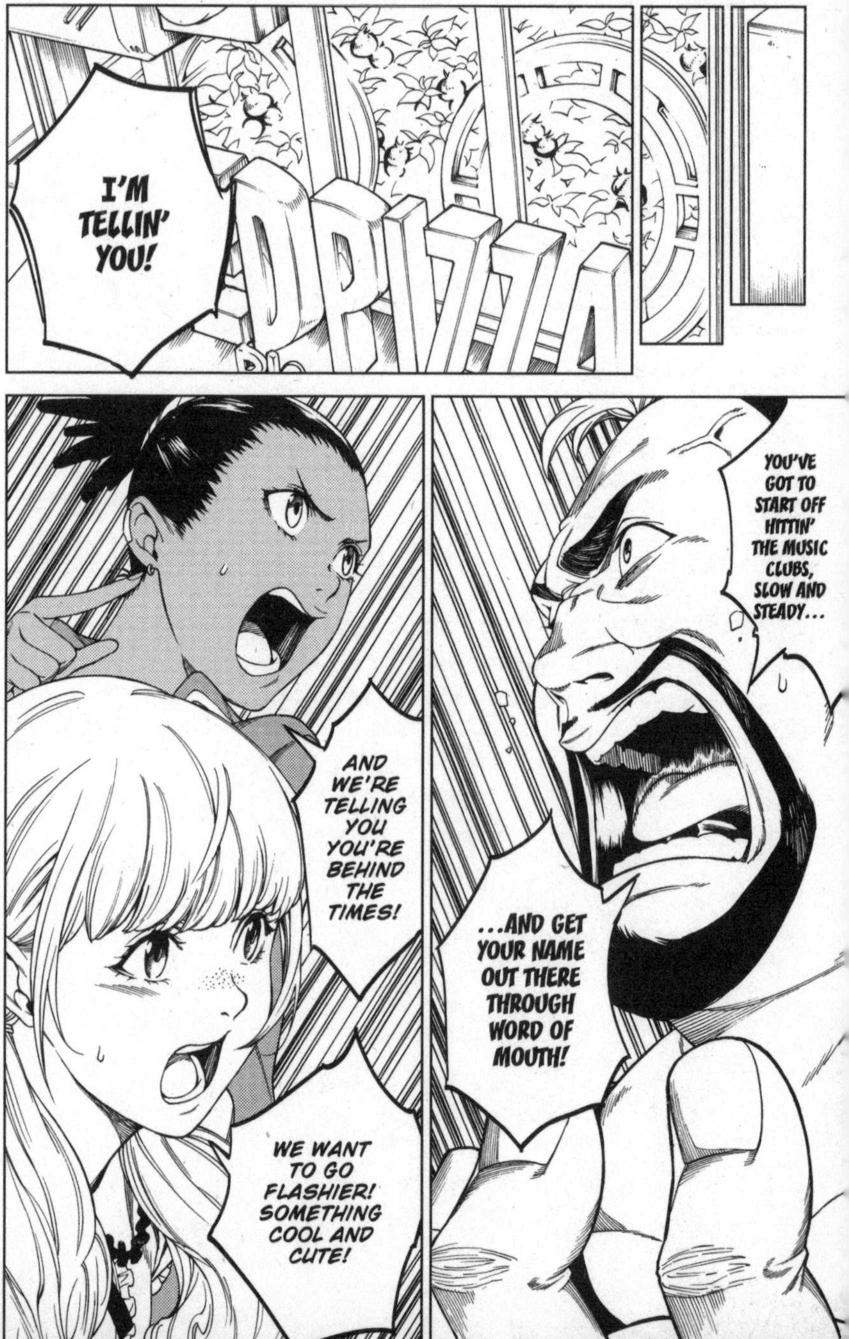
I'M TELLIN' YOU!
YOU'VE GOT TO START OFF HITTIN' THE MUSIC CLUBS, SLOW AND STEADY...
...AND GET YOUR NAME OUT THERE THROUGH WORD OF MOUTH!
AND WE'RE TELLING YOU YOU'RE BEHIND THE TIMES!
WE WANT TO GO FLASHIER! SOMETHING COOL AND CUTE!

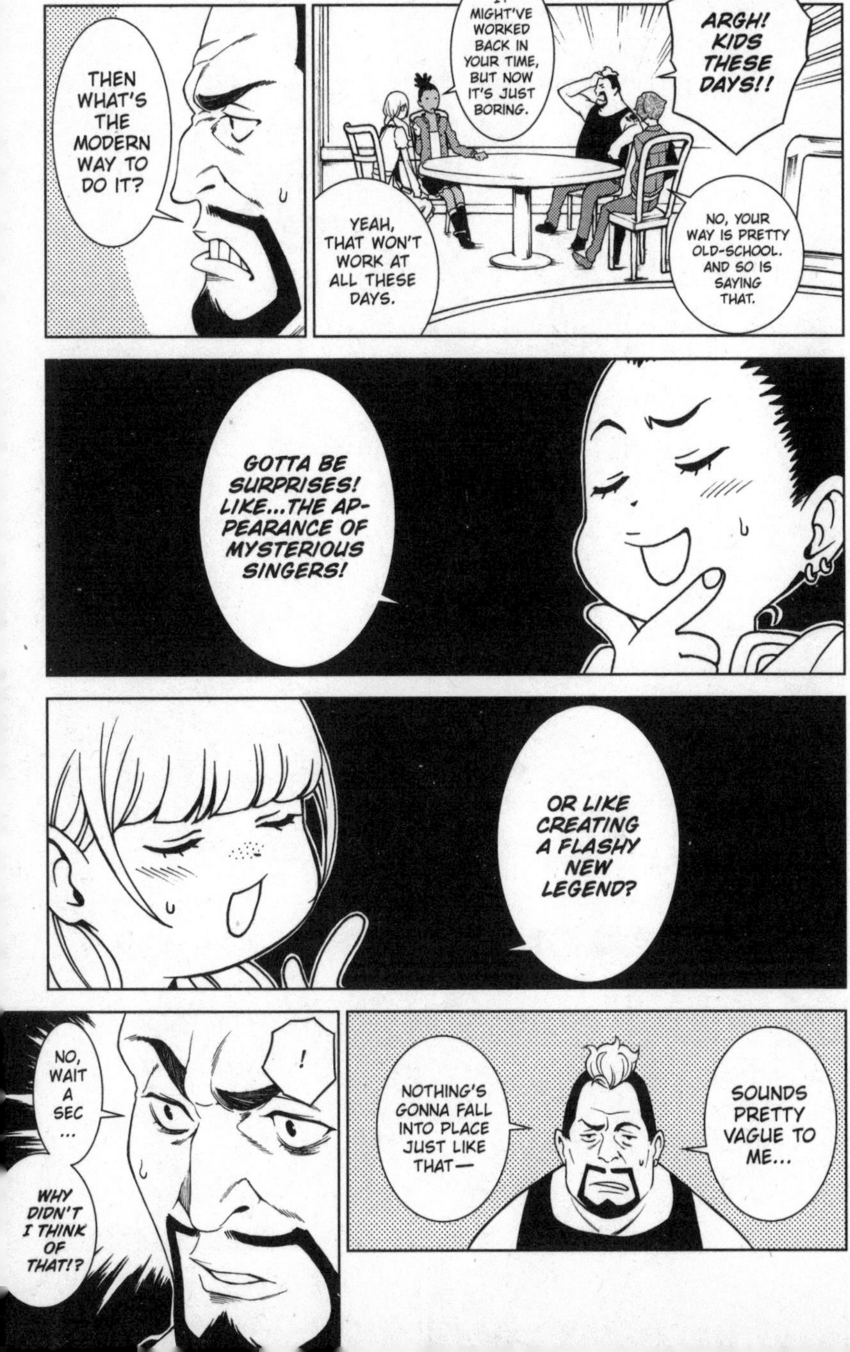
ARGH! KIDS THESE DAYS!!
IT MIGHT'VE WORKED BACK IN YOUR TIME, BUT NOW IT'S JUST BORING.
NO, YOUR WAY IS PRETTY OLD-SCHOOL. AND SO IS SAYING THAT.
YEAH, THAT WON'T WORK AT ALL THESE DAYS.
THEN WHAT'S THE MODERN WAY TO DO IT?
GOTTA BE SURPRISES! LIKE...THE AP-PEARANCE OF MYSTERIOUS SINGERS!
OR LIKE CREATING A FLASHY NEW LEGEND?
SOUNDS PRETTY VAGUE TO ME...
NOTHING'S GONNA FALL INTO PLACE JUST LIKE THAT—
!
NO, WAIT A SEC ...
WHY DIDN'T I THINK OF THAT!?

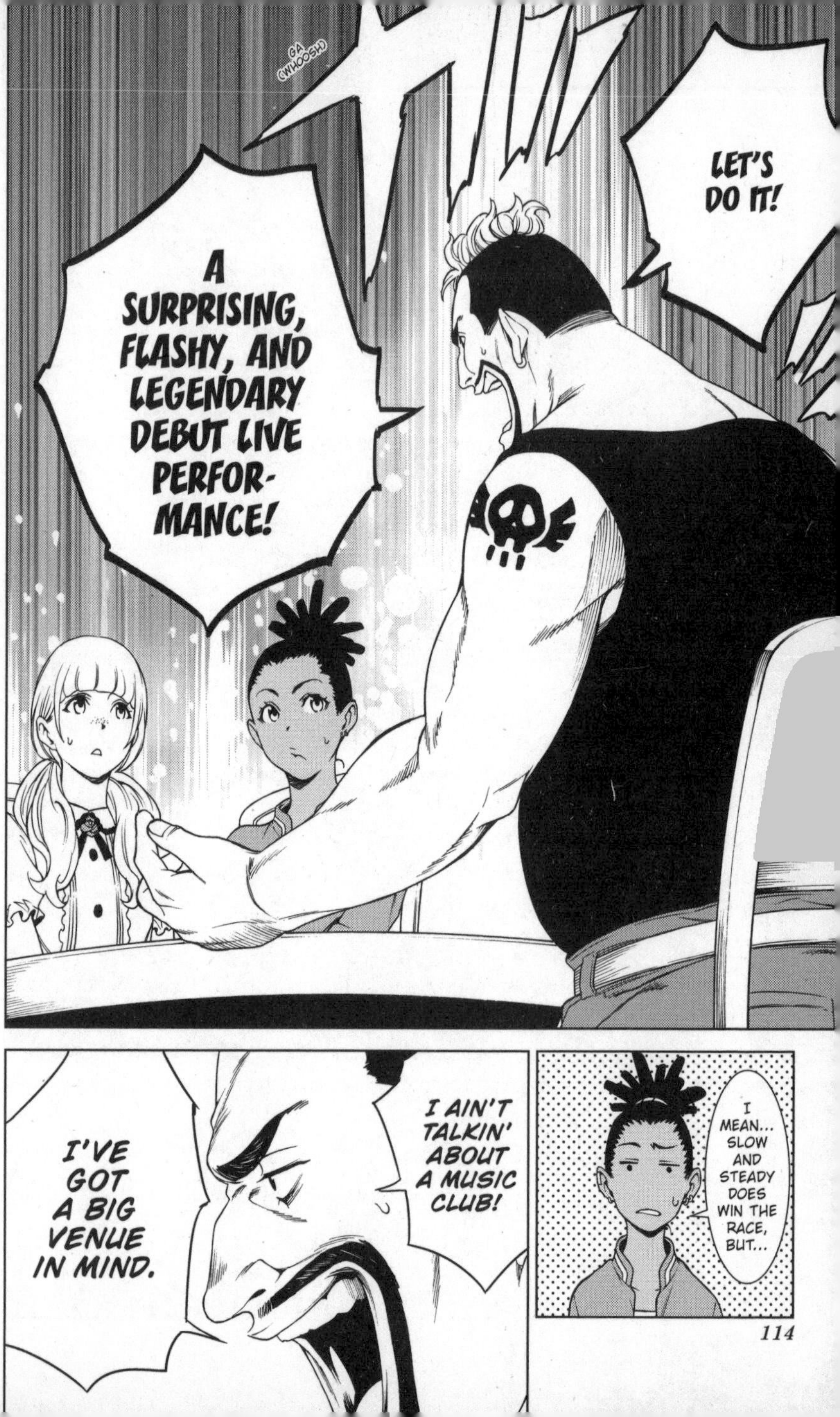
LET'S DO IT!
GA (WHOOSH)
A SURPRISING, FLASHY, AND LEGENDARY DEBUT LIVE PERFORMANCE!
I MEAN... SLOW AND STEADY DOES WIN THE RACE, BUT...
I AIN'T TALKIN' ABOUT A MUSIC CLUB!
I'VE GOT A BIG VENUE IN MIND.

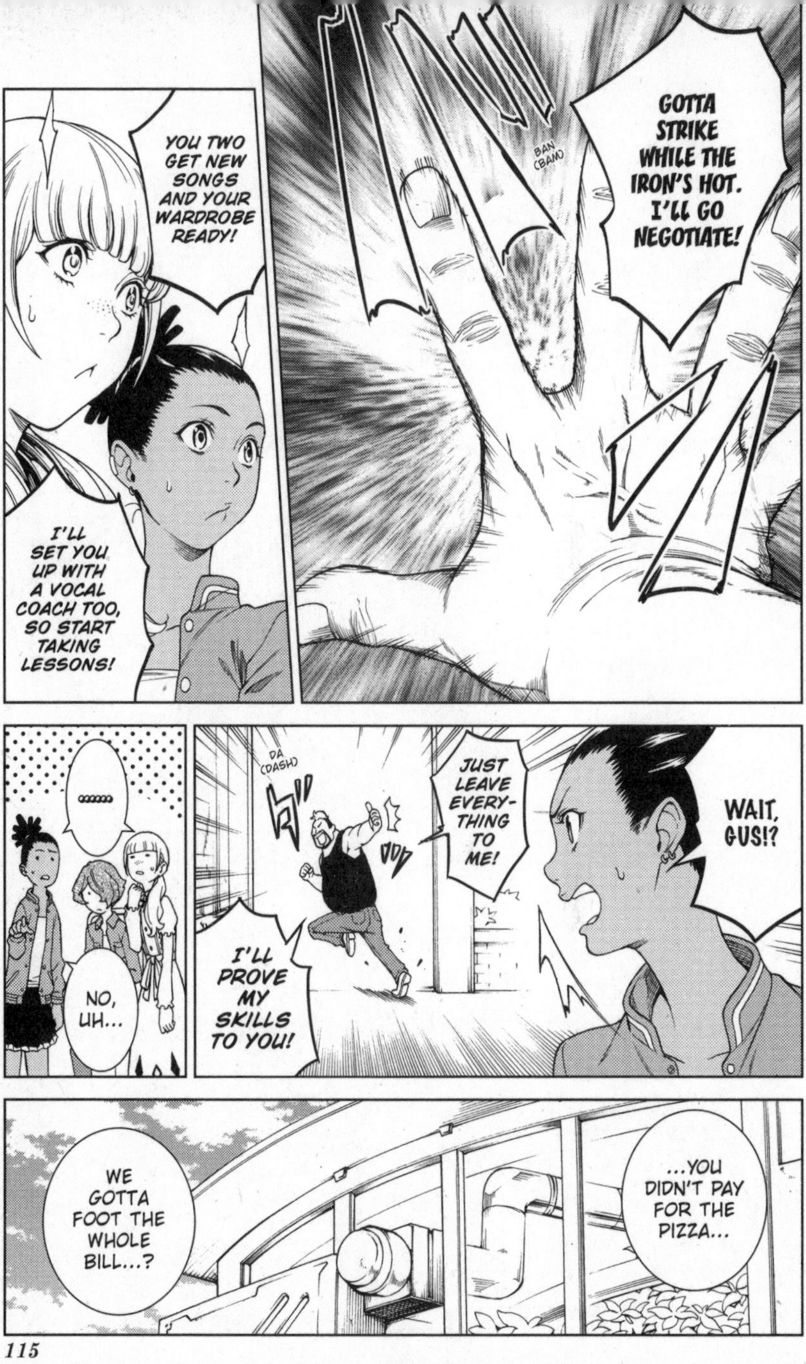
GOTTA STRIKE WHILE THE IRON'S HOT. I'LL GO NEGOTIATE!
BAN (BAM)
YOU TWO GET NEW SONGS AND YOUR WARDROBE READY!
I'LL SET YOU UP WITH A VOCAL COACH TOO, SO START TAKING LESSONS!
WAIT, GUS!?
JUST LEAVE EVERYTHING TO ME!
DA (DASH)
I'LL PROVE MY SKILLS TO YOU!
......
NO, UH...
...YOU DIDN'T PAY FOR THE PIZZA...
WE GOTTA FOOT THE WHOLE BILL...?

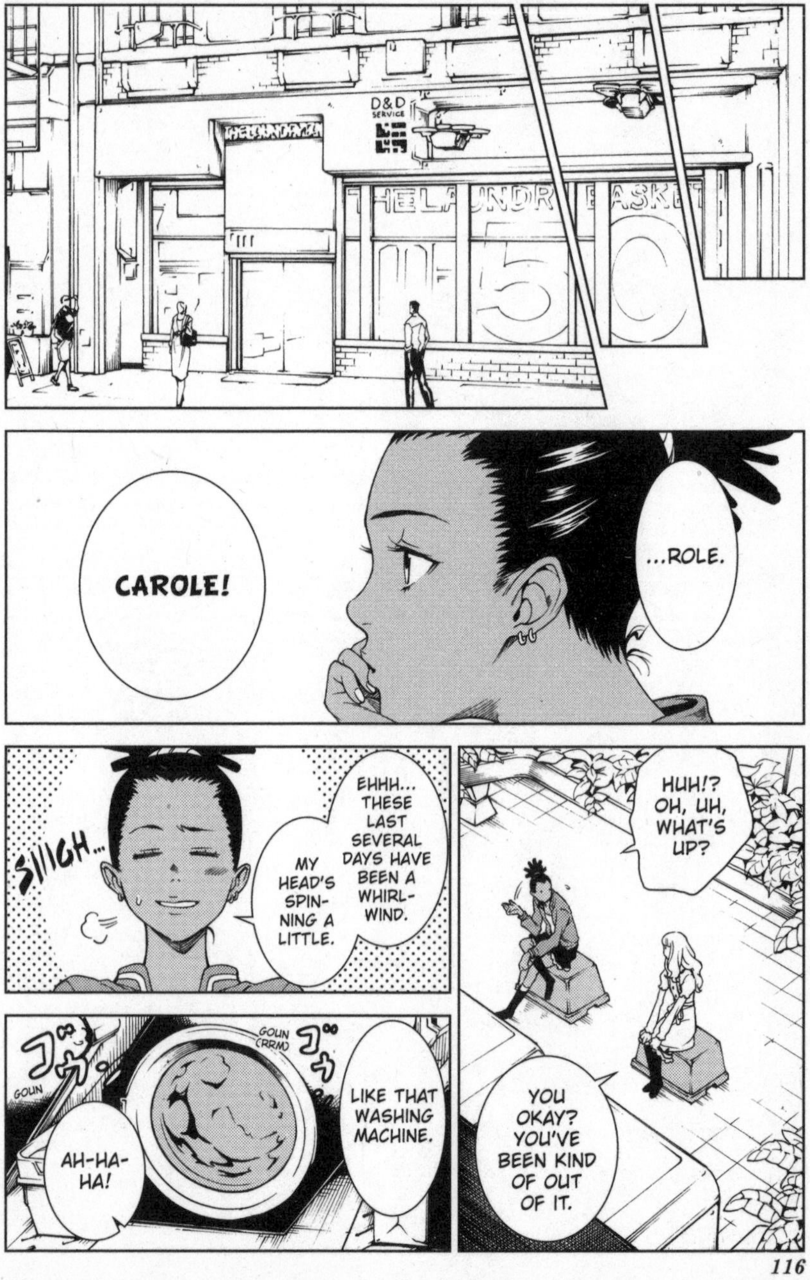
D&D SERVICE
...ROLE.
CAROLE!
HUH!? OH, UH, WHAT'S UP?
YOU OKAY? YOU'VE BEEN KIND OF OUT OF IT.
EHHH... THESE LAST SEVERAL DAYS HAVE BEEN A WHIRLWIND.
MY HEAD'S SPIN-NING A LITTLE.
SIIIGH...
GOUN (CRRM)
LIKE THAT WASHING MACHINE.
GOUN
AH-HA-HA!

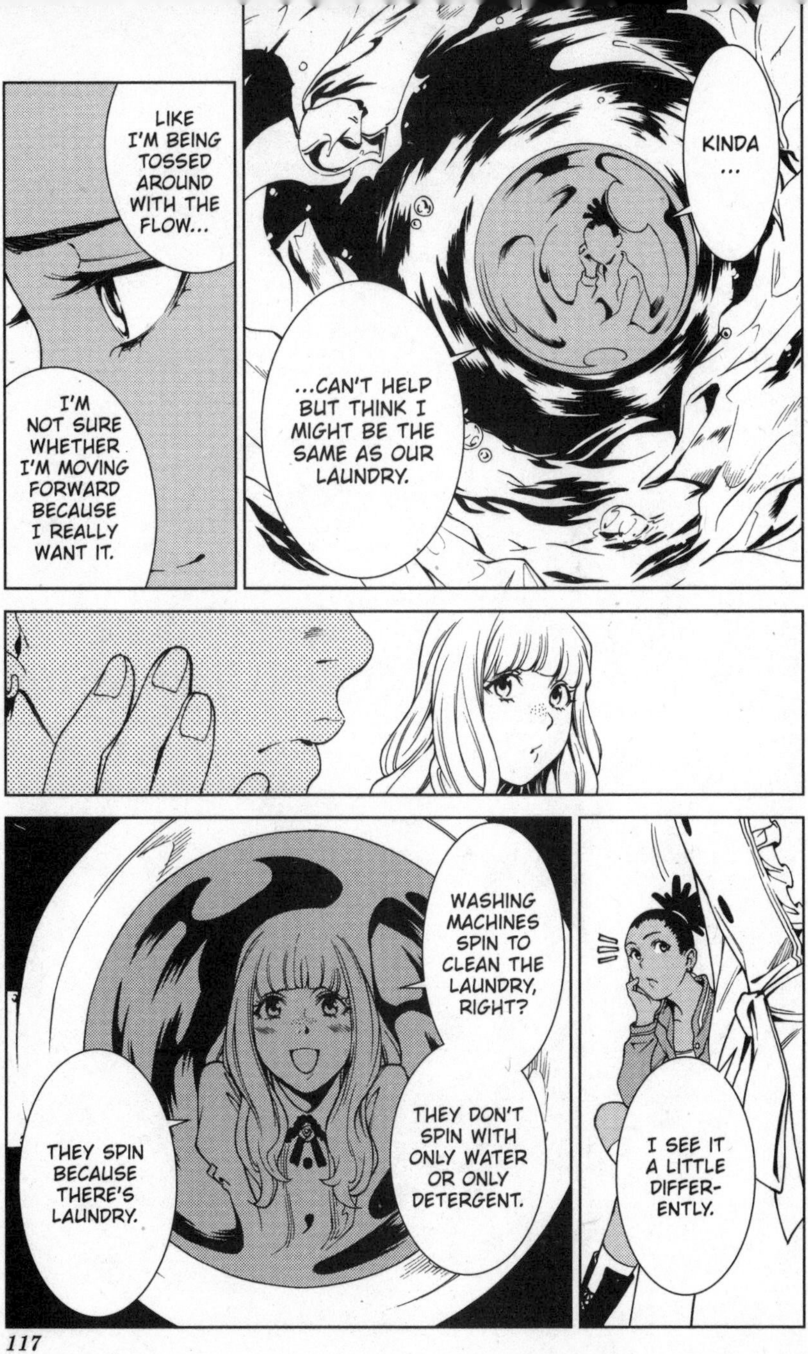
KINDA...
...CAN'T HELP BUT THINK I MIGHT BE THE SAME AS OUR LAUNDRY.
LIKE I'M BEING TOSSED AROUND WITH THE FLOW...
I'M NOT SURE WHETHER I'M MOVING FORWARD BECAUSE I REALLY WANT IT.
I SEE IT A LITTLE DIFFER-ENTLY.
WASHING MACHINES SPIN TO CLEAN THE LAUNDRY, RIGHT?
THEY DON'T SPIN WITH ONLY WATER OR ONLY DETERGENT.
THEY SPIN BECAUSE THERE'S LAUNDRY.

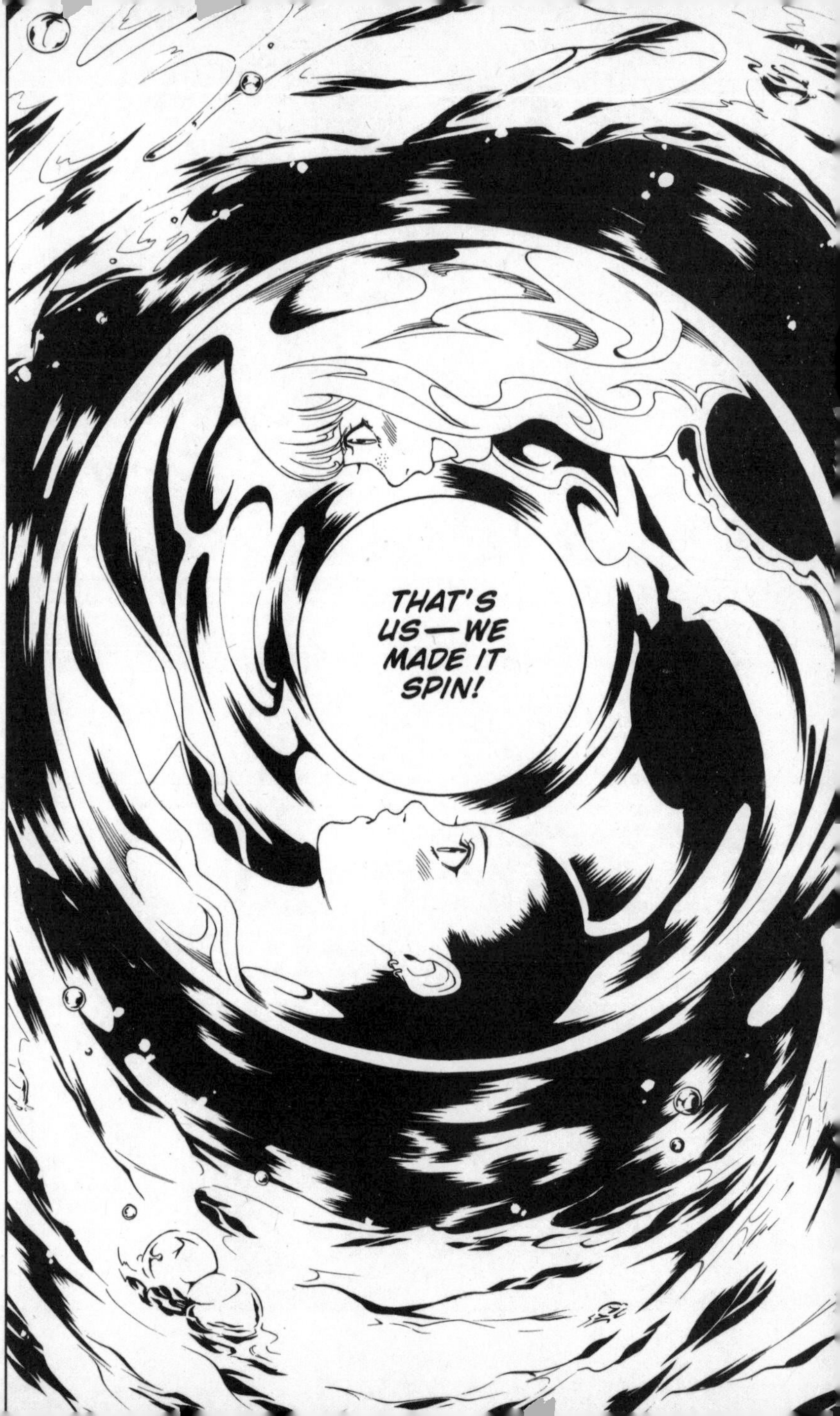
THAT'S US—WE MADE IT SPIN!

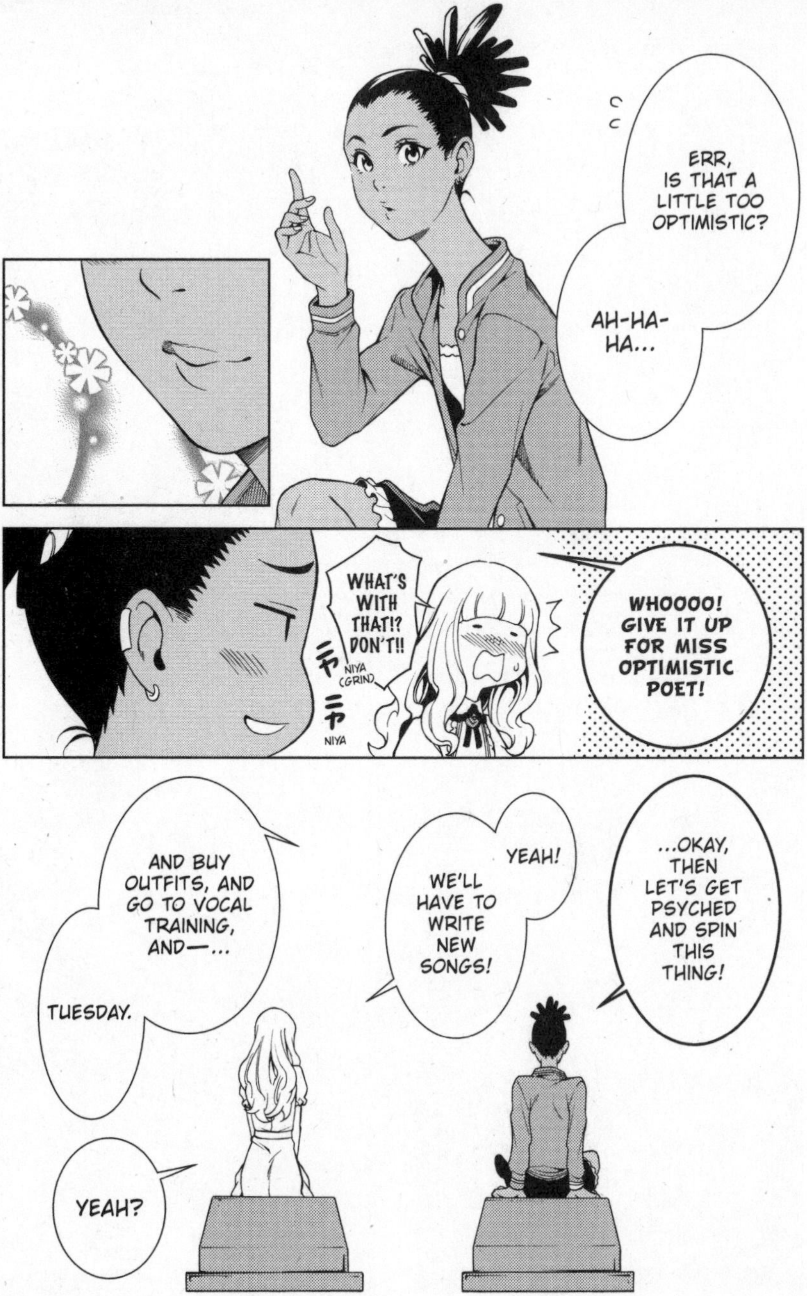
ERR, IS THAT A LITTLE TOO OPTIMISTIC?
AH-HA-HA...
WHOOOO! GIVE IT UP FOR MISS OPTIMISTIC POET!
WHAT'S WITH THAT!? DON'T!!
ニヤ NIYA (GRIN)
ニヤ NIYA
...OKAY, THEN LET'S GET PSYCHED AND SPIN THIS THING!
YEAH!
WE'LL HAVE TO WRITE NEW SONGS!
AND BUY OUTFITS, AND GO TO VOCAL TRAINING, AND—...
TUESDAY.
YEAH?

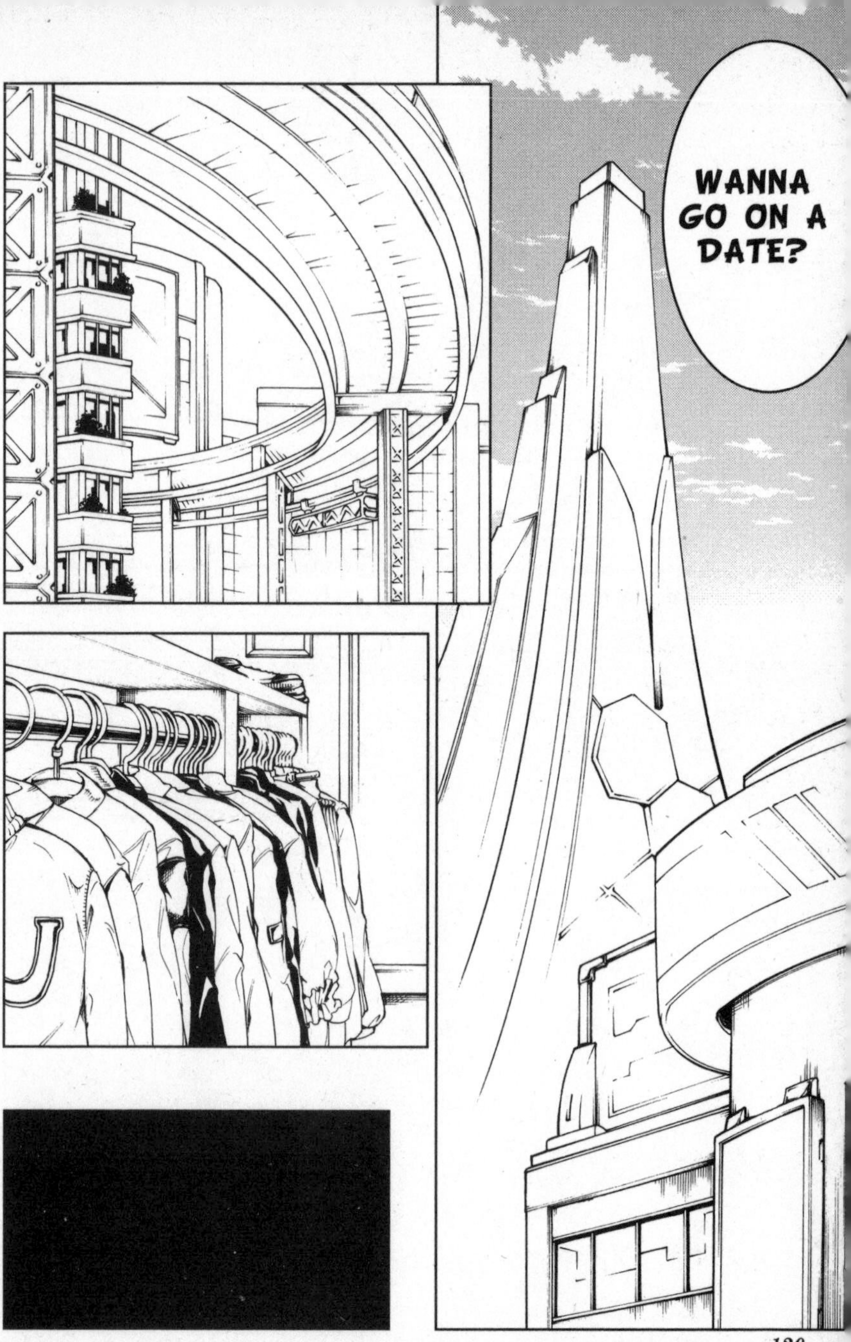
WANNA GO ON A DATE?

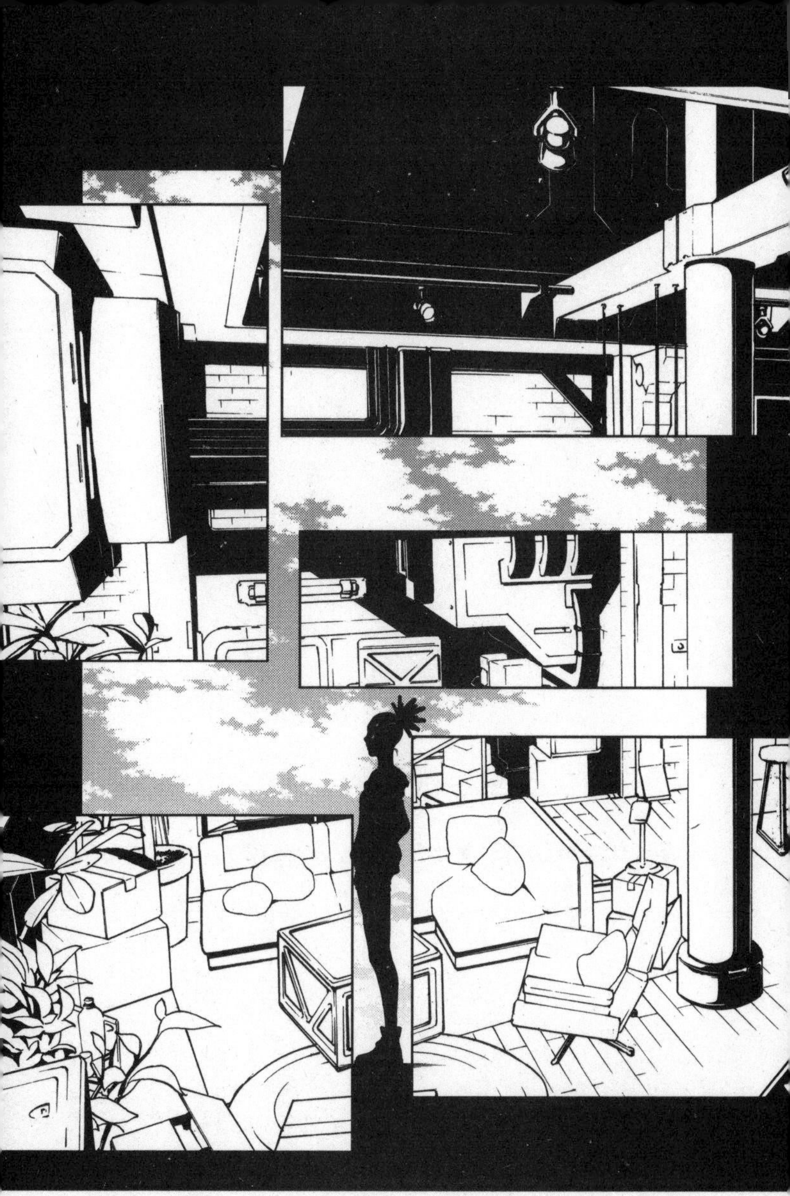

FOR ME, BEING ALONE WAS JUST A FACT OF LIFE.

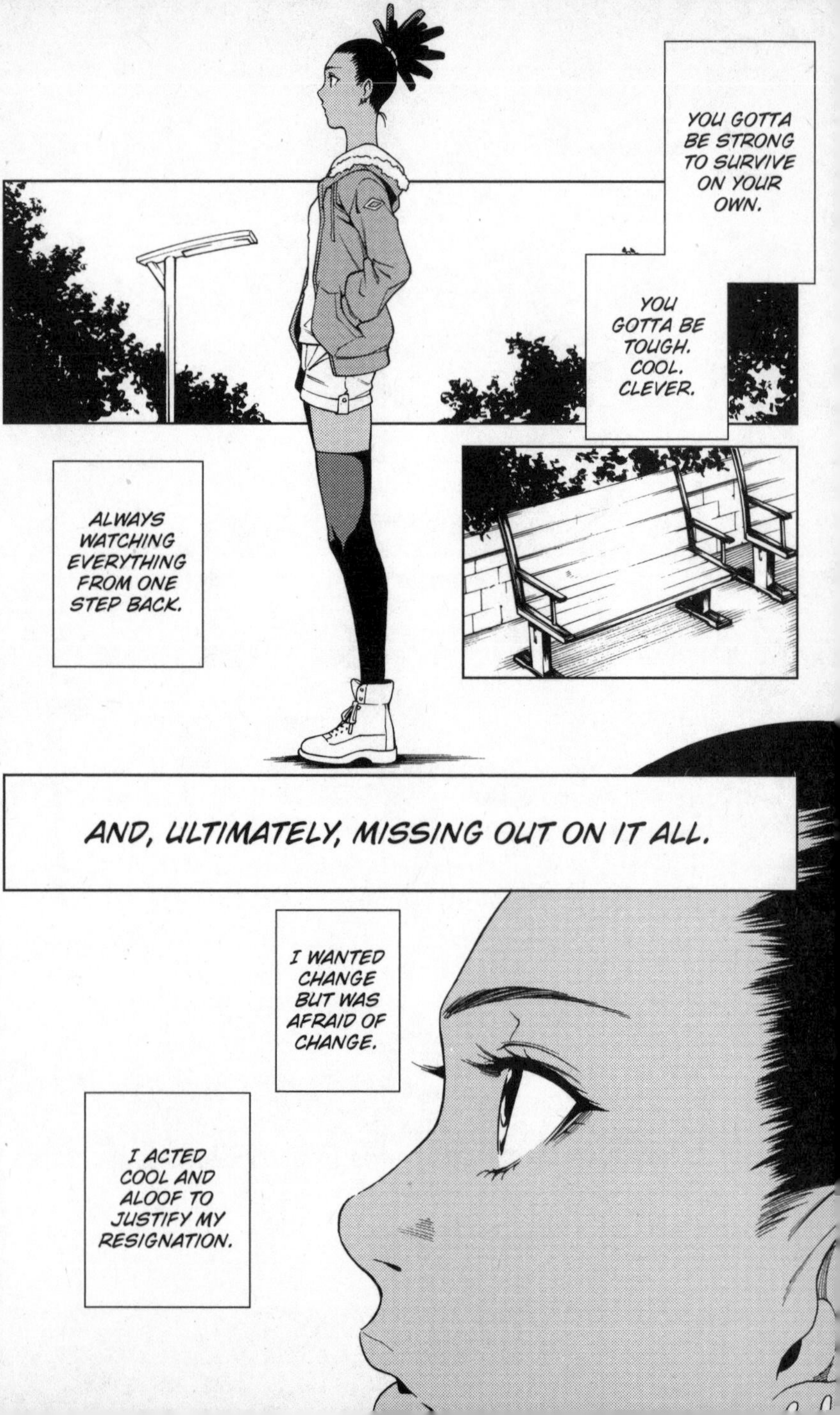
YOU GOTTA BE STRONG TO SURVIVE ON YOUR OWN.
YOU GOTTA BE TOUGH. COOL. CLEVER.
ALWAYS WATCHING EVERYTHING FROM ONE STEP BACK.
AND, ULTIMATELY, MISSING OUT ON IT ALL.
I WANTED CHANGE BUT WAS AFRAID OF CHANGE.
I ACTED COOL AND ALOOF TO JUSTIFY MY RESIGNATION.

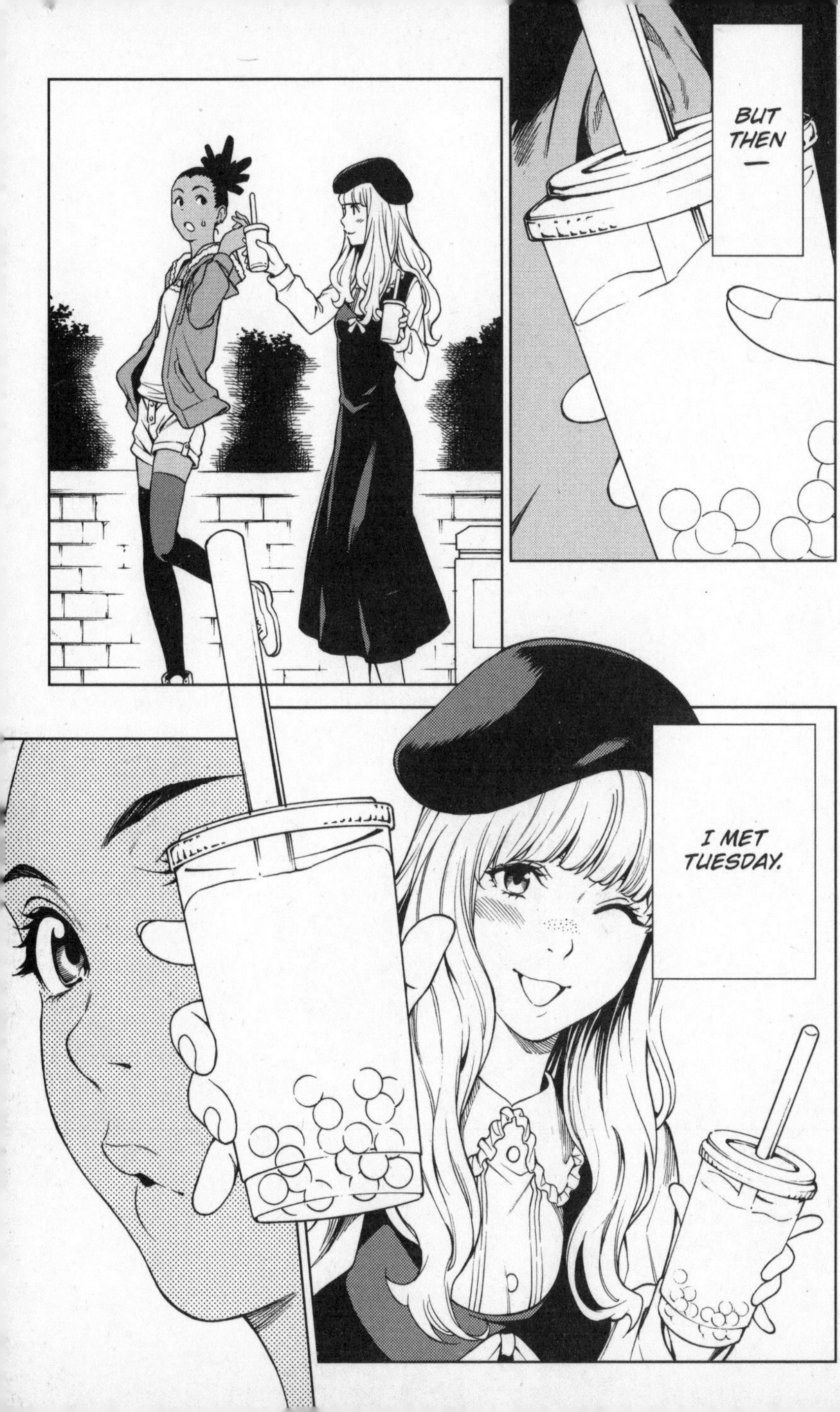
BUT THEN —
I MET TUESDAY.

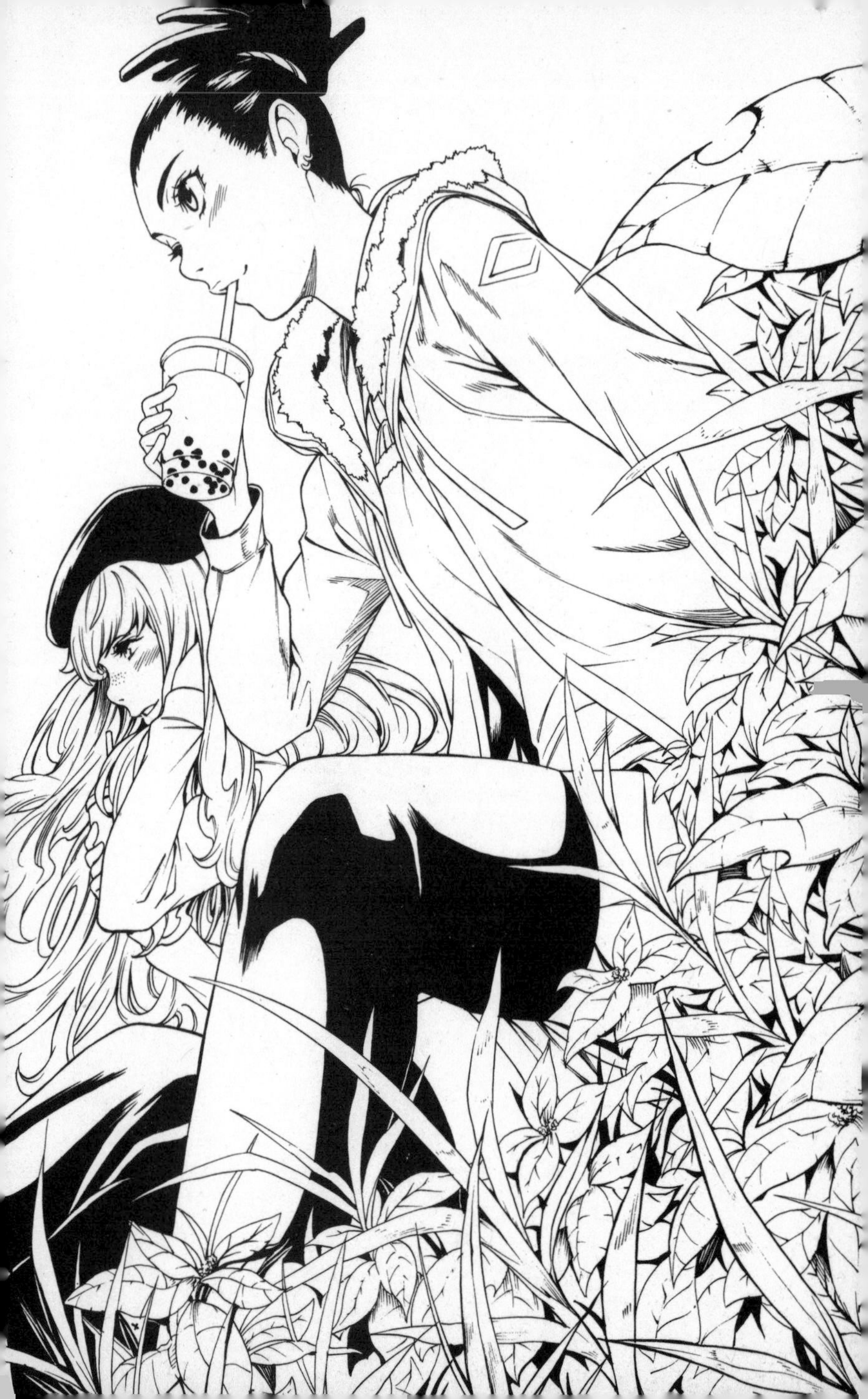

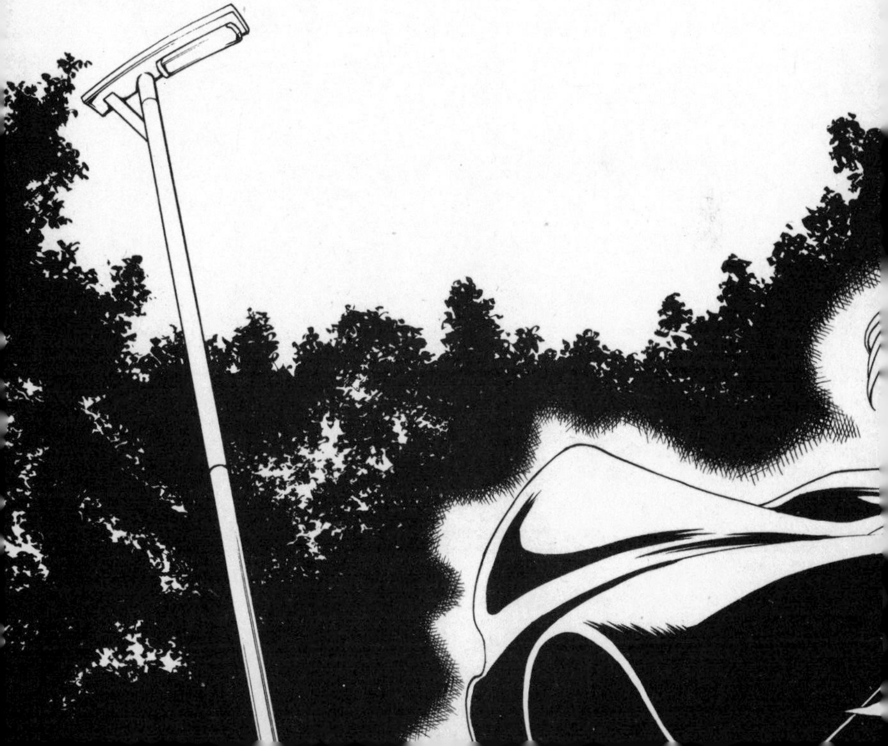

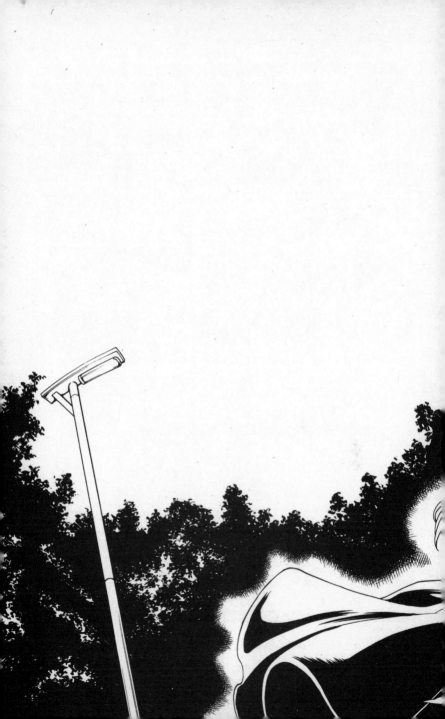

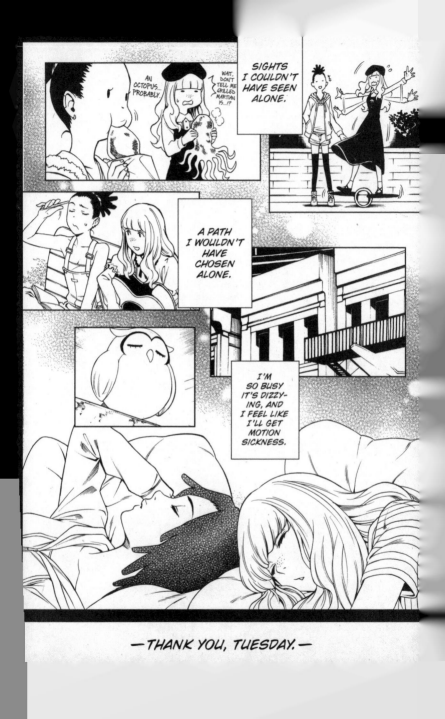

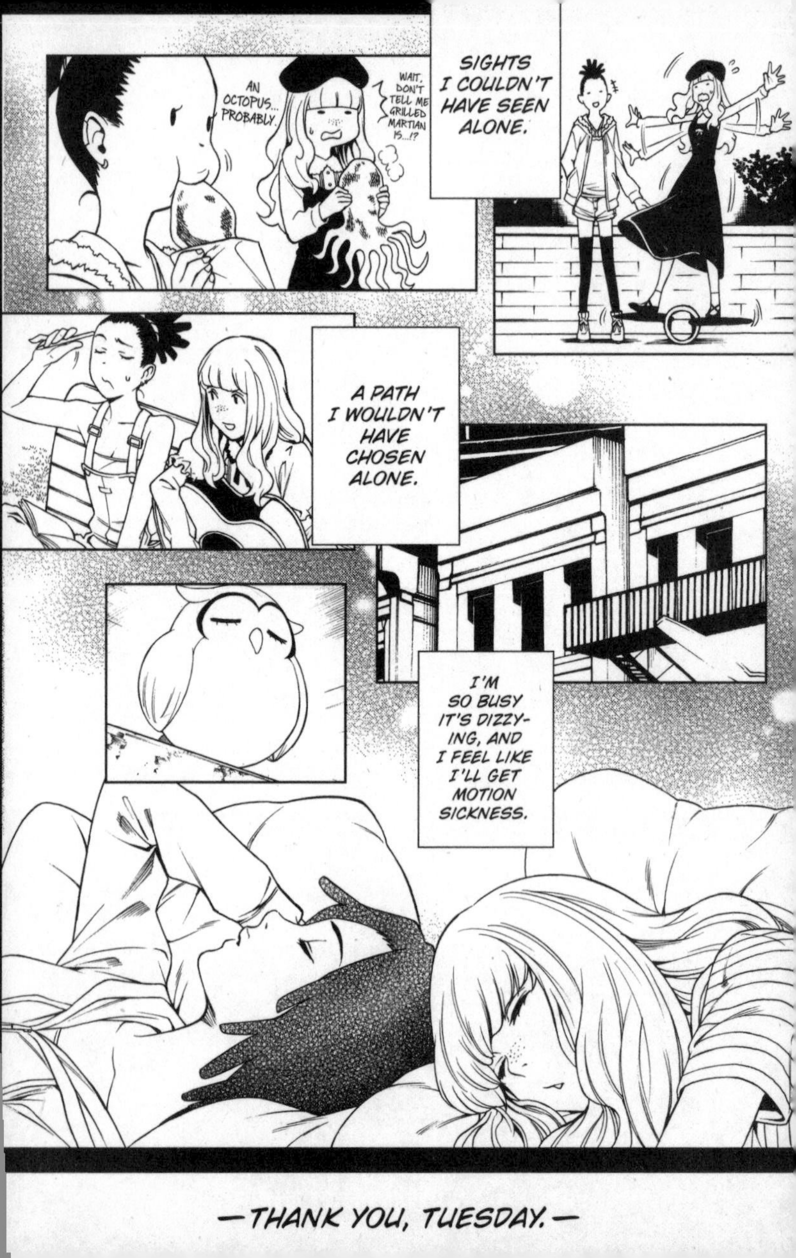
SIGHTS I COULDN'T HAVE SEEN ALONE.
WAIT, DON'T TELL ME GRILLED MARTIAN IS...!?
AN OCTOPUS... PROBABLY.
A PATH I WOULDN'T HAVE CHOSEN ALONE.
I'M SO BUSY IT'S DIZZYING, AND I FEEL LIKE I'LL GET MOTION SICKNESS.

—THANK YOU, TUESDAY.—

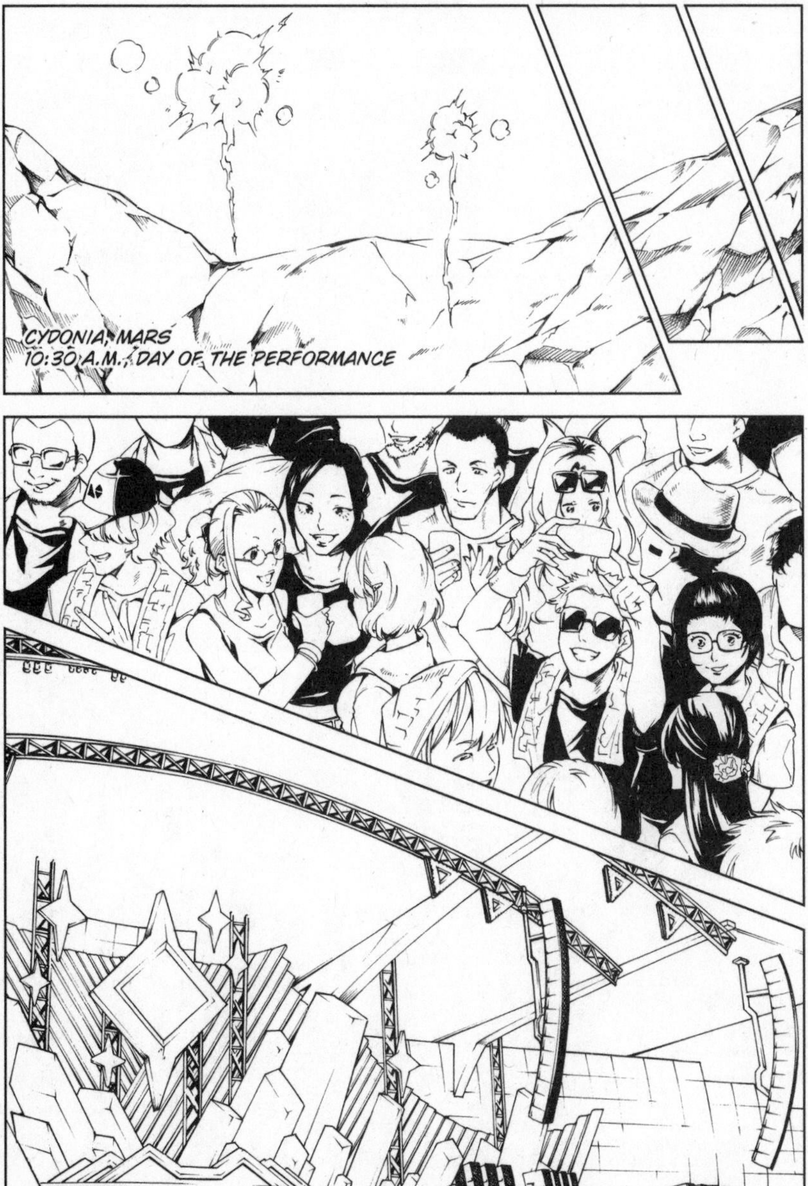
CYDONIA, MARS
10:30 A.M., DAY OF THE PERFORMANCE

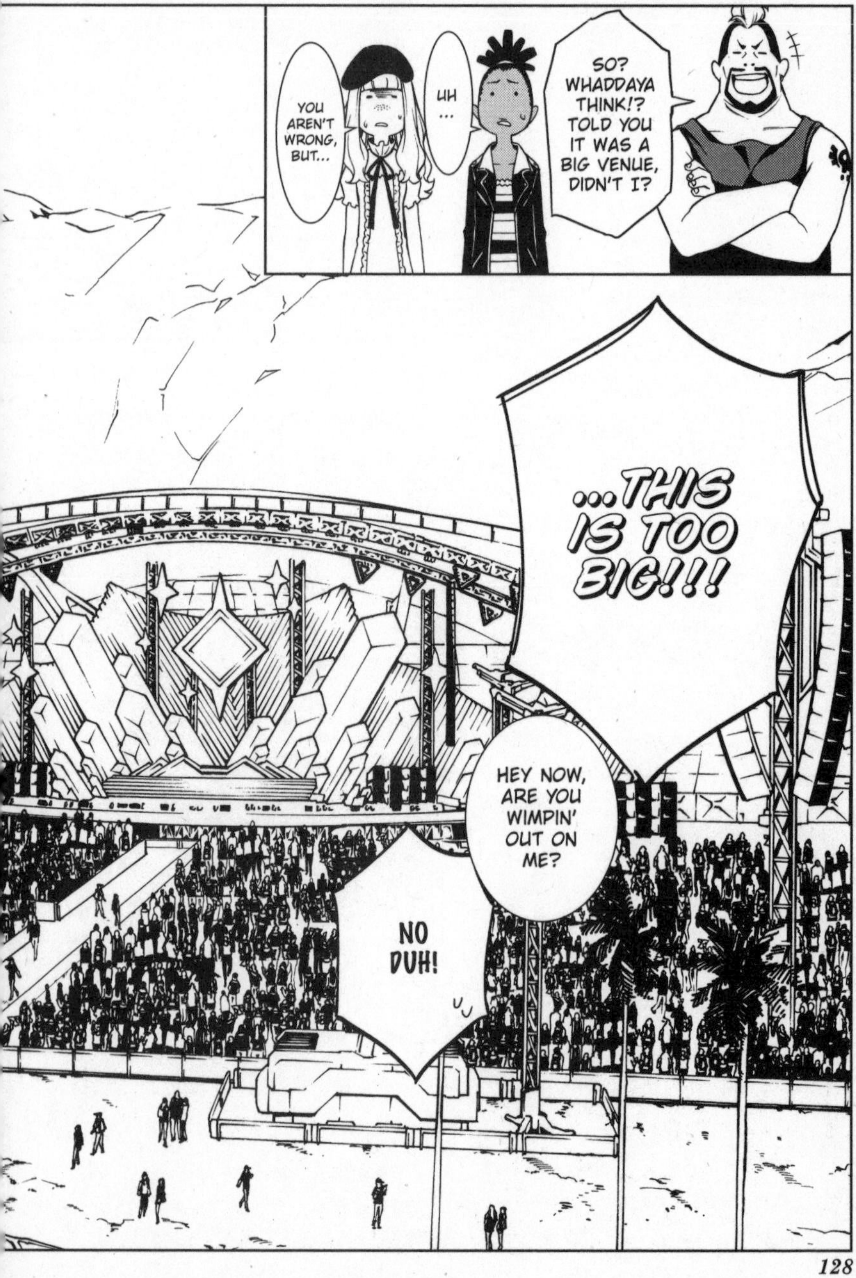
SO? WHADDAYA THINK!? TOLD YOU IT WAS A BIG VENUE, DIDN'T I?
UH ...
YOU AREN'T WRONG, BUT...
...THIS IS TOO BIG!!!
HEY NOW, ARE YOU WIMPIN' OUT ON ME?
NO DUH!

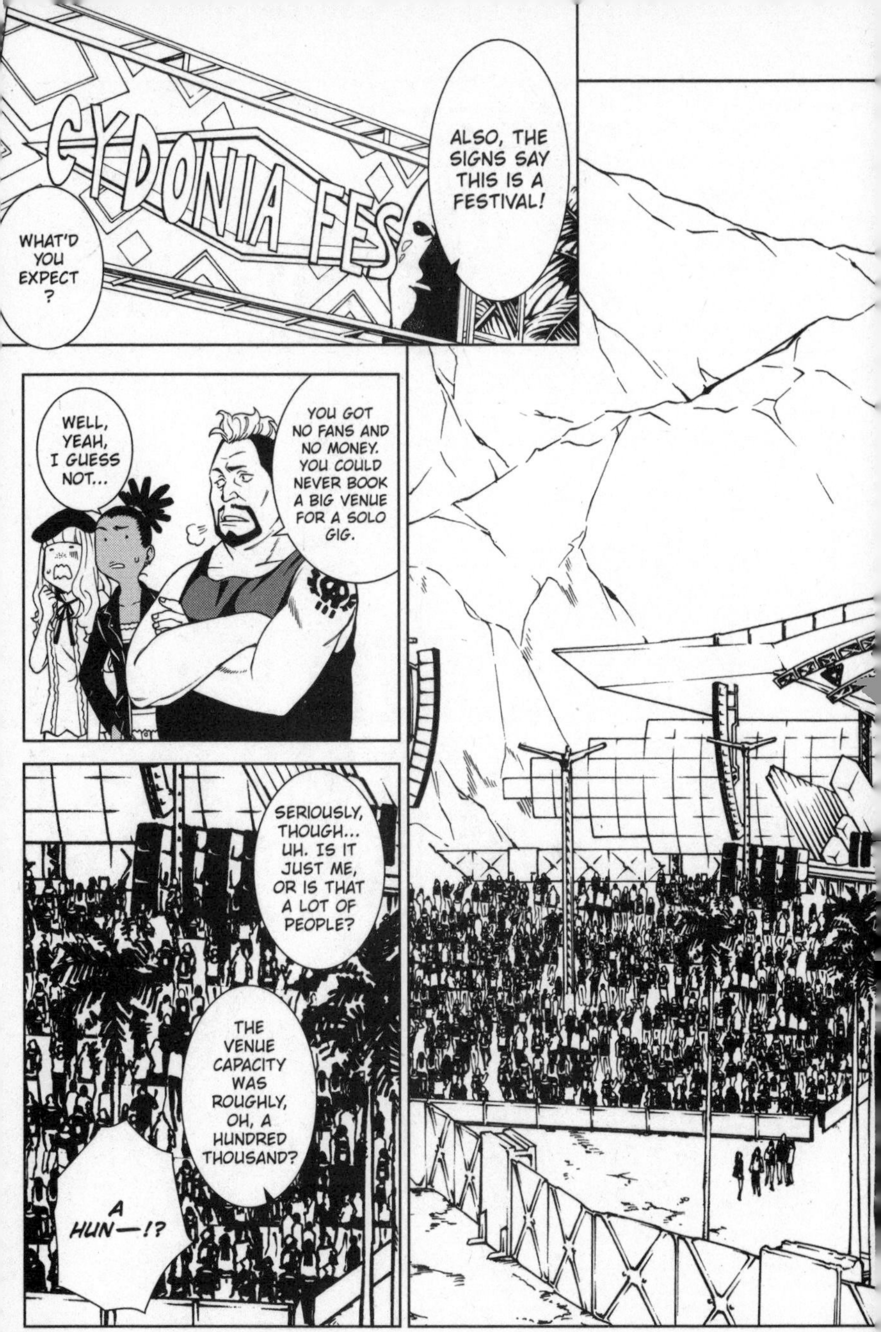
CYDONIA FES
ALSO, THE SIGNS SAY THIS IS A FESTIVAL!
WHAT'D YOU EXPECT?
YOU GOT NO FANS AND NO MONEY. YOU COULD NEVER BOOK A BIG VENUE FOR A SOLO GIG.
WELL, YEAH, I GUESS NOT...
SERIOUSLY, THOUGH... UH. IS IT JUST ME, OR IS THAT A LOT OF PEOPLE?
THE VENUE CAPACITY WAS ROUGHLY, OH, A HUNDRED THOUSAND?
A HUN—!?

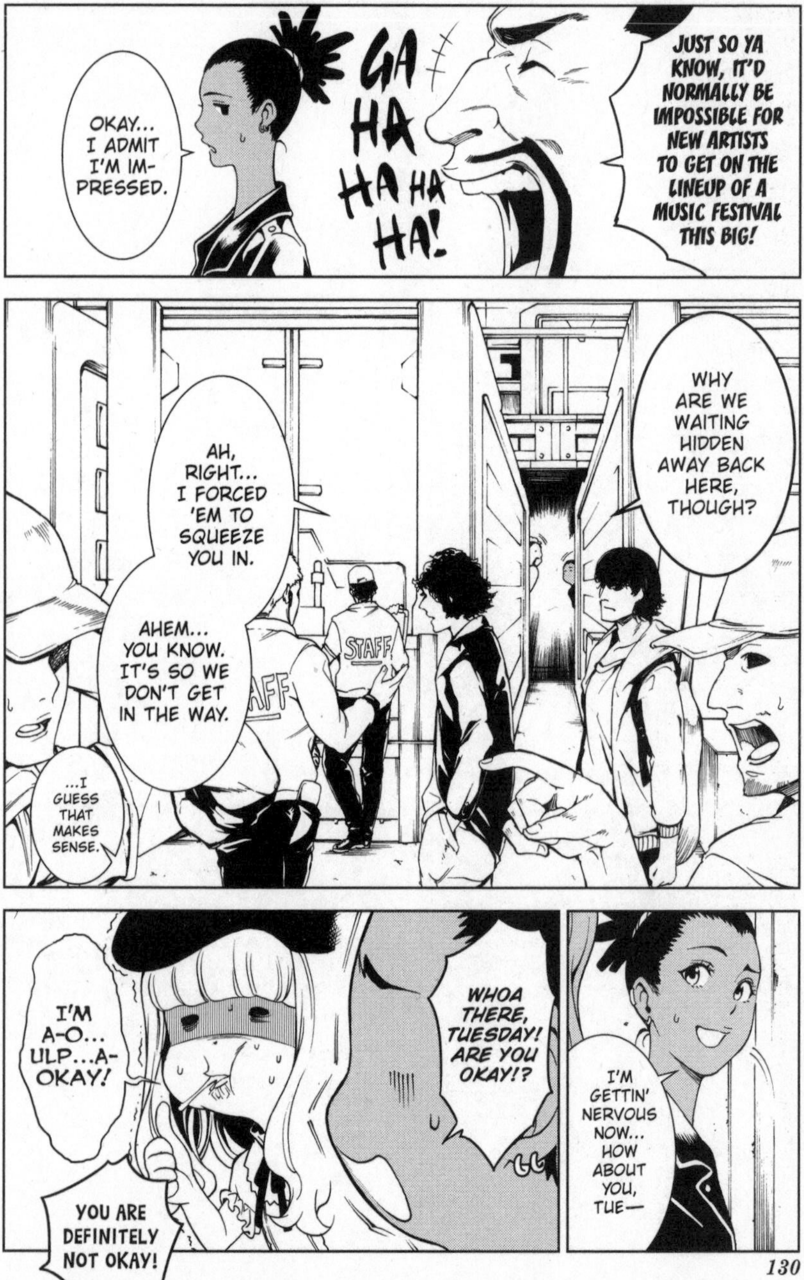
JUST SO YA KNOW, IT'D NORMALLY BE IMPOSSIBLE FOR NEW ARTISTS TO GET ON THE LINEUP OF A MUSIC FESTIVAL THIS BIG!
GA HA HA HA HA!
OKAY... I ADMIT I'M IM-PRESSED.
WHY ARE WE WAITING HIDDEN AWAY BACK HERE, THOUGH?
AH, RIGHT... I FORCED 'EM TO SQUEEZE YOU IN.
AHEM... YOU KNOW. IT'S SO WE DON'T GET IN THE WAY.
STAFF
...I GUESS THAT MAKES SENSE.
I'M GETTIN' NERVOUS NOW... HOW ABOUT YOU, TUE—
WHOA THERE, TUESDAY! ARE YOU OKAY!?
I'M A-O... ULP...A-OKAY!
YOU ARE DEFINITELY NOT OKAY!

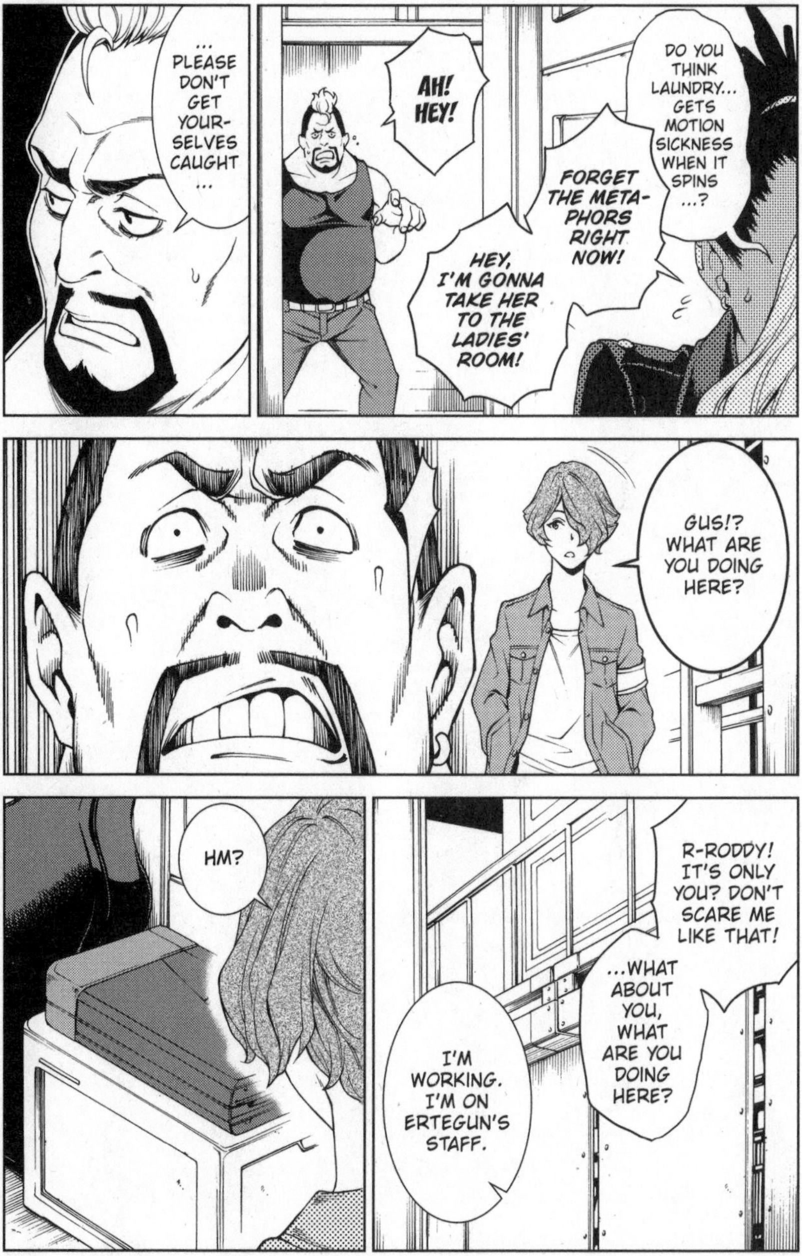
DO YOU THINK LAUNDRY... GETS MOTION SICKNESS WHEN IT SPINS ...?
FORGET THE METAPHORS RIGHT NOW!
HEY, I'M GONNA TAKE HER TO THE LADIES' ROOM!
AH! HEY!
...PLEASE DON'T GET YOURSELVES CAUGHT...
GUS!? WHAT ARE YOU DOING HERE?
R-RODDY! IT'S ONLY YOU? DON'T SCARE ME LIKE THAT!
...WHAT ABOUT YOU, WHAT ARE YOU DOING HERE?
I'M WORKING. I'M ON ERTEGUN'S STAFF.
HM?

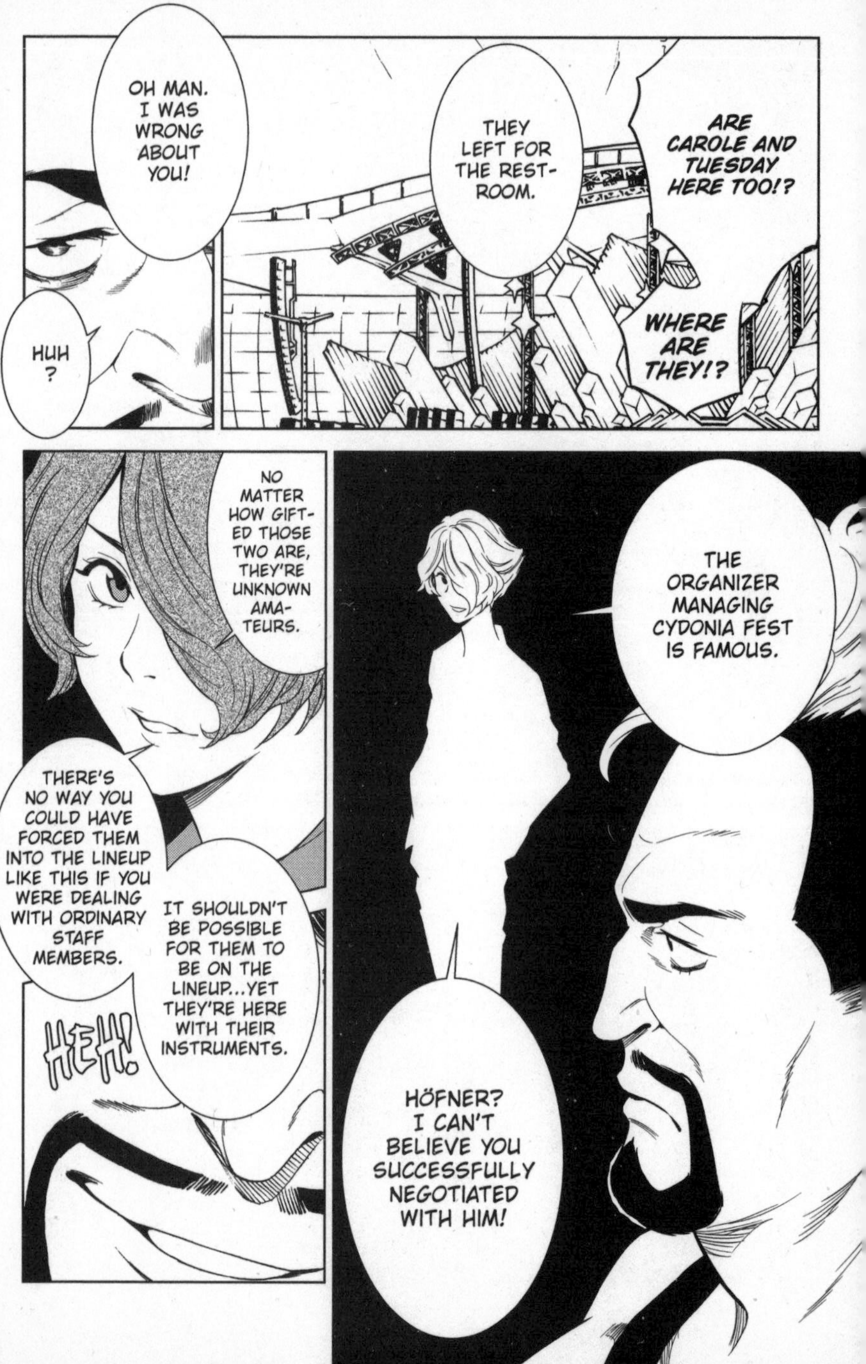
ARE CAROLE AND TUESDAY HERE TOO!?
WHERE ARE THEY!?
THEY LEFT FOR THE REST-ROOM.
OH MAN. I WAS WRONG ABOUT YOU!
HUH?
THE ORGANIZER MANAGING CYDONIA FEST IS FAMOUS.
HÖFNER? I CAN'T BELIEVE YOU SUCCESSFULLY NEGOTIATED WITH HIM!
NO MATTER HOW GIFT-ED THOSE TWO ARE, THEY'RE UNKNOWN AMA-TEURS.
THERE'S NO WAY YOU COULD HAVE FORCED THEM INTO THE LINEUP LIKE THIS IF YOU WERE DEALING WITH ORDINARY STAFF MEMBERS.
IT SHOULDN'T BE POSSIBLE FOR THEM TO BE ON THE LINEUP...YET THEY'RE HERE WITH THEIR INSTRUMENTS.
HEH!

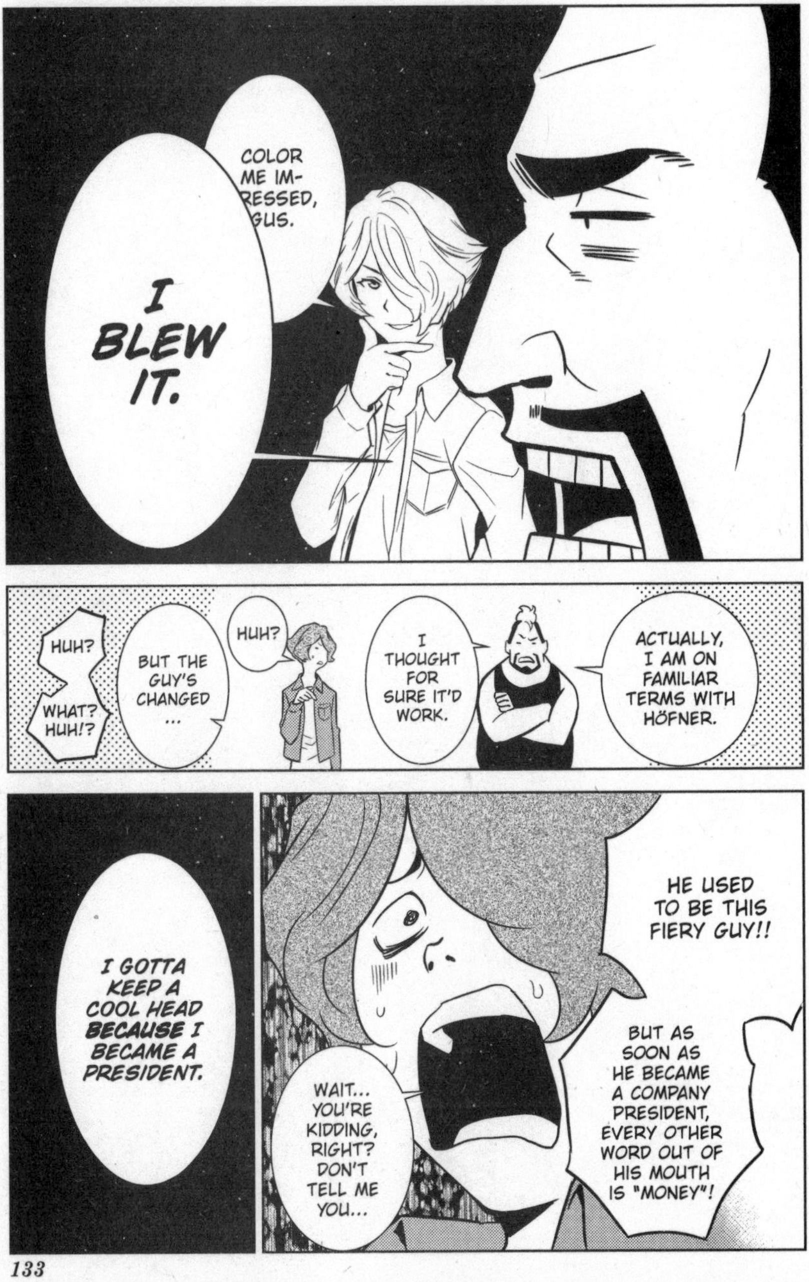

COLOR ME IM-RESSED, GUS.
I BLEW IT.
ACTUALLY, I AM ON FAMILIAR TERMS WITH HÖFNER.
I THOUGHT FOR SURE IT'D WORK.
HUH?
BUT THE GUY'S CHANGED ...
HUH? WHAT? HUH!?
HE USED TO BE THIS FIERY GUY!!
BUT AS SOON AS HE BECAME A COMPANY PRESIDENT, EVERY OTHER WORD OUT OF HIS MOUTH IS "MONEY"!
WAIT... YOU'RE KIDDING, RIGHT? DON'T TELL ME YOU...
I GOTTA KEEP A COOL HEAD BECAUSE I BECAME A PRESIDENT.

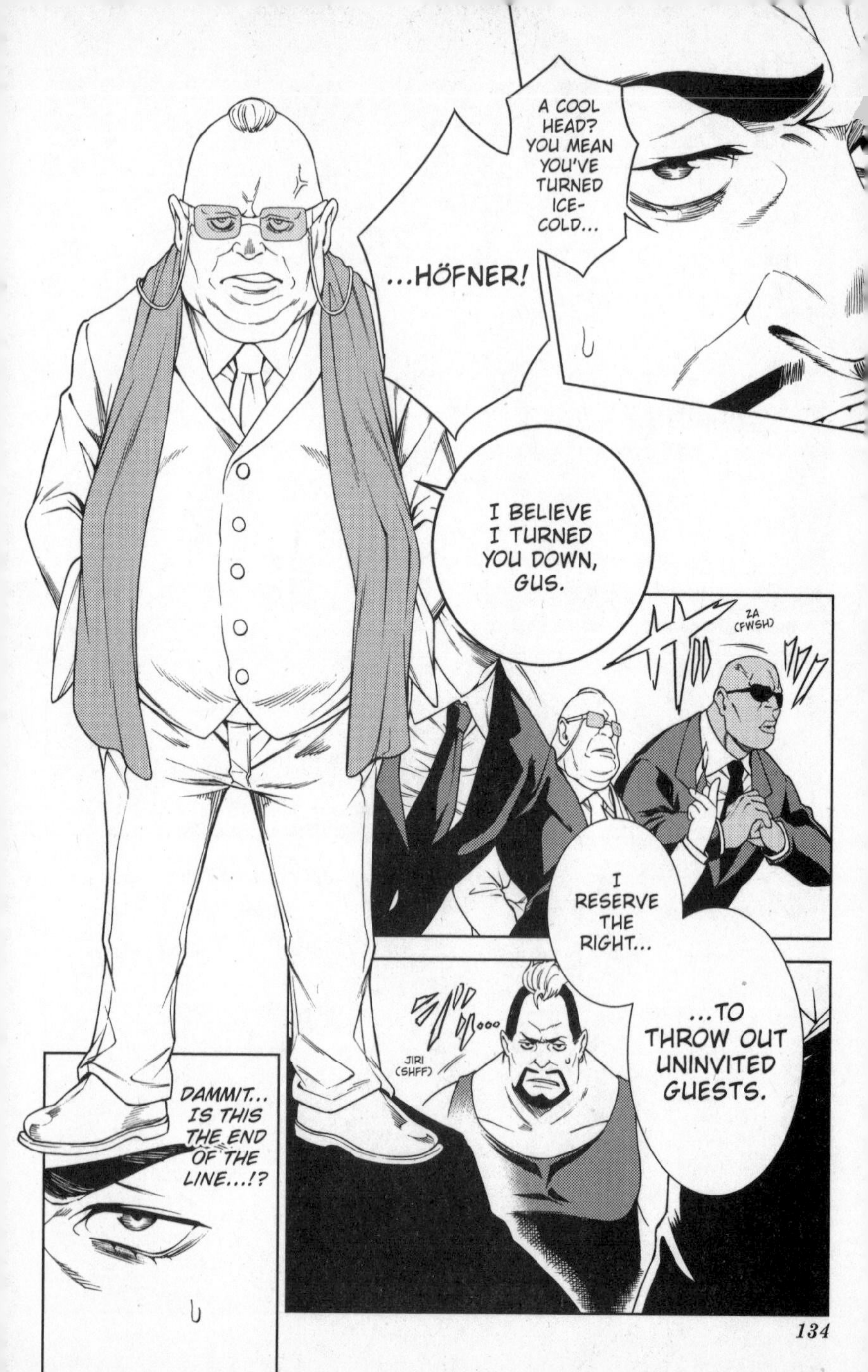
A COOL HEAD? YOU MEAN YOU'VE TURNED ICE-COLD...
...HÖFNER!
I BELIEVE I TURNED YOU DOWN, GUS.
ZA (FWSH)
I RESERVE THE RIGHT...
JIRI (SHFF)
...TO THROW OUT UNINVITED GUESTS.
DAMMIT... IS THIS THE END OF THE LINE...!?

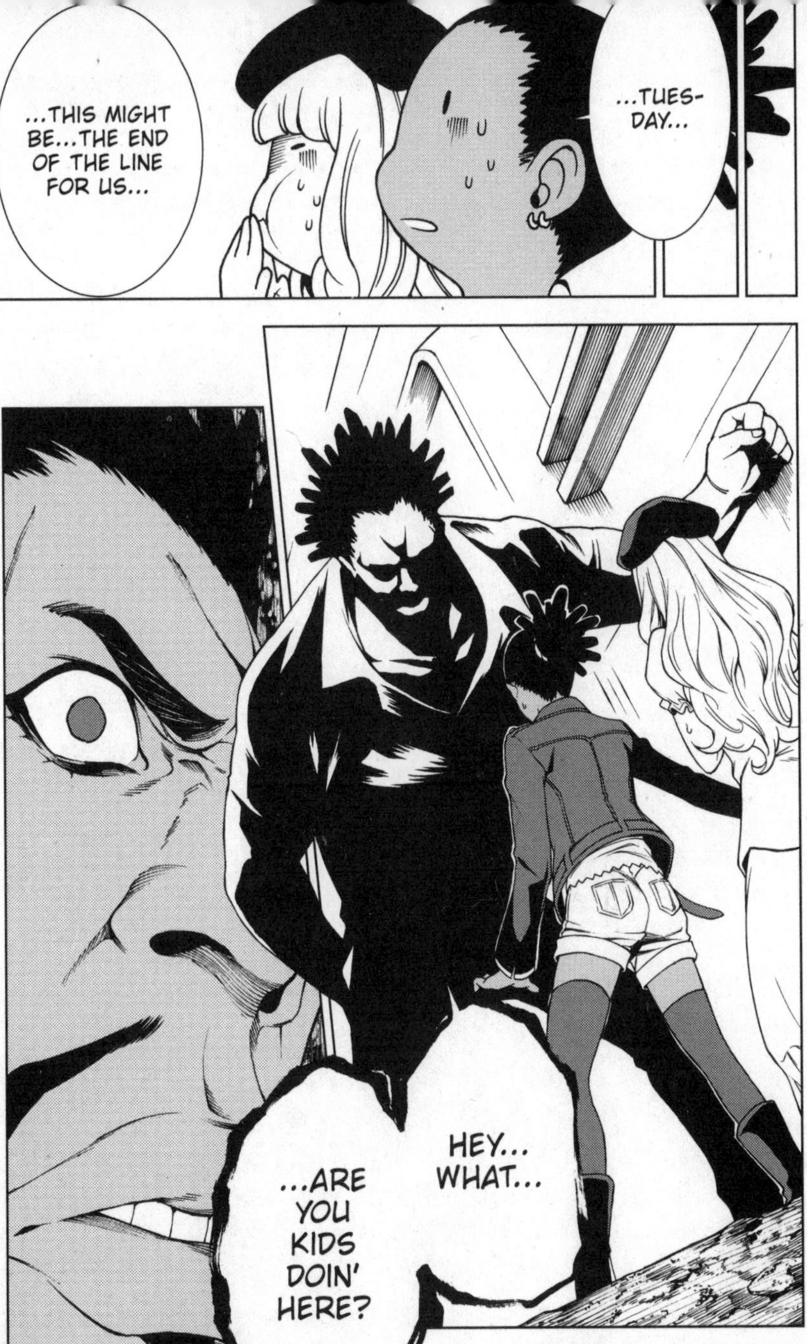
...TUES-DAY...
...THIS MIGHT BE...THE END OF THE LINE FOR US...
HEY... WHAT...
...ARE YOU KIDS DOIN' HERE?

END

CAROLE
& TUESDAY

episode 4: Life Is a Carnival

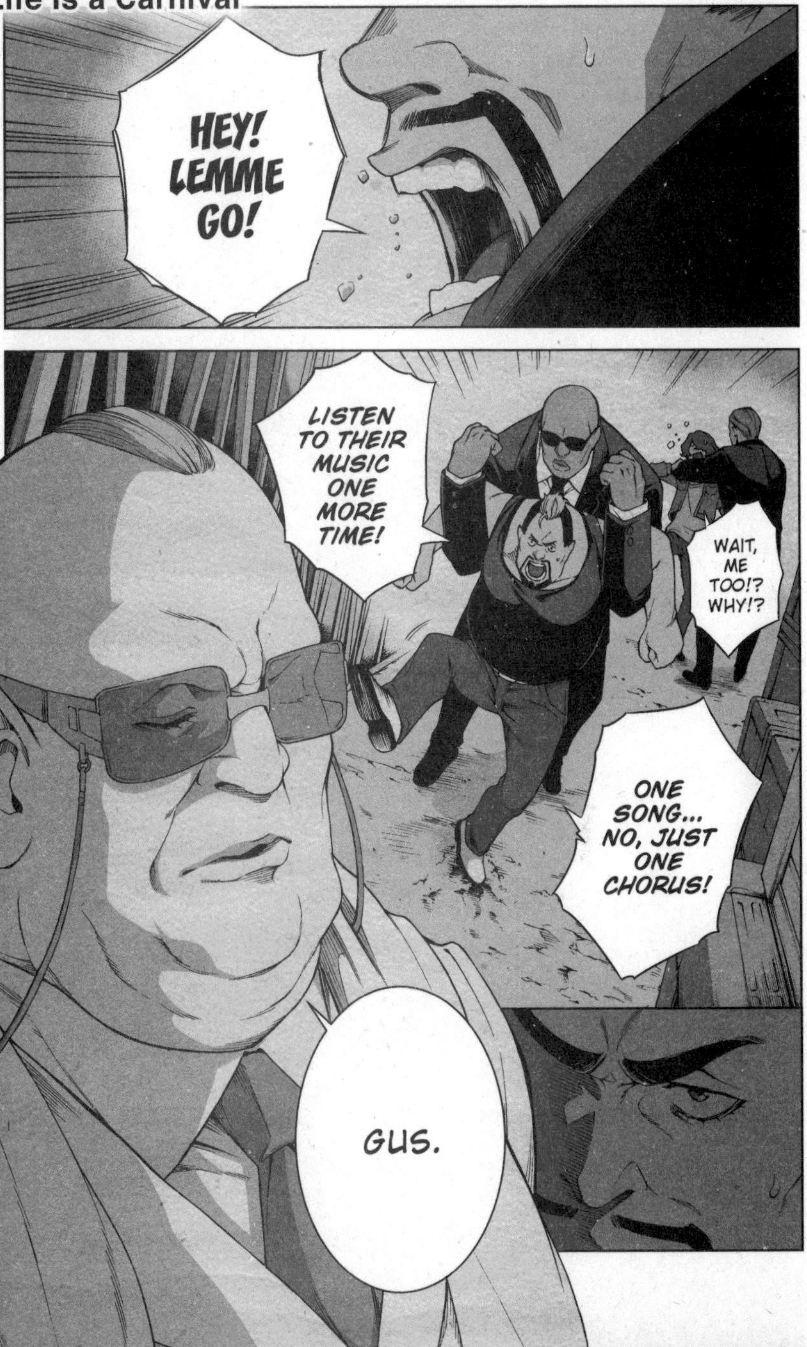
HEY! LEMME GO!
LISTEN TO THEIR MUSIC ONE MORE TIME!
WAIT, ME TOO!? WHY!?
ONE SONG... NO, JUST ONE CHORUS!
GUS.

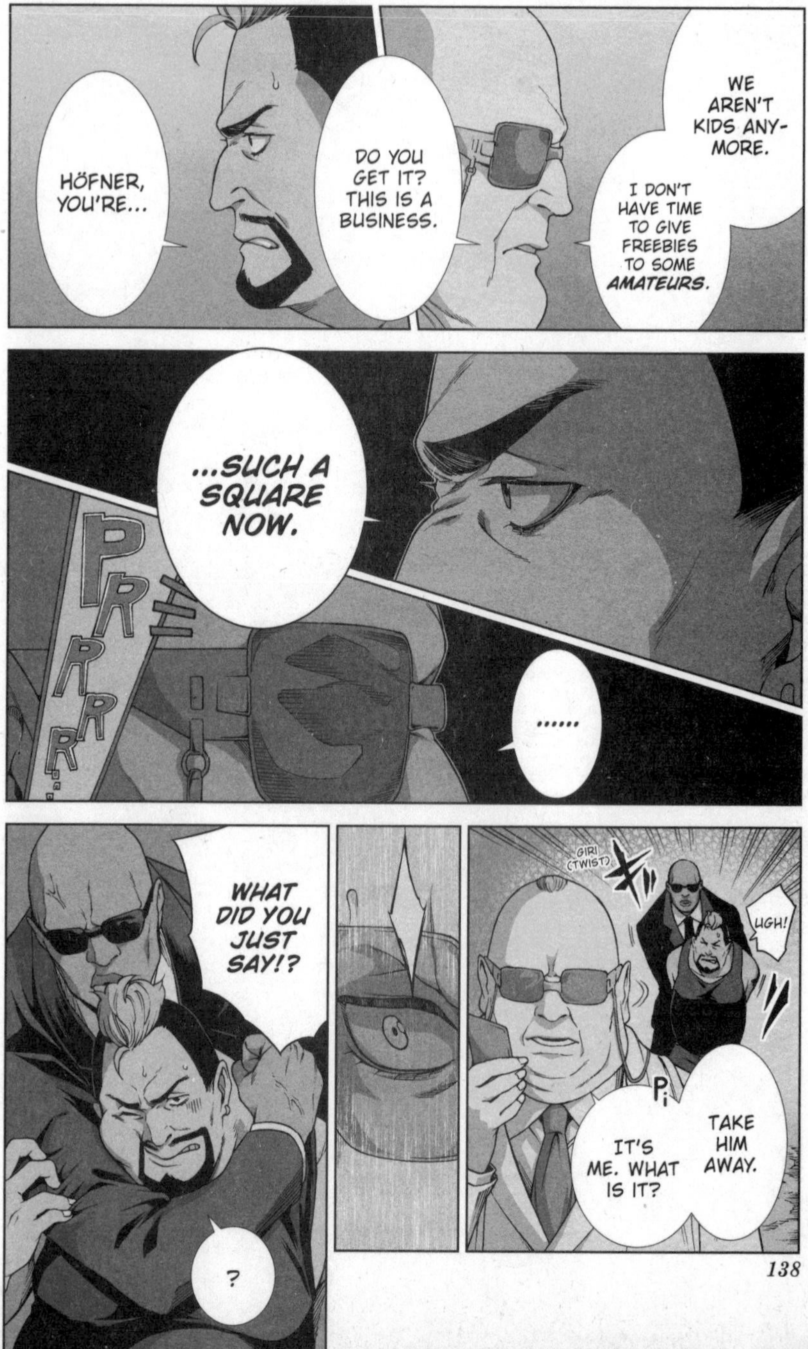
WE AREN'T KIDS ANYMORE.
I DON'T HAVE TIME TO GIVE FREEBIES TO SOME AMATEURS.
DO YOU GET IT? THIS IS A BUSINESS.
HÖFNER, YOU'RE...
...SUCH A SQUARE NOW.
......
PRRRR
GIRI (TWIST)
UGH!
TAKE HIM AWAY.
Pi
IT'S ME. WHAT IS IT?
WHAT DID YOU JUST SAY!?
?

episode 4:
Life Is a Carnival

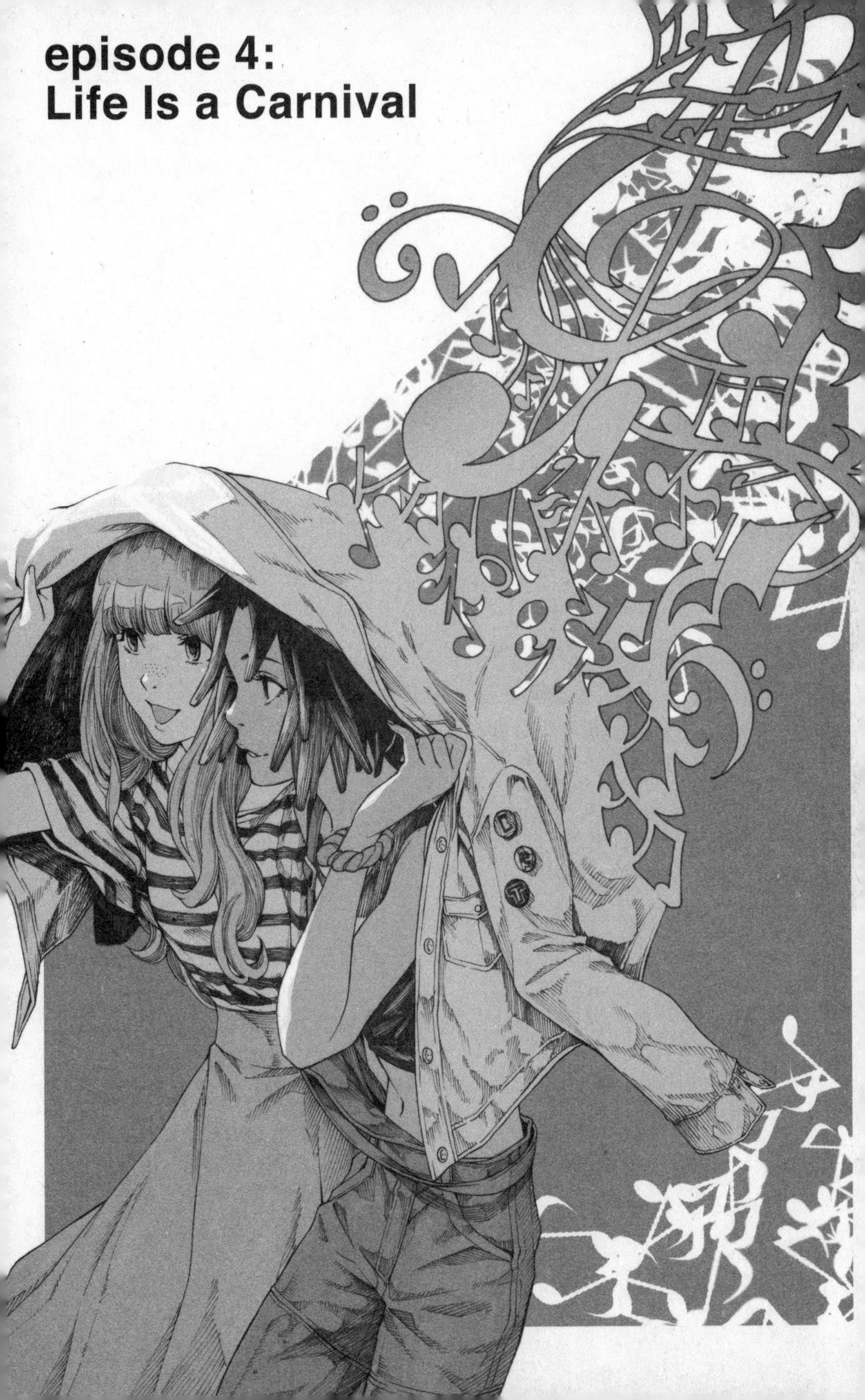

CAROLE
& TUESDAY

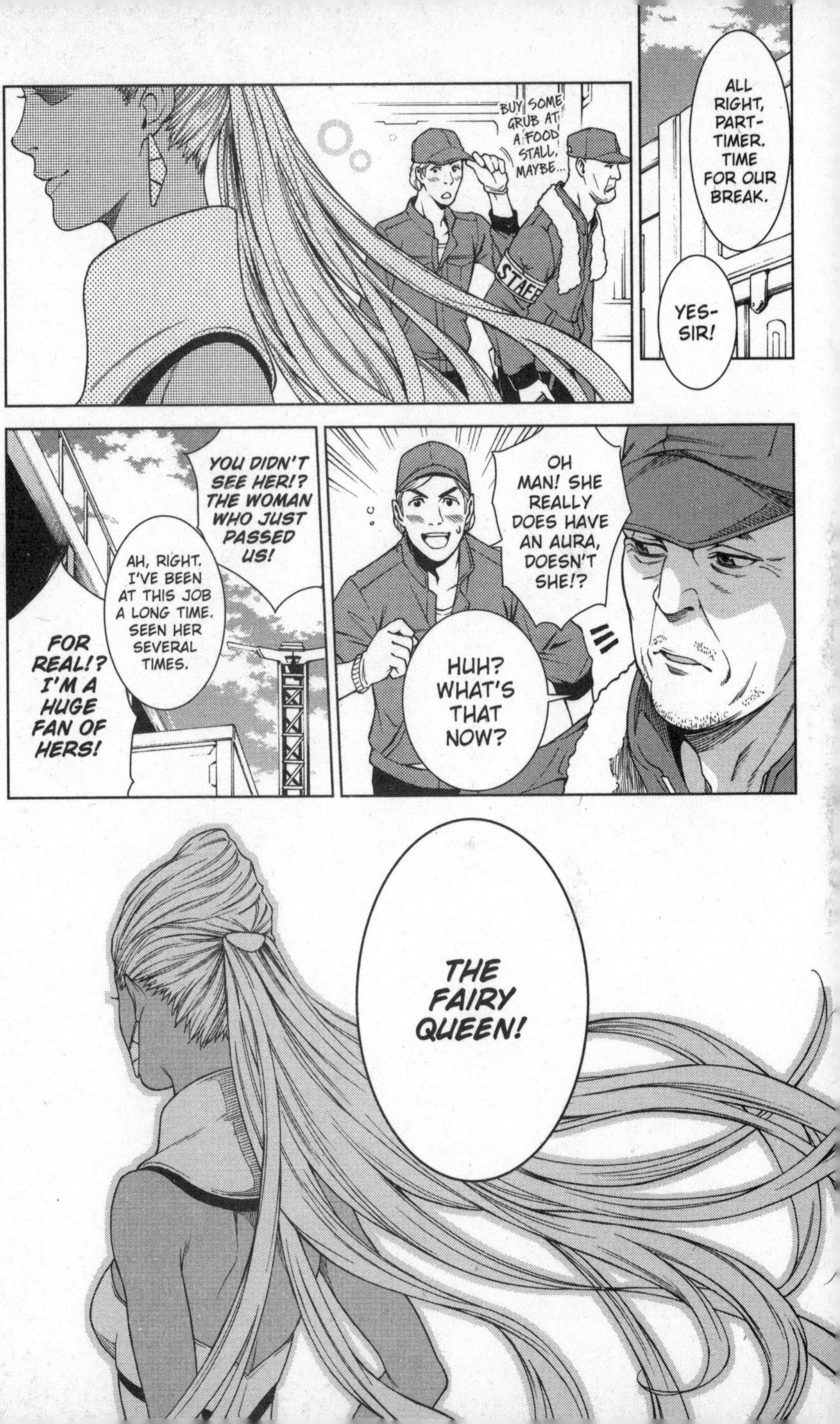
ALL RIGHT, PART-TIMER. TIME FOR OUR BREAK.
YES-SIR!
BUY SOME GRUB AT A FOOD STALL, MAYBE...
STAFF
OH MAN! SHE REALLY DOES HAVE AN AURA, DOESN'T SHE!?
HUH? WHAT'S THAT NOW?
YOU DIDN'T SEE HER!? THE WOMAN WHO JUST PASSED US!
AH, RIGHT. I'VE BEEN AT THIS JOB A LONG TIME. SEEN HER SEVERAL TIMES.
FOR REAL!? I'M A HUGE FAN OF HERS!
THE FAIRY QUEEN!

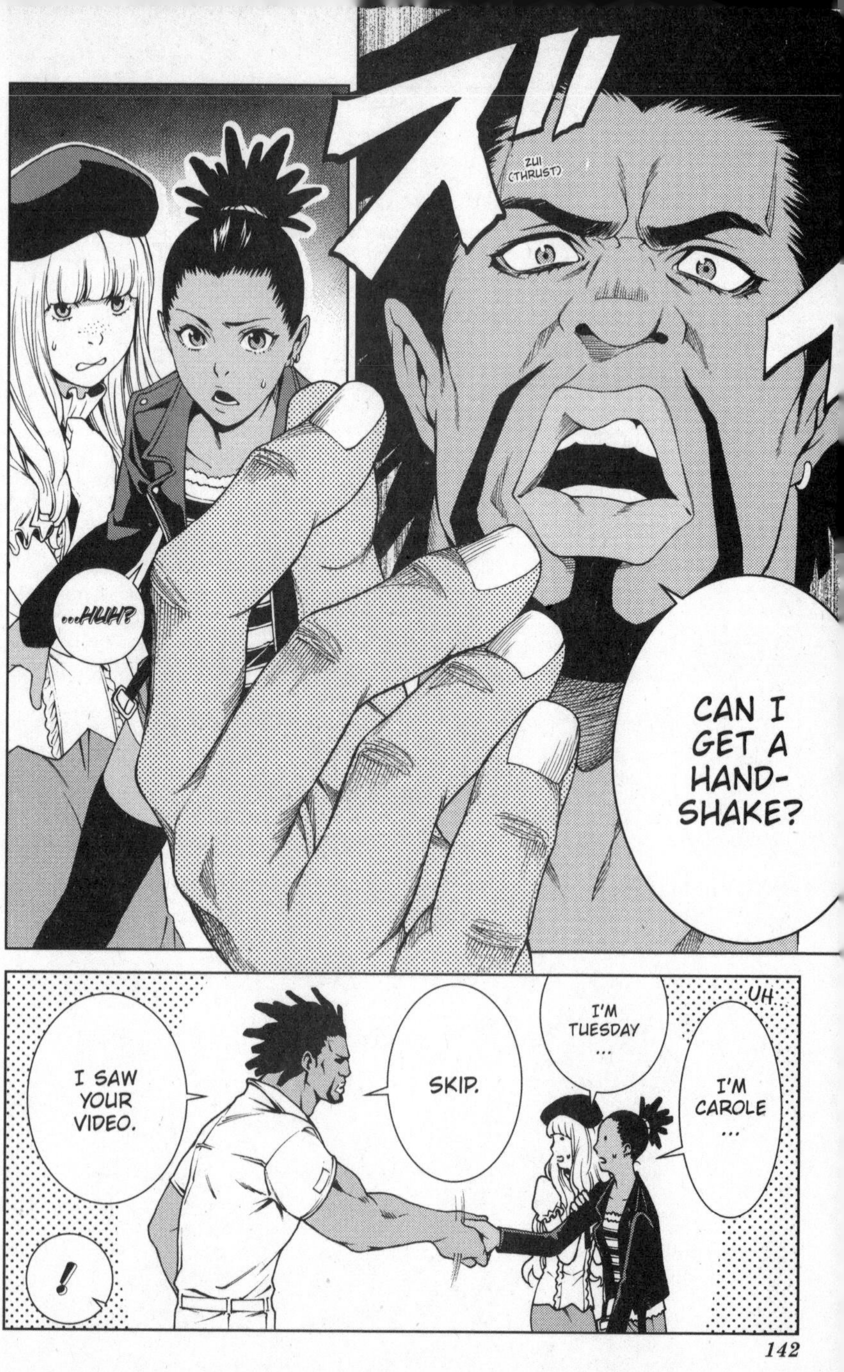
ZUI (THRUST)
CAN I GET A HAND-SHAKE?
...HUH?
UH
I'M CAROLE ...
I'M TUESDAY ...
SKIP.
I SAW YOUR VIDEO.
!

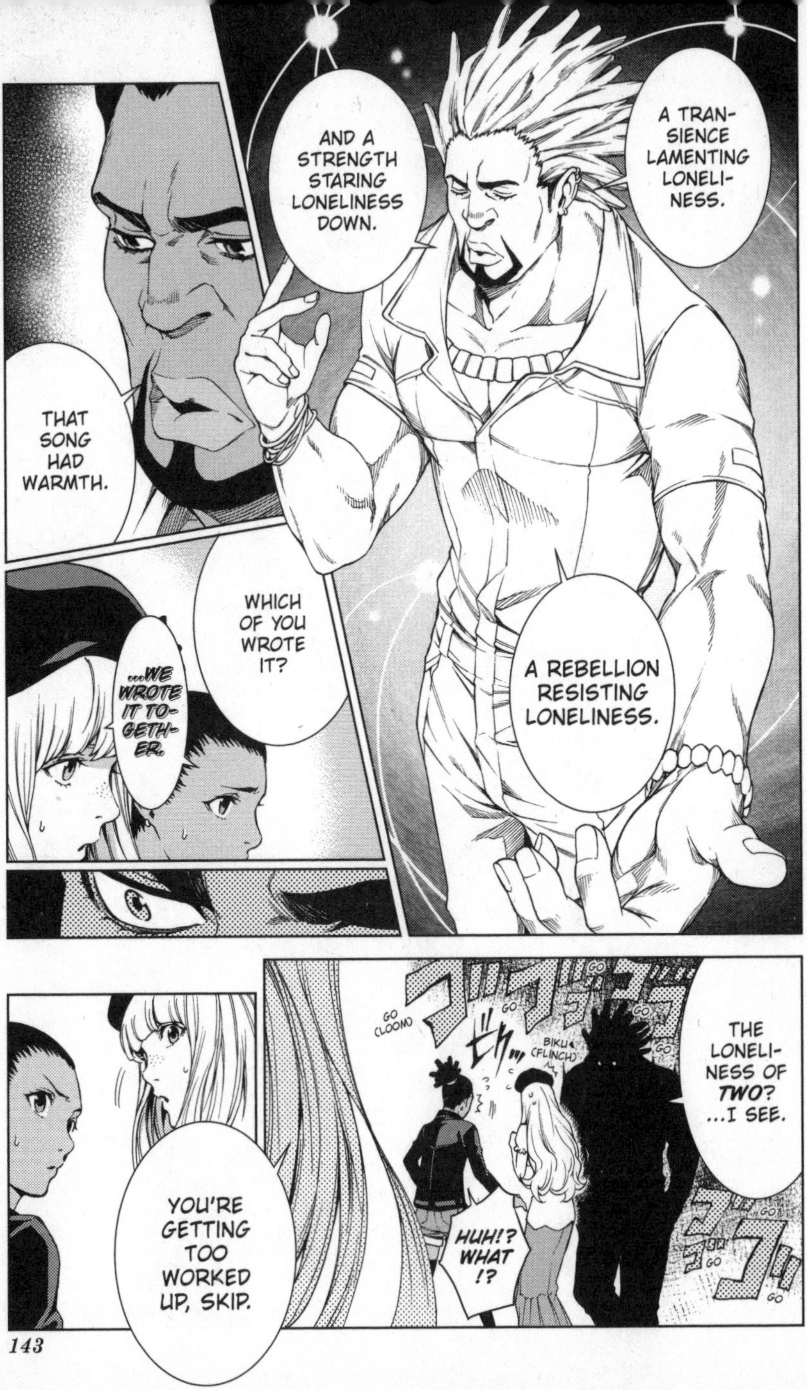
A TRANSIENCE LAMENTING LONELINESS.
AND A STRENGTH STARING LONELINESS DOWN.
A REBELLION RESISTING LONELINESS.
THAT SONG HAD WARMTH.
WHICH OF YOU WROTE IT?
...WE WROTE IT TOGETHER.
GO GO GO GO GO
THE LONELINESS OF TWO? ...I SEE.
GO (CLOOM)
BIKU (FLINCH)
HUH!? WHAT!?
GO GO GO
YOU'RE GETTING TOO WORKED UP, SKIP.

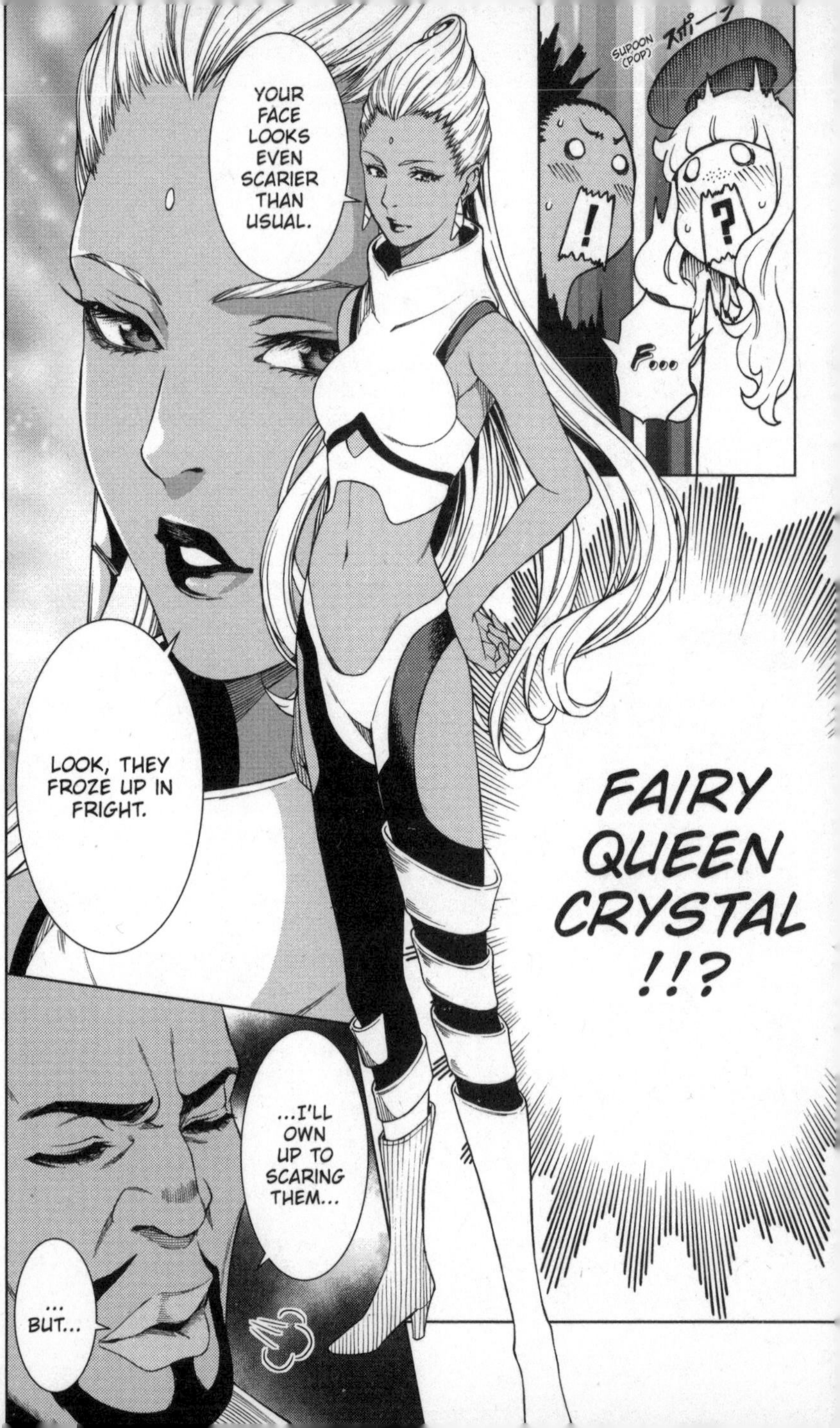
SUPOON (POP)
F...
!
?
FAIRY QUEEN CRYSTAL !!?
YOUR FACE LOOKS EVEN SCARIER THAN USUAL.
LOOK, THEY FROZE UP IN FRIGHT.
...I'LL OWN UP TO SCARING THEM...
... BUT...

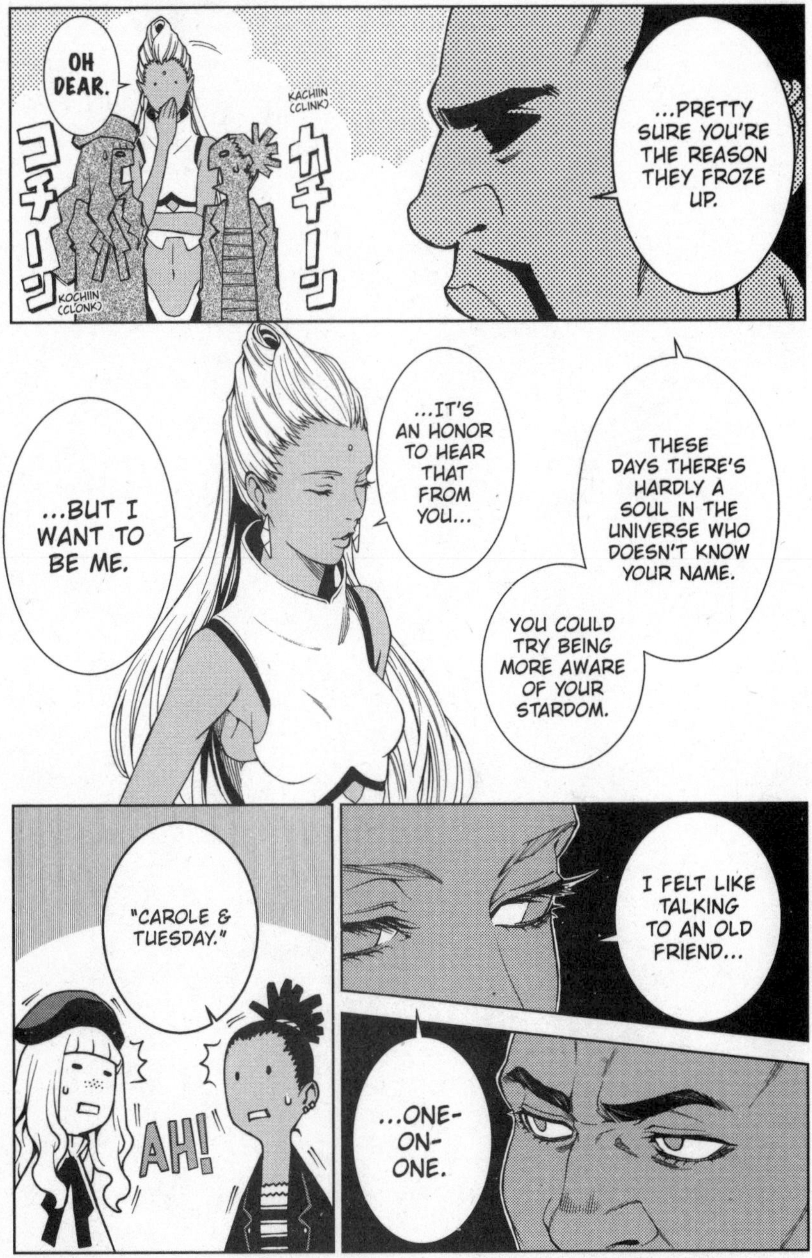
...PRETTY SURE YOU'RE THE REASON THEY FROZE UP.
OH DEAR.
カチーン
KACHIIN (CLINK)
コチーン
KOCHIIN (CLONK)
THESE DAYS THERE'S HARDLY A SOUL IN THE UNIVERSE WHO DOESN'T KNOW YOUR NAME.
YOU COULD TRY BEING MORE AWARE OF YOUR STARDOM.
...IT'S AN HONOR TO HEAR THAT FROM YOU...
...BUT I WANT TO BE ME.
I FELT LIKE TALKING TO AN OLD FRIEND...
...ONE-ON-ONE.
"CAROLE & TUESDAY."
AH!

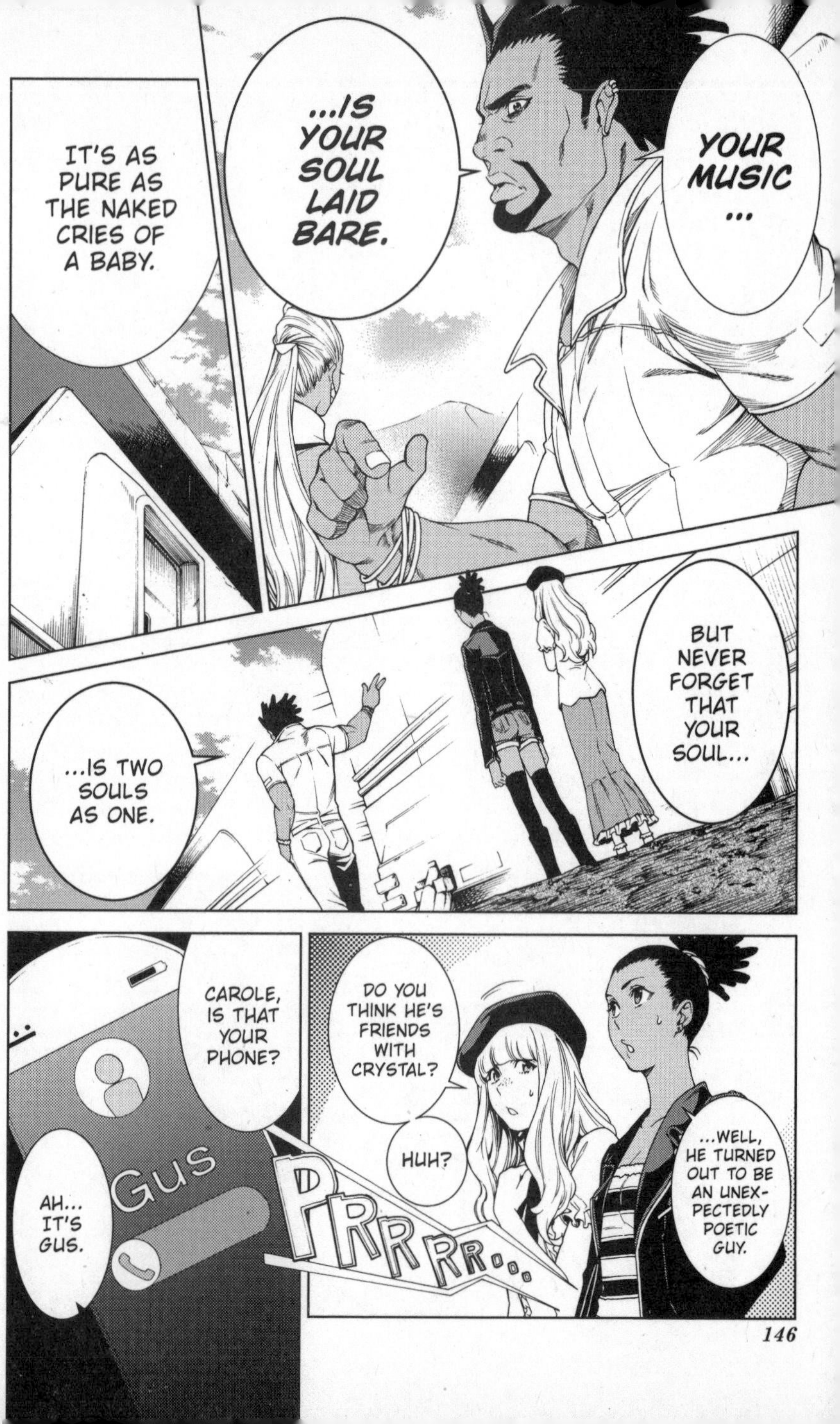
YOUR MUSIC...
...IS YOUR SOUL LAID BARE.
IT'S AS PURE AS THE NAKED CRIES OF A BABY.
BUT NEVER FORGET THAT YOUR SOUL...
...IS TWO SOULS AS ONE.
...WELL, HE TURNED OUT TO BE AN UNEX-PECTEDLY POETIC GUY.
DO YOU THINK HE'S FRIENDS WITH CRYSTAL?
HUH?
PRRRRR...
CAROLE, IS THAT YOUR PHONE?
Gus
AH... IT'S GUS.

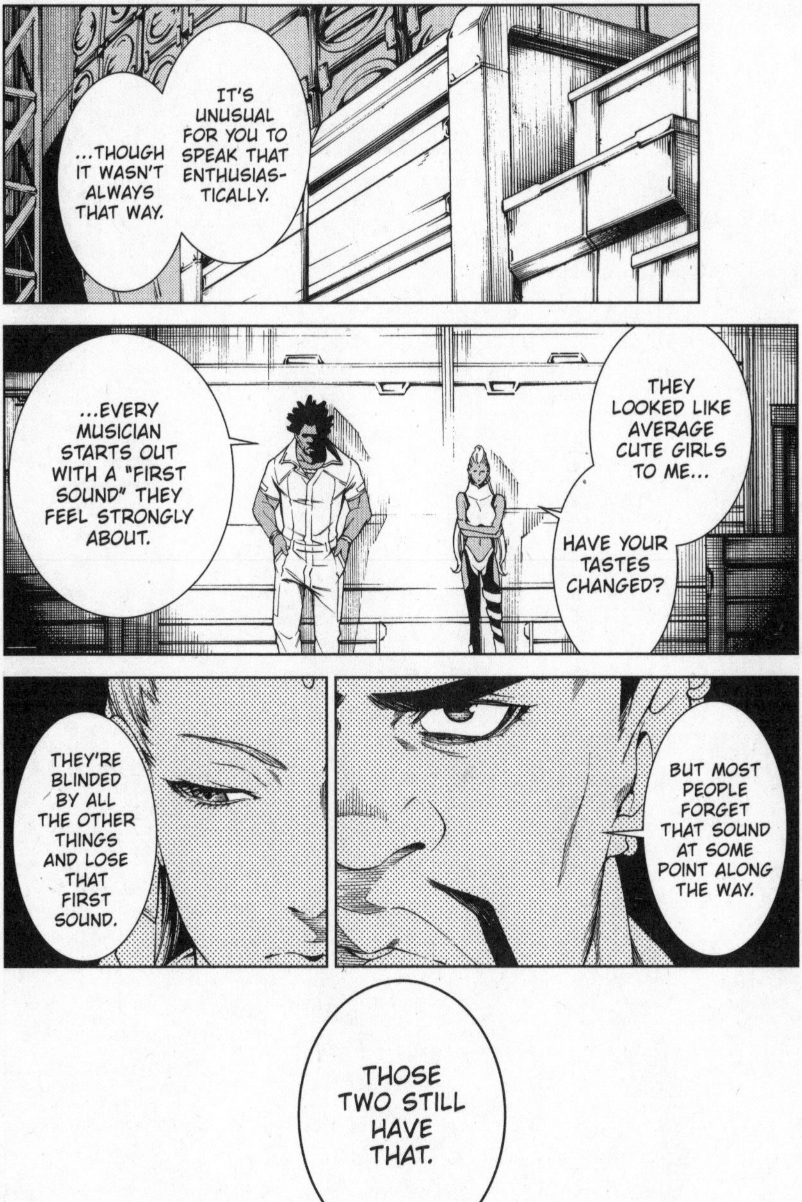
IT'S UNUSUAL FOR YOU TO SPEAK THAT ENTHUSIASTICALLY.
...THOUGH IT WASN'T ALWAYS THAT WAY.
THEY LOOKED LIKE AVERAGE CUTE GIRLS TO ME...
HAVE YOUR TASTES CHANGED?
...EVERY MUSICIAN STARTS OUT WITH A "FIRST SOUND" THEY FEEL STRONGLY ABOUT.
BUT MOST PEOPLE FORGET THAT SOUND AT SOME POINT ALONG THE WAY.
THEY'RE BLINDED BY ALL THE OTHER THINGS AND LOSE THAT FIRST SOUND.
THOSE TWO STILL HAVE THAT.

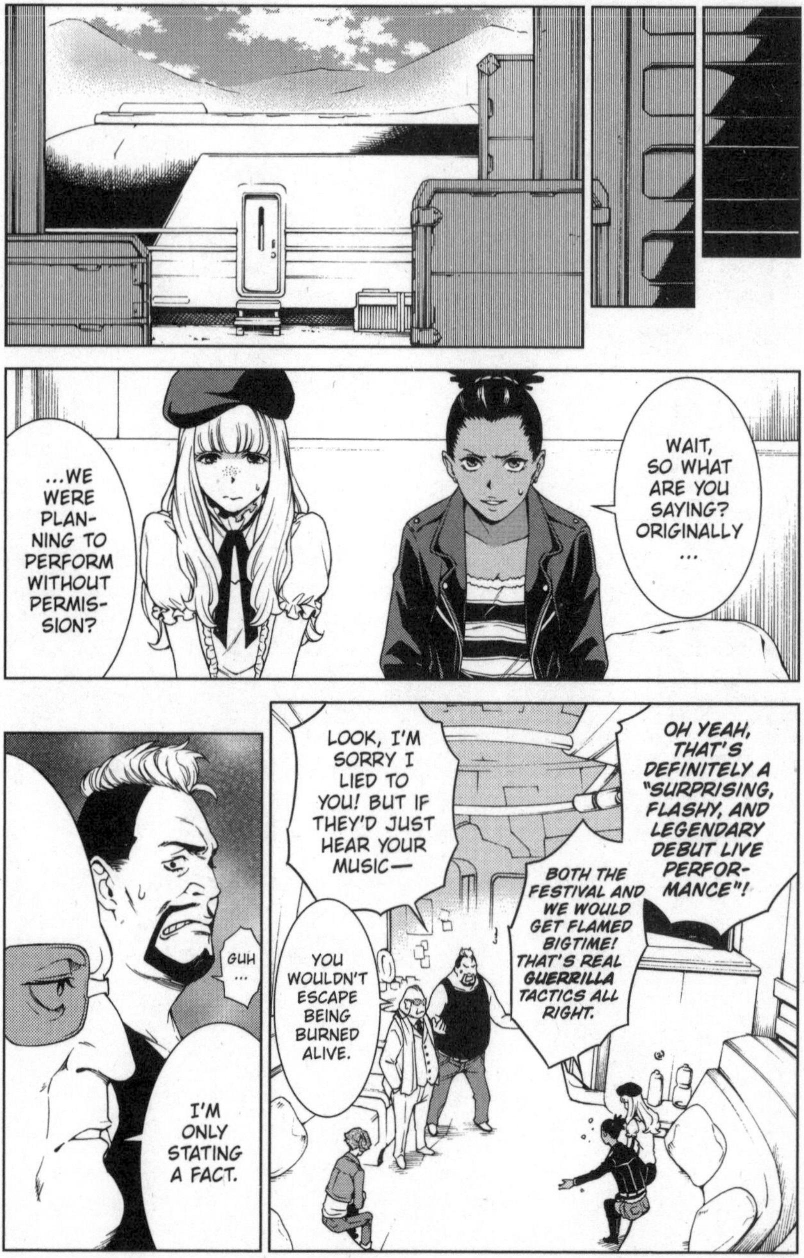
WAIT, SO WHAT ARE YOU SAYING? ORIGINALLY ...
...WE WERE PLAN-NING TO PERFORM WITHOUT PERMIS-SION?
OH YEAH, THAT'S DEFINITELY A "SURPRISING, FLASHY, AND LEGENDARY DEBUT LIVE PERFOR-MANCE"!
LOOK, I'M SORRY I LIED TO YOU! BUT IF THEY'D JUST HEAR YOUR MUSIC—
BOTH THE FESTIVAL AND WE WOULD GET FLAMED BIGTIME! THAT'S REAL GUERRILLA TACTICS ALL RIGHT.
YOU WOULDN'T ESCAPE BEING BURNED ALIVE.
GUH ...
I'M ONLY STATING A FACT.

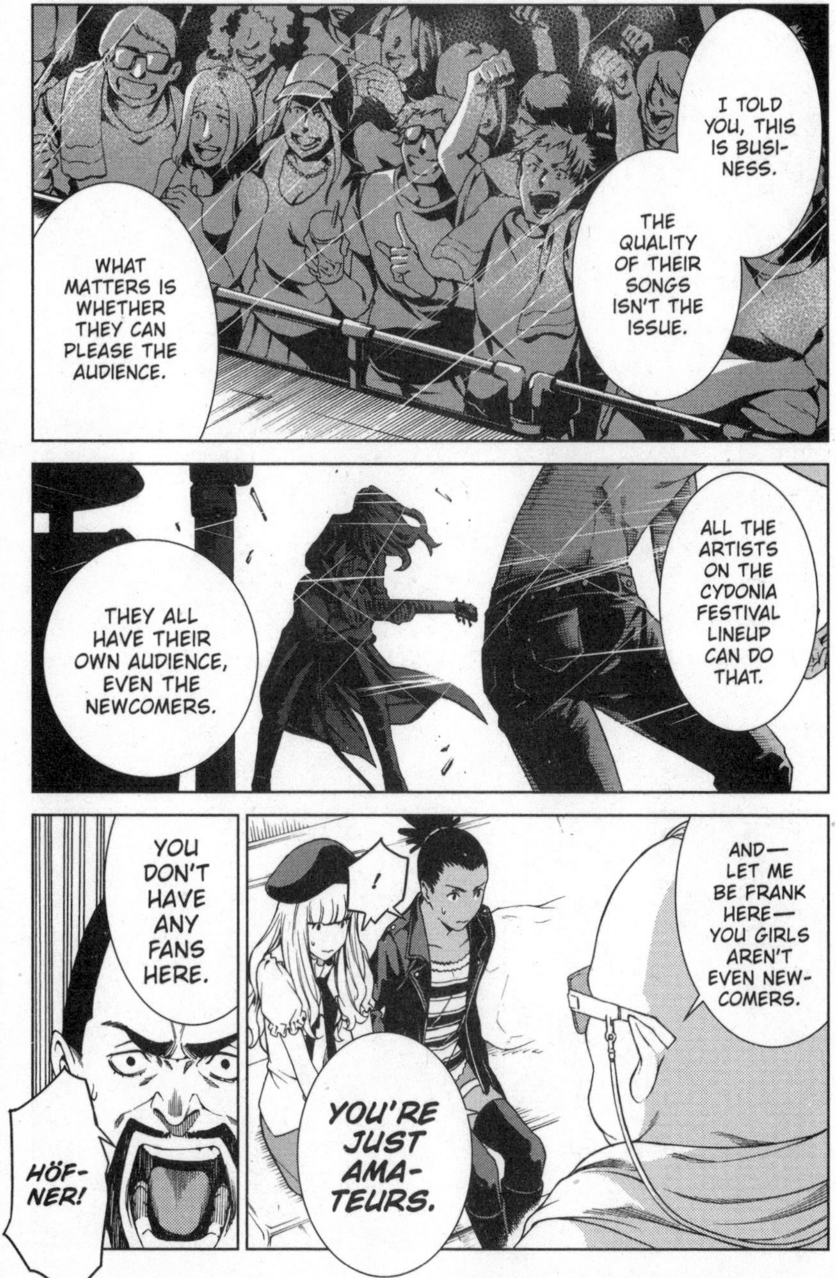
I TOLD YOU, THIS IS BUSINESS.
THE QUALITY OF THEIR SONGS ISN'T THE ISSUE.
WHAT MATTERS IS WHETHER THEY CAN PLEASE THE AUDIENCE.
ALL THE ARTISTS ON THE CYDONIA FESTIVAL LINEUP CAN DO THAT.
THEY ALL HAVE THEIR OWN AUDIENCE, EVEN THE NEWCOMERS.
AND—LET ME BE FRANK HERE—YOU GIRLS AREN'T EVEN NEWCOMERS.
!
YOU'RE JUST AMATEURS.
YOU DON'T HAVE ANY FANS HERE.
HÖFNER!

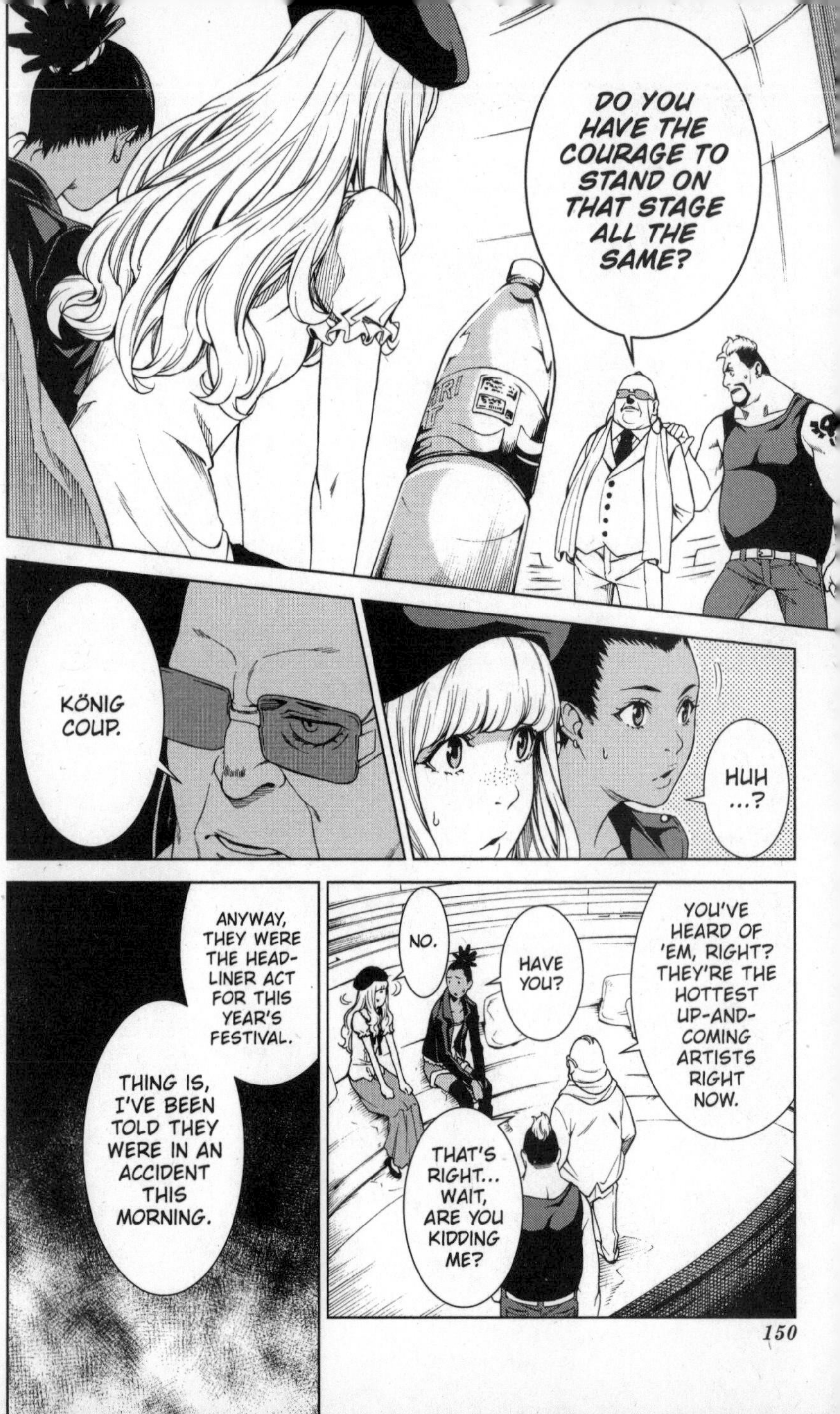
DO YOU HAVE THE COURAGE TO STAND ON THAT STAGE ALL THE SAME?
HUH ...?
KÖNIG COUP.
YOU'VE HEARD OF 'EM, RIGHT? THEY'RE THE HOTTEST UP-AND-COMING ARTISTS RIGHT NOW.
HAVE YOU?
NO.
THAT'S RIGHT... WAIT, ARE YOU KIDDING ME?
ANYWAY, THEY WERE THE HEAD-LINER ACT FOR THIS YEAR'S FESTIVAL.
THING IS, I'VE BEEN TOLD THEY WERE IN AN ACCIDENT THIS MORNING.

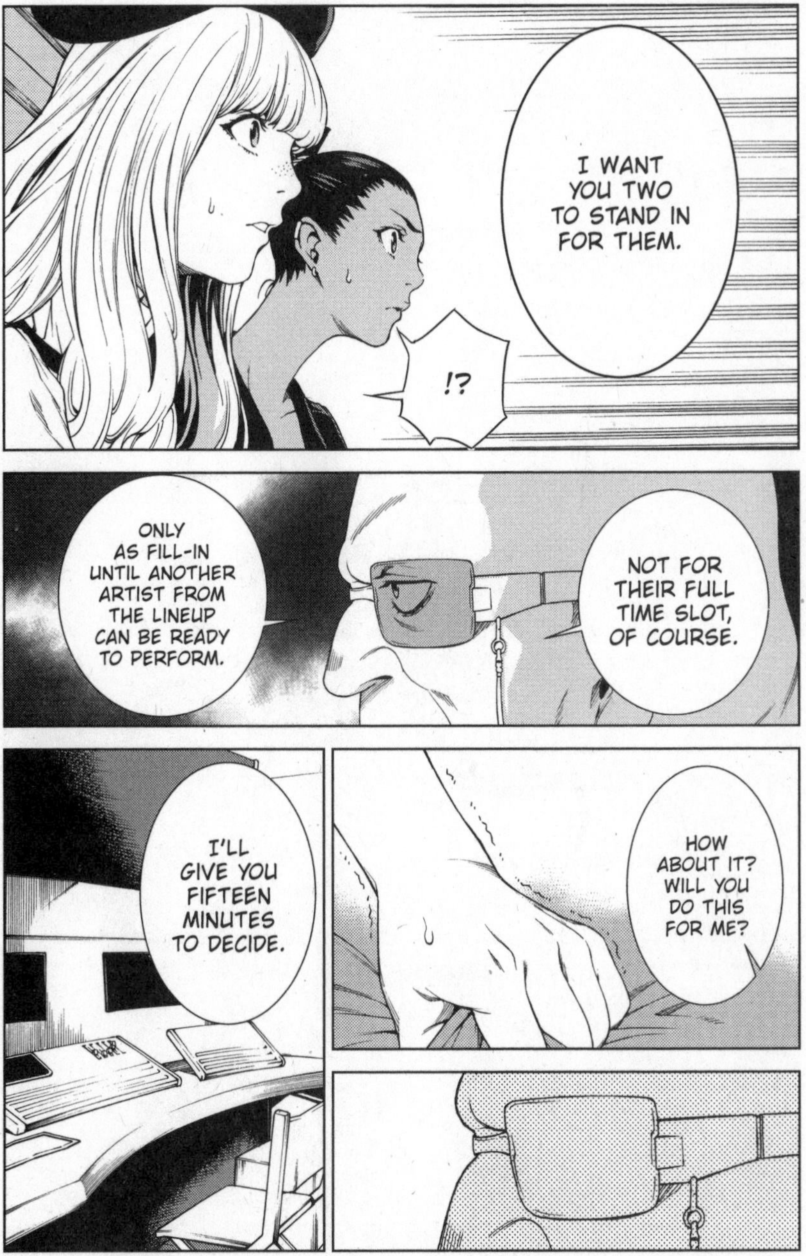
I WANT YOU TWO TO STAND IN FOR THEM.
!?
NOT FOR THEIR FULL TIME SLOT, OF COURSE.
ONLY AS FILL-IN UNTIL ANOTHER ARTIST FROM THE LINEUP CAN BE READY TO PERFORM.
HOW ABOUT IT? WILL YOU DO THIS FOR ME?
I'LL GIVE YOU FIFTEEN MINUTES TO DECIDE.

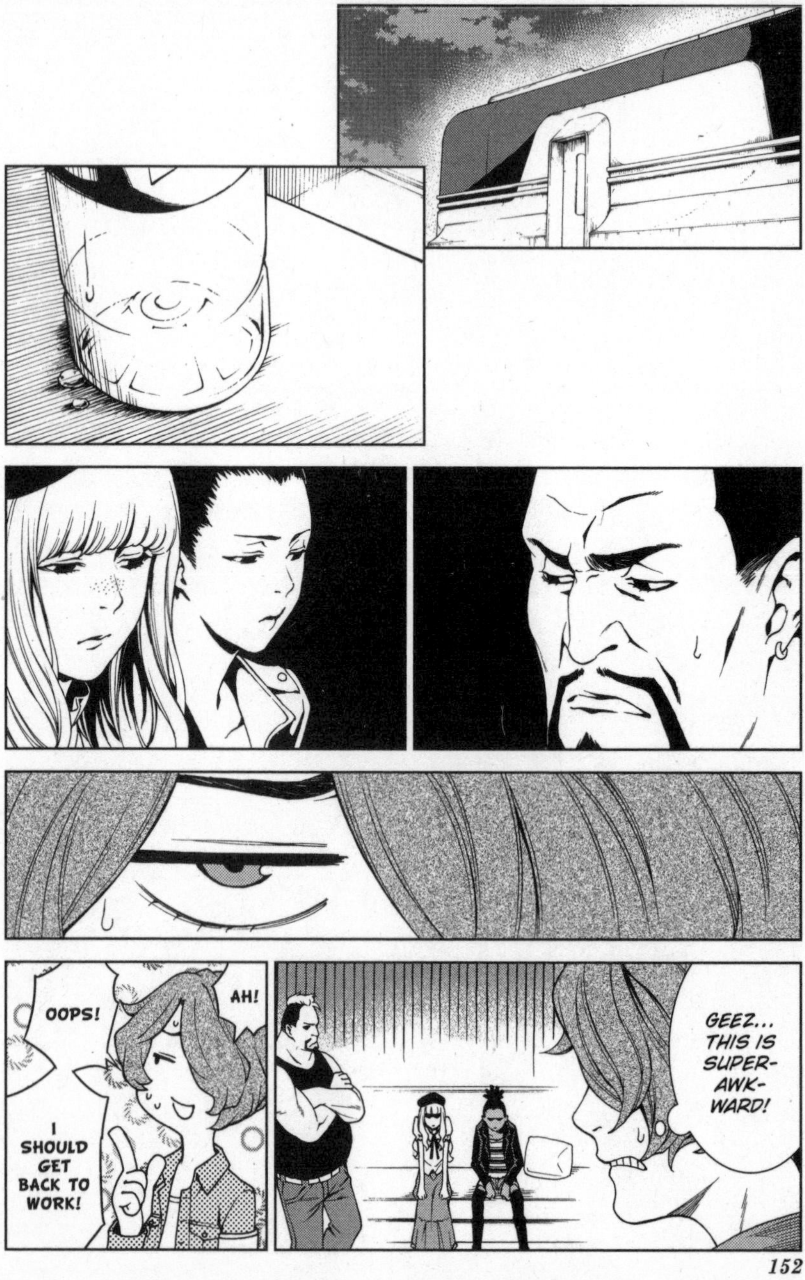
GEEZ... THIS IS SUPER-AWK-WARD!
AH!
OOPS!
I SHOULD GET BACK TO WORK!

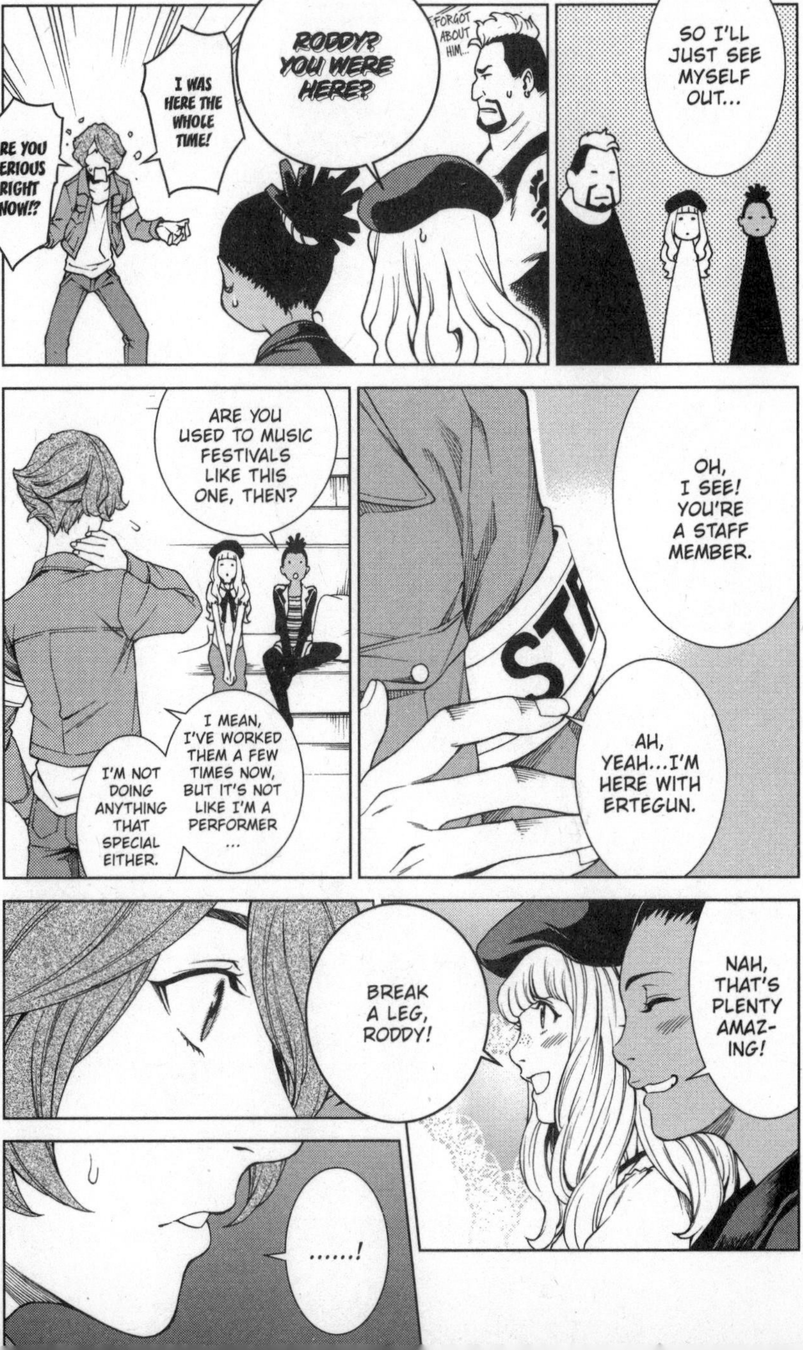
SO I'LL JUST SEE MYSELF OUT...
FORGOT ABOUT HIM...
RODDY? YOU WERE HERE?
I WAS HERE THE WHOLE TIME!
ARE YOU SERIOUS RIGHT NOW!?
OH, I SEE! YOU'RE A STAFF MEMBER.
AH, YEAH...I'M HERE WITH ERTEGUN.
ARE YOU USED TO MUSIC FESTIVALS LIKE THIS ONE, THEN?
I MEAN, I'VE WORKED THEM A FEW TIMES NOW, BUT IT'S NOT LIKE I'M A PERFORMER...
I'M NOT DOING ANYTHING THAT SPECIAL EITHER.
NAH, THAT'S PLENTY AMAZ-ING!
BREAK A LEG, RODDY!
......!

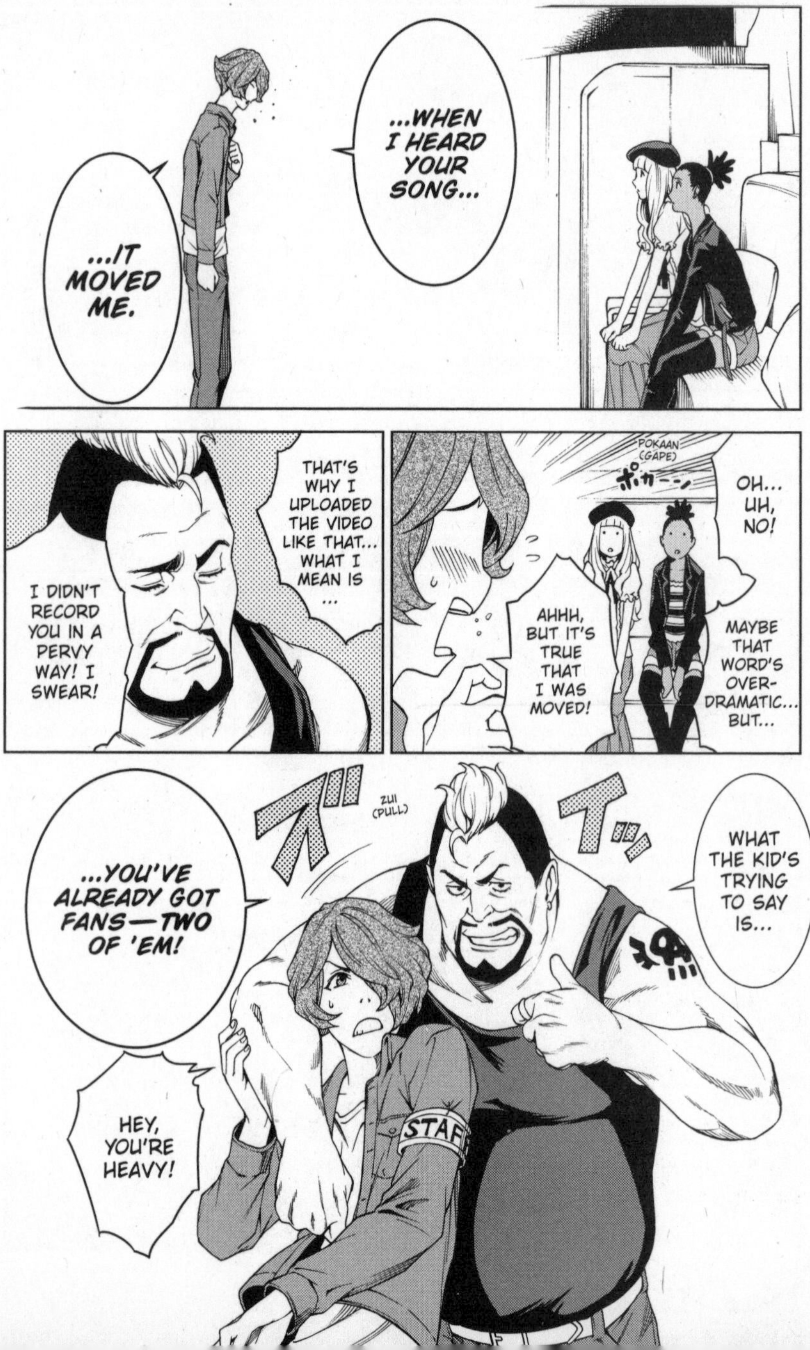
...WHEN I HEARD YOUR SONG...
...IT MOVED ME.
POKAAN (GAPE)
OH... UH, NO!
MAYBE THAT WORD'S OVER-DRAMATIC... BUT...
AHHH, BUT IT'S TRUE THAT I WAS MOVED!
THAT'S WHY I UPLOADED THE VIDEO LIKE THAT... WHAT I MEAN IS ...
I DIDN'T RECORD YOU IN A PERVY WAY! I SWEAR!
WHAT THE KID'S TRYING TO SAY IS...
ZUI (PULL)
...YOU'VE ALREADY GOT FANS—TWO OF 'EM!
HEY, YOU'RE HEAVY!

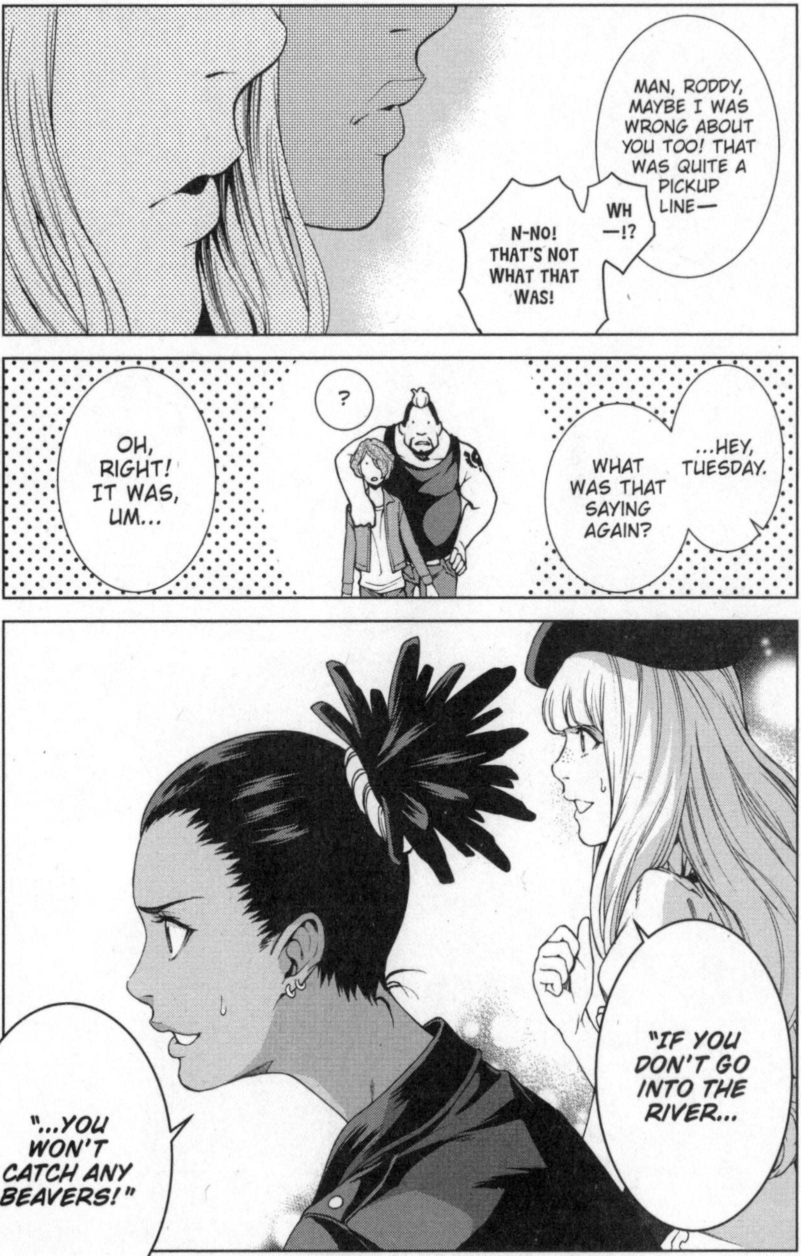
MAN, RODDY, MAYBE I WAS WRONG ABOUT YOU TOO! THAT WAS QUITE A PICKUP LINE—
WH—!?
N-NO! THAT'S NOT WHAT THAT WAS!
...HEY, TUESDAY.
WHAT WAS THAT SAYING AGAIN?
?
OH, RIGHT! IT WAS, UM...
"IF YOU DON'T GO INTO THE RIVER...
"...YOU WON'T CATCH ANY BEAVERS!"

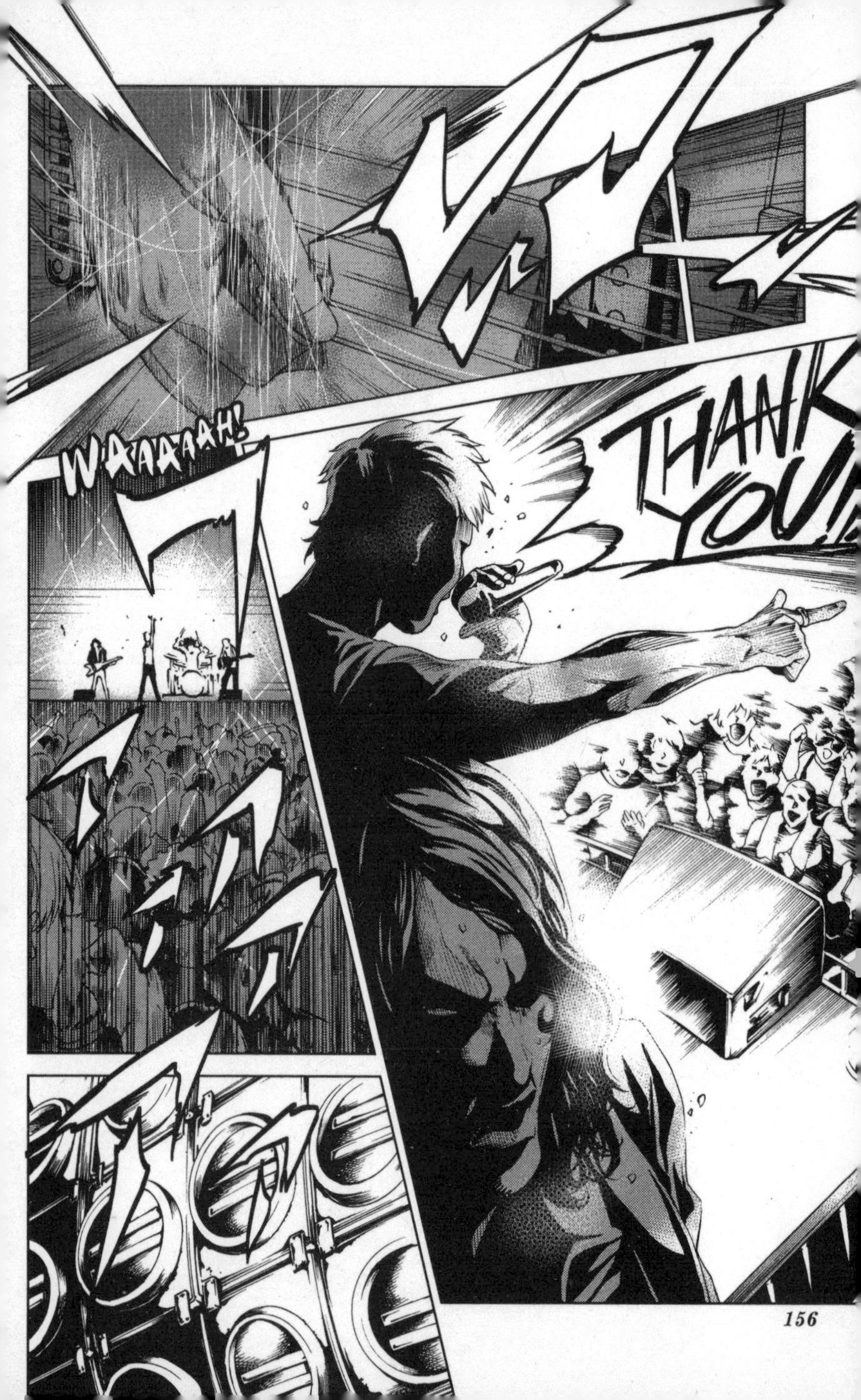
THANK YOU!!
WAAAAAH!

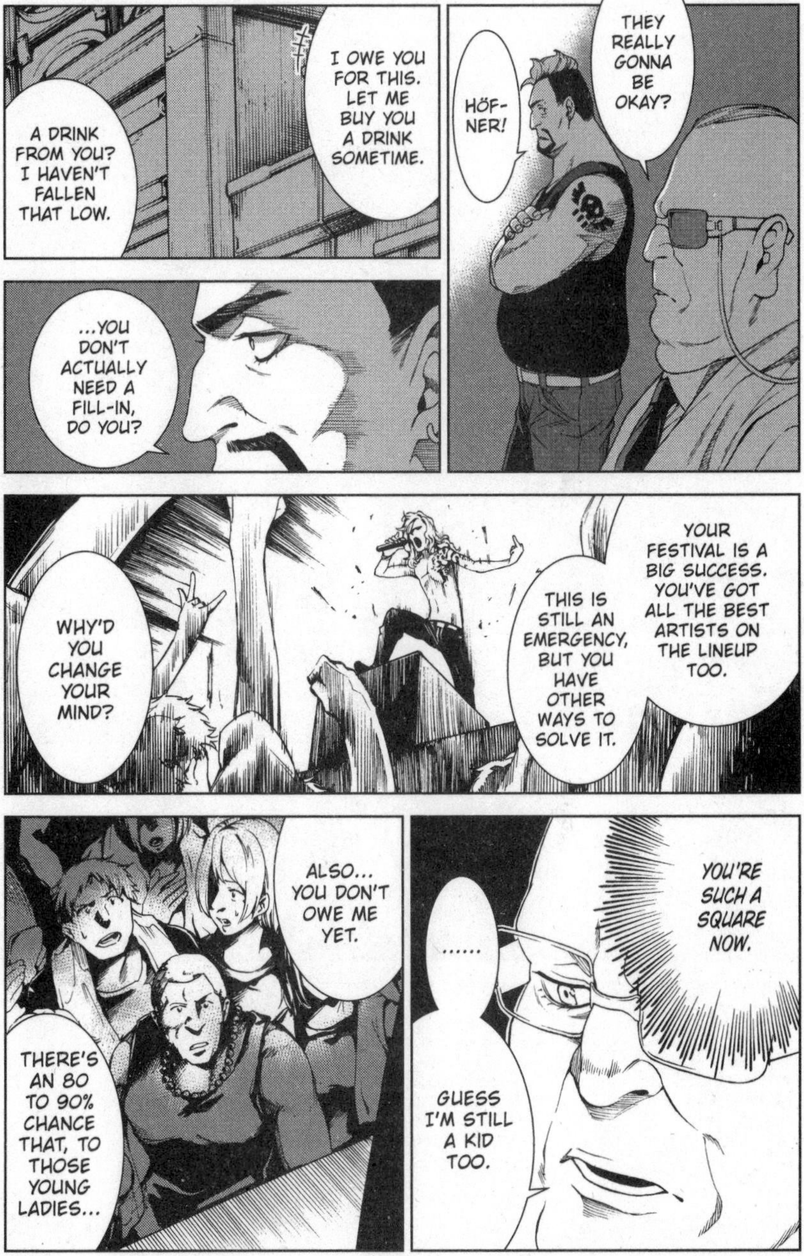
THEY REALLY GONNA BE OKAY?
HÖF-NER!
I OWE YOU FOR THIS. LET ME BUY YOU A DRINK SOMETIME.
A DRINK FROM YOU? I HAVEN'T FALLEN THAT LOW.
...YOU DON'T ACTUALLY NEED A FILL-IN, DO YOU?
YOUR FESTIVAL IS A BIG SUCCESS. YOU'VE GOT ALL THE BEST ARTISTS ON THE LINEUP TOO.
THIS IS STILL AN EMERGENCY, BUT YOU HAVE OTHER WAYS TO SOLVE IT.
WHY'D YOU CHANGE YOUR MIND?
YOU'RE SUCH A SQUARE NOW.
......
GUESS I'M STILL A KID TOO.
ALSO... YOU DON'T OWE ME YET.
THERE'S AN 80 TO 90% CHANCE THAT, TO THOSE YOUNG LADIES...

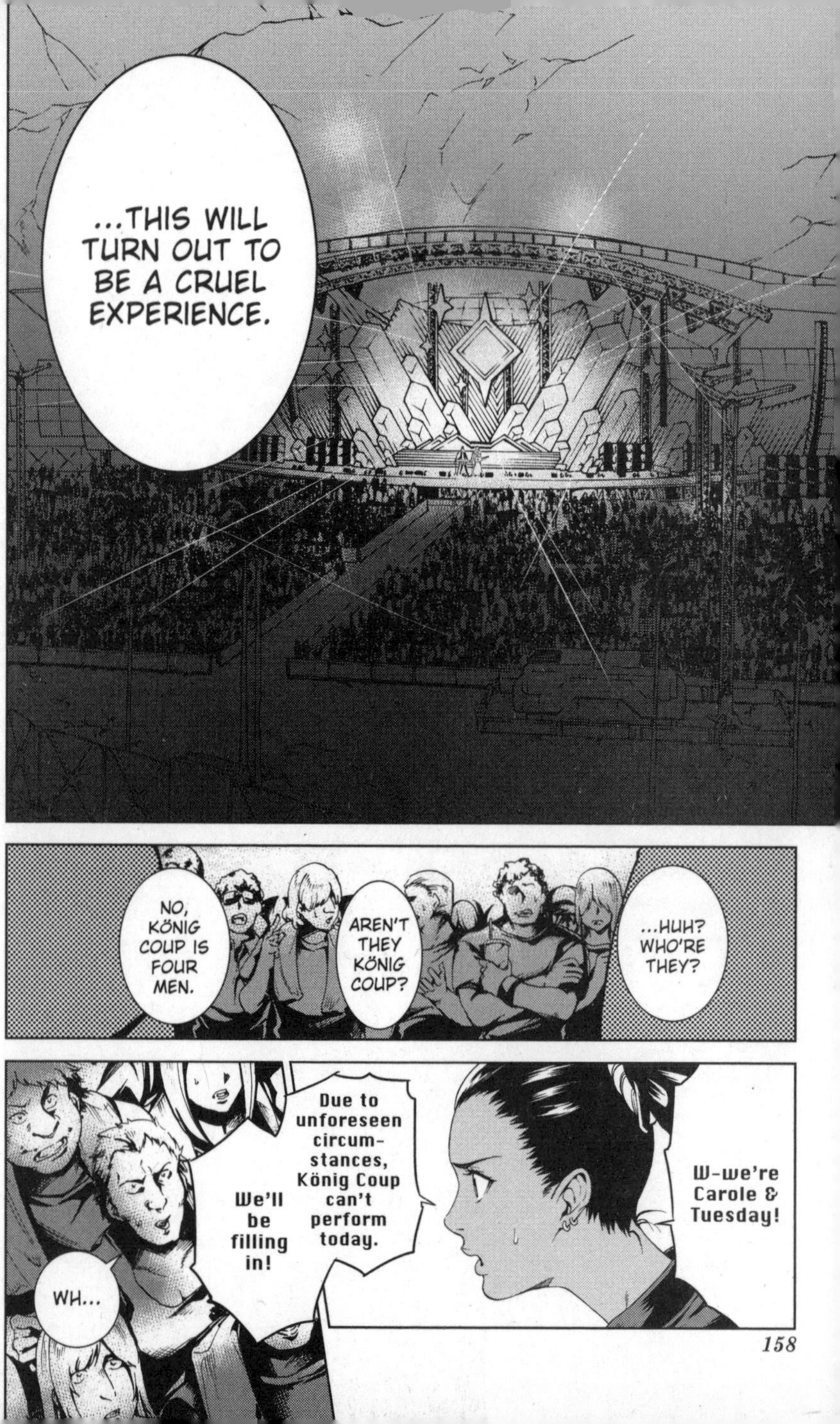
...THIS WILL TURN OUT TO BE A CRUEL EXPERIENCE.
...HUH? WHO'RE THEY?
AREN'T THEY KÖNIG COUP?
NO, KÖNIG COUP IS FOUR MEN.
W-we're Carole & Tuesday!
Due to unforeseen circumstances, König Coup can't perform today.
We'll be filling in!
WH...

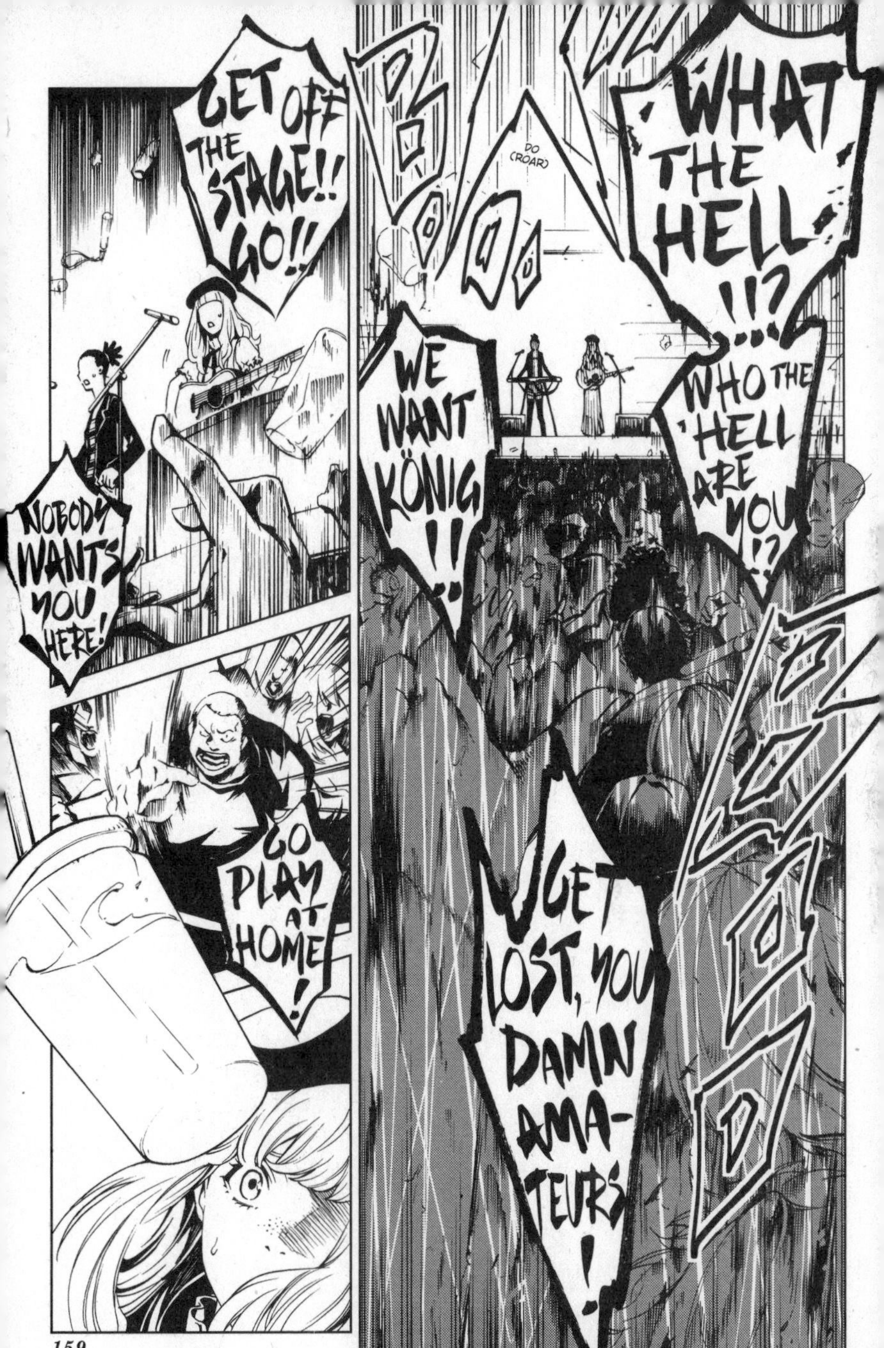
WHAT THE HELL!!?...
DO (ROAR)
WHO THE HELL ARE YOU!?
WE WANT KÖNIG!!
GET LOST, YOU DAMN AMATEURS!
GET OFF THE STAGE!! GO!!
NOBODY WANTS YOU HERE!
GO PLAY AT HOME!

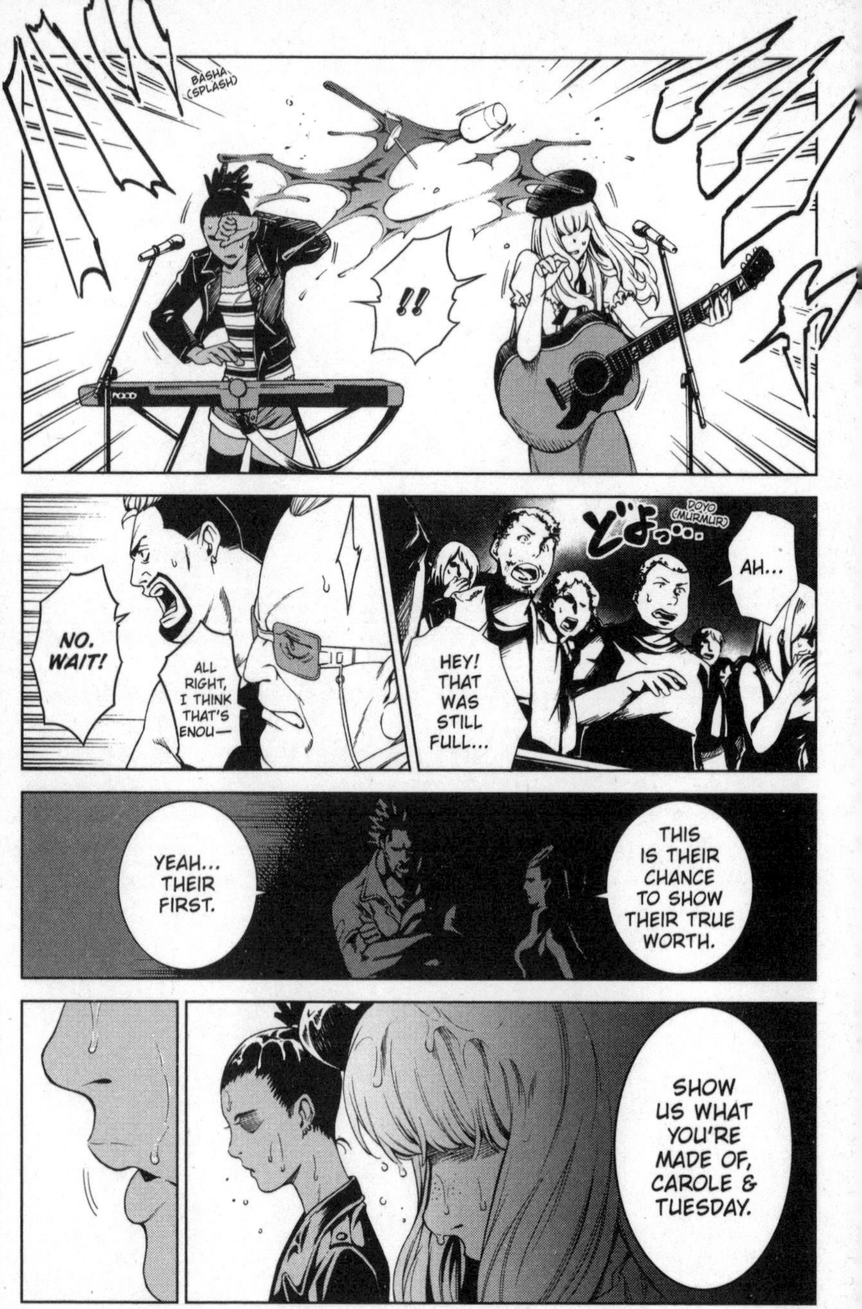
BASHA (SPLASH)
!!
DOYO (MURMUR)
どよっ…
AH...
HEY! THAT WAS STILL FULL...
ALL RIGHT, I THINK THAT'S ENOU—
NO. WAIT!
THIS IS THEIR CHANCE TO SHOW THEIR TRUE WORTH.
YEAH... THEIR FIRST.
SHOW US WHAT YOU'RE MADE OF, CAROLE & TUESDAY.

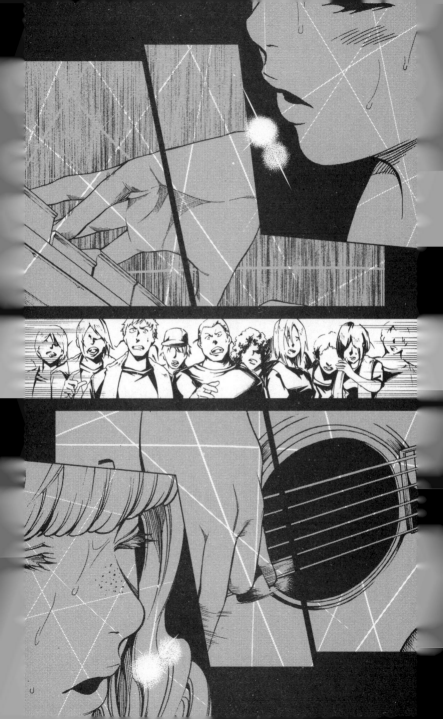

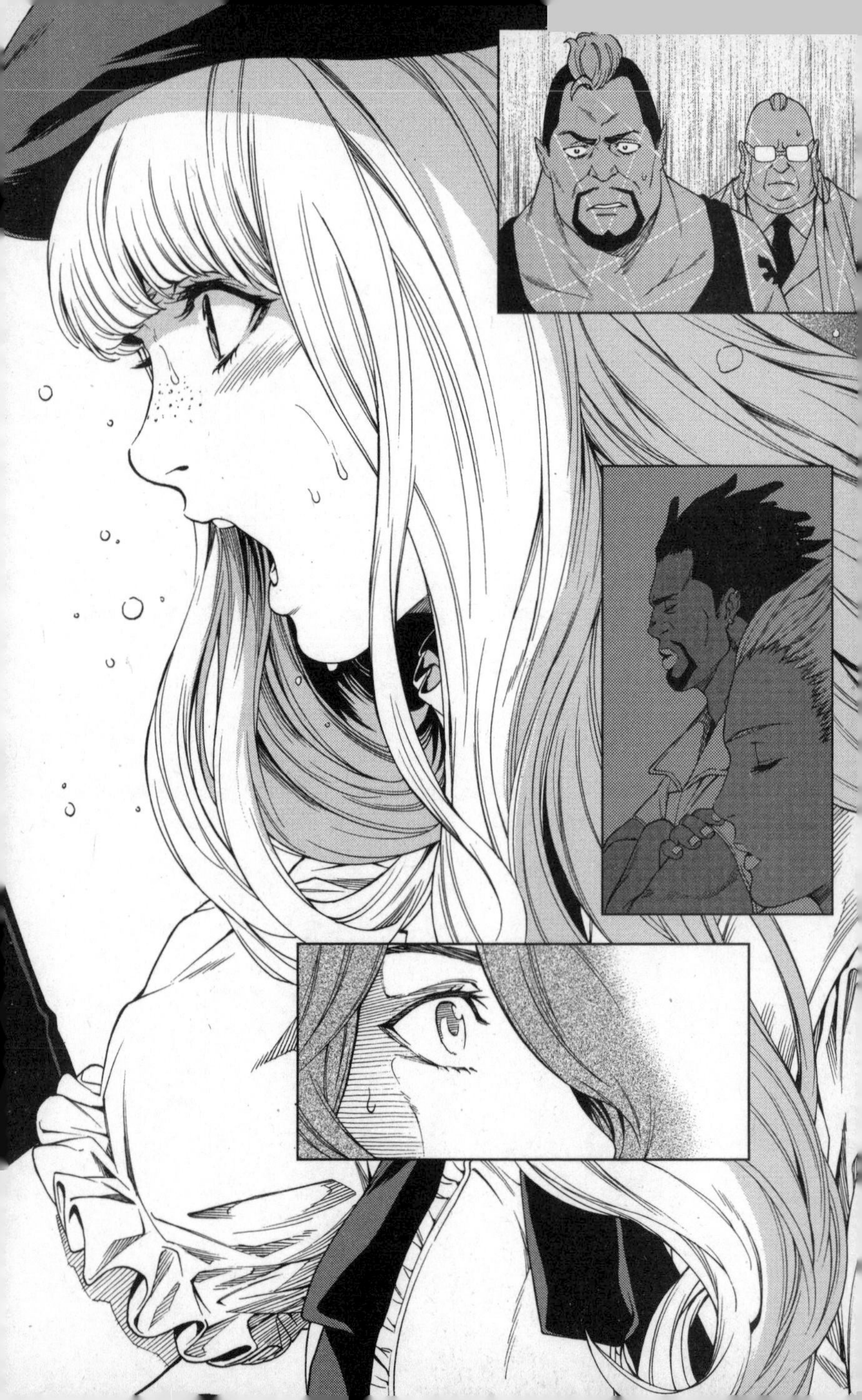

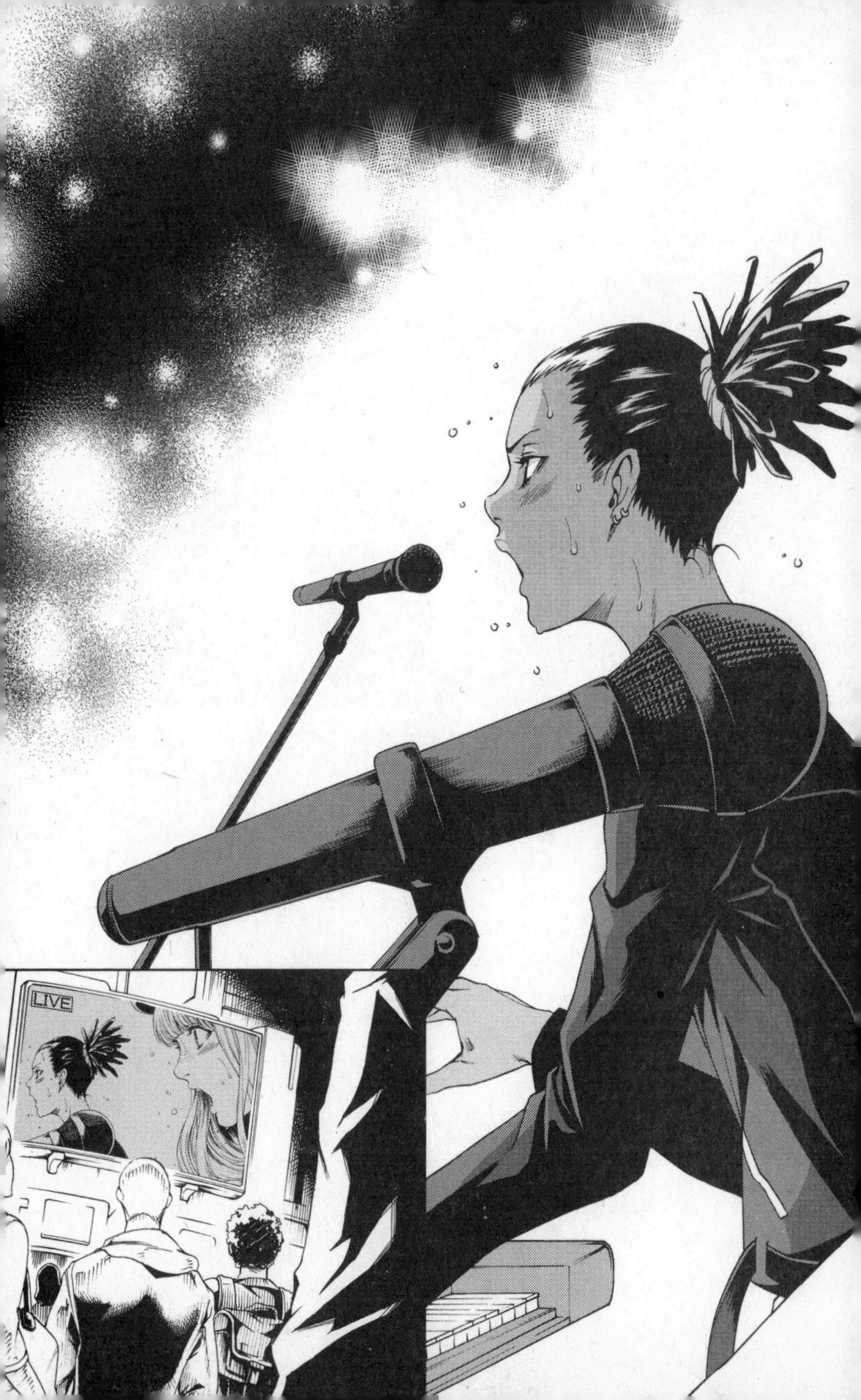
LIVE

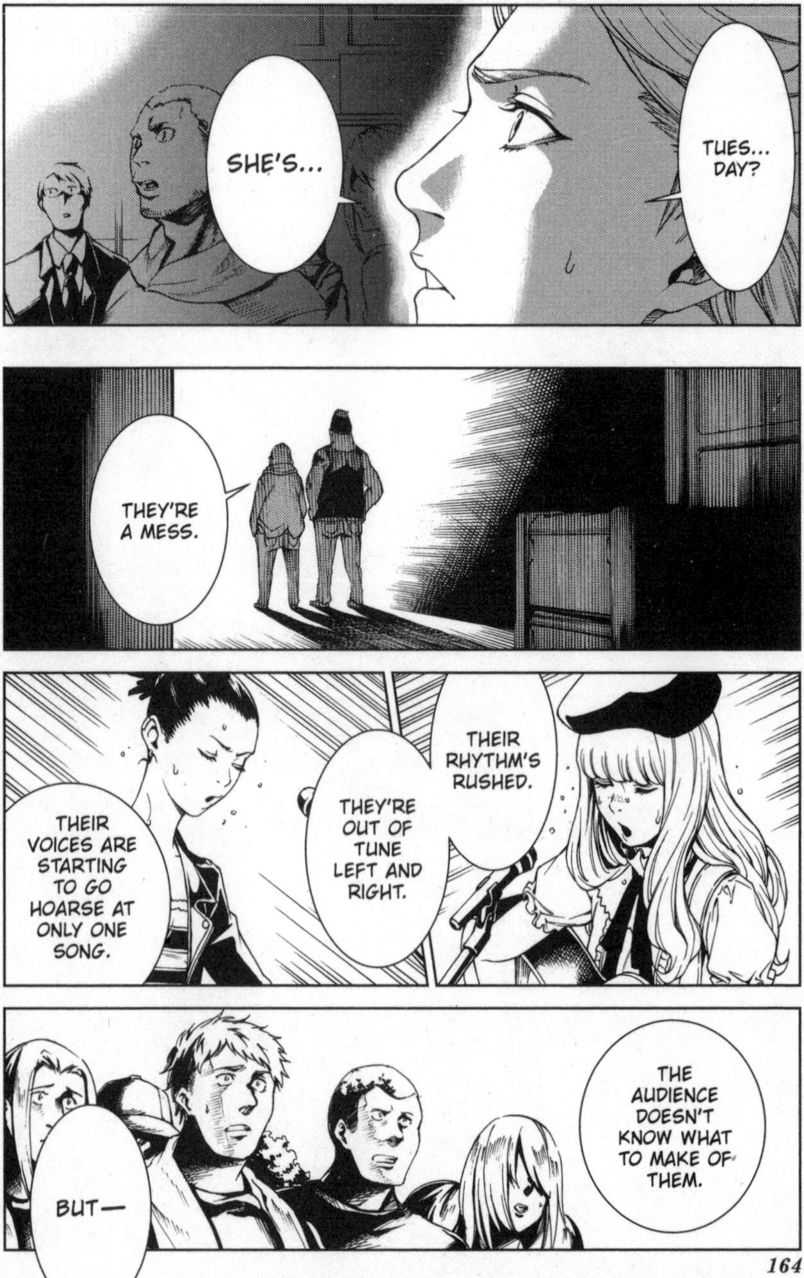
TUES... DAY?
SHE'S...
THEY'RE A MESS.
THEIR RHYTHM'S RUSHED.
THEY'RE OUT OF TUNE LEFT AND RIGHT.
THEIR VOICES ARE STARTING TO GO HOARSE AT ONLY ONE SONG.
THE AUDIENCE DOESN'T KNOW WHAT TO MAKE OF THEM.
BUT—

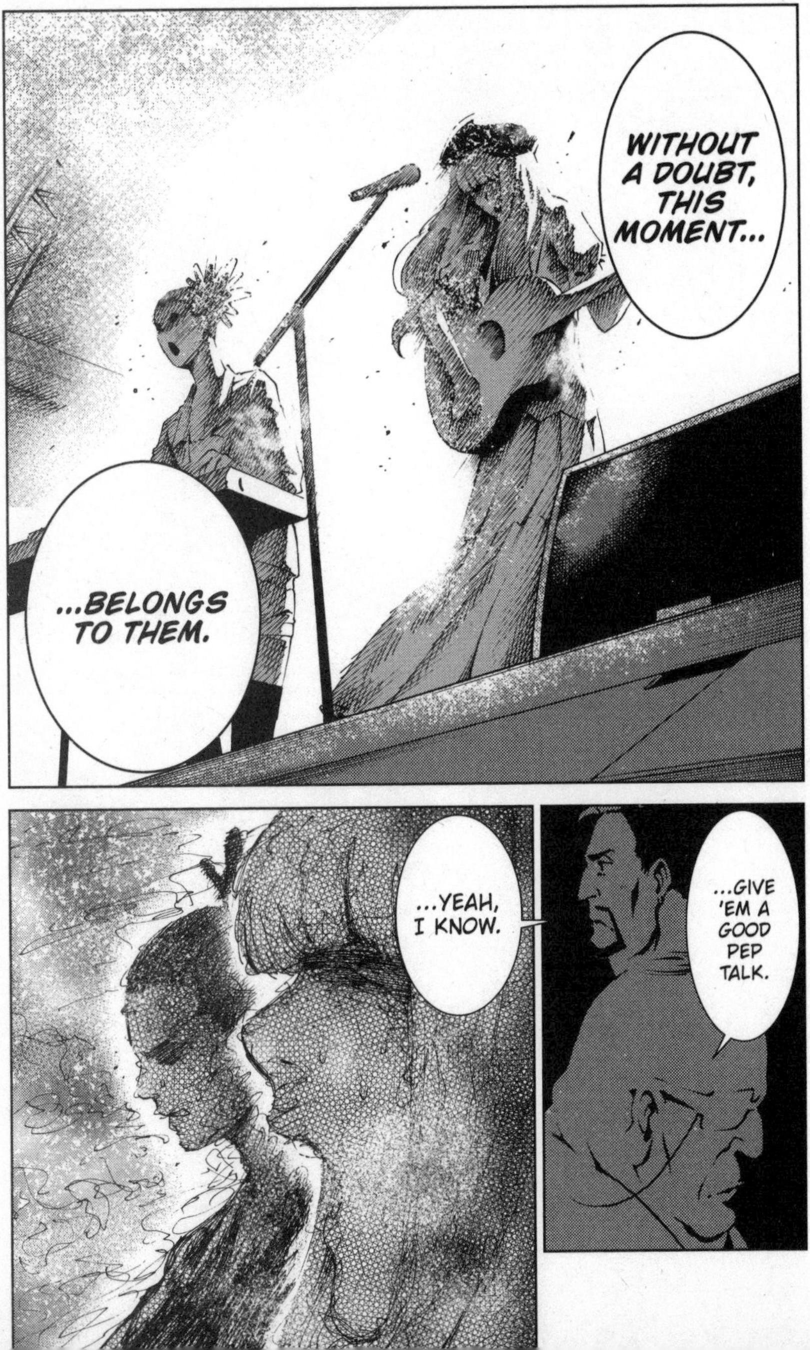
WITHOUT A DOUBT, THIS MOMENT...
...BELONGS TO THEM.
...GIVE 'EM A GOOD PEP TALK.
...YEAH, I KNOW.

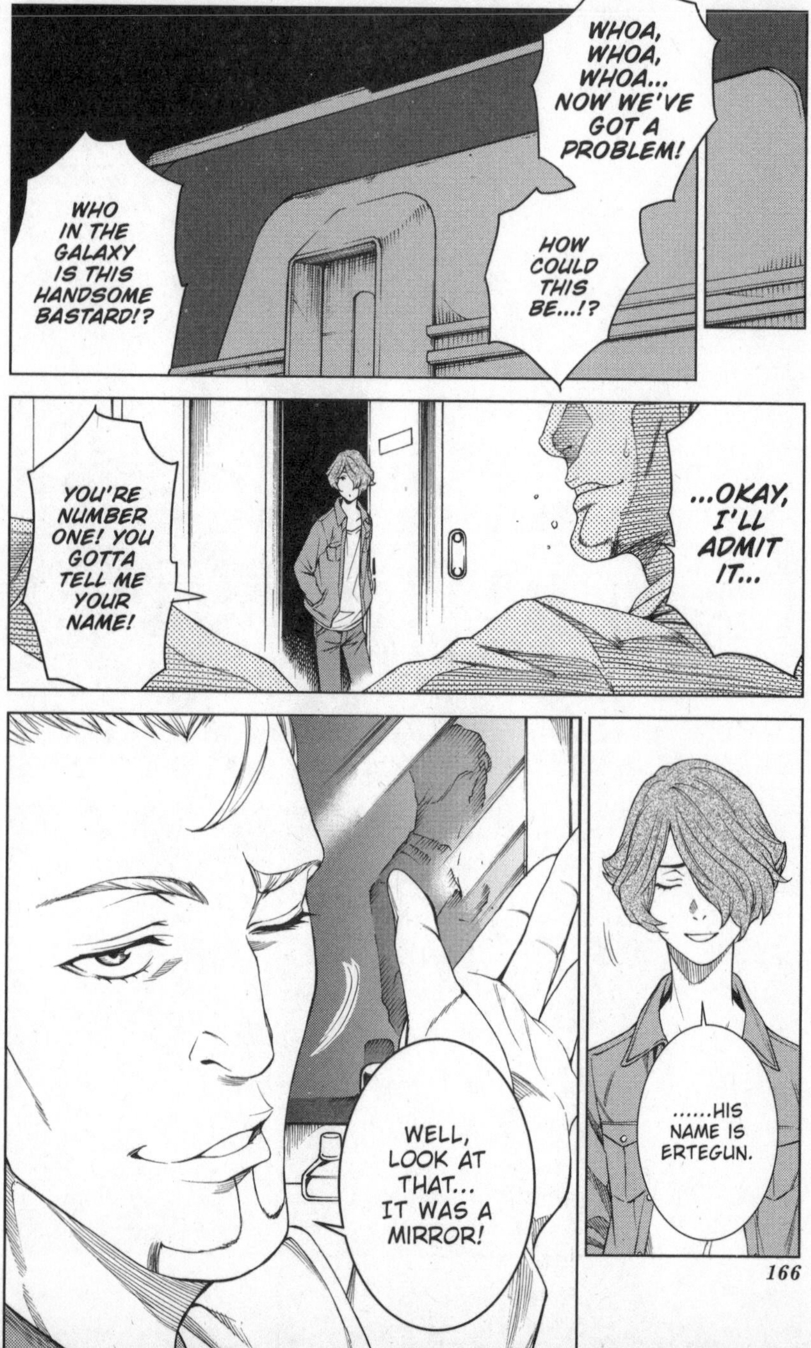
WHOA, WHOA, WHOA... NOW WE'VE GOT A PROBLEM!
HOW COULD THIS BE...!?
WHO IN THE GALAXY IS THIS HANDSOME BASTARD!?
...OKAY, I'LL ADMIT IT...
YOU'RE NUMBER ONE! YOU GOTTA TELL ME YOUR NAME!
......HIS NAME IS ERTEGUN.
WELL, LOOK AT THAT... IT WAS A MIRROR!

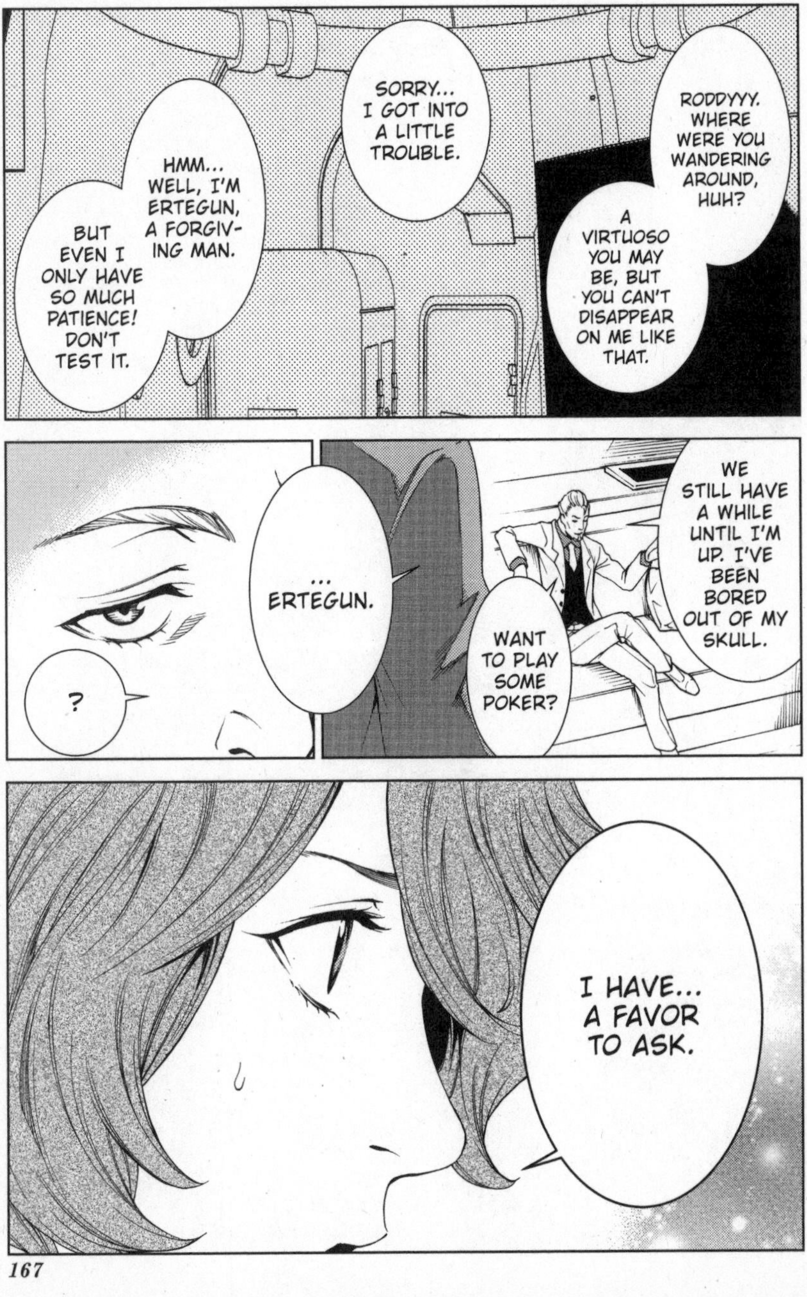
RODDYYY. WHERE WERE YOU WANDERING AROUND, HUH?
A VIRTUOSO YOU MAY BE, BUT YOU CAN'T DISAPPEAR ON ME LIKE THAT.
SORRY... I GOT INTO A LITTLE TROUBLE.
HMM... WELL, I'M ERTEGUN, A FORGIVING MAN.
BUT EVEN I ONLY HAVE SO MUCH PATIENCE! DON'T TEST IT.
WE STILL HAVE A WHILE UNTIL I'M UP. I'VE BEEN BORED OUT OF MY SKULL.
WANT TO PLAY SOME POKER?
... ERTEGUN.
?
I HAVE... A FAVOR TO ASK.

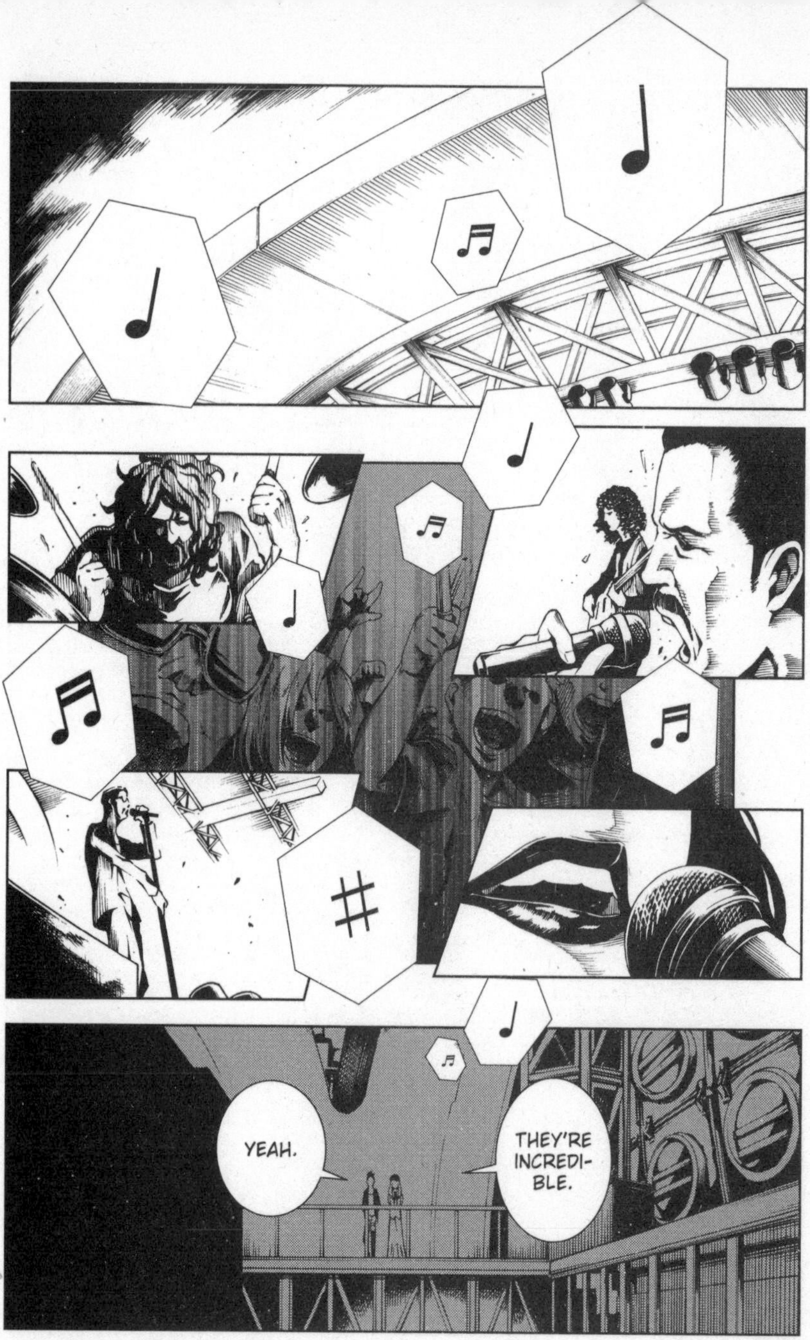
THEY'RE INCREDI-BLE.
YEAH.

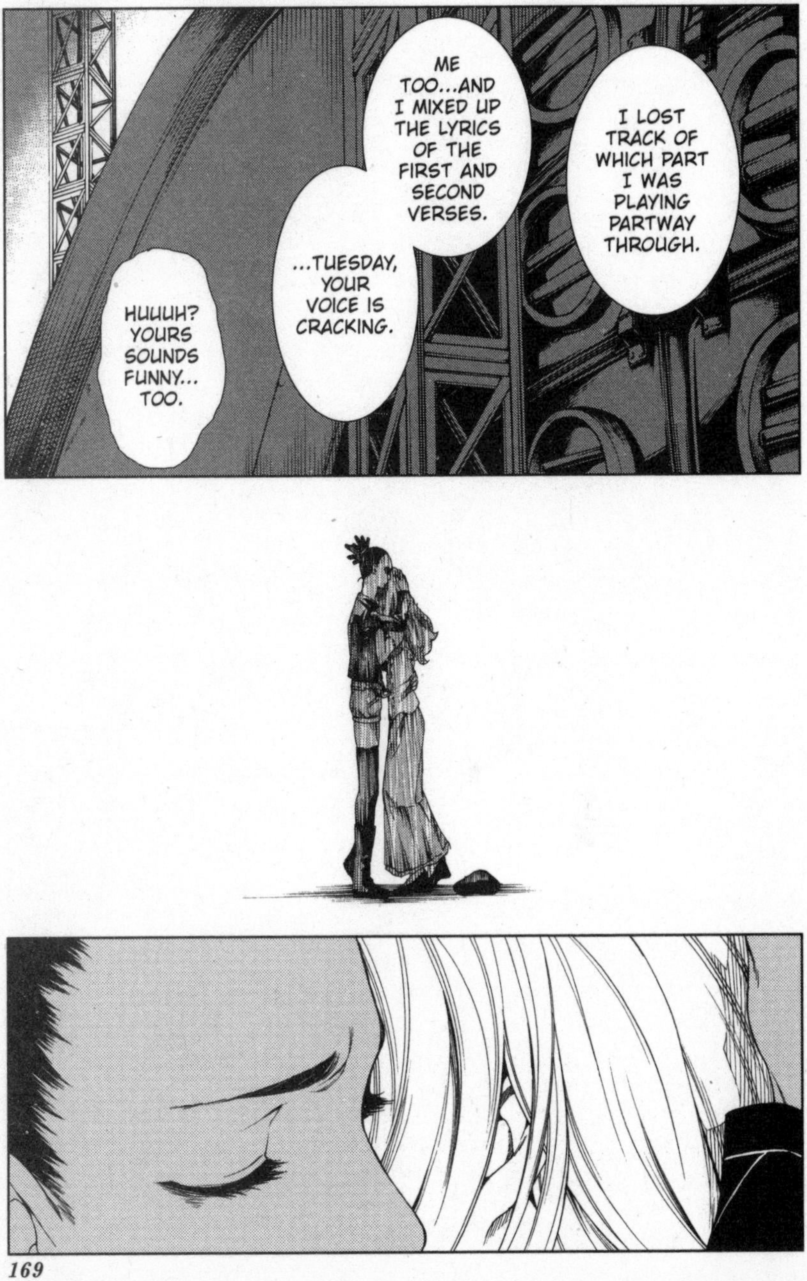
I LOST TRACK OF WHICH PART I WAS PLAYING PARTWAY THROUGH.
ME TOO...AND I MIXED UP THE LYRICS OF THE FIRST AND SECOND VERSES.
...TUESDAY, YOUR VOICE IS CRACKING.
HUUUH? YOURS SOUNDS FUNNY... TOO.

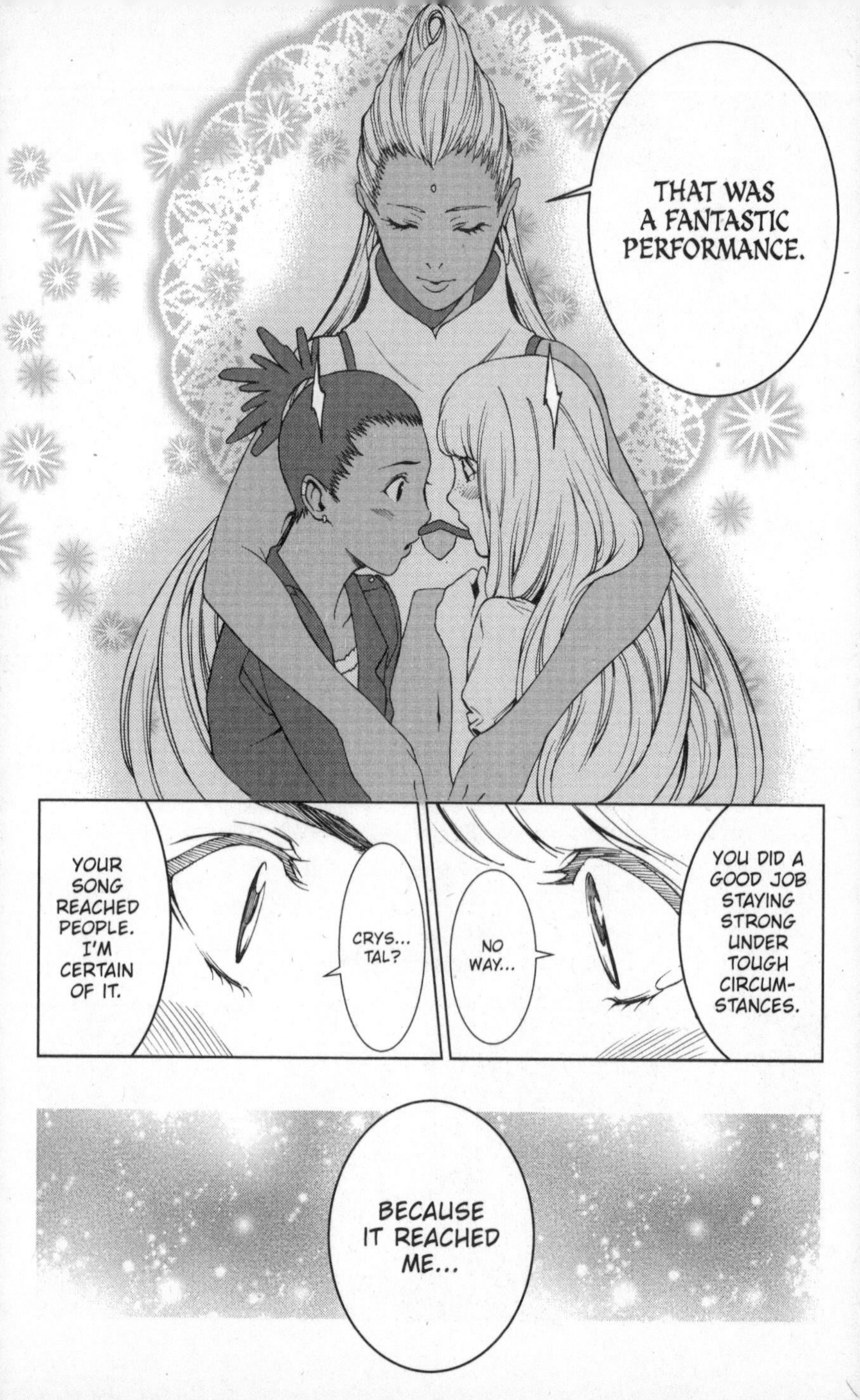
THAT WAS A FANTASTIC PERFORMANCE.
YOU DID A GOOD JOB STAYING STRONG UNDER TOUGH CIRCUM-STANCES.
NO WAY...
CRYS... TAL?
YOUR SONG REACHED PEOPLE. I'M CERTAIN OF IT.
BECAUSE IT REACHED ME...

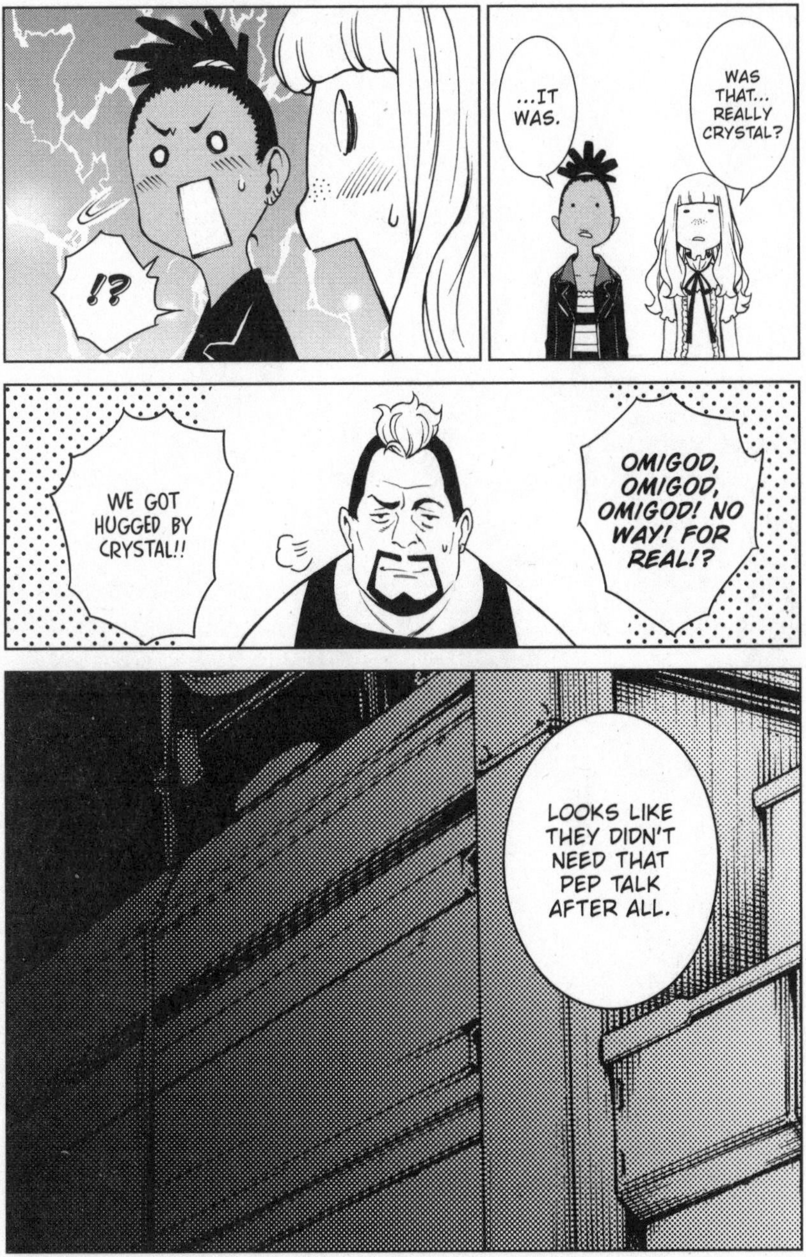
WAS THAT... REALLY CRYSTAL?
...IT WAS.
!?
OMIGOD, OMIGOD, OMIGOD! NO WAY! FOR REAL!?
WE GOT HUGGED BY CRYSTAL!!
LOOKS LIKE THEY DIDN'T NEED THAT PEP TALK AFTER ALL.

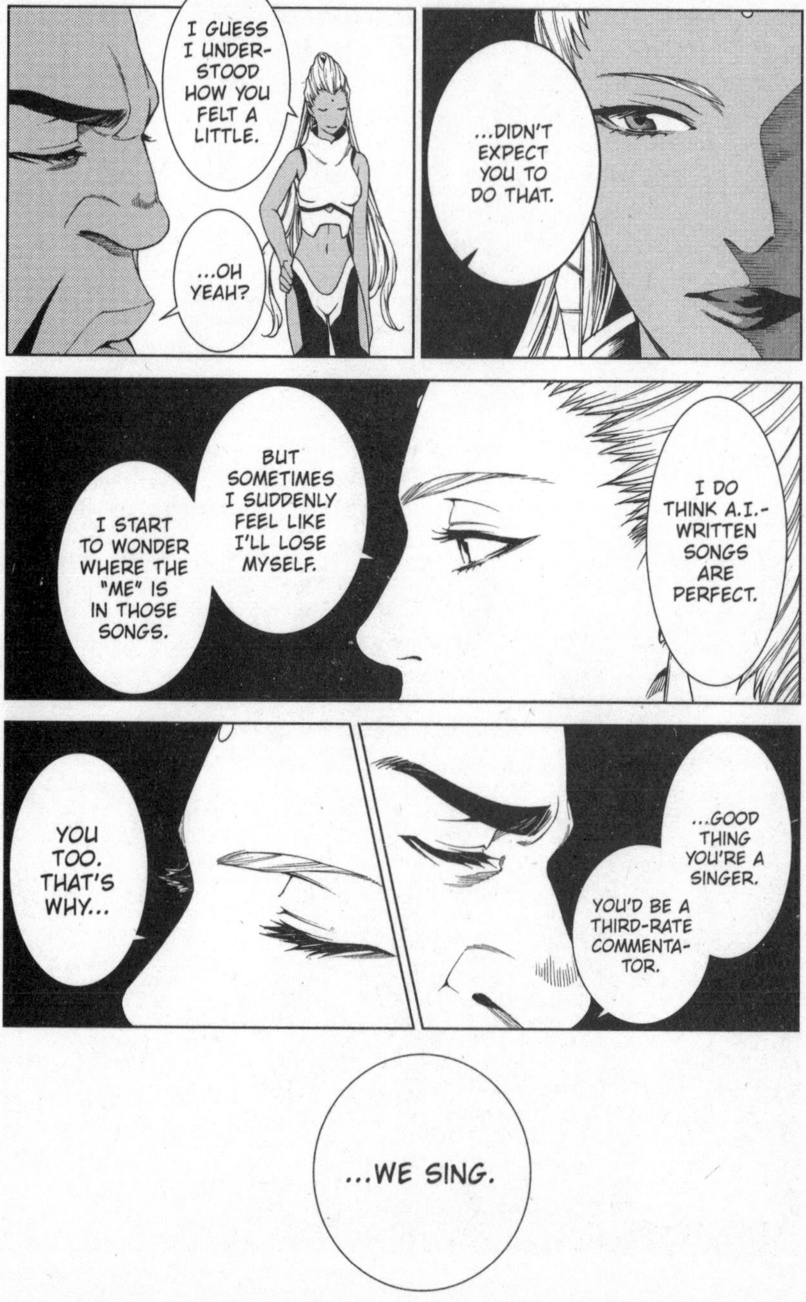
...DIDN'T EXPECT YOU TO DO THAT.
I GUESS I UNDER-STOOD HOW YOU FELT A LITTLE.
...OH YEAH?
I DO THINK A.I.-WRITTEN SONGS ARE PERFECT.
BUT SOMETIMES I SUDDENLY FEEL LIKE I'LL LOSE MYSELF.
I START TO WONDER WHERE THE "ME" IS IN THOSE SONGS.
...GOOD THING YOU'RE A SINGER.
YOU'D BE A THIRD-RATE COMMENTA-TOR.
YOU TOO. THAT'S WHY...
...WE SING.

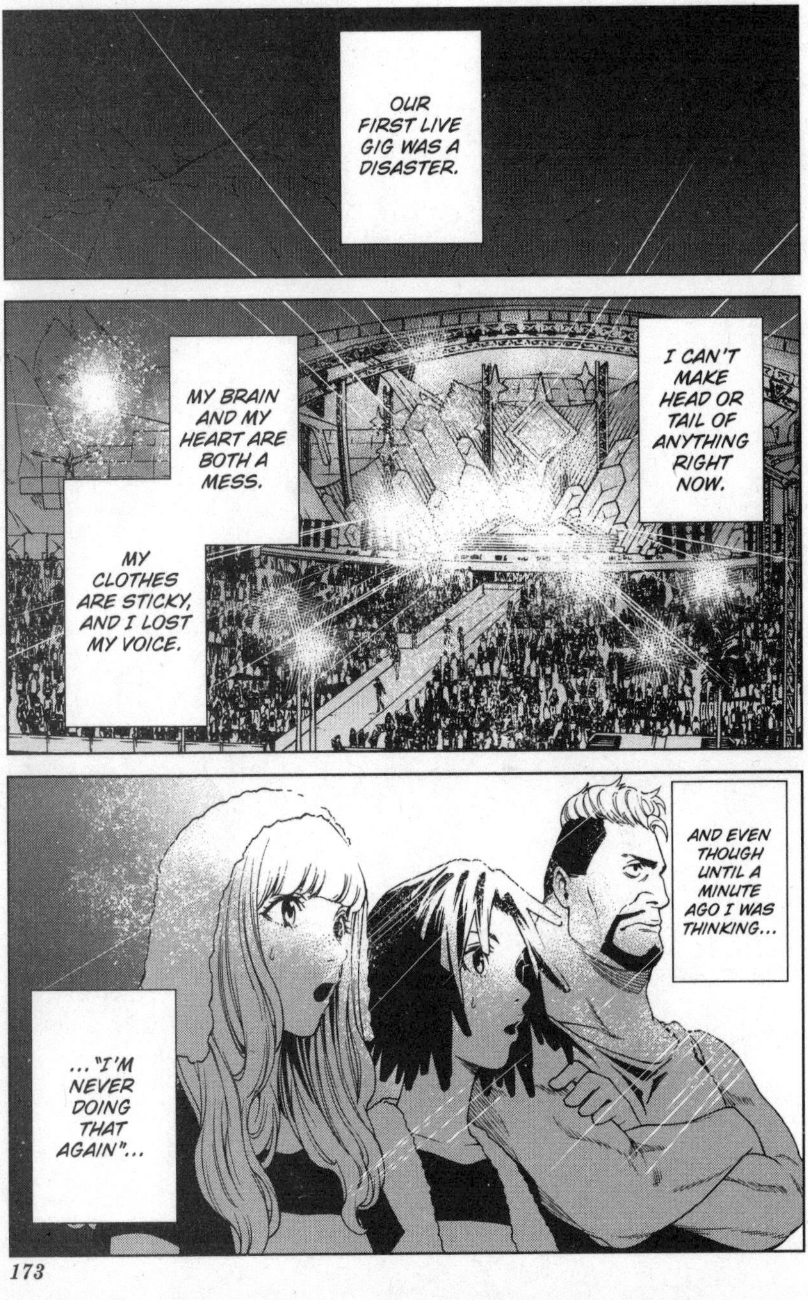
OUR FIRST LIVE GIG WAS A DISASTER.
I CAN'T MAKE HEAD OR TAIL OF ANYTHING RIGHT NOW.
MY BRAIN AND MY HEART ARE BOTH A MESS.
MY CLOTHES ARE STICKY, AND I LOST MY VOICE.
AND EVEN THOUGH UNTIL A MINUTE AGO I WAS THINKING...
..."I'M NEVER DOING THAT AGAIN"...

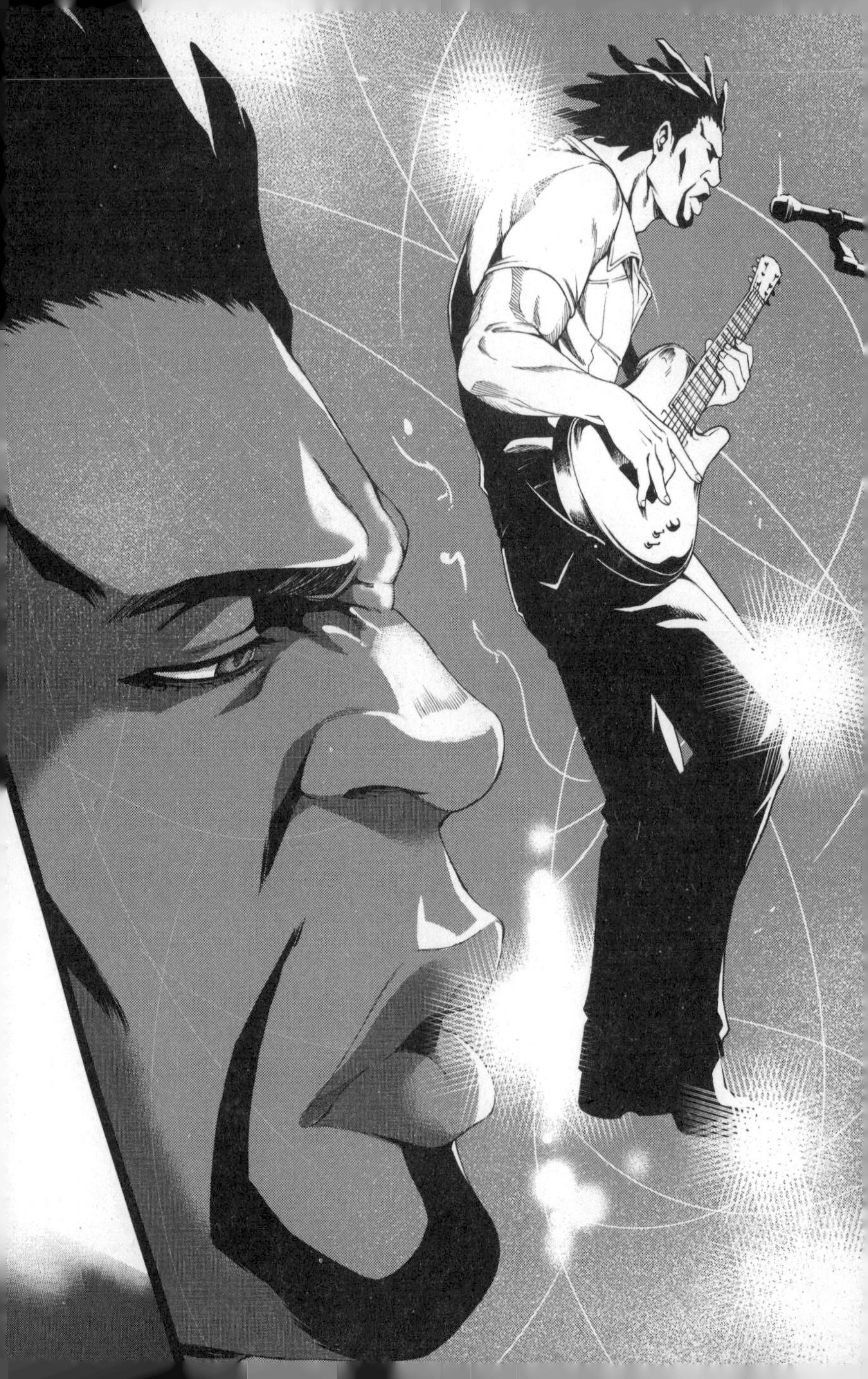

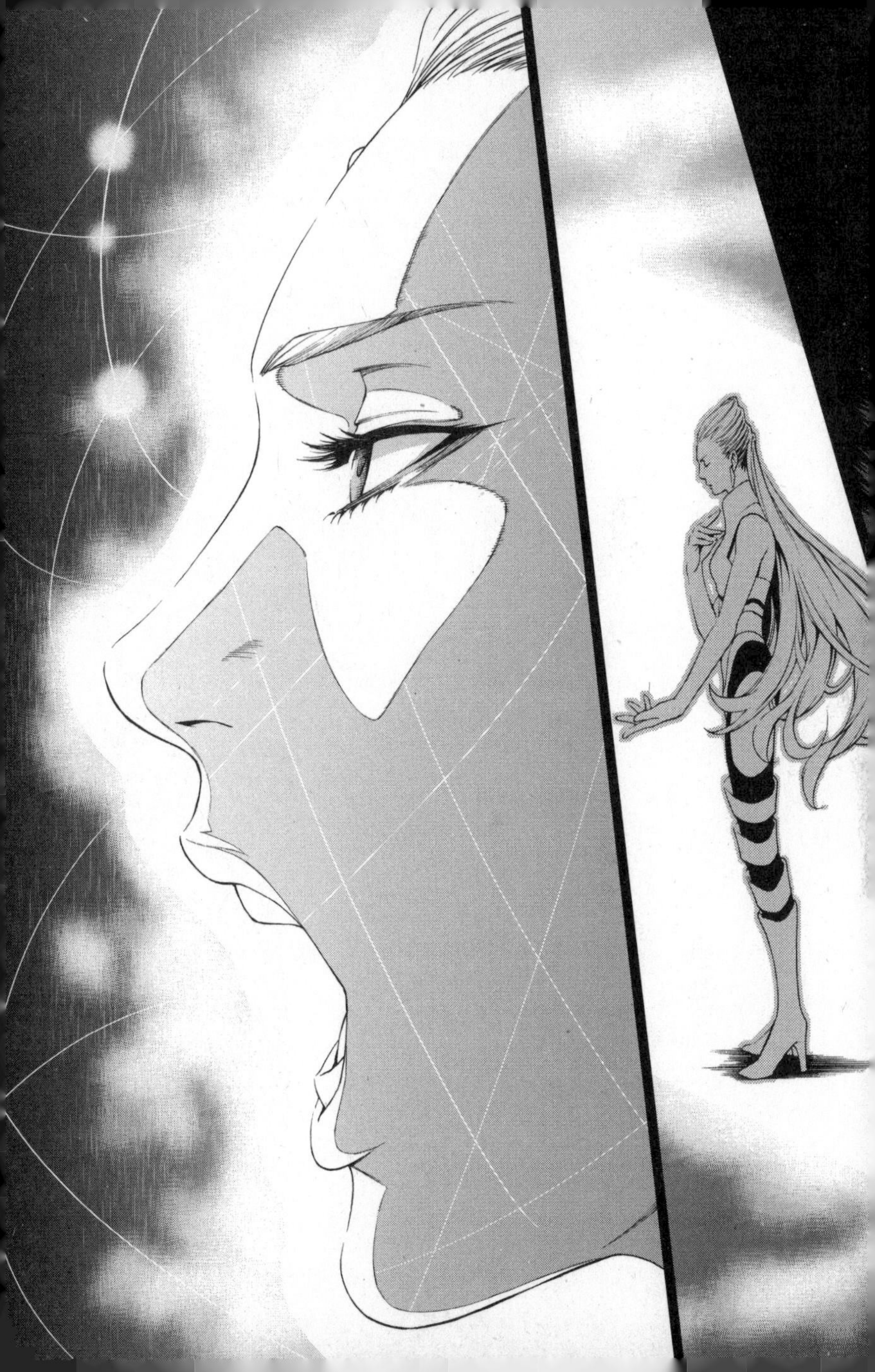

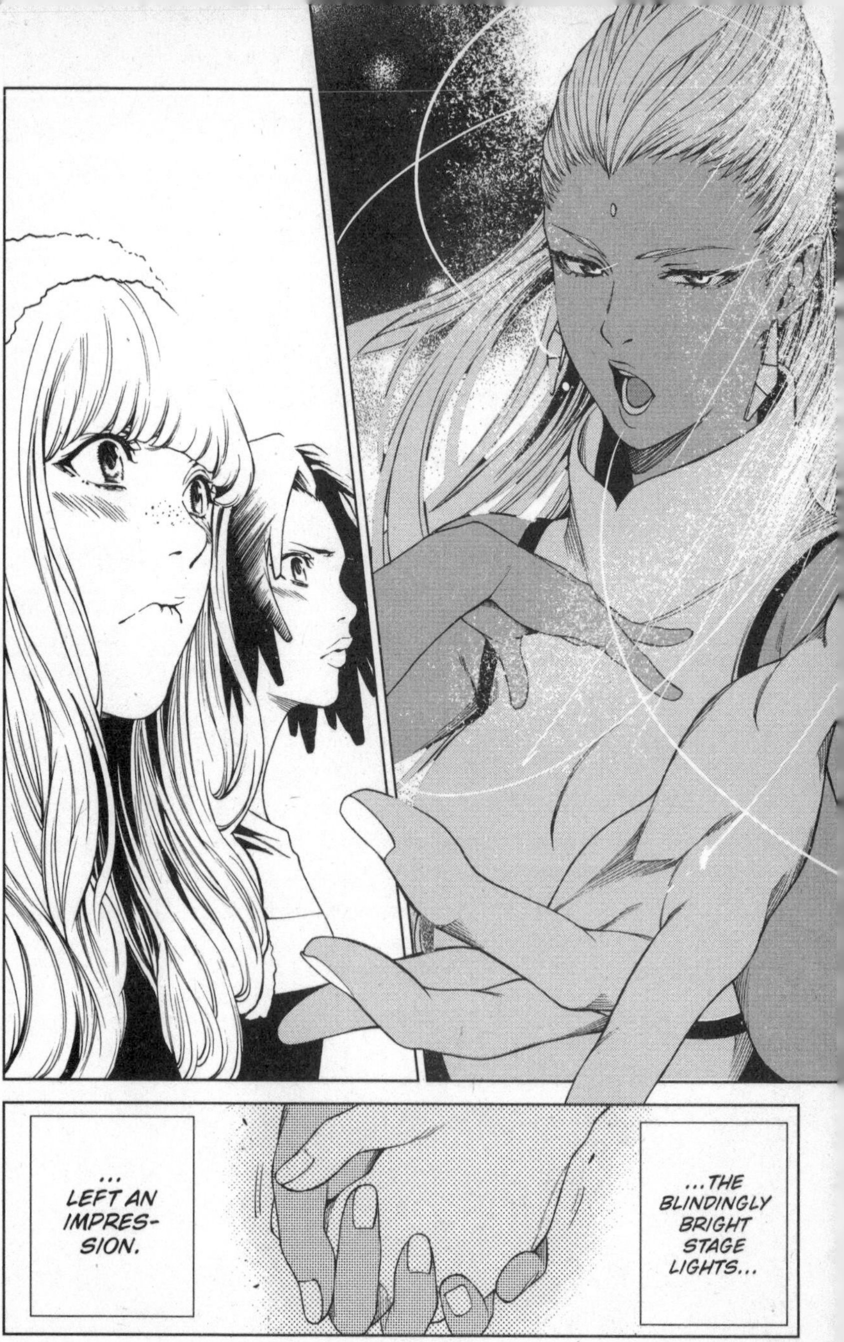
...THE BLINDINGLY BRIGHT STAGE LIGHTS...
... LEFT AN IMPRES- SION.

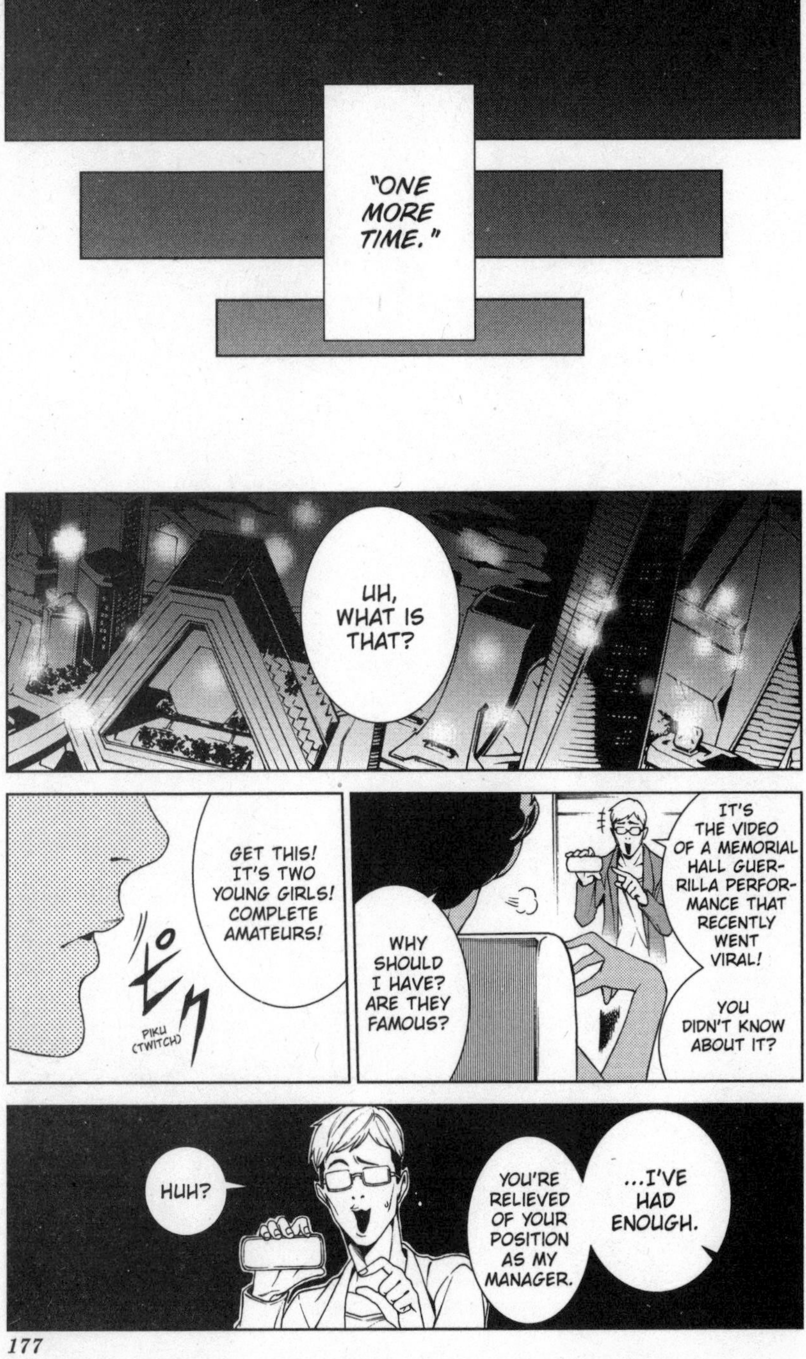
"ONE MORE TIME."
UH, WHAT IS THAT?
IT'S THE VIDEO OF A MEMORIAL HALL GUERRILLA PERFORMANCE THAT RECENTLY WENT VIRAL!
YOU DIDN'T KNOW ABOUT IT?
WHY SHOULD I HAVE? ARE THEY FAMOUS?
GET THIS! IT'S TWO YOUNG GIRLS! COMPLETE AMATEURS!
PIKU (TWITCH)
...I'VE HAD ENOUGH.
YOU'RE RELIEVED OF YOUR POSITION AS MY MANAGER.
HUH?

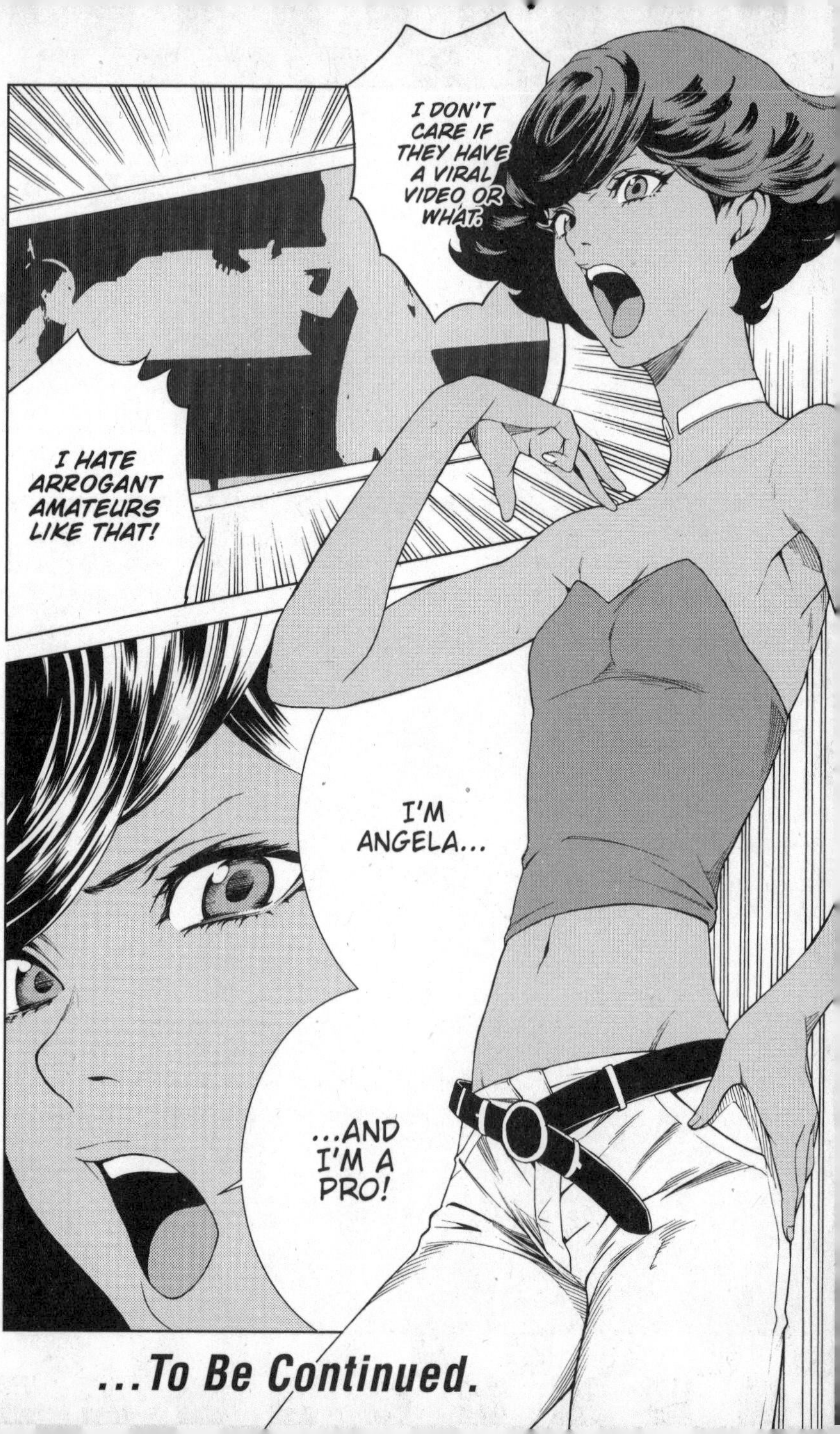
I DON'T CARE IF THEY HAVE A VIRAL VIDEO OR WHAT.
I HATE ARROGANT AMATEURS LIKE THAT!
I'M ANGELA...
...AND I'M A PRO!
...To Be Continued.

Afterword

Thank you so much for picking up the first volume of Carole & Tuesday the manga.

Hello. I'm Morito Yamataka.

I'm having a total blast drawing this series. Really, I'm serious. It isn't just lip service! Carole & Tuesday has given me many new experiences.

I've always liked listening to music and singing, and while I can...barely play instruments, I enjoy that too. But not so much that I ever planned on drawing a manga about music. The same applies to the characters. Carole's and Tuesday's quirks are different in both visual design and personality than any characters I've created myself up to this point.

It's full of things I think I'd never have created on my own. That's exactly what makes it all so fresh and fun and new.

...I say that, but as someone being serialized in a manga magazine, it's not like I create it on my own in the first place (lol)!

Carole and Tuesday. Maybe them meeting is the same thing. They each have their own sound. It could be those sounds are really similar, but they definitely aren't the same. Naturally, that might cause differences, but you can only create a harmony with different sounds.

I hope this adaptation turned out to be in harmony with the original Carole & Tuesday anime. This is Yamataka, signing off.

See you in Volume 2!

<SPECIAL THANKS>
Shinichiro Watanabe
The Staff of BONES
Tsuyoshi Kusano
My editor

<STAFF>
Kyousuke Nishiki

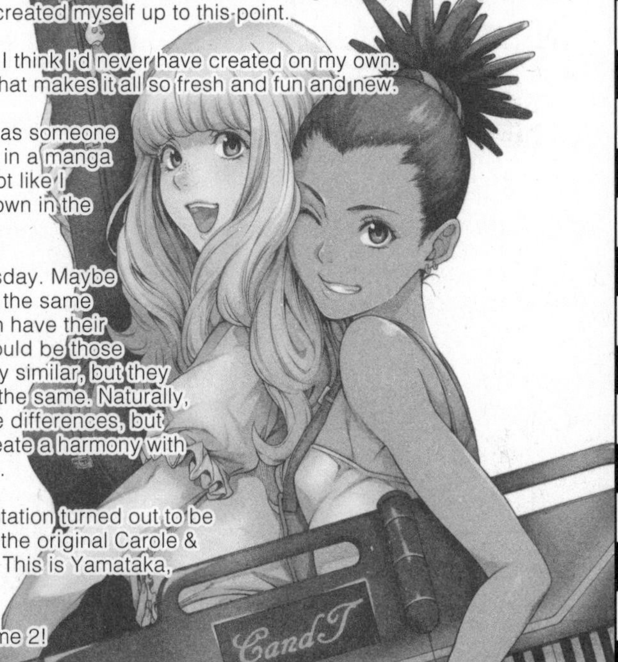
CandT

CAROLE & TUESDAY

1

ART
Morito Yamataka
ORIGINAL STORY
BONES, Shinichiro Watanabe

Translation: **Amanda Haley** | Lettering: **Lys Blakeslee**

CAROLE & TUESDAY, vol. 1
© Morito Yamataka 2019
© BONES, Shinichiro Watanabe 2019
First published in Japan in 2019 by KADOKAWA CORPORATION, Tokyo.
English translation rights arranged with KADOKAWA CORPORATION, Tokyo
and Yen Press, LLC through Tuttle-Mori Agency, Inc.

English translation © 2020 by Yen Press, LLC

Yen Press
150 West 30th Street, 19th Floor
New York, NY 10001

Visit us at yenpress.com ♫ facebook.com/yenpress ♫
twitter.com/yenpress ♫ yenpress.tumblr.com ♫ instagram.com/yenpress

First Yen Press Edition: December 2020

Yen Press is an imprint of Yen Press, LLC.
The Yen Press name and logo are trademarks of Yen Press, LLC.

Library of Congress Control Number: 2020933563

ISBNs: 978-1-9753-1302-9 (paperback)
       978-1-9753-1301-2 (ebook)

10 9 8 7 6 5 4 3 2 1

WOR

Printed in the United States of America